THE
BLACK MALE
IN
AMERICA

THE
BLACK MALE
IN
AMERICA

PERSPECTIVES ON HIS STATUS IN CONTEMPORARY SOCIETY

DORIS Y. WILKINSON
RONALD L. TAYLOR

NELSON-HALL • CHICAGO

LIBRARY OF CONGRESS CATALOGING IN PUBLICATION DATA
Main entry under title:

The Black male in America.

    Bibliography: p.
    Includes indexes.
    1. Afro-Americans—Psychology.   2. Afro-American
families.   I. Wilkinson, Doris Yvonne.   II. Taylor,
Ronald Lewis, 1942–
E185.625.B56   301.45′19′6073   76–44310
ISBN 0–88229–227–7 (cloth)
ISBN 0–88229–409–1 (paper)

Manufactured in the United States of America.

CONTENTS

PREFACE

Doris Y. Wilkinson

The dynamics of the teaching-learning encounter in courses focusing on racial and ethnic relations, black history, stratification systems based on color differentiation, and the sociology of minorities, are often characterized by an intense dissatisfaction with accompanying standard basic textbooks. These are described as too diffuse in coverage, too conventional in orientation, and/or irrelevant to specific and pertinent social issues which reflect the intricate character of interracial and intra-racial exchange. Expressing their interest in realistic and meaningful substantive areas, concerned and critical students voice the need for examination of the topic of black-white relations from current and pertinent political and psycho-cultural frames of reference. They indicate an interest in analyses of the impact of economic and political networks on racial statuses and role enactments; of cultural definitions of sex role relationships; evolution of color stratification, and measurable forms of dominant-subordinate interactional relations. Combined with this is often an expression of concern with institutional aspects of racism and sexism, primarily the empirical components of racist ideologies. "In what *specific ways* are blacks oppressed?" is frequently asked. Apparently a more well-delineated perspective and substantive focus, which would permit the student an understanding of reality-based concepts, is what is being sought.

Recently there has appeared a plethora of anthologies and original literature on the specific topic of sex roles and color focusing on the black female. Notable among these are, Toni Cade's *The Black Woman*, 1970; Joyce Ladner's *Tomorrow's Tomorrow: The Black Woman*, 1971; Robert Staples' *The Black Woman in America*, 1973; and Gerda Lerner's (ed.) *Black Women in White America: A Documentary History*, 1973. In addition there have been related large-scale research projects like the Wilkinson combined sociological and literary analysis of *images of black women in twentieth century fiction.** This volume places emphasis on a relatively uninventoried subject area. Including a number of original contributions, the work has been carefully delimited to focus upon the social positions and role enactments of African American males. It is also interdisciplinary in scope; and in this sense is unique. Selections include not only the contributions of sociologists, but also social psychologists, anthropologists, and psychiatrists. The extensive bibliography includes empirical studies and literature by and about black males from a variety of disciplines.

Essentially our compilation represents a synthesis of substantively related materials with the purpose of offering a realistic and contemporary examination of the American black male. With respect to the coverage of this interdisciplinary treatment, the following areas are examined: socialization to the black male role in the ghetto and its accompanying street culture; the statuses and role performances of black fathers; historical and contemporary myths about the psychology and biology of African American males; processes such as stigmatization and fragmentization or dissection of role performance; motivations and legal issues related to interracial mating and marriage; socio-economic factors operative in black family structure and life styles; and lastly the future role expectations of African American males in "post industrial" society.

Examination of the position of the black male in the present social system should be of intrinsic interest to college students and instructors of all racial groups. It is hoped that this volume will stimulate analytic and objective thinking about the socio-political interactional processes occurring between black males and other members of American society. Though the reader may not agree with all of the various perspectives represented, it is hoped that the diversity of the selections will contribute to understanding.

Our project began with the many helpful suggestions received from interested colleagues and was sustained by support from contributors. Without their efforts, this work would not have been completed. To these persons and to the University of Connecticut Research Foundation for its support, we are grateful.

---

*See: Patricia Kane and Doris Y. Wilkinson, "Survival Strategies: Black Women in *Ollie Miss* and *Cotton Comes to Harlem,*" *Critique: Studies in Modern Fiction* 16 (1974): 101–109.

1

SOCIALIZATION TO THE BLACK MALE ROLE

Ronald L. Taylor

The public image of the black male coalesces around three interrelated postulates: 1) that the black male has been emasculated by white society (both literally and figuratively) ; 2) that the emasculation process has prevented him from coming to full emotional maturity; and 3) as a result of these processes, the black male tends to be a poor husband and father. These postulates are grounded in the experience of slavery and its residual effects, in the contemporary situation in which black males are handicapped by macrostructural forces in performing satisfactorily as husbands and fathers, and in certain socialization practices which tend to convey a view of masculinity that is essentially "deviant," or "psychopathological" in extreme.

The institution of slavery is generally assumed to have been destructive to the institution of marriage in that it flagrantly subverted the relations between the sexes. The system is believed to have imposed responsibilities on black women that were inconsistent with the conventional feminine role vis-à-vis the masculine role, and granted to them an "unnatural" superiority over black men. More-

1

over, the dual role of husband/father was institutionally obliterated, thus denying to black men a significant place and function in the family. In short, the black male was put in a predicament in which conformity to masculine norms was all but impossible, and then he was, in effect, both rewarded and punished for not conforming to them. The inferior role in which he was cast—docile, humble, and irresponsible—is alleged to have compromised and severely damaged his masculinity. Indeed, the role he came to play with such admirable skill was itself an adaptive device purchased at considerable psychic cost. Hence, the process of emasculation begun under slavery was compounded and intensified by the relationship to women it imposed, and a somewhat similar set of circumstances produced the same effects on subsequent generations of black men.

While the second and third postulates share an historical continuity with the first, they place emphasis on presently operating causes of the black male's role and status. The view stressed here is that a combination of contemporary social and economic factors conspire to limit the black male's access to status and economic resources so that his ability to perform as husband and father is greatly undermined. Accordingly, his contribution to the family as breadwinner is relatively less than that of his spouse. Since the allocation of authority and prestige in the family is typically assessed on the relative contribution of each partner to the marriage, the black male's influence and status in the family is correspondingly reduced. The effect is an expansion in the role and influence of the female in the household at the expense of the male. The inability to function successfully in the male role, it is claimed, may be experienced as a loss in masculinity and social identity, which he may attempt to recoup by active involvement in the life of the streets, or, not infrequently, by leaving the household unit.

The often antagonistic relationship between black husbands and wives is assumed to influence the way in which black children are frequently socialized. Consequently, girls may come to hold an exaggerated view of female self-sufficiency, while boys may come to more fully appreciate their marginal status and the difficulties involved in assuming a self-satisfying masculine posture. However, the latter's difficulties are said to be compounded should the father leave the home. Boys reared in fatherless families are reported to be less socially responsible, less achievement oriented, and more susceptible to delinquency than other youth. In addition, they are said to experience greater difficulty in differentiating the roles of the sexes, and to be more submissive and dependent, and less mature at any given age. The danger, it is assumed, is that in the absence of the father, the black male child may identify too closely with the mother, the results of which are expressed in ambivalence over sexual identity and overt homosexuality. More typically, however, confusion over sexual identity is thought to be compensated for in the form of exaggerated masculinity (e.g., toughness and strong language), or various defense mechanisms (e.g., aggressive independence). In any case, it is alleged that the black male youth is frequently forced to develop his sense of being a man largely outside the home and under the tutelage of his peers, who present a model of masculinity often at variance with the mainstream model. Further, the nature of socialization that goes on in the peer group tends to reflect the generalized relationship between the sexes.

One of the most important effects, it is claimed, of fatherless socialization is revealed in the failure to develop in young boys a "marital aptitude," i.e., an ability to maintain stable marital relationships. Anxieties arising out of their unresolved status frequently drive black men to destructive activities that result in further rejection by women. Violence and alcoholism are seen as by-products of the black male's identity problems, but are also seen as the sources of much strain and conflict in the marital relationship. Infidelity is considered the more common source of discord and disruption in marriage, however. Prodigious promiscuity is alleged to be a positive value among black males, combined with a lively sense of sexual exploitation. Hence, this male orientation is seen as contributing toward the deterioration of the relationship between the sexes as revealed in shifting union, divorce, and female-based households.

It is for all these reasons, then, that both black males and females are said to hold negative views of marriage. For their part, women are said to view men as irresponsible, exploitative, aggressive—even depraved. Black men, on the other hand, may view women as domineering, untrustworthy, and often indifferent to their plight. These views in turn poison the relationship between them and serve as strong impediments against stable and gratifying relationships. And given the more influential role of the black mother in the family, her attitudes (often hostile) toward males are more likely to prevail and to be passed on to the children—thus the cycle of matriarchy—male emasculation—family instability begins again.

Growing up as a black male is thus assumed to involve a number of social and psychological impediments. Boys become embroiled in the "battle of the sexes" long before they come of age, and come of age before they are prepared to do battle. In the black community, then, more than in the white, the child is the father of the man.

This, in its simple and complex form, is the stuff of which the popular image of the black male is made (all exceptions granted). It is this image, together with the circumstances (and myths) that produced and sustain it, that undergo critical examination in the selections assembled in Part One (and again in Part Two).

In the selection, "Coming Up as a Boy in the Ghetto," Schulz presents the orthodox interpretation of the nature of black male socialization in matrifocal families. Specifically, he examines some of the problems black youth encounter in the world of the urban ghetto as they strive to assert their masculinity and negotiate the harsh realities of that world. He contends that the problems of these youth, in a community where matrifocality is common, is not so much a matter of the absence of a father or older male figures with whom they may identify as it is a lack of "adequate" masculine role models enabling successful "adaptation" to the norms and values of the larger culture. Lacking such models in the home, boys must discover how to become men outside the home and under the negative influence of their peers. By the end of adolescence, boys are well on their way toward developing the modes of behavior characteristic of the ghetto-specific male role celebrated in street life. Hence, Schulz argues for the existence of a ghetto subculture and a "deviant" male role to which black youth are socialized.

The article by Schulz sets the stage for a more critical examination of the empirical evidence and underlying assumptions of conventional interpretations of black male socialization. Hannerz notes that much of the data adduced in support of the effects of fatherless families is misleading and inapplicable to the actual circumstances under which many black male youth are socialized. He contends that fatherless households need not be maleless as is often assumed, and that mothers frequently instruct boys in manly behavior—mainstream and ghetto-specific. The interpretation of "playing the dozens" as a reaction-formation of boys protesting female domination is also scrutinized. Playing the dozens is seen as part of the interaction idiom among peers, a game to be mastered if the youth expects to be a successful member of the peer group. Hannerz contends that ghetto youth are not only socialized into a ghetto-specific sex role but are "biculturated", i.e., instructed in mainstream culture as well via the school, home, and mass media. Which sex role model becomes salient depends upon the sociocultural context; a conclusion which leads Hannerz to suggest that the ghetto-specific male role deserves to be studied as a cultural entity in its own right.

The cultural aspects of the ghetto male role alluded to by Hannerz are developed more thoroughly in the selection by Keil. He contends that there is a distinctive black culture characterized by the "battle of the sexes," unique kinship patterns, values, and styles of life. These cultural themes, he asserts, are most clearly expressed in the music of the urban bluesman. Keil argues that if we are to understand urban black culture we must come to view entertainers as culture heroes, for one can find in their performance the essence of black culture as a whole. It is our failure to recognize the existence of black culture, he contends, that has led to disastrous conclusions about the role of males in the black community.

Robert Coles, a psychiatrist of national reputation, presents a rather sympathetic account of black fathers he has encountered during his extensive investigations of the poor throughout America. These are urban black fathers found in such cities as Boston, New York, Chicago, and Cleveland, who migrated from the South in search of a better life. Their daily struggles to support their families make them unavailable when scientific observers come to do their work. But they present another side to the rather dismal picture painted by many such writers. They are proud men, strong husbands and fathers, who are hopeful that their children will be able to lead better lives than they themselves have been forced to live. Their children apparently respect them and so, too, their wives. In his interviews with these men, Coles was frequently met with the question: "Why is it that men like us never seem to catch the eye of people who talk about the black man and say all these things about us?" Why indeed?

In the final selection, Parker and Kleiner attempt to ascertain the extent to which the family role performance of the black male can be explained in terms of accommodation to social and economic barriers and a high probability of failure, as against the view that it represents conformity to a "deviant" normative family role system. The authors hypothesize that the existence of a deviant normative family role system would suggest that the family norms of lower class blacks are markedly different from those of stable white or black middle class families, in which case family role deviation among lower class black males would not be associated with psychological stress. Conversely, if such a subcultural orientation is not assumed to exist then there should be no class-related differences in family norms, and deviation from majority (middle-class) standards would be accompanied by feelings of psychological stress. The results from their study, based on the responses of married black males (between 20 and 60 years of age) from a representative sample of a Philadelphia community, suggest that family norms held by married black males do not differ markedly from these generally assumed to be associated with stable family life, and that those males who perceived discrepancies in family role performance tended to experience some degree of stress. Thus the data support the hypothesis that obstacles encountered by the black male in such areas as employment, housing, and general opportunity are more powerful as explanatory variables in determining his performance than conformity to subcultural norms.

COMING UP AS A BOY
IN THE GHETTO*

David A. Schulz

While the feminine role is associated with respectability, dependability, the family, and the home, masculinity is more often associated with the reverse of these and its locus is the street. A boy strives to achieve a "rep" on the street because he perceives that he does not have much status in the home. He strives to assert his masculinity against almost overwhelming handicaps. His father still remembers his "place," but his mother is a recognized pillar of the family and the church and is the one who sees to it that he at least makes an effort in school. If he is in his late teens, he has seen in himself what he feared he saw all along in his father—a person ill-prepared to "go it alone." He sees himself more destined for the dependance of welfare than the independence of manhood. Coming up as a boy in the ghetto is thus a most difficult process indeed.

BOYHOOD AND BLACKNESS IN RECOLLECTION

A part of the environment in which a boy becomes a man is his father's recollection of his own boyhood. Edward Patterson (forty-five) remembers his youth in Kentucky and southern Missouri:

> I mostly had a life of my own.... I traveled around quite a bit with my dad when I was a child.... From the time I can remember up until about twelve years old ... [my father] was a fair speaking and understandable type of person. *He respected people and wanted to be*

*From David A. Schulz, *Coming Up Black: Patterns of Ghetto Socialization*, © 1969, pp. 59–87. Reprinted with permission from Prentice-Hall, Inc., Englewood Cliffs, New Jersey.

respected. He more or less believed in minding his own affairs and anything that didn't concern him, just wasn't any use for it. Definitely speaking, I believe that he thought like myself that it was a lot easier for him to get in other people's way than it was for them to get in his way because he was able to walk around [them] where the other person probably wouldn't agree to do such things.

Edward was a sickly child but helped out on the farm when he could. When he married, he farmed until he was twenty-four. In the back of his mind there was always the dream of owning a trailer and being able to travel so that he could "go where the work was available." His ideal was to have "a couple of kids"; he now has thirteen. His mother died when he was eleven, and his father took up with a girlfriend:

> It was a lady who lived nearby. [My older siblings] wouldn't agree to have another mother.... One could cook, the other could keep the house,... the two of us [boys] could bring enough in for us to have lunch and everything. So I guess we were just a very successful family.

When Edward was eighteen, his father died. Edward married when he was twenty-one, bringing to his marriage one illegitimate child, Herbert, whose mother had died in childbirth.

Arthur Washington (fifty-one) was born in Arkansas and moved into the boot-heel of Missouri as a young boy. His father was "a very industrious man" who sharecropped. "He was a good provider, a good church man, and was well liked by everyone." He died when Arthur was only sixteen. As he was coming up, Arthur had very little to do around the house. "The biggest we did was fish; we had no responsibility at all. Whatever my father said do, that's what we did."

A quite different boyhood is remembered by Stanley Billit (forty-four) :

> I started plowing when I was eight... [with] horses and mules.... I could plow all day. [My father] was nothing but a farmer. He's still farming. He is a pretty good man.... Anybody could get along with him until he got mad. He'd just go crazy.... He could have five or six hundred dollars in his pocket and if you ask him for a dime, he'd swear he didn't have a dime.

Stanley didn't get very much schooling because he was always in the fields. He says that his father caught him playing hookey so much that he said: "Well, I'm just going to keep you to work since you don't want to go to school." Living in the city has convinced him that he ought to have gotten a better education, but now it is, as he sees it, too late for that. He left home when he was twenty-one to marry a girl from Mississippi. Both of his parents are still alive.

When he was nine, Andrew Buchanan (fifty-five) ran away from home. He lived by his "mother wit," sometimes visiting relatives, but often completely on his own. His father died shortly before he left home. Early life, for Andrew, was pretty much a matter of freewheeling, living off the land and the women encountered.

Andrew remembers his father:

> . . . mild, gentle, good—very good—just the type of a father a boy would want. Just one thing that was wrong with my father; he just wasn't home enough. . . . He worked in all types of capacities as a cook—that is, in hotels, restaurants, and even went on hunting parties with the hotel owner. He was a chief cook in a hotel. The owner of this hotel was going on a hunting trip and wanted him to go because he was also a barber and a good huntsman. I understand that he was a left-handed man and he shot very well. This seemed to be some kind of advantage because the people that he worked for never went on a hunting trip without taking him. Whenever they couldn't get a deer or bear, he did, and of course it was their bear. Not only that, he could cut their hair, shave them, all this kind of thing while he was on the hunting trip. It made him feel *almost essential to their hunting party.* This way he was away from home three to four weeks, a month at a time. Then they had boats and they had friends who had boats and they would go on excursions on the Mississippi on the *Kate Adams*—if I can remember right—in later years the *Jeff Hicks.* . . and daddy either cooked or waited tables on this party on these boats and he was away from home. Of course when he was home he seemed to me and my boyish ways to have plenty of money and was nice to me.

Andrew's own career reflects his father's. Once, while helping with a coat, he remarked: "I've had a lot of experience doing this. I'm pretty good as a shoeshine boy." He also followed up his father's interest in cooking, but not hunting.

Finally, Lester Frazier remembers his father, who was a sharecropper in Mississippi:

> [He] was a curious man. . . . He was good to his children and his wife. . . . Lots of men, they take the living out of the children's mouths and throw it away. . . . He worked the share because he wasn't able to afford to rent and take care of us.

Lester is particularly sensitive about his status as a Negro, and he makes explicit what is implied in all of the above remarks that speak of a father as a man who knows how to get along with people:

> I never did have no trouble out of white people. Didn't no white people ever beat on me or never cussed me. I always talked right to white people. I know how to treat anybody. I talked nice to them, I stayed in my place and wanted them to stay in their place. . . . Ain't none never attempted to hit me. The only thing is they just wouldn't pay me.

The components of masculinity revealed in these recollections of childhood indicate an early work orientation centering around the fields or unskilled labor on road gangs; or, as in Andrew's case, they reflect a father whose service was "almost essential" to his employer, who for all the world treated him as a slave "set free." They reflect a minimum of responsibility around the home. A boy's chores might be to bring in the wood for the fire and to milk the cows if there were any, but housework was women's work.

Lester could think of his father as peculiar because, in the experience of these men, it was not uncommon for a father to fail to care for his wife and children. It is perhaps significant that none of these men reports his own father as a derelict. Three of the five, however, lost their fathers before they were out of their teens. Combined with the enforced necessity of knowing one's place, the lack of an adequate male model undoubtedly contributed to their conception of handling situations passively by getting out of people's way or letting them run over you if need be.

While none of these men ever talked about their father "beating on" their mothers, several of the mothers who were described in the previous chapter stressed this fact about their fathers. A man frustrated in his relationship with the world outside his family takes it out on his wife and children, and this would seem to be quite often the case in project families.

These men, furthermore, are handicapped in teaching their sons a legitimate means of earning a living because the work that they did in the country is not available in the city or is of such low status that no young boy coming up would want "to be what his father was." They are also handicapped in helping their sons develop responsible behavior around the home as a direct consequence of this fact.

The problem of the Negro lower-class family—from the inevitably biased point of view of the dominant middle class—is, therefore, not so much a matter of the absence of a father as it is the absence of an *adequate* masculine role model *enabling adaptation* to the *values* of the larger culture. Most fathers do not seem to influence their sons significantly until the boy has begun to break away from the dominance of his mother and to move under the tutelage of his peers.

BABYHOOD AND BOYHOOD IN THE PROJECT

Freedom from Responsibility

As far as the three babies (one girl and two boys) born during the course of this study are concerned, no differential socialization by sex could be detected. As babies, boys and girls receive the same treatment. A great deal of affection and attention is given them until they begin to achieve some degree of autonomy. Then their siblings begin to lose interest in them. Babies are like dolls, things to play with and cuddle, but they soon become more trouble than they are worth. Only one child, the last child, can play the role of "family pet" for any length of time; the rest must quickly relinquish babyhood and the center of attention in the family world.

Birth order does not seem to be as important a factor affecting the early experience of boys as it does in the case of girls. Even the firstborn boy is relieved of work around the house when he is living in the city. He must discover how a boy becomes a man outside of the family under the influence of his peers, while his sisters learn feminine roles close at home. Furthermore, mothers favor their girls more than their boys, both because of the girls' greater utility around the house and because men have numerous "pathologies" peculiar to their sex. A woman's experience of being exploited by men influences her attitude toward her sons.

Thus a boy must develop his sense of being a person and a man largely outside of the home and under the negative evaluation of his mother. He must further do this where the father is often missing or, if present, is likely to be preoccupied with the attempt to cover his own deep sense of failure with a facade of competence and rough hewn masculinity manifested in his physical, if not psychological, domination of his wife. Quite likely the male model provided by his father and older brothers is totally inadequate as a model for achieving mobility in the larger society. These older males may, on the other hand, be greatly admired as persons able to provide invaluable instruction in survival techniques for life in the ghetto. When this male role model is focused on his mother's boyfriend, the boy is made further aware of the possibilities of being a man without assuming full responsibility for a family. Some boyfriends, however, are amazingly competent as surrogate fathers.

The small boy in the project is made aware of his mother's preference for his sisters in numerous ways. Jerry Parvin, for example, knows this is true because his mother characteristically denies him the treats which she permits her daughters to have.

> *Jerry*: Can I have some can'y?
> *Lilly*: No!
> *Jerry*: (whines and sulks around behind his mother pleading for some candy) : Umm, Ummm, Canieeee, Ummm.
> [Jerry goes several times to the refrigerator, each time taking out the bag of candy and bringing it to his mother. Each time his mother refuses. He tries to ride a trike; she tells him to get off. Stephanie, his sister, watches with interest. She takes the trike away from Jerry and rides around the living room.]
> *Lilly*: I told you to put that trike in the closet. Did you hear me, Stephanie? Put that trike in the closet. You just riding it because you heard him say he wanted to. Neither of you can ride that trike.
> [Stephanie takes the trike and goes out into the hall. She rides around a while then comes in and goes to the refrigerator, takes out the bag of orange slices, and gives some to a neighbor's child who has come into the apartment.]
> *Lilly*: Come here, Stephanie Ann.
> [Stephanie takes the bag of candy and gives some to all of the children present except Jerry. Jerry tries to take some candy himself.]
> *Lilly* (shouting) : Didn't I tell you not to get into that candy?
> [Jerry stares hungrily at the candy. His mother goes out of the room for a few minutes. He takes a piece of candy and is chewing it when his mother comes back into the room. Lilly makes no comment although she has seen that he has taken a piece.]

In this instance Lilly's official permission was denied to both Jerry and his sister, but from past experience Stephanie knows that she can get away with such activities in open defiance of her mother's wishes. Jerry, if he is to be successful, must do it behind his mother's back. Stephanie enjoys such a privileged position in her family because she is a girl, and although only ten, she takes a great deal of the work that is done around the house off her mother's hands. Jerry does nothing, is not required to do anything, and is treated accordingly.

Lilly also sees in Jerry his father's evils. At the age of nine he is, in his mother's eyes, already a little man who must be prevented from stepping into his father's shoes. On another occasion Jerry was aggressively acting out an attempted robbery which he claimed actually happened to the Parvin family. He kicked and shouted at the unseen assailant and then, exhausted, sat down to put on a pair of oversize shoes. His sister shouted a warning: "Them's men's shoes, them's men's shoes," and looked sheepishly at her mother when asked to explain. Her mother volunteered: "She means them shoes too big for Jerry. He's trying to be a little man now. He thinks he is a man." That this fact has highly symbolic overtones for Lilly was revealed a bit later when she remarked:

> Jerry, he don't want to mind at all. I try to send him to the store with Stephanie and them so he can get some fresh air sometimes, and he don't want to go. A man told me he's watching me.... Somebody put Jerry up to watching me.... Anyway, I been trying to get him out of here because I think you should play like little kids should play.
> Q: Why would Jerry be watching you?
> I don't know. I know I don't have a husband or nothing.... I think that kinda keeps me upset.... One day I was getting ready to go to the store and he began aggravating me and getting on my nerves.... I went over there to the door and he start talking like he been planning something.

In her illness Lilly exaggerates sentiments held by other mothers in the project to the point where she imagines that her son is a potential rapist. She further projects the responsibility for all of the evils she observes in him on various male relatives. His uncle taught him homosexual play; his father is responsible for his aggressiveness. Jerry Parvin's case is the case of every boy in the project writ large and explicit, rather than covertly expressed in subtle preferences and avoidances.

Breaking Away from Mother: The Dozens

The masculine struggle against the feminine domination of the "stable," respectable world of the family is dramatized most clearly in the custom of "playing the dozens." Project residents believe that boys begin to play the dozens when they are about eleven years old and girls when they are about a half year older (Table 1-1). While the game is played by both boys and girls, it is preeminently a male activity in which the mother is made the target of ridicule and satire.[1]

Table 1-1 Average Age at Which Respondents Think Project Youth (Under Age 25) Begin Various Activities*

Activity	Girls (Per Cent†)						Boys (Per Cent†)					
	Ave. Age	−2 yr.	−1 yr.	Ave.	+1 yr.	+2 yr.	Ave. Age	−2 yr.	−1 yr.	Ave.	+1 yr.	+2 yr.
Dropped a bottle out of window on concrete below	7.8	13.3	13.3	13.7	7.9	11.5	8.5	10.0	12.8	9.5	10.9	14.7
Stole something from a store	8.9	7.1	11.2	8.0	17.4	15.6	10.9	5.9	10.9	13.6	5.9	12.7
Knew how to jive, play the dirty dozens	10.8	8.0	6.2	13.3	6.2	14.2	11.5	3.6	12.6	4.9	16.6	8.1
Danced with a girl (boy)	11.2	5.6	12.2	8.7	23.5	12.2	11.5	1.3	8.3	10.5	23.6	17.8
Played hookey from school for two or three days at a time	11.7	7.5	14.9	7.0	16.7	11.4	12.9	11.7	3.2	19.4	15.3	18.0
Kissed and felt up a girl (kissed and was felt up by a boy)	12.9	7.9	5.7	22.0	14.5	16.3	12.8	9.3	12.0	20.4	12.8	12.4
Smoked cigarettes fairly often	12.7	9.5	6.9	17.7	12.5	19.4	13.4	6.1	18.2	18.2	22.1	15.6
Had sexual relations with a girl or woman (boy or man)	14.2	9.8	13.0	20.1	25.0	17.0	13.8	4.0	15.1	18.7	17.8	23.1
Drank enough wine, beer, or whiskey to get high	14.2	10.0	11.8	21.8	22.7	15.3	15.1	9.3	18.6	18.6	23.4	11.1
Got into a fight in which someone was badly hurt	14.8	8.8	9.7	15.4	19.3	18.9	14.5	8.5	11.7	17.9	19.3	17.9
Made a girl pregnant (got pregnant)	15.6	5.8	13.3	25.3	23.1	22.2	14.2	8.8	24.7	24.2	21.2	14.9
Smoked marihuana	15.6	7.9	9.4	18.3	21.8	17.8	15.9	8.0	14.6	13.7	21.1	15.6
Had homosexual relations with a girl or woman (boy or man)	15.7	6.1	9.7	14.6	16.4	5.5	16.2	10.2	10.8	15.6	6.6	25.2

*This is a modified version of the data presented in Stromberg, "Perspectives on Pathology . . .", p. 27.

†Percentages are calculated for each full year. Thus if the average age is 7.8, 13.7 per cent of the respondents felt the average age was between 7 & 7.9 years & 7.9 per cent felt it was between 8 & 8.9 years (listed under +1).

Even when girls play, the imagery retains an assertion of masculine virility, as evidenced by this rhyme given by a six-year-old girl:

> I was walking through the jungle
> With my dick in my hand
> I was the baddest motherfucker
> In the jungle land.
> I looked up in the tree
> And what did I see
> Your little black mama
> Trying to piss on me.
> I picked up a rock
> And hit her in the cock
> And knocked that bitch
> A half a block.[2]

Abrahams notes that in his experience "one occasionally finds girls making dozen-type remarks, but for the most part not in the organized fashion of the boys."[3] One function of the dozens common to both sexes is the training in verbal ability which is a necessary part of the male-female interchange of the late teens and early adulthood.

For the boy entering puberty, however, the dozens has a very specific function. It enables him to break free from the world of the mother and enter the world of the man, expressed in its earliest form in the project as the "gang."

In playing the dozens the boy can subject the mother, who is the chief dispenser of love and care, as well as discipline and authority, to criticism and abuse within the confines of a rigidly defined rhythmic game which prevents the volatile activity from getting out of hand. Playing the dozens occurs at the point when the boy is about to enter puberty and suffer his greatest rejection from his mother as a result of his becoming a man. The dozens enables him to develop a defense against this rejection and provides a vehicle for his transition into the manipulative world of the street dominated by masculine values expressed in gang life. By the end of adolescence the incipient mistrust between the sexes becomes an overt and central aspect of a way of life for both men and women. The dozens is thus a "ritualized exorcism" enabling the combatants to break away from the family dominated by the mother and to establish their own image of male superiority celebrated in street life.[4]

The dozens also functions to inform both sexes of some of the aspects of sexuality at an early age. These verbal contests acquaint

children with many details of sexuality, often before they are otherwise aware of them. They are a kind of primer imparting information
about the sex act, sexual deviance, sexual anatomy, and mores which
serves as basic guidelines for children who are exposed to sexuality
early and completely without being reared in a home where the matters of sex are commonly talked about.

The Perceived Trajectory of Boyhood: Problems and Privileges

Boys become problems at an earlier age than girls in the eyes
of project residents (Table 1–1). They are more difficult to manage,
engage in such activities as dropping bottles out of windows (sometimes aimed at persons below), stealing, playing hookey from school,
smoking cigarettes, drinking to get drunk, smoking marihuana, and
engaging in homosexual activities at an earlier age than girls. They
are not seen, however, as engaging in most heterosexual activities at
an earlier age. Girls and boys begin dancing and kissing at about the
same age, but girls experience the sex act at an earlier age and consequently become pregnant earlier than boys engage in sex and become responsible for making a girl pregnant.

Boys demonstrate their lack of fear and begin to cultivate their
aggressiveness in such activities as dropping objects on people from
the gallery windows and stealing small objects from the store. Often
the items a boy steals are not used or sold. They are stolen "just for
kicks." A girl, on the other hand, begins to steal later because she steals
items she uses, such as clothing and make-up. These become important
to her when she begins to consider her chances with the other sex.

However, the activities engaged in by both sexes before the age
of fourteen—or about the time most project youngsters are getting
out of grade school—are not activities that are going to get them into
much trouble with "the man," nor bring much trouble into the home.
The objects stolen in the early years are usually small and can be returned or paid for if the child is caught. Trouble comes in mid-teens,
and then it often comes as a surprise, even though the child has been
gradually developing a deviant career for almost seven years.[5]

The likelihood of a boy being labeled as a deviant while he is
in his teens is thus great.[6] This label, however, in the ghetto becomes
not a mark of rebuke but a medal and a further indication of having
a "rep." Police records, plus the prized ability to "make out," are at
one and the same time rejections of the values of the white world from
which one is barred by virtue of race, and the respectable home from

which one is barred by feminine values enforced by a rejecting mother and taunting sisters. A boy has no other choice in his struggle to become a man than to reject the home or conform to feminine and/or white values. He achieves his identity, therefore, as a Negro and as a man in the street by earning a "rep" because he has not been able to develop an identity as a respected member of his household.

Not all boys follow this deviant trajectory, but a significant number—perhaps a majority—do. In the group of teenagers in these families, only one, possibly two, boys (Richard Frazier and Jeremiah Brown) seem to be consistently following a "more acceptable" line of development, earning their spending money at odd jobs and preferring their own company to that of their peers. Even they, however, ran with a "gang" for a while before deciding that they did not want to "run with people who had trouble on their minds."

Gangs and Running Buddies

Although the gang in the classical sense is not a part of boyhood in the project, informal groups which are called "gangs" are. These gangs are rarely given names, they do not have emblems on their backs, or formal structures, though they usually have recognized leaders and may dress alike to the extent that all will wear a particular style of hat. Nicknames like "Daddio," "Big Pops," and "Coco" serve to identify a close relationship among members, or to define a significant aspect of a member's personality. The gang is usually a group of from seven to fifteen boys in their early to mid-teens who hang around together for a summer or two and whose apparent main objectives are stealing and fighting.

Richard Frazier (fifteen) gives this account of his experience:

> I know when I was running with a gang about thirteen of us were together and with me it was fourteen. They was going to steal something. They said, "Man, we're going to make him [Richard] go in there and get it." I said, "Naw you ain't going to make me go there 'cause I'm fixing to go.... This is my last night with you." They said, "It don't make us no difference. We should make you go in there and get it anyway." After I saw them getting in trouble, I just came on back. ... I don't follow people that have trouble on their minds.

Boys more than girls are under the influence of their peer group when coming up, and the tendency of this influence is to foster deviant behavior. If a boy is going to get into trouble, project residents believe that he will get into quite a few "serious troubles" by the time he is sixteen.

Robbing, stealing, drinking, teenage fighting, promiscuity, and having children before marriage are seen as both serious and frequent troubles.[7] The joy ride, drinking party, "gang bang," and purse snatching episodes are quite often part of the activities of these gangs.

Gangs, like friends, however, do not stay together very long. The membership changes, gets older, ends up in reform school, or simply loses interest in running with each other, and so the gang disbands. Gerald Buchanan claims that in the early sixties there were several large gangs in the project, but these disbanded when their leaders were "sent up." When they disbanded, no organized group replaced them, but project boys still hang around together and seek their kicks where they can find them.

Another group that is characteristic of the teenage boy is the singing group. The fields of entertainment and athletics have thus far offered the most conspicuous avenues for upward mobility for Negro ghetto youth. One very apparent indicator of the extent to which these youth desire mobility is the number of teenagers in the project who train for these fields. Many never reach an audition or a tryout, but the effort they exert as amateurs testifies to their not having opted out of the struggle for success.

Four or five boys and occasionally a girl or two will get together quite regularly and practice. One group, the Mellmonts, sings in apartments, downstairs janitors' rooms, or anywhere it can gather an audience. The songs sung are about the problems of love, the hardships of life, and occasionally a bit of the blues, although the blues are generally recognized as a sign of both "old age" and a rural background. Most teenagers here, as everywhere, prefer rock and roll. Disappointment in love is the most common theme:

> Two stupid feet set down beside you
> You wring my heart in two
> But till they discover
> You really love another
> Two stupid feet walk back to you.

Because large groups of any character tend to be undependable, a boy seeks a close running buddy to help him in his fighting and help him out in life's troubles. These dyadic relationships tend to be more stable than larger ones, but even they are not of long duration because the expectations boys have of a running buddy are usually beyond his ability to fulfill. A buddy doesn't have the money you need when you need it; he is almost as prone to steal your girl as any one else, and when it comes right down to it, he doesn't trust you any more than you really trust him. All relationships with one's peers, therefore, are tenuous, and the boy in his late teens, while he may have one or more running buddies, is generally prepared to face life on its own terms alone. Hammond writes:

> "Go for yourself" means in a sense do what you're big enough to do because you are the one who must suffer the consequences in a culture that says you can do as much "wrong" as you like, but shame on you if you get caught. In this setting, limits are where the individual doers put them. What would be considered in middle-class terms as deviant behavior is highly tolerated.[8]

Gerald's Perspective

Gerald Buchanan was fifteen when the study began. The problems of teenage boys are well presented in his career. From this one teenager's point of view, many things are "natural" that might, from a middle-class point of view, be considered deviant. Thus there is the matter of vandalism:

> You know kids. They used to be real high fences and then they cut them down, half size. And that did it. The kids got tired of walking around. They would kick one of em loose and just start throwing it, doing everything. . . . I can't feel too bad about this because I do it myself. I don't feel too bad about it. I feel neutral about it.

And of course sexual intercourse is considered natural even for a thirteen-year-old. Gerald was once asked, "How do you view girls that get pregnant at thirteen?" He replied:

> I think of them the same way I thought of them before they were pregnant 'cause myself, I like to get a little just like the next one. I think the fella's usually in a mess because he ain't got no job and he can't support her. So the mother usually have to take care of the girl. And she did it once . . . well she'll be the wiser.

Part of the problem of adolescence is running with the wrong crowd. There are so many temptations in this environment and so many kids on the loose that it is difficult not to run with the wrong crowd. Gerald was asked if he ever belonged to a gang and he replied much like Richard Frazier (see p. 17):

> Ah, I used to be with them say a lot. I used to be with them, but I never did when they go to steal something. I go home . . . [and] they start

telling some other of their friends about Gerald, "Gerald ain't nothing, man, that nigger scared. We got ready to go steal some money over on Newberry. He wouldn't even go with us." I wasn't interested, so they passed the word and I got popular by being unpopular with them.

Thus Gerald does not consider himself to be one of the "thuggish" crowd. But he has been in constant contact with the police nevertheless.

He has been taken down to police headquarters on several occasions. He brags, "I been to Ram Street once, I been to Ninth, I been to Eight, Gotham. . . . I got tooken down the Eighth District for curfews [being out after 1:00]." He also has made many trips to Central. Gerald claims, however, that he has never been convicted. His exploits seem to be pretty typical of boys in the project. For example:

> There was a laundry truck down there in front of Opal's home and me and my buddy were snatching clothes out of it and we started running. There was a police car right around there talking to a project policeman named M. . . . They were over there. [They] took out their gun and thought maybe they were going to shoot somebody so I stopped. So M., he calls you "little punk," . . . he choked me and then he told me [them] "Take this little punk and get on down" and then I got in the car and they took me down there [Main]. The one that took me down, he was nice. He was going to let me go, but seeing that I been down there before he didn't let me go, so I stayed four hours.

He also tells of another run-in with the police:

> One day me and a boy named Ike, we were downtown. I didn't go downtown with him. I saw him down there. He was stealing stuff, and a boy named Arthur he was with him, and they left outside the building. The man brought in a shipment of Knoxs, and set it outside the building and Arthur grabbed a box and I grabbed a box and so they caught me, but he got away. They took me over to Central District, and you know, they will try to make you tell a lie. They say I went down there with him . . . that I purposely came down there to see him. That wasn't it at all. Since I saw a chance like that I went and took it. If they think you lying and you keep on sticking to what you saying, they get mad and hit you.

Thus stealing, like other deviant behavior, is very much a part of the teenager's way of life, although in general more rationalization is required to justify such activity. Gerald himself has a record of four arrests for petty theft and joyriding.

The conviction that one is going to end up in jail is neither uncommon nor unrealistic. One of Gerald's running buddies, Samuel, was asked, "What do you think will happen to you?" and he replied, "I'll end up in the pen somewhere." "What makes you think that?" "Sometimes I be thinking that. . . . My mother always talking, she say, 'You need to be put somewhere where you can stay out of trouble.'" Sam was sentenced to nine months in the State Reformatory for Boys in the summer of 1965 for his part in an armed robbery where another boy was knifed. He took part in a riot in the Reformatory and was sentenced to six months more and thus is still in detention.

From Gerald's point of view his mother is his biggest problem as a teenager because she constantly tries to "mother" him. "She tries to kiss me and do all that before you go anywhere." He handles this by provoking her to anger:

> I joke with her. She tell me, "Mind your manner." I say, "Aw shut up." I be playing with her and stuff like that. I don't mean it. I aggravate her, you know, trying to get her back out of here. I aggravate her again. She say she going to hit me, but she never do.

And so he won't ask his mother for money, but rather turns to his father who also gives him an understanding ear:

> He understands you. He used to tell me he had the same trouble most every trouble I have had, he'd have so you know when he was small. He said, I dealing with it all right. Therefore I come to him a whole lot.

> Q: Do you think he's a special father?

> Well, used to be, but not any more. You know, I told him I want to learn to drive and he ain't got round to it yet. I'm kinda mad at him.

At the end of the study Gerald was nineteen, a high school graduate by virtue of the equivalency exam, unemployed, separated from a wife and two children, and unable to join the Air Force because of his police record. He has thus experienced frustration, failure, and fatherhood before he has come of age.

EARLY ATTEMPTS AT EARNING MONEY LEGITIMATELY

While the boy is not expected to do much work around the house, there is some expectation that he will at least make the effort to find part-time work. Most boys in their teens have done some work for pay, though the majority do not have regular part-time jobs. Richard Frazier (fifteen) has the most regular work history of the younger boys, having held a job in a grocery store as a carry out clerk for several months. T. J. Patterson (nineteen), a high school graduate, has perhaps made the best job adjustment of the older boys, although he is at present out of a job. He worked for a local packing company for about a year and for a nearby refrigerator company for a few weeks. In both he performed only manual work. Although he is the only member of his family to finish high school, present job opportunities look no better for him than they do for his other siblings, so he is taking night school courses and trying to improve his education. He remains hopeful that his education will eventually improve his job opportunities. Gerald Buchanan has had numerous jobs, including helping clean up the project through the Youth Corps, working in the local assembly plant, and taking training under programs offered in the Job Corps. He has not stayed more than a few weeks at any one job. He works until he gets a couple of pay checks and then lays off to play pool (to the consternation of his parents). Gerald has found his high school equivalency diploma to be useless in getting him the job he wants. The Washington boys, Levan (nineteen), Jerry (sixteen), Lee (eighteen), and Howard (fifteen), have helped their father out on his truck, and have also been employed in several part-time jobs outside the family. (Only one of eight teenage daughters, Barbara Wards, is presently working, and in fact she has been working regularly at a local department store for almost two years.)

Most boys have a fuzzy notion about what they want to be, or else they want to be like someone they see regularly and who, they fancy, must live an exciting existence. For example, Richard claims, along with Sam, that he wants to be a policeman.[9] Gerald has aspirations of being an electrical engineer, by which he means someone who repairs appliances or airplanes, whichever he can find training to become. Several of the boys find the Army a way out of their job problems. James Perry (seventeen) and Nathan Patterson are now in the service. As we have seen, Gerald tried to get into the Air Force, but his police record kept him out. He has not applied for induction into the Army. By and large the services are not very attractive to the boys in the project.

Richard Frazier

For the boy who has recently moved to the city, the contrast between the expectations of his parents and what he is able to provide in the way of help is often a source of conflict. This is best exemplified in the case of Richard Frazier. He is quite a contrast to his parents. While they are of the country, he has quickly picked up city ways. At fifteen he is a sharp dresser from his Knox hat to his highly polished shoes. Richard remembers Mississippi somewhat differently than his parents, who tend to romanticize it:

> You have to pick cotton down there but up here you know it's different. . . . You don't have to do up here as you do down there because [there] you come back out of the field [and cook lunch or dinner and go right back out in the field] . . . [and the] stores down there are different to me. . . . Shoes down there and up here look like to me they're two different pairs. . . . You can get better shoes up here.

The city has meant freedom from field work and chores, as well as access to things like new clothes and many new acquaintances. His father stands with the comfortable casualness of a farm hand, whereas Richard stands tall, pulls precisely at a cigarette, and looks you over with the air of deceptive confidence characteristic of the street. He is often to be found slouching teenage fashion in the living room club chair, talking to friends on the phone. His father does not feel at ease talking over a phone.

Having already acquired more than three times the formal education of either of his parents by virtue of being a sophomore in high school, he is often called upon to carry out the necessary family business. Bills from creditors, doctor's prescriptions, instructions from government agencies like Welfare pass through his hands. He is especially useful in answering the many notes from the school regarding himself and his brothers and sisters. For a while he had managed to convince his parents that he was going to graduate this year, but they discovered their error and are trying to convince him that he ought to stay in school until he finishes high school. He decided, finally, to complete school.

Richard thus has a certain status in the family by virtue of being such an important link with the outside world. His younger sister Rosie Joe shares some of this, but she is much more reticent and less well prepared to handle such important matters. It is not an easy thing for his parents to accept their dependence upon him, a dependence that they probably would not have felt as acutely if they were still living in the country.

THE STRATEGY OF COOL[10]

Playing it cool is an important aspect of what Rainwater has called "the expressive life style."[11] This survival technique is an attempt to "make yourself interesting and attractive to others so that you are better able to manipulate their behavior along lines that will provide some immediate gratification."[12] When a person "loses his cool," he has become victimized by this strategy or "put in a trick." Playing it cool is thus a defense against exploitation.

Learning to lie effectively is central to the notion of "cool" and the expressive life style. Children are taught early that it does not pay to tell the truth, particularly to strangers who might be bill collectors, plain clothes "fuzz," or simply someone interested in some personal and immediate gratification. The following is an attempted deception undertaken by two eight-year-olds:

> Annette then went over to the window in the living room and put her hand behind the curtain and was looking out. She put her hand behind her and turned to me and said: "I lost my quarter."
>
> "How did you do that?"
>
> "It fell out the window. Give me another one."
>
> "No! I don't have another one to give you."
>
> "But mine's gone."
>
> Clinton then went over to where she was and said: "No you didn't; you still got it."
>
> Annette grinned and reached behind the curtain and opened her hand and brought it back and said, "See, I found my quarter."
>
> Clinton tried the same thing and said: "I lost my nickel."
>
> "Did you? What happened?"
>
> "It fell."
>
> Annette said: "You didn't lose it either."
>
> Clinton then came over to where I was and pushed his quarter underneath a stand and said: "I lose mine. Give me another."[13]

What appears to be an impossible deception to an outside observer is not considered as such by Clinton, who has seen equally obvious lies frequently rewarded. This is especially true in the small matter of begging for pennies—a constant activity of the children in the project. Sometimes the necessity for giving the gift is implied in the situation with a stranger, who ought to be able to perceive that you are poor and therefore in need. Often the encounter is simply initiated: "Give me a penny." One young ten-year-old boy was asked in return, "Why, do many people give you pennies?" His reply was: "Yes, because I do things for them." This he said while dancing away chanting: "Wash the car, clean out the garage...," knowing full well that what he was saying was untrue and that he was begging for pennies without ever having done anything to earn what he received. In this situation, however, he was unable to continue the pretense and made as graceful an exit as he could.

Another important function of the lie in the ghetto is "face saving." The Cadillac, the forty-five dollar shoes, the one hundred and twenty dollar suit tell the world, "I'm a success and I've been around," although the reality is ordinarily quite grim. Gerald Buchanan carried this off quite well in a small way when he remarked at a restaurant that he had tasted all of the twelve or thirteen wines on the wine list except the ruby port which he selected.

This need to create a world with the appearance of success and personal competence has interesting repercussions. On one occasion Mrs. Buchanan claimed, "Gerald is in Indiana. He's in Job Corps training now," despite the fact that he was at the time in the bedroom and soon came out to say hello. For her son to have been in Indiana was very important to Betty Re because it marked for her the beginning of his assuming responsibility for his wife and children. In this instance the word "lie" is perhaps not quite accurate to describe what took place, as it may well have been an expression of a deep wish fervently believed in and not an intentional deception.

The hustler is the epitome of this phenomenon and an idol of the "cool" world. The hustler is aware of his front, but in less stressful situations a man of the ghetto may well assume a front and afterward come to believe in it, not as a game, but as a part of himself.

Working Game

The manipulative, aggressive aspect of "cool" is seen in working game. The verbal dexterity required for working game is developed in playing the dozens. Several teenage boys constantly worked the author for small change while he was in the project, and they always had a ready reason for needing the money. They needed "carfare to get to grandfather's house" or to the "draft board" or "to look for a job" or to "buy lunch," usually adding that if they didn't get what they needed, something serious would happen to them. They begged money on the pretense of needing food only a few times, but when they were successful, they often turned it into wine or beer.

The following gives an example of their game:

Gerald: Give me a quarter.

Interviewer: Why?

G: Well, see, I gotta go to work tomorrow, and I don't have carfare.

I: Did you get a job?

G: Yeah, I got a job on Middlebury and Park.

I: Doing what?

G: Well, washing woodwork and things.

I: How much do you get paid?

G: Forty-five dollars a week.

I: How long do you have to work for that?

G: From nine until four-thirty.

I: How did you get the job?

G: Well, a man in the building, on the elevator that I know, he talking about it one night and he works out there and he got me a job.

[At this point the interviewer decided to give Gerald the quarter for the heck of it and tossed it to him.]

Sam: I need a quarter too.

I: Why do you need a quarter?

S: I ain't got nothing to eat.

G: You can see what he's trying to eat can't ya [boiled egg sandwich]?

I: How is it that you don't have anything to eat at this time of day?

S: Well, my mother left and she went to work and she didn't leave any money in the house and I don't have anything to get lunch with.

I: Aw come on now Sam; you can do better than that.

S: No, honest, that's the truth, ain't it, Gerald?

G: Sure is.

The author gave Sam a quarter; they took their money and left, presumably to buy food. The author stayed behind with Mary, Gerald's girlfriend, assuring them he would remain only a few minutes. In about fifteen minutes they returned with a bag and went into the bedroom. Mary said that Gerald "is embarrassed to eat in front of people, so he's gonna eat in the bedroom."

Feeling that he knew the boys well enough, the author decided to visit them in the bedroom where he found them drinking beer and wine. They were totally unmoved at being unmasked, for by their teens they had been well trained in playing it cool.

The author asked, "Why didn't you tell me that you wanted to buy some beer?" He had done this several times for them in the past. Gerald replied: "Because we didn't think you'd give us the money." Of course, Gerald did not have a job at all, but since the author was interested in his getting a job, he frequently used this as a cover to hide his real intentions when he did not want to be bothered by the author, or when he wanted something from him. In contrast to the example of Annette and Clinton, Mary and Sam decided to support Gerald in his deception. Thus the maintenance of a lie often becomes a group activity that may well pay off to more than one member.

While this example could be interpreted merely as the common mode of treatment given to white outsiders, it is also a very common form of interaction between members themselves. This is particularly true in rapping or jiving a girl in order to obtain her sexual favors.[14] Sometimes the manipulation of the other is carried out with a minimum of verbal interaction. Thus Mr. Buchanan frequently obtains small change from friends by pocketing change for drinks when the friends are too drunk to know the difference.

The Pimp

In the cool world the ideal relationship (from the young male's point of view) between the sexes is achieved by the man who "pimps" a woman.[15] In this type of relationship the woman supports the man. In the classic understanding of the term, a pimp may live off the labors of several prostitutes, getting a stylish living in return for services such as protection, banking for jail bond and saving purposes, and "fix" procurement in the case of legal action. This type is still prevalent. Thus Sam tells of his friend who has diamond rings and Cadillacs derived from the income of five prostitutes who live with him and his wife and children, but conduct their business elsewhere. Andrew Buchanan (fifty-five) confides that for about three years he enjoyed the life of a pimp as a young man and remembers that he always had several hundred dollars in his pocket and always dressed in the best of style:

> Due to the time, the economics of the time ... I didn't have no money. If you found a girl who had a nice big house (they had seven or eight other girls in there), maybe she was working, maybe her old man was a chauffeur for the same family, had a whole lot of income coming. You wouldn't have to worry about a place to stay and no food or clothes. And if you was diligent enough you could have some money. These girls made fifteen or twenty dollars a night. [They] didn't do a thing but drink it up and buy some stockings. I didn't drink so I could stash some money and it kept me with a nice bankroll when I got situated. I could go around and play a little policy, do some cheap gambling, have a suit on every day, have a cigar and be dressed up. Kept forty, fifty dollars all the time. After becoming acquainted with these girls, I guess my very character and the way I carried myself, they trusted me. So, therefore, all the money they had left, maybe one dollar, maybe fifty cents, they would give to me for the bank. So that made me a big bankroll—a hundred dollars or so in my pocket. Say there came a girl, some kind of saintly too, some had families they had to support, they would like to save their money until Friday or Saturday. They tell their mama they been working (they should have been going to school). I would give them their money, which was minus fifty cents or a dollar. Then some of them (the older ones didn't have anybody to give any money to particularly) they save their money for the time they might get arrested. At that time about fifteen dollars would take them down to court, and if they would go into the workhouse, fifteen dollars would take them out. So they would save money.

However, the term also covers the more general situation where a man lives off a woman who is not a prostitute and who earns her living legitimately as a professional, a well-paid clerk or domestic, or a welfare recipient. Hence, the excitement of "Mother's Day," the tenth of the month when the welfare checks come in the mail and "the eagle flies." Pimping seems to be the younger man's approach to the dilemma of poverty, low status in the larger culture, and unemployment. In the language of the street, a "cat" is usually a pimp. Thus Mary (eighteen) says that a "cat" can:

> ... be a girl or a boy and they wants to be cool, wants to be hip, jive, you know. If it's a boy, he try to pimp off a woman. He going to lovey dovey up on her ... if she got some money ... they gonna use their

power to get the money from you. . . . You know, like telling the girl that she got "Cleopatra eyes" and that she be "sweeter than a cherry." . . . She probably buy him clothes and he ain't giving her nothing but a little love and stuff like that. . . . For instance a lot of these cats gets a woman about thirty-nine or something and she not married and do have a good job.

The role of the pimp, then, is most characteristically that of a young man seeking an older woman who may have a comfortable income and feels that her powers of attraction are fading. Sam explains the willingness of a woman to "pimp a man" under the rubric of "she loves him." Love, for Sam, implies a willingness to do anything for the person who is loved, including "bringing them their slippers, lighting their cigarettes. . . . Man, if a woman loves you, you got it made, there ain't nothing you have to do . . . you don't have to lift your little finger."

This conception of love is in keeping with a general tendency to demand evidence of concern, even, as here, to the point of exploitation in the small matters of everyday life. Irvin (seventeen) explains the problems of city life in terms of a declining emphasis upon concrete and traditional expressions of love. He believes that kids are so bad these days because they are raised on cow's milk rather than their mother's milk; they have been placed more often in the hands of baby-sitters, and as infants no longer receive their food premasticated from their mother's mouth. The pimp takes advantage of this need to concretize relationships. He constantly demands that his woman demonstrate her affection by providing him with a high standard of living (by ghetto standards) while he demonstrates his by his capacity as a lover.

Mary Perry maintains that she knows a boy, "who is nineteen years old and he got a woman [thirty-nine] 'up tight.' . . . She's a nurse and she gets paid every month . . . and he gets just about half of her check and comes and spends it on us." The final insult of the pimp—and the fear of any woman keeping one—is that he will take her money and spend it on other women, demonstrating that despite her care for him, he cares not a whit for her. The pimp is, in some sense, the urban counterpart of the relationships between rural women and the wandering men who moved from lumber camp to lumber camp living off the women they could find in each. There the exchange, however, was rarely of money, but rather an exchange of intimacies.

"Pimping" is but one of several non-marital roles a man can

play. He can in certain unusual situations take full advantage of a woman's holdings and exploit her with even less reciprocity. Thus Lilly Parvin claims Ronnie tries to rape her occasionally and sometimes succeeds. Other relationships that indicate a greater degree of commitment and reciprocity on the part of the male will be discussed under the role of the boyfriend in the next chapter.

Learning "Cool"

"Playing it cool" is thus primarily the way of the street, but it extends into the family as well and results in some painful paradoxes. If the mother is to train her child for survival on the street, she must train him in the arts of manipulation and deception. The following is an excellent account of the process by which a young boy is ushered into the cool world by his mother:

> Darryl, age seven, tells his mother that he needs a quarter so he can attend the movies in school. Mary, his sister, age eight, then tells her mother not to listen to him because he is lying so he can have the money for himself. She goes to the same school and she assures her mother that no money is necessary to see the movies. Darryl stands quietly with a sheepish grin on his face. His mother asks if he really needs money. Darryl says very meekly that he does. Mary shouts: "No he doesn't; he's lying."

> His mother practically shouts back: "DARRYL BE A MAN! Speak up for yourself, boy."

> It was obvious from the expression on Darryl's face that he was lying —that fact seemed to be understood by everyone. His mother asks him again if he needs the money. This time a little louder, still not very manly, he says: "I sure do," and now he adds a few embellishments. "My teacher told me to bring the money, 'cause if I don't I can't go to the movies and all the other kids are going."

> His mother is now satisfied, not that he isn't lying, but that he has learned to lie a little better than he did before. She gives Darryl the money, and as an afterthought, she tells him to return the money if he doesn't need it for the movies. The whole family knows that Darryl won't think of returning the money and that's the way it should be.[16]

Playing it cool is a survival technique *par excellence*. Nevertheless, the matter of socialization is not simply training for the cool world as though that world existed in a social vacuum, for that socialization conflicts with those portions of the ghetto world still maintaining working-class orientations and aspirations. Such a world is focused in the mother and the "stable family."

Looking at the street from "inside" the family, one is more aware of the striving for respectability—and the actual accomplishment of the task with certain families at certain times and places. The problem is that at least two, perhaps many more, value configurations or "cultures" influence the lives of those in the ghetto. Which one is given expression at any one time is a matter of circumstance, and which one is dominant or subordinate is not at all clear unless one is willing to acknowledge observable behavior as the only dimension of factuality.

Nevertheless, the problems posed for the young ghetto Negro male by the "cool world" are great, because "being cool" may be an asset in surviving in the street, but it is not a source of deep pleasure. It is rather a source of a great amount of disappointment and sometimes violence, particularly as related to the deception of "cutting out on a spouse." Furthermore, the extent to which a man submerges himself in the cool world is a measure of the acceptance of defeat not only in the interpersonal realm, but also in the social realm where mobility is still an aspiration. The cool man is not, however, the bowery man who needs assurance from his compatriots that "Man you can't do no better." The cool man has pretentious aspirations in both areas, and the matter of moving up either legitimately or illegitimately is very much a matter of his concern. The need for intimate, affectionate relationships with the opposite sex, while undoubtedly inhibited by the rubric of "cool," nevertheless is there and seeks expression in warm human relationships.

Some of these relationships are quite durable. The family, with all of its internal stresses and strains, exists in spite of the street, though it can never be cut off from it. That it exists with any stability at all in the light of such circumstances is a point that has caused more than one researcher to pause. The argot of cool, the image of the pimp, the life of the street are all too obvious and are on the lips and in the souls of the ghetto dwellers constantly, and yet the solidarity of the family is not completely destroyed.

NOTES

1. John Dollard, "The Dozens: The Dialect of Insult," *American Imago,* I (1939), 3–24.
2. Boone Hammond, "The Contest System: A Survival Technique" (St.

Louis: Washington University Essay Series in Sociology, December 1965), p. 23.

3. Roger D. Abrahams, "Playing the Dozens," *Journal of American Folklore,* LXXV (July 1962), 207–20.

4. *Ibid.,* p. 214.

5. Howard Becker's concept of a deviant career and the importance of "labeling" as marking a significant turning point in that career is highly relevant here. Howard Becker, *The Outsiders: Studies in the Sociology of Deviance* (New York: The Macmillan Company, 1966), pp. 25 ff.

6. In this group of teenagers, 61 per cent of the boys have police records, 29 per cent of the girls, or 48 per cent of the total teenage population.

7. Jerome Stromberg, "Perspectives on Pathology, Socialization, Religion and World View of Project Residents," p. 10.

8. Hammond, *op. cit.,* p. 9.

9. The implications of this fact are more fully explored in David A. Schulz, "Some Aspects of the Policeman's Role as It Impinges Upon the Lower-Class Negro Family" (Paper presented to the American Sociological Association, Boston, August 1968).

10. The following definition of cool is offered by Robert H. DeCoy in his *The Nigger Bible* (Los Angeles: Holloway House Publishing Co., 1967), p. 30: "Cool, n.v.—In control, wise, aloof, detached. A state of being in admirable possession of one's wit and emotions."

11. Lee Rainwater, "Work and Identity in the Lower Class," in *Planning for a Nation of Cities,* ed. Sam H. Warner (Cambridge: M.I.T. Press, 1967). For a succinct picture of street life, see John Horton, "Time and Colored People," *Trans-action,* IV (April 1967), 5–12.

12. Lee Rainwater, "Crucible of Identity: The Negro Lower-Class Family," *Daedalus,* XCV (Winter, 1966), 206.

13. These notes on the Buchanan family were made by a colleague, Miss Gwendolyn Jones.

14. Greater detail is to be found in Hammond, *op. cit.,* pp. 35–42.

15. The more general term covering the situation where a woman supports a man is not acceptable usage to a professional pimp, who calls these persons "studs" and claims they have no expertise or professional skills.

16. Barry Dworkin and Susan Dworkin, "Cool: Young Adults in the Ghetto" (Columbia, Mo.: University of Missouri), p. 4.

GROWING UP MALE*

Ulf Hannerz

In this final chapter on sex roles, and in particular on the male role, we will take a look at some social and cultural data concerning the life of ghetto boys as a context for raising anew a question to which some people apparently feel they already have a satisfactory answer. The question, in its most general form, is, "What is the character of sex role socialization for young lower-class black males in a community where matrifocality is common?" It seems important to point out that we are really only raising the question and examining it. To give a definite answer to it, for one thing, one would need a degree of psychological sophistication which is outside the area of competence of at least this social anthropologist. The reason for taking another look at this complex, then, is that some of the pronouncements on it have been somewhat deficient in their considerations of culture and social relations, and these are the facets which will be examined here.

Our point of departure is the commonly accepted opinion that a boy growing up in a household where the father is more or less absent comes to suffer from confusion over his sexual identity. First of all, the person with whom the boy ought to identify is missing, so the boy has no appropriate model for his sex role. The information about the nature of masculinity which a father would transmit unintentionally to his sons merely by going about his life at home is lacking. Furthermore, the adult who is available, the mother, is inappropriate as a role model for him; if he starts to identify with her, he will sooner

*From Ulf Hannerz, *Soulside: Inquiries Into Ghetto Culture and Community,* © 1969. Reprinted with permission from Columbia University Press.

or later find out that he has made a mistake. ("Identification" is here taken, perhaps somewhat simplistically, to stand for perception of real or desired similarity between model and observer, leading to the observer's acting in imitation of the model.) This misidentification with mother would lead the young males to become more feminine. Some commentators on black family structure do indeed cite examples of men out of matrifocal families of orientation inclined toward feminine behavior: Dai (1949:450) writes of a psychiatric patient who ever since early childhood had wished to be a girl and who acquired such feminine interests as playing with dolls, doing house work, and being his mother's helpmaid. Rohrer and Edmonson (1964:165–167) describe more extensively the case of Roland, who stayed with his mother until her death and devoted his life completely to caring for her. He took a "womanly pride," as the two authors put it, in the furnishings of his apartment and their care, and seemed to have little to do with other men. His psychological test responses showed confusion over his sex role, and it appeared that he had largely taken over his mother's position in the home and in the family.

Cases such as these would serve as examples of rather overt tendencies toward femininity among some men coming out of matrifocal families. Very casual observations in the ghetto also lead one to believe that male homosexuality is not particularly infrequent in the community. Small ghetto boys are well aware of what a "faggot" is (but also of what a "bulldagger"—lesbian—is; there are obviously sociopsychological forces propelling toward female homosexuality as well). However, all sex role confusion does not take this course. Brody and his collaborators (Brody 1961; Derbyshire *et al.* 1963) mention such identification problems as a contributing cause of schizophrenia (sometimes occurring in conjunction with homosexuality) among black mental patients. Many more writers, however, see as the final consequence of this early misidentification and confusion a compulsively masculine reaction, in that males from matrifocal families of orientation come to embrace a very conspicuously male role definition—of the type we first delineated as a ghetto-specific male alternative in chapter 4. In this view, the male peer group, as the locus of shows of anxious masculinity, has developed as a response to the male need for a forum where identity problems of this kind can be resolved. Walter B. Miller is one of those scholars who have pointed to such a relationship between matrifocality and the type of masculine expression we find in the black ghetto (1958:9; 1959:227). Roger D. Abrahams (1964:32 ff.) is another. Rohrer and Edmonson write that although the peer group is a necessary institution, it is only a poor substitute for family security and stability. Yet without the group, the self-doubts and insecurity of the male would be even stronger and more crippling; in the peer group they can be shared by the frightened and confused little boys and the tough but embattled "mama's men" they grow into (Rohrer and Edmonson 1964:167–168).

This is the kind of depiction of the process of growing up male in the ghetto which we will discuss here. It is rooted in an implicit or explicit microsociological notion of what goes on in domestic life under matrifocality. Restated in a perhaps somewhat extreme form, the interpretation is that there is a male model vacuum, and even a risk that the little boy will start striving to become more feminine like his mother. When he belatedly discovers his mistake—and this "discovery," of course, need not be on a high level of awareness—he strives hard to compensate by being extremely masculine, but traces of the identification with mother are hard to destroy, so the process of ostentatious male identity definition has to go on continuously, as a kind of rhetoric of behavior directed as much at oneself as at anybody else.

Are we to believe this?

In the face of a lot of evidence, this view of male identity development cannot easily be rejected altogether. There are points in the story, however, where modifications may be suggested, question marks inserted, and alternative interpretations proposed.

First of all one may want to point out that the problems of identification and re-identification are not qualitatively unique to the boy in the black ghetto matrifocal family. It is, of course, a commonplace and generally accepted tenet of psychoanalytic theory that infants first identify with the mother and that boys later have to change their identification to the father as the major available male. The necessity of some kind of change of identification for boys is thus far from peculiar to the ghetto; what is unusual, if we follow the interpretation summarized above, is the problem of finding someone to reidentify with. Furthermore, however, and more noteworthy, there have been claims set forth that precisely this kind of difficulty in finding a useful model is characteristic of white urban middle class in American society. Parsons points out that girls can be initiated into a female role from an early age because their mothers are usually continuously at home doing things which are tangible and meaningful to the children, while fathers do not work at home so that their role enactment remains to a large extent unobserved, inaccessible and relatively unknown. Girls can help their mothers with many domestic activities and thus get sex role training; the boys have little chance to emulate their fathers in action, partly because of the abstract and intangible nature of many middle class male tasks (Parsons 1942: 605). Elsewhere Parsons views the peer groups of white middle class boys quite similarly to the way other commentators have looked at the peer groups of boys from black matrifocal families; these groups are seen as a focus of compulsive masculinity where boys reinforce one another's reaction formations (in Parsons and Bales 1955:116).

The gap between white mainstream and ghetto matrifocality thus appears to have narrowed down even more as far as the socialization experiences of boys are concerned. Yet the observers of matrifocal families cited above obviously consider this difference great enough for the boys involved to have particular problems in arriving at a satisfactory definition of their male identity. To give some opportunity for evaluating this view, we will take a look at the typical contexts of potential sex role socialization of ghetto boys from matrifocal families, starting by paying particular attention to that extreme case of matrifocality, the husbandless household.

Socialization at Home

Several factors are obviously involved in determining what kind of sex role learning for young males goes on in the household. One of them is whether adult male role models are really as unavailable as they are presumed to be, although the father is absent. In previous chapters we have indicated that husbandless households need not be maleless—many of them have boarders, others include a mother's brother. In a great many cases, the boys' mothers have male friends who make regular visits; some households are not strictly husbandless in that the mother has a resident male friend, common-law husband or ordinary husband, who is not her children's father. Quite frequently, then, the adult male vacuum within the household is less than complete. It should be possible to some extent to use these men as role models, so that the boys can make some sense of what is "typically male" from their behavior. The question to what extent the boys really fashion their own behavior after these potential models cannot be conclusively answered here. As we have noted earlier, the relationship between these men and the children of the dominant woman (or women) in the household is not usually particularly close. (It may be added here too that in many cases the difference between such households and matrifocal families with a resident husband-father may not be great. In the household of Harry and Patricia Jones of Winston Street, the closest relationship is undoubtedly that of Patricia Jones and her teenage daughter. This is not at all balanced by Harry Jones' relationship to his sons, for as he readily admits, he seldom speaks to them except to ask them to run errands, keep quiet, or get out of his way. On the other hand, he is also quite attached to the teenage daughter, whom he often takes along when he goes for a car ride with a friend or when he goes bowling. The sons tend to turn to their mother or older sister for help or advice rather than to their father.) It may be that this relatively non-nurturant quality of the relationship of men to boys in matrifocal families makes it unlikely that it will be a basis for identification and role modeling, but there is also some evidence that in general, nurturance is not a necessary antecedent of imitative learning (cf. Bandura and Walters 1963:95). Other writers on identification, like Parsons (in Parsons and Bales 1955), have assumed that the person of power in the household is the major model for the children, everything else held equal. If this is valid for the ghetto matrifocal family, the mother may indeed be a more important model for the boys than any domestically peripheral male figure. Yet it should be noted here that the woman in a matrifocal household far from always is in a position of uncontested dominance over the adult males—husband, male friend, or brother in residence—and this could tend to blur her image of power for the children. In addition, we should remind ourselves that the degree of control a woman in a matrifocal household really has over members in the household oriented toward participation in street life is often quite limited. Thus even if there is no other adult in the household, the children may not become overawed by maternal powerfulness.

Burton and Whiting (1951) present another approach to the nature of identification in what they call the "status envy hypothesis," according to which identification consists of the covert practice, in fantasy or in play, of the role of an envied status. In a husbandless household, they see the mother as the person to be envied, as she controls the resources sometimes withheld from children—resources which are thus to be envied her. Burton and Whiting cite the studies of Miller and of Rohrer and Edmonson which were discussed above, and accepting the interpretations of compulsive masculinity in peer groups as made by these authors, they see this as evidence for the status envy hypothesis; obviously the boys must have overidentified with their mothers to arrive at such a strong reaction formation.

However, even here the evidence from ghetto matrifocality is not quite as clearcut as it may seem. Burton and Whiting point out that the Oedipal situation is only a special case of the status envy hypothesis, and if ghetto mothers have male friends on whom they spend some of their affection because they are, if nothing else, desirable company, then there is an Oedipal situation in which the boys' object of envy is another male—to be identified with according to the hypothesis. Again the necessity of identifying only with mother is not quite as obvious as it might have appeared at the outset.

Another issue which we will leave largely unresolved is whether the relatively asymmetrical character of a functioning father-son relationship, as in a mainstream American family, really provides the optimal conditions for a son to learn his male role. As the father assumes his leader and authority role, the son becomes assigned to a complementary dependent and submissive role. The central position of an adult male in the household could also conceivably lessen the boy's chance of practicing his male role by providing too stiff competition. Yet it may be that we are introducing a red herring here. First of all, father-son relationships are not necessarily forced into a rigid mold of dominance and submission; according to an early paper by Gregory Bateson (1942), there is a noticeable difference in this respect between English and American mainstream culture in that American children are encouraged by their parents toward independence and even a certain boastfulness. Furthermore, and at least as important, the child's imitation of the adult need not take place in the direct interaction with that adult. Rather, he may pick up the adult's behavior covertly in the process of role taking which goes on continuously in interaction, rehearse it to himself, and display it in quite different relationships. Even in a dominance-submission relationship can thus the submissive party learn to be dominant. Finally, as Parsons points out (in Parsons and Bales 1955:59), the socializing agent plays at least a dual role in relation to the socializee. In his direct relationship he may motivate the latter to take him for a model, but the modes of behavior he models may be taken out of quite different social contexts and relationships which the socializee may observe only as a non-participant or a participant not directly interacting with the model.

These points may lead us to doubt that the mainstream household is inferior to the matrifocal household as a male role socialization milieu as far as the influence of paternal presence is concerned. But neither can we state conclusively that the matrifocal household is devoid of potential role models, or that these potential models do not really function as such, even if circumstances are such that their modeling efficiency is probably not optimal.

Another major question is what kind of influence the mother (or any other adult woman in the household acting in some way like a mother) actually has on a boy. For one thing, there seems to be some danger here that those commentators who have most strongly drawn the attention toward the possibility of socialization into non-masculine behavior in a female-headed household have made too facile an inference from childrearing in female-headed households which are possibly quite different from those in the ghetto. Pettigrew, for instance, cites evidence from studies of white American boys whose fathers were absent from family life during World War II, and of Norwegian sailors' sons. These boys were reported as clearly more immature, submissive, dependent, and effeminate than other boys (Pettigrew 1964: 18). But here the strong possibility must be noted that these boys had very different relationships to their mothers than many ghetto boys in matrifocal families have. A housewife with few children and relatively limited everyday contacts with other adults is likely to devote a great deal of time to nurturant interaction with the children, and her relationship to them is thus likely to become intensive and quite possibly overprotective. If the boys then turn out as described by Pettigrew there is little reason for surprise. Obviously there are instances of such mother-child relationships in the ghetto; the case of Roland described by Rohrer and Edmonson and cited above may well have been one of them. But those who worry about ghetto boys becoming more immature, submissive, dependent, and effeminate on account of mother's influence might have done well to give more heed to the comment on this topic in one of the pioneering anthropological studies of black Americans, Hortense Powdermaker's *After Freedom.* Writing of a Mississippi town, Powdermaker points out that the black mother in households where there is no father either works outside the home or is busy at home with her own work, thus having little spare time and energy to lavish on her children. Powdermaker also notes that the women have outside sexual contacts and thus do not make the children emotional substitutes for a mate (Powdermaker 1939:197).

The matrifocal households in the Winston Street neighborhood are in many ways like those described by Powdermaker. They often contain large numbers of children, and taking care of domestic chores for such large households—and with so limited resources—makes it rather difficult for the mother to engage actively in very intensive emotional relationships with the children. Furthermore, many of the mothers have—aside from possible male friends—female friends among relatives and neighbors with whom they tend to spend spare time. Thus the possibility that boys would continue to identify too strongly with the mother is somewhat weakened by the quality she gives—willingly or not—to her interaction with them.

Another facet of maternal influence on the identity of young males involves her actions in instructing them, knowingly or not, about masculinity. Cannot the mother, in her domestic behavior, get her distinction between her own sex category and that of her son across to him, and thereby contribute to having him choose other models? Of course she can, to some extent, and we have already in an earlier chapter noted that the ghetto-specific public imagery about sex roles tends to influence mothers in their behavior toward their children; for instance, they appear to prefer to have daughters, and they have other expectations for their sons' behavior than for that of their daughters. This is how one single mother of three boys and two girls expresses it:

> "You know, you just got to act a little bit tougher with boys than with girls, 'cause they just ain't the same. Girls do what you tell them to do and don't get into no trouble, but you just can't be sure about boys. I mean, you think they're OK and next thing you find out they're playing hookey and drinking wine and maybe stealing things from cars and what not. There's just something bad about boys here, you know. But what can you say when many of them are just like their daddies? That's the man in them coming out. You can't really fight it, you know that's the way it is. They know, too. But you just got to be tougher."

So the women are tougher toward their sons, and they expect their sons to be tougher than their daughters. They feel this is as it should be; a boy who is not tough in his overt behavior may be ridiculed as a "sissy" not only by his peers but also by the women of his household, and his mother admonishes him to act like a boy.

This should not be taken to mean that women consciously and exclusively socialize their sons toward ghetto-specific masculinity. On the contrary, one may be quite certain that most of the instruction mothers are aware of giving is in line with mainstream norms. But even in the domestic context there is some ghetto-specific male role socialization because the women in the household—primarily the mother, but also a grandmother, an aunt, or sisters if they are present —have their behavior toward boys colored by the implicit or explicit notions of the typical characteristics of masculinity. As the socialization relationship in some ways comes to reflect the generalized relationship between men and women in the community, it is to a certain extent a question of an antagonistic socialization. The women are much more concerned to warn sons than daughters against drinking, stealing, staying away from school, and so forth, as they perceive these as male activities; they warn both boys and girls against having too much to do with the other sex, but they make it perfectly clear that boys should refrain from initiatives, while girls need only be on guard against such initiatives. One may speculate that there is an element of self-fulfilling prophecy in such instruction, as the women thus make explicit to the boys what can be expected from a male. This suspicion would seem to have much less support if all mothers were quite consistently and unambiguously negative in their response when such behavior occurs. However, like their older counterparts, young ghetto males, correctly or not, seem rather often to perceive some ambivalence and contradictoriness in the views held by women concerning what males should be like. One may in fact occasionally discern an admiring undertone in complaints by mothers about their sons, just as in those by women about their male friends. One young man in his late teens, still living at home, made this comment about his mother:

> "Sometimes my mother makes a big deal out of it when I have a taste and says I shouldn't drink and I'm turning into a bum and that kind of stuff, you know what I mean. And she acts real angry and says I shouldn't be running around so much, and one day I might get in trouble and all that stuff, you know. And then I hear her talking to all her old women friends about how I go out with all those girls and how I'm really going strong, and once she came and offered me a taste, big smile on her face you know, and then she said she found the bottle in my room a week ago! Shi-it, I'm sure I'm just the way she wants me to be. Women just want to make themselves look good, you know, so they keep fussing about you and showing off."

For an additional fragment of evidence that ghetto women's response to shows of ghetto-specific masculinity on the part of young males is not uniformly rejective one may turn again to ghetto entertainment;

there is an enthusiastic reception from the female audience, adolescents and upwards, to youthful stage personalities showing such behavior. For instance, the child prodigy Little Dion—a song and dance boy—and the youngest member of the young rock-and-roll group Alvin Cash and the Registers, both sometime stars of that series of ghetto stages known as "the chitterling circuit," had a choreography with a heavy sexual load, entered into aggressive verbal contests with the emcees, and put on a *blasé* air about affairs with women, while the mothers in the audience rocked with laughter at this expression of masculinity.

There seems to be some indication, then, that ghetto mothers differentiate between the sexes in the socialization which goes on within the domestic domain; perhaps they do so more strongly than other mothers because the social cleavage between the sexes is so pronounced in the ghetto and is seen as a very fundamental social fact. This differentiated socialization can at least make it obvious to the boy that the mother is not an appropriate role model for him; to some extent it may, largely quite unintentionally, show the road to ghetto-specific masculinity. Rohrer and Edmonson note this (1964:161–162), but they attach little weight to it in their over-all view. Yet, all in all, the phenomena we have pointed to here may lead us to believe that the sex role vacuum for the socialization of males in the matrifocal family is considerably less than complete. This need not mean that a ghetto family of such a structure is just as efficient as the mainstream family in socializing males toward a culturally appropriate form of masculinity. But perhaps we may find it reasonable to doubt that the difference between them is as great as it is sometimes made out to be.

Socialization in the Street

Anyway, these notes on what goes on in the matrifocal family as far as male role socialization is concerned are of somewhat marginal importance when compared to the point at which the absent-model view of male role development can be most strongly criticized. In an earlier chapter, we cited Birdwhistell's (1966) comment on what he called the "sentimental model" of family life; Birdwhistell pointed out that much thinking about the family, among social scientists as well as among the general public, is based on an idealized image which need not be a very accurate reflection of family life in reality. One of the characteristics of the "sentimental model" is that the family is depicted as relatively self-sufficient. It is implied that most of the members' psychological needs are met in interaction with other members.

Theoretical frameworks for socialization research seem often to be based on the unquestioned assumption that the "sentimental model" is a correct representation of reality—see for instance Kagan's review article (1964:145). This assumption may be reinforced by the strong influence that Freudian thinking has had on the study of family processes; it may be, of course, that this model was closer to real life in Freud's days, and in Freud's milieu, than it may be now, particularly in the ghetto community. According to the "sentimental model" it is natural that if the family does not socialize its boys to masculinity, nobody does. But as we have already pointed out, it is characteristic of many ghetto dwellers, in particular of that segment of the community where matrifocality occurs most frequently, that they participate intensively in the social life of the street, and they start to do so at an early age. And when young boys start taking part in street life, they are exposed to a great number of males, even if there is little by way of an adult male presence at home. As we have noted before, there is no lack of males in the ghetto community, although many of them are no more than loosely attached to any child-rearing household. True, in seeing the behavior of their adult male neighbors, young boys get a number of potential role models who show great variability in behavior between themselves, as several life styles co-exist in the community. This may well contribute to variation, compromises, and drift in the boys' behavior. But the men showing ghetto-specific masculinity are in a majority among those who hang out at the street corner, in the alley, or at the carry-out. Thus there is a tendency for the boys to be more strongly exposed to this kind of masculinity than to any other as they start to spend much of their lives away from the household, in territory they share with these men. Again, of course, we come back to the question whether the interaction between the boys and the men is such that it will influence the boys significantly in ordering their behavior. Here we can only note that the men are at least no amorphous mass of anonymous individuals, seen once and then never again; many of them are known neighborhood residents whom the children see practically every day. The men are also familiar with the children. As we have said before, they often keep a watchful eye on the children's play; they tell the children not to play too close to the traffic, they serve as an audience for games, they break up a fight occasionally, and sometimes they give a little instruction for instance in boxing. Now and then they send a boy away on an errand to the store, for a nickel or a dime. Such interaction may lead the boys to experience these men as significant others and perhaps as role models. And in the context of the street corner, if nowhere else, these men—or some of them, at least—may have their share of power and success which might make them seem enviable persons.

The Company of Peers

However, adult men are not the only role models ghetto boys may find in street life. The peer group is a highly influential phenomenon in the patterning of their existence, and its importance begins to be felt early in life. Mothers in ghetto families, both matrifocal and others, often have many children and much to do, so they frequently let older children take care of their younger siblings; particularly often, it seems, those of the same sex. This may mean that one older male whom a small boy may take as a role model is his older brother. More generally, however, the boy is thus introduced at an early age to the all-male peer group. For other boys the link to such a group may be slightly more difficult to achieve so early, but even for them the initiation into the peer group context soon comes. Peer group life, of course, brings boys into contact with others of the same age, so that they can seek concerted solutions to common problems. However, the groups are not severely age graded; the members' ages span over a few years. Thus boys may participate both in groups where they are among the younger members and in groups where they are among the older, and a great many boys are in both positions at the same time, in relation to different groups.

In these groups, of course, there is intensive interaction between members. Much of the activity in the boys' groups may be viewed as "just ordinary children's play"—ball games, roller skating, and so forth. It is noticeable, however, that much of the behavior evinced in the peer group context is of the type we have described as ghetto-specific masculinity, typical of many adult men in the community. There is the concern with sex; already boys less than ten years old talk in the group context about "getting some pussy" (or "some leg" as boys in Washington started saying about 1967), and although there is undoubtedly the same kind of exaggeration in their claims of which one might suspect some of the older males, there is little question that many of the boys start sexual experimentation early, with the girls who form separate but somewhat more loosely knit groups parallel to those of the boys. Many boys also eagerly grasp for opportunities to taste liquor. A streetcorner man may let them have a little, but they may also manage to get it some other way, from somebody's house, from a parked car, or from some intoxicated streetcorner alcoholic who is in no shape to guard his belongings. There is fighting for fun or in all seriousness, and there are intensive involvements in verbal contests, as we shall discuss at greater length below. The interest in male clothing fashions is also there—this is the comment of a man in the Winston Street neighborhood on his young neighbors:

> "These kids criticize your clothes even if their own clothes are the raggediest things you ever saw. Leroy kept talking about my shoes the other day, and there wasn't one thing right about them the way he carried on. And his own shoes hardly got soles underneath!"

The proponents of that view of male role socialization which emphasizes the lack of paternal role models at home interpret these masculine concerns in the peer group in a manner consistent with their overall analysis, as we have already seen. Peer group formation is seen to be simply a response to the discovery that the identification with mother is all wrong; the boys get together to enhance their masculinity. According to the vocabulary in which this kind of interpretation is usually formulated, this is a reaction formation of compulsive masculinity. Rohrer's and Edmonson's delineation of the characteristics of peer group members were cited above; they couch it in such terms as "self-doubts," "insecurity," and "frightened and confused little boys." The peer group is seen as a "second-rate substitute" for family life.

There seems to be a certain weakness in this kind of view of peer group life, at least in its most clearcut form. First of all, one may wonder whether the "sentimental model" of the family is not rearing its head from below the surface of the analysis here. Is this model not a significant ideological underpinning for the judgment of the peer group's worth relative to that of the family? Despite the strength of the mainstream family model in the ghetto community, it is obvious that many of its male members, on the basis of their experience, turn the entire thing around and consider the family a poor substitute for the peer group as far as satisfactions are concerned. Furthermore, the interpretation exemplified by Rohrer and Edmonson seems to contain a fair amount of psychological reductionism in the explanation of the genesis of peer groups, and this reductionism may be open to some questioning. In this view of ghetto male behavior, it appears that the peer group is born again and again, like a Phoenix arising from those ashes of mother identification perhaps not completely burned to the end, out of a sheer psychological need for a place where masculinity can be celebrated. An alternative or at least complementary view of peer group functioning ought to be stated.

We may speculate that peer groups originally became an important component of the structure of the black community precisely because there was a need for them of this kind, and we can assume that they continue to meet such a need. It is very questionable, however, if it is an accurate representation of the continuity of the ghetto social structure to claim that peer groups emerge repeatedly independently of one another. As we pointed out above, small children are usually inducted into relationships with already existing groups of slightly older children, and there is constantly the idea of the peer groups as a natural context of children's life. Parents, neighbors, and older siblings contribute in making boys members of peer groups. The young males easily end up in these whatever are their families of origin and their psychological needs, and as ghetto-specific masculinity tends to be an idiom of interaction in the peer groups these serve as cultural equalizers for boys starting from different points and moving toward different goals. We have noted in an earlier chapter that generations of one family may show different life styles, and that peer groups may have an important influence in causing such changes; but even if boys later move toward mainstreamer lives, a great many of them have established some competence in ghetto-specific masculinity during their period of more intensive peer group participation. This may be helpful even for a mainstreamer member of the ghetto community, for instance in interaction with streetcorner men.

The craving for an arena for masculinity need thus not be *the* motive for entering into the first stage of that series of age graded groups which always exists in the ghetto. Any thoroughgoing psychological reductionism in accounting for the existence of male peer groups is, if not unfounded, at least too one-sided.

At this point one may also ask whether some of the psychological characterizations of peer group members are not couched in too strong terms in order to make them fit with the rest of the interpretation. The fact that children of large ghetto families are left to take care of their own entertainment, or in the company of an older sibling rather

than in that of the mother, seems to constitute an independence training, intended or not, which seems quite successful in the case of most
children in the Winston Street neighborhood. (It was an early impression in field work that the small children's way of life reminded one
of the *Peanuts* comic strip. Later it was realized that this was probably
because most of them seemed very independent and self-confident, and
handled their interaction without much of the parental mediation
which has a relatively large place in small middle-class white children's
play.) Thus it seems hard to vouch for the general applicability of
a description of small ghetto boys as "frightened" and "confused."

The other view of how boys come to participate in peer groups,
as stated above, does not explain the intensity of masculine expression,
as does the reaction formation view. It is necessary, therefore, to interpret this in some other way. The most obvious explanation is again
that of role modeling. The older members of a peer group tend to be
somewhat dominant to the younger ones, and it is thus likely that the
older ones are perceived as role models; but at the same time these
older boys participate as junior partners in relationship to boys older
than they. It is likely, therefore, that adult concepts of masculinity are
continuously trickling down through the age grades through a series
of role model relationships where the boy who is the socializee in one
relationship is the model in the next. At the same time, of course, there
is the direct influence of adult role models.

We may also note that peer groups may take up the masculine
theme and elaborate on it in their own way because their members
can easily perceive that public imagery is preoccupied with the differences and the relationships between the sexes. There is probably a less
significant discontinuity between childhood and adulthood in this regard in the ghetto than there is in mainstream society. While mainstream children are often somehow "protected" from knowledge of
adult interest in matters of sex, ghetto children easily learn a great
deal about this topic by listening to adult conversations. Even if the
adults try to avoid this, the lack of privacy in ghetto homes makes it
difficult to shield the children both from overhearing such exchanges
and from witnessing sexual behavior of one type or another. Besides,
ghetto children are intensively exposed to the broadcasts of black
radio stations, blaring continuously in many households and often out
on the sidewalks as well—one index of this exposure is that they often
know the texts of the top tunes word for word. The rock-and-roll tunes
as well as the disc jockeys' talk are primarily aimed at adults and older

teenagers and have some rather obvious sexual content. In this way, too, the younger boys may learn their concern with masculinity and sex from age groups above them. Borrowing a concept from Cloward and Ohlin (1960), we may say that the ghetto community provides a relatively open learning structure for the ghetto-specific male role.

Rituals of Obscenity

We pointed out above that verbal contests occur among young males as well as among their adult counterparts. Here we will halt for a while to consider one of the forms these contests take, both because in its elaborateness it provides a conspicuous example of ghetto-specific culture and because it is of interest in illuminating our two alternative perspectives toward ghetto male role socialization. This is the phenomenon which has become most known as "the dozens," but it is also known as "sounding" and under some other local names. The term most often used in Washington, D.C., is "joning," which we will therefore use here.

Joning is an exchange of insults. It has been described earlier at some length by Dollard (1939) and Abrahams (1962); since the latter also includes a representative collection of the kind of statements involved, we need only give a few examples here, from the repertoire of boys in the Winston Street neighborhood. The boundaries of the concept are a little fuzzy; there is some tendency to view as joning any exchange of insults of a more or less jocular type in sociable interaction among children and adolescents. Joning is definitely closely associated with joking. For most smaller boys it seems to shade imperceptibly into the category of "cracking jokes," and when joning occurs in a peer group sociable session it is often preceded or followed by other kinds of jokes. These are also often exchanged in a manner resembling a contest, and some of them have a form and content somewhat similar to jones, as for instance these two show:

Batman was flying in the air
when he lost his underwear
Batman said, I don't care
Robin, bring me another pair!

—What do you do when a girl ask you for something?
—?
—You tell her to lie down and then you give it to her!

The type of joning which may be taken as the most central referent of the term, however, consists of disparaging statements about the opponent's family, most often its female members and particularly frequently the mother. Some of the statements are simple one-liners, such as the following:

> Your mother play baseball for the U.S. Navy
> Your mother smoke a pipe
> Anybody can get pussy from your mother
> Your mother a prostitute
> Your mother ate a cockroach sandwich with mayonnaise on it
> Your sister live in a alley
> Your sister a bulldagger
> Your sister name Crazy leg Sally

However, there are also quite elaborate rhymed jones such as the following:

> I fucked your mother on top of a wall
> that woman had pussy like a basketball
>
> I fucked your mother from house to house
> she thought my dick was Mighty Mouse
>
> I fucked your mother from tree to tree
> The tree split
> and she shit
> I didn't get nothing but a little bit
>
> I fucked your mother on a car
> she said, Tim—you're going too far!
>
> I fucked your mother in a Jeep
> she said, Kenny—you're going too deep!
>
> I fucked your mother on a red heater
> I missed her pussy and burned my peter

Quite similar in context to such jones are certain songs occasionally sung in the peer group context—either by a single boy or in unison—of which the following two may be regarded as representative. The first is quite short:

> Your mama ain't pretty
> she got meatballs for her titties
> she got scrambled eggs
> between her legs

The other song, like a few others, has many verses:

A ha ha baby I know
you get'em from the peanut man
Ye Ye Ye Ye
ha ha baby I know
you get'em anywhere you can

See that girl
aha
in the pink
aha
I betcha five dollars your mother stink
A ha ha baby I know . . .
(refrain repeated)

See that man
aha
in the blue
aha
I betcha five dollars your mother sleep in a shoe
A ha ha baby I know . . .
(refrain repeated)

See that man
aha
in the white
aha
I betcha five dollars your mother smoke a pipe
A ha ha baby I know . . .
(refrain repeated)

See that man
aha
in the black
aha
I betcha five dollars your mother live in a shack
A ha ha baby I know . . .
(refrain repeated)

See that girl
aha
dressed in white
aha
I betcha five dollars your mother ride in a Cadillac
A ha ha baby I know . . .
(refrain repeated)

See that girl
aha
in the red
aha
I betcha five dollar your mother pee in bed
A ha ha baby I know...
(refrain repeated)

See that boy
aha
all in gray
aha
I betcha five dollars your mother sleep in the hay
A ha ha baby I know...
(refrain repeated)

The latter song obviously allows for some variability in performance. One does not always run through the whole list of colors,
and the colors are not always matched with the same persons—boy,
girl, man, or woman. Sometimes there are mismatches; in the version
transcribed above, "Cadillac" should probably rhyme with "black"
rather than with "white." This also means that there are alternative
rhymes for some colors, as "black" had already been rhymed with
"shack."

These songs are noted here rather parenthetically, as another
expressive form containing the themes encountered in joning. As far
as the content of the regular jones is concerned, it is all more or less
humiliating, in one way or other, to the person mentioned. Particularly the elaborate rhymed kind involves sex; jones are generally seen
in the ghetto community as obscene, "nasty," and some boys are obviously too inhibited to become adept at joning. The rhymes are frequently of a rather nonsensical kind—rhyming takes precedence to
making absolute sense—but are not always quite exact, although at
least in some of these cases they may be understood to be exact in the
ghetto dialect. The performer who claims to have had intercourse
with his opponent's mother often depicts himself more or less as a
sexual athlete, by indulging in sex in odd settings if in no other way.
What is perhaps the most conspicuous feature of these jones, however,
is that the mother involved—or sometimes the sister—is usually seen
to be guilty of some kind of moral deviation from her idealized woman's role, and the deviation is of either of the two kinds often im-
puted to females in the public imagery of ghetto males, as described

in a preceding chapter. She is not as "good" as she ought to be, in that she engages in sex with quite inappropriate partners, or she has taken over too much of the male sex role—smoking a pipe or playing baseball for the U.S. Navy, for instance. (Probably riding a Cadillac is also too masculine for a woman; there hardly seems to be anything else wrong with it from a ghetto dweller's point of view.) Other themes of joning are degradation (the cockroach sandwich) and ugliness (the sister named Crazy leg Sally); occasionally a jone appears to have more than one level of meaning, but one cannot at all be sure that the boys are aware of this.

The practice of joning is quite prevalent among young ghetto dwellers, although not much talked about since it is considered "nasty." There are many girls who are skilled at joining, but it is in particular a phenomenon of boys' peer group life. Men who can be made to reminisce about it usually say they were most involved in it when they were in junior high school, that is, in early adolescence. However, some of the boys in the Winston Street neighborhood who are best at joning are several years younger, but intensively engaged in peer group life. The exchanges can occur between two boys who are alone, and it is even possible for them to jone on some third absent person, usually one of their peers, but the typical situation involves a group of boys; while a series of exchanges may engage one pair of boys after another, most members of the crowd function as audience, inciters, and judges—laughing, commenting on the "scoring," and urging the participants on:

> He's talking about YOUR mother so bad
> he's making ME mad

Usually the joning just stops after a while, as the participants' repertoire has been used up, as no good new ideas about insults seem to be forthcoming, or as the contestants simply get tired of it. The boys in the Winston Street neighborhood appear to have rather similar repertoires (although some know more jones than others) which indicates that a great many of especially the more elaborate obscene rhymes have become traditional cultural artifacts. (However, if collected on a nation-wide basis, their number may turn out to be very large; none of those rhymed jones quoted above as examples is identical to any one of those offered by Abrahams (1962), although the third represents only a minor variation from one of his, and the fifth and the sixth have a recurrent theme which can be found also in Abrahams' collection.) This may explain why joners themselves are sometimes not sure of the meaning of the jones.

There are times when joning is transformed into fighting, but this happens relatively seldom. It should be added, too, that this is often only playful wrestling, only a slight escalation of the non-serious activity of joning. For after all, it is all a game. The insults are generally stereotyped, and there is relatively seldom any need for a boy to get very personally upset; some informants claim, however, that a boy whose mother is dead might get in an angry mood if someone should jone on her. All in all, it would seem that the boys' own interpretation of how an insult should be taken depends much on the social relationship within which it is uttered. An enemy who jones on you becomes a little more of an enemy, as your resentment grows, but a friend who is joning is a friend you are playing a game with.

As the boys become men they gradually cease to amuse themselves with joning. Although verbal aggression continues, it becomes less patterned; the insults contain hardly any references to mothers any more, and if a man, often by chance rather than intentionally, should say anything which could be construed as an abuse of another's mother, the latter might simply say, "I don't play that game no more."

The question now emerges, how are we to understand joning in terms of either role modeling or masculine reaction formation? It is clear in this case that the boys are not modeling themselves closely on the pattern of adult males, as the latter have stopped rhyming about their mothers. Early adolescence, we have said, is the high point of joning. Role modeling can exist in this instance only in the sense that the boys have time to pick up their skills from slightly older boys, before these start getting out of practice. But the reason for the involvement with joning at this age cannot be just "reaching for the adult role," pure and simple—at least the locus of joning in this age grade must be accounted for in some other way.

On the other hand there appears to be a rather nice fit with the thesis of reaction formation. The boys have supposedly just found out that they have identified with the wrong person, the mother. Now they must do their utmost to ridicule her and thus convince everybody and themselves—but particularly themselves—of their masculinity and independence. (Only since they are not yet daring enough to attack their own mothers, they attack somebody else's instead, thus setting the stage for him to go to work on their own.) Rohrer and

Edmonson draw an analogy between joning—which they term "the dozens" but give only brief mention—and brainwashing (1964:162), and Abrahams (1962) also makes a bow in the direction of seeing joning as a way of dealing with an unsatisfactory sense of sex identity. By indulging in joning, the boys fashion for themselves a collective ritual cleansing in which they point out each other's weaknesses, so that they can finally all emerge as better males.

Again, we need not reject such a view altogether in order to suggest another perspective which is again more closely connected with the emphasis on role modeling. The reaction formation view seems to see joning as primarily a backward-looking ritual—in order to arrive at a "normal' male identity, the boys have to purge themselves of mistakes made in early childhood. One may consider the other possibility that the boys are looking forward, and seeing a community with a major social division between males and females whose relationships to each other are often rharacterized by conflists and ambivalence. Up to the point of adolescence, their closest relationships to females have been to those at home, above all to the mother but also to sisters and possibly to others. These relationships, whatever they are like, are not relationships between potential sexual partners; however, that is the kind of relationship the boys envisage for themselves in the future, and which is at the basis of the generalized male-female relationship and the public imagery pertaining to it in the community. It is also at about this age that boys start using epithets such as "bitch," "gypsy," and "whore" in referring to females. It may not be an altogether improbable interpretation of joning, then, to see it as a rite of passage whereby boys train themselves for the particular adult relationship between the sexes which exists in the ghetto community, not only as one whereby they unlearn peculiarities picked up in matrifocality. As far as the relationship to the mother is concerned, we may add that she is also aware that her son is moving into the adult male category, and this contributes to making the mother-son relationship more tense than it has been at earlier points. This may well be another reason for boys to express hostility in joning. Perhaps one could express this in terms of identification and reaction formation, but there may be a danger of exaggerating the case if one does so.

Adolescence, then, may be an age in which male role socialization becomes intensified because the initiation into the final adult role is imminent, and this is why a particular cultural complex such as joning is stored in this transitional age grade. Making mothers and, to a lesser extent, other close female kin the topic of joning could thus serve the purpose of driving home the point that to a man, all women are alike in their characteristics. Of course, by claiming to be the sexual partner of a peer's mother or older sister, a boy also states a claim of more or less mature status while at the same time putting down his opponent who must then strive to come back to at least equality by answering in kind. At the same time, of course, joning may be seen as an attack on the collective family honor—not necessarily only that of the mother—which no real male can let pass.

Clearly the view sketched here and the reaction formation perspective toward joning are not mutually exclusive. However, we may now feel less sure that problems with the male identity arising out of matrifocality constitute the only reason why ghetto boys should indulge in joning. Another problem with such an explanation arises out of the fact that some girls take part in joning exchanges, as noted above, often in interaction with boys; the girls are not likely to have the problems with the male identity that boys have. Obviously this form of cultural expression has simply diffused to the girls. But if there can be such a diffusion process between the sexes, why not within the male sex? It is much more likely, of course, that boys who participate in the same peer groups should take on joning as an interaction idiom although they have no matrifocality problems, than that girls, interacting much less with boys in such contexts, should do so. Thus it is likely that although some of the boys who jone may have sex identity problems, others take part in the ritual simply because it is part of peer group culture, to be mastered if personal success in the group is to be ensured. (Unless, of course, they are motivated to jone by their perspective of the future.) Among the boys in the Winston Street neighborhood, some of the boys who are good at joning are not from husbandless households, or even from two-parent households dominated by the mother. On the other hand, they have central positions in their peer groups. This would indicate that household structure and peer group participation are variables relatively independent of one another, and that possibly the latter is at least as important as the former for a boy's involvement and skill in joning.

The Alternatives in Review

This chapter has been openly partisan in order to point out what look like weak points in a well-known view of the process of growing up male in the ghetto. We would not serve this purpose well

by denying or passing over points in favor of that argument altogether; it should be noted, therefore, that many of the streetcorner
men out of matrifocal families of orientation have a strong attachment to their mothers, although the relationship is not free from conflicts. Fats, unemployed, a heavy drinker, and a streetcorner strong-
man, claims he is a Muslim and is in constant conflict with his mother
who is an old-fashioned Baptist. Yet he leaves the rent for his apartment for her to keep for him over the weekend before he goes out on
Friday night; "So I can't take from it," he explains with a slightly embarrassed smile. Another Friday evening, the two Preston brothers were
fighting and threatening each other, in the family's house and all the
way down Winston Street. The neighbors explained it in terms of
their mother's illness: "They never got along good, but they're very
upset now 'cause their mother is in the hospital, and so they just break
down you see." Both brothers are close to sixty years old and alcoholics. One may note, also, that when a marriage breaks up, it is often
the man who moves home to mother; and many streetcorner men
readily condemn their fathers who left their mothers alone, although
they have behaved similarly themselves. Finally, we may observe with
Abrahams (1964:261–262) that the word "motherfucker" and its deriv-
atives are used in a curiously ambivalent way, sometimes in statements
of admiration and at other times in a thoroughly pejorative sense.

In this context it should also be pointed out that there are expressions of a kind of fascination with sexual deviation. "Faggot" is
in frequent use as a term of abuse among men, "sissy" and "punk"
(with a less clear reference to homosexuality) more often among boys.
The "Jewel Box Revue," a transvestite show, travels regularly on the
chitterling circuit, including appearances at the Howard Theatre.
Thus it can hardly be denied that there is an apparent concern with
sex role problems in the ghetto.

It is questionable, however, whether they can all be laid at the
door of matrifocality. It would seem rather likely that sex role deviations, and a concern with such deviations, could occur rather frequently in a community where ambivalent and conflict-ridden relationships between the sexes are understood to be prevalent, where one
of the alternative male roles is difficult to live up to because of severe
macrostructural constraints, and the other alternative is as personally
demanding as the ghetto-specific role may be to some. If there is anything in the guess that such factors may also be at work, the influence

of matrifocality may have been overestimated even in the shaping of those sexual deviations which ghetto dwellers themselves recognize.

The major goal of this chapter, however, is not to pose an alternative explanation of a "pathology," but to throw in doubt the existence of much of it. For it seems that the thesis which has been criticized throughout this chapter is one which constantly views the ghetto-specific male role as a kind of psychopathology; because the matrifocal family does not conform to the mainstream model and because the ghetto-specific male role does not either, one "deviation" is said to cause the other by way of first a lack of role models, then a compulsive masculine reaction continuing into adulthood. To reach this result one employs a framework of interpretation loaded with mainstream assumptions, about what a man should be like—a mainstream male, of course— and about the kind of relationship which sex role socialization needs if it is to occur—the father-son relationship, of course. In both cases, it seems likely that the normative bias makes the scheme of interpretation unfair to a community with a different social organization and different cultural norms. To a considerable extent, it seems to be a spurious claim that ghetto boys have no role models, and it seems quite possible that the ghetto-specific male role recurs in generation after generation in the manner sex roles are usually transmitted, through role modeling and in other ways. In the interpretive scheme of sex role confusion and compulsive male reaction formation, little or nothing is said about the ghetto-specific male role as a cultural entity in its own right, because adult males are largely absent from the picture until they appear as grown boys, embattled "mama's men"—the imagery here seems to have the child as the father of the man, as reaction formation seems to carry on into infinity. The existence of a ghetto-specific male pattern of behavior seems to be only a recurrent accident caused by matrifocality.

The alternative perspective set forth here and foreshadowed in preceding chapters holds that the ghetto-specific male role is dependent on macrostructural factors not just because these make males disappear from the arena where they should be role models, but because these factors have forced ghetto men to redefine their sex role in a ghetto-specific way. After this role has been defined in accordance with circumstances, however, the man may well be the father of the child, in a socializing sense—that is, the role modeling process is at work.

The criticisms made in this chapter may well have been shaped by the typical predilections of a social anthropologist, vaguely uneasy with a more complex use of psychological arguments. in explaining social forms while at the same time ready to challenge any point of view which takes cultural invariance for granted and which assumes that a certain function, such as role modeling, can only be vested in a particular structure, such as the nuclear family. Obviously the ghetto is not the most clearcut possible example of cultural difference; the picture is complicated by the fact that the community has so little autonomy but is under pressure to idealize a set of cultural norms to which many of its members can hardly conform. Thus ghetto boys, according to this social anthropological perspective, are socialized not only into their ghetto-specific sex role—rather, they are biculturated At home and in school, and through diverse mass media, they are instructed in mainstream culture, with its attendant proper behavior for boys. There are also the ghetto's own mainstreamers who acquaint the boys with this cultural alternative by their sheer presence, and furthermore there is some personal contact with the surrounding society. Yet this involvement with mainstream culture on the part of ghetto dwellers provides no excuse for ignoring the facts of life peculiar to the ghetto, or taking such a narrow view of which of them are relevant that possibly significant social and cultural relationships are left out. If the kind of argument about male growth which has been questioned here is carried too far, it lends itself to facile judgments about "solving the masculinity crisis" which are more than a little bizarre. It may be claimed, for instance, that since the father is not around, the model vacuum can be filled with male school teachers and social workers. Whether ghetto boys would really be given to modeling themselves on the representatives of these two categories seems highly uncertain, and one may wonder why they should be able to beat all other men outside the family out of the competition. But it may well be that the commentators who suggest such solutions see in the mainstream manner of man not just the only proper model, but also the only possible model—persons differing from it are seen as "confused," and thus nobody would bother to take them as models.

The lack of awareness of the possibility of ghetto-specific culture can also be seen in attempts to measure the "femininity" of ghetto males with far from culture-free psychological instruments, according to which it is feminine to agree with such statements as "I think that I feel more intensely than most people do" and "I would like to be a singer" (cited by Pettigrew 1964:19). The first index ignores the fact that black people have simply had a great deal to feel intensely about, something they now identify quite consciously in their self-conception, as embodied in the vocubulary of "soul." The other takes no note of the general great concern with music in the black community, nor of the fact that singing is generally recognized as a road to success, more open to a black man than are many others.

There is no need to claim that all interpretations of ghetto masculinity in terms of misidentification with mother, followed by compulsive masculinity, are so culturally naive. As we have pointed out above, facts remain which favor such an interpretation. We must also be aware that boys from matrifocal families may have quite different experiences, and that individuals may evince the same behavior and participate in the same institutions for quite different reasons. It may well be that neither the thesis criticized here nor the one outlined as an alternative can alone provide an understanding of how ghetto boys become ghetto men; they, and perhaps other interpretations as well, may be needed as complementary perspectives rather than as alternatives. But even so—or perhaps particularly in such a case—it is necessary to point out exactly how far one single mode of interpretation may go, and what are its weaknesses. This is particularly necessary when the correctness and completeness of one of them become taken for granted, and when there is a tendency to pursue it to extreme and untenable positions, as seems to have happened in this case.

THE EXPRESSIVE BLACK MALE ROLE: THE BLUESMAN*

Charles Keil

I am primarily concerned with an expressive male role within urban lower-class Negro culture—that of the contemporary bluesman.

The terminology of this statement of purpose needs some clarification, for what an anthropologist calls his "conceptual vocabulary" is sometimes labeled "unnecessary jargon" by anyone who is not a social scientist, and might well be considered just plain "signifying" or "off-the-wall jive" by the people I'm writing about. Since I share the points of view of the latter more often than not, my definitions of these terms and others like them that appear in these pages tend to be simple and can usually be taken at face value. For example, urban lower-class people, as far as I am concerned, are those who live in big cities and have very little money.[1]

The term "role" is used here in the conventional theatrical sense for the most part—a person playing the role of Hamlet is supposed to act like Hamlet; a man who calls himself a father, a friend, or a blues singer is expected to act the part or parts. These expectations define each role. An expressive role obligates the person who fills it to express something—the prayer of the priest, the joke of the comedian, the composition of an artist. What does the Negro audience expect of a bluesman today, and what does he express for them in his performance?

My attempts to answer these questions in the following pages

*From Charles Keil, *Urban Blues,* © 1966, pp. 1–29. Reprinted with permission from the University of Chicago Press.

have forced a confrontation with two problematic fundamentals: Negro culture, and the Negro male. It is the exploration of these components in my statement of purpose and the issues they raise that I would like to emphasize in this introduction.

There are fancier definitions, but essentially a culture is a way of life. In this sense, every individual is a cultured individual. Every child rapidly acquires the language, the eating habits, the religious beliefs, the gestures, the technology, the notions of common sense, the attitudes toward sex, the concepts of beauty and justice, the responses to pleasure and pain, of the people who raise him. These general guidelines for living vary remarkably from culture to culture. What seems pleasurable or just to an Eskimo may seem painful or criminal to me; but once a person has acquired a particular framework of values, beliefs, and attitudes, it is devilishly difficult to modify and impossible to erase entirely. Individuals come and go; cultures remain. To be sure, cultures change—sometimes rapidly—but the process is usually measured, if at all, in generations and centuries.

A basic axiom that underlies anthropological thought is that culture is always learned and never inherited. Anthropologists have long recognized this clear distinction between race and culture. But, judging by the current vocabulary of "race relations," the distinction is still not generally understood. I cannot think of a single respected or self-respecting anthropologist or geneticist who will seriously question its validity. Yet there has been no mass conversion to this principle, no general understanding of its implications; those who have accepted the distinction intellectually sometimes find it difficult to do so emotionally.

The facts on "race" are readily available elsewhere and need not be summarized extensively here. Scientists use the term to denote a shared gene pool—that is, any group of people who breed (exchange genes) with each other more often than they breed with outsiders. Americans, Hawaiians, hillbillies, Asians, Navahos, Negroes, the inhabitants of most small towns, Catholics, Brooklyn Jews are examples of such groups. Since people who share the same culture or locale are more likely to intermarry, the American race (or any other national gene pool which is in the process of formation) contains a great many genetic puddles and streams. Insofar as we can speak intelligently of a Negro race at all, it is something rather vague and, like the American race of which it is a part, only beginning to take recognizable genetic shape. The scientist's flexible classifications are based upon

measurable genetic factors, usually discrete blood and plasma characteristics, since racial classifications based upon appearances have been
found to be extremely unreliable. Racists of course employ the latter
criteria when they designate groups of people who "look different and
act different" as races. This designation reveals a double or compound
ignorance for it brings together dubious appearance criteria and totally irrelevant cultural factors—"acting different." This compound
ignorance has given firm support to slavery, genocide, imperialism,
and all the most hideous crimes of the past few centuries.

I, for one, would like to see the term "race" abandoned altogether and with it the pernicious rhetoric of race relations, racial conflict, race riot, struggle for racial equality, *ad nauseam.* Can a shared
gene pool riot? No. Can it relate in any meaningful way to another
bunch of genes? No. Nor can races conflict; but cultures can, and in
this shrinking world they clash with increasing frequency. Racial
equality is an established fact; the struggle is for cultural pluralism.

What are we to make of the "so-called Negro"? The Black Muslim phrase is particularly apropos, for the man called Negro is apparently three men: a genetic man, a cultural man, and a colored man.
"Spelled with a capital 'N' by most publications (one of the important early victories of my own people in their fight for self-definition)
the term describes a people whose origin began with the introduction
of African slaves to the American colonies in 1619."[2] The capital "N"
may represent a pyrrhic victory, however, for by insisting upon equality with Caucasians (another highly ambiguous category) proponents
of the upper case would seem to have further obscured the crucial
distinction between race and culture, to the detriment of the latter,
as we shall see. There is still a third definition of "Negro" to contend
with—the infamous social definition. A man may not fit a geneticist's
definition of "Negro"; he may not participate in Negro culture, in
fact he may have blue eyes, fair complexion, and a fully developed
set of white American middle-class values. Yet American society will still
label him "colored" or "Negro" if he has or is rumored to have an
African ancestor or two—the proverbial touch of the tarbrush. I don't
think it would be pedantic or petty at this point to insist that in the
interests of rational discussion we begin to use three different terms
in place of the indiscriminate (and therefore discriminatory) category
"Negro." Perhaps "Negro" best fits the genetic definition, "negro"
could be used for the irrational social concept, and in the cultural
context "Afro-American" might be considered more appropriate. Since

I am writing almost exclusively about cultural matters, I see no reason to force this terminology upon the reader. I would, however, like it to be perfectly clear that I use the term "Negro" in connection with a way of life, a culture, and in no other sense. Note that this usage allows me to include a few so-called white Negroes in my discussion if I care to, while excluding a number of black Americans who identify with the majority culture.

The social definition of the Negro—the fact that he is colored and an outcast—has almost hidden the fact that Negroes have a culture. Twenty-five years ago Melville Herskovits did a rather thorough job of debunking the American myth that "the Negro is a man without a past."[3] Although this myth is still prevalent, a much more dangerous revision of it current today is that the Negro has no culture or at least no viable culture worthy of attention. Yesterday's rural Negro may have had something like a folk culture, so the myth goes, but today's urban Negro can be found only in a set of sociological statistics on crime, unemployment, illegitimacy, desertion, and welfare payments. The social scientists would have us believe that the Negro is psychologically maladjusted, socially disorganized and culturally deprived. Others tell us that any Negro way of life that may exist is nothing more than a product of poverty and fear.[4] From an initial assumption that the Negro is only an American, a long string of insults and injuries inevitably flows. Remove the assumption, recognize a Negro culture, and many of the alleged pathologies disappear while others become subject to new and difficult verification.

Nat Hentoff writes:

> Not one of the many book reviews I read of Nathan Glazer's and Daniel Moynihan's *Beyond the Melting Pot* took exception to their overwhelmingly ignorant assertion that "the Negro is only an American and nothing else. He has no values and culture to guard and protect." That two such sophisticated social scientists were able to be so myopic is a measure, of course, of how ignorant most of us continue to be about what Ralph Ellison called the Negro American style, or rather, styles. As Ellison peristently points out, the complexity and subtlety of Negro experience in America have produced infinitely more diverse individualities among Negroes than their friends, enemies, and attending sociologists and psychologists have ever recognized.[5]

Ellison's magnificent novel *Invisible Man* and his recent collection of essays *Shadow and Act* establish him in my estimation as one of the most perceptive analysts of Negro culture writing today. Unlike most of the authors considered here, he is well aware of his heritage and the intricate strategies developed by Negroes in an effort to cope with America. Yet even Ellison shies away from Negro culture per se and prefers to speak of "an American Negro sub-culture" or "American Negro styles" with the accent on "American," "styles" and "sub-culture." Some statements from an Ellison essay written in 1958 illustrate this emphasis.

> Thus, since most so-called "Negro cultures" outside Africa are necessarily amalgams, it would seem more profitable to stress the term "culture" and leave the term "Negro" out of the discussion.

> Nor should the existence of a specifically "Negro" idiom in any way be confused with the vague racist terms "white culture" or "black culture"; rather it is a matter of diversity within unity.

> Culturally this people represents one of the many sub-cultures which make up that great amalgam of European and native American sub-cultures which is the culture of the United States.[6]

If Negroes are not the least amalgamated of all Americans, then what is the current struggle all about? The melting-pot tone of Ellison's remarks would lead us to believe that Negro culture is only one minor variation among many on the major American theme. I disagree.

There is an important sense, discussed below, in which the Negro is the most American of all Americans, but I must take strong exception to Ellison's statement that

> Its [the Negro people's] spiritual outlook is basically Protestant, its system of kinship is Western, its time and historical sense are American (United States), and its secular values are those professed, ideally at least, by all of the people of the United States.[7]

These generalizations may have validity when applied to the "black bourgeoisie"[8] and to a cluster of Negro intellectuals, but have little or nothing to do with the vast majority of Negroes living in the Northern ghettos and rural South.

Speaking in tongues, prophecy, healing, trance, "possession," a staff of nurses to assist those "filled with the Holy Ghost," frenzied dancing, hand clapping, tambourine playing, instrumental groups, fluctuating musical styles, singing-screaming sermons, constant audience participation—these and many other features of Negro church services are completely foreign to the prevailing conception of Protestantism. White Holy Roller churches still exist in many parts of the country, Southern snake-handling cults are occasionally reported,[9] and a few Yale Divinity School students have been dabbling in "glossolaly" recently. But ecstatic communion with "the living God" as practiced in the Negro store-front churches of Chicago is clearly far removed from the staid and stolid Puritanism that has dominated the American Protestant tradition. Significantly, it is only the Black Muslims (approximately twenty thousand in number) and a few other tiny sects who adhere faithfully to the Protestant ethic, and the Muslims are explicitly opposed to all manifestations of traditional American Negro culture (probably the principal reason that their membership isn't closer to the two hundred thousand they claim). The values usually associated with Protestantism—thrift, sobriety, "inner-directedness," strictly codified sexual behavior (better to marry than to burn), and a strong insistence on respectability—tend to be reversed in the Negro cultural framework. Preachers and elderly Negro women love to give these values lip service, but that's usually as far as conventional Protestantism goes.

To say that Negro kinship is Western, Ellison must overlook the most striking feature of Negro social structure—the battle of the sexes. Or, alternatively, he must disregard the essence of middle-class kinship in America—that is, the core concept of marital companionship and the primacy of the nuclear family over all other kinship ties. For the vast majority of Negroes, the battle of the sexes is no mere figure of speech. In the ghetto, men and women are considered to be separate and antagonistic species, and this division "overrides the minor distinctions of creed, class and color."[10] Men are "by nature" primarily interested in sexual satisfaction and independence (money will get you both); they are "strong" sexually, and will take favors from anyone who will grant them. Women are said to be primarily interested in emotional support and their families (money is needed to keep the household intact); they are "weak" sexually, and tend to become attached to one or two men at a time. Men call women self-righteous, money-grabbing, treacherous, and domineering. Women simply say that all men are no good. Relationships between the sexes are usually governed by variations of the "finance-romance"[11] equation that appears in so many blues lyrics. This equation covers a gamut of ties ranging from May-December marriages for security (with a lover on the side for the May partner), through "getting help from my ol' man," to casual, semi-professional and professional prostitution.

The female forces on one side of the battle line consist of units like mother and daughter, sister and sister, niece and aunt, wife and mother-in-law, a matriarch with her daughters and grandchildren. Facing this formidable opposition is the independent Negro male who seeks allies where he can—in the gang, pool hall, blues bar, and barber shop. Moralizing types—Negro women in particular and white Americans generally—see him as lazy, shiftless, and irresponsible. White liberals see him as jobless and demoralized. Norman Mailer[12] portrays him as an existentialist stud, hedonistically at home in a world of violence, drugs, wine, women, and song. Apparently Ellison doesn't see him at all—an invisible man perhaps. However we characterize the anomalous position of the Negro male, he doesn't seem to fit gracefully into a conventional American or Western kinship system. Nor, for that matter, do the basic features of lower-class Negro kinship patterns match well with any non-Western kinship system that anthropologists have encountered. The battle of the sexes can of course be found raging in many slums around the world—for example, Athens, Mexico City, Liverpool, Johannesburg—but in most of these "cultures of poverty"[13] the battle tends to be resolved in terms of male authoritarianism rather than "mother-centeredness."[14] The study of lower-class culture (slum culture, culture of poverty, underculture, as you prefer) is in its infancy, and it is hazardous to make comparisons; but it would seem that the Negro male is on the whole farthest removed from both his family of origin—Mama excepted—and his family of procreation. The resultant kinship patterns are different in degree if not in kind from any others.

I do not want to leave the reader with the impression that every Negro is fatherless or that every Negro family is matrifocal, but the patterns sketched above are normative if not normal. That is, working-class or lower-class Negro couples who manage to stick together, as well as families in the emergent Negro middle class, define themselves and their ideals in contradistinction to these well-known ghetto conditions and are, in this antagonistic respect at least, a part of Negro culture. Finally, we can note that every urban culture of poverty is a product of Western industrialization or the beginnings of it, but I don't think that this is the point that Ellison has tried to make.

What about Ralph Waldo Ellison's contention that the Negro's "time and historical sense are American (United States)"? Again I must insist that Ellison speaks for himself but not for the man in the street. The writer-in-residence usually shows up for his literature classes on time. He writes cogent essays relating the past to the present and the future. And he knows that he has two historical traditions to draw upon in his work—the slavery and post-slavery experience of his immediate forebears, and the history in which his namesake Ralph Waldo Emerson played such a prominent part. The black man on the street corner, like most slum dwellers everywhere, lives for the present and tends to drift with events rather than show up for appointments, assuming that he has any. His historical perspective is epitomized in the adage "The white man's heaven is the black man's hell," lyricized so tenderly by the reformed calypsonian and Black Muslim minister Louis X. The heavenly history found in high-school textbooks is mostly meaningless drivel to him, and what he knows of the history of hell he would just as soon forget. To plan for the future is probably futile; Emerson is unknown; and Negro History Week, promoted by middle-class strivers, is a bad joke. His history is American (United States) to be sure, but it is upside down.

The Negro's "secular values are those professed, ideally at least, by all of the people of the United States." The ironic shading of "ideally at least" suggests that the secular values Ellison has in mind are freedom, justice, and equality rather than wine, women, and song. The manner in which these two sets of values coexist and interpenetrate in Negro culture is given some attention in the present book, but I should like to pursue for a moment the notion of freedom, justice, and equality and the related view expressed by many leading authorities that the Negro is the most American of all Americans.

It is certainly true that the traditional American ideals have been given an urgently needed rehabilitation from time to time by a few black citizens audacious enough to blurt out some strong complaints concerning America's long-standing and pervasive hypocrisy. A very small minority within the minority legitimately qualify as most American, I think, when they not only cling to the ideals of the American Revolution but go so far as to act on those ideals in the face of an affluent, complacent populace that, by and large, couldn't care less —throw them a law, a crumb, a prize, or something, just get them off the streets! If Negroes try to remind Americans of their spiritual heritage, they also offer an awful parody of the traditional American lust for material possessions. The American status-symbol quest becomes an obsession in the Negro community, where conspicuous consumption— the acquisition of the biggest cars and the flashiest clothes—sometimes takes precedence over adequate food and shelter. Like his fellow Americans, the Negro is addicted to TV, loves baseball, and to a certain extent he even loathes and fears the Negro.

Elkins[15] and many others, including Ellison, have noted the similarities between Negroes in America and the prisoners in a concentration camp who tend to adjust to the brainwashing cruelties and degradations of life there by identifying with the oppressor. They mimic their godlike guards in viewing each other as less than men, and act accordingly. To the extent that Negro culture is a concentration-camp culture—and I am not sure that the analogy is all that valid—the Negro is very American indeed. When so-called Negro spokesmen and white liberals speak of the Negro's Americanness, however, the concentration-camp analogy and ugly facts of slum life are often dispensed with in favor of the dangerous illusion that the Negro is an all-American boy at heart, with a pleasant Protestant outlook and a nice Western kinship system, upholding "our" secular values and sharing "our" sense of time and history.

Almost any Negro in the presence of a white or black bourgeois interviewer or social worker can recite a stream of conventional American values and beliefs without a hitch, halt, or second thought. Yet it is also true that these are rarely the cultural guidelines by which the person reciting them lives. The art of the "put on" has of necessity been developed to an exceptionally high level in Negro culture,[16] and the researcher or leader who reports recited values at face value may be putting us all on twice over.

It is not at all easy to probe beneath the shucking and jiving of Negroes and Negro experts for an unclouded view of Negro culture and man's place in it. My rebuttal to Ellison's generalizations, for example, is only a preliminary outline of urban lower-class Negro culture and a slightly lopsided one at that. It could be classified, I suspect, with the grim-reality genre of writing on the Negro problem as exemplified by Charles Silberman's socio-economic study *Crisis in Black and White*[17] and by Kardiner and Ovesey's psychodynamic analysis *Mark of Oppression*.[18] These analysts fail to do what Ellison has done so well. Concerned primarily with the pathological side of Negro life—what whites have done to Negroes—they ignore or obscure what Negroes have done for themselves.

In the late 1940's Abram Kardiner and Lionel Ovesey compiled a thoroughly depressing assortment of psychoanalytic case histories based upon information given by twenty-five residents of Harlem. The individual histories themselves are certainly of value in assessing the

impact of oppression upon Negroes in America, but the chapters preceding and following the personal stories are marred by false premises
and ignorance of Negro survival techniques. A long concluding chapter
on "The Expressions of Negro Personality" dwells on crime and broken homes, devotes a few paragraphs to Father Divine, and overlooks
completely such essential forms of expression as jazz, blues, and comedy. The authors' passing comments on folklore, religion, and Negro
culture as a whole are indicative:

> He had no culture, and he was quite green in his semi-acculturated
> state in the new one. He did not know his way about and had no
> intrapsychic defenses—no pride, no group solidarity, no tradition.
> This was enough to cause panic. The marks of his previous status
> were still upon him—socially, psychologically and emotionally. *And
> from these he has never since freed himself* [emphasis added].[19]

> We have seen little evidence of genuine religiosity among Negroes.
> They have invented no religion of their own.[20]

> The Br'er Rabbit and Uncle Remus tales are the only remnants of
> anything that can be called folklore.[21]

> These Spirituals and folk tales do not belong to the contemporary
> scene, and hence, cannot be used in any way to supplement our study
> of the present-day Negro personality. Where, then, can we look for
> such expression?[22]

If the authors had left their offices and gone out into the Negro
community, this question as well as a number of omissions and silly
assertions might have been avoided.

Charles Silberman, probably the most candid and sensible
while American to express himself on "the crisis" in recent years, feels
there is little hope for American democracy unless Negroes obtain quality education (particularly at the pre-school and primary-school levels), strong community self-help organizations, and a viable identity.
I agree wholeheartedly. Silberman's discussions of Martin Deutsch's
revolutionary pre-school program and Saul Alinsky's equally radical
self-helping organizational techniques are strong and to the point. But
his chapter on "The Problem of Identification" is rather pessimistic
and only partly successful, since he too denigrates Negro culture and
seems largely unaware of the resources available to the Negro in shaping a positive identity:

> In contrast to European immigrants, who brought rich cultures and

long histories with them, the Negro has been completely stripped of his past and severed from any culture save that of the United States.[23]

Negroes are both more than an ethnic group and less; though their color makes them far more identifiable than any ethnic group, they lack the common history and cultural traditions which the other groups share. The Negro's central problem is to discover his identity, or to create an identity for himself. What history suggests is that when the Negro solves his problem of identity, he will have gone a long way towards finding the means of relating himself to every other American group.[24]

The central problem is not so much to discover or create a new identity as, first, to accept an identity that is already available and, second, to transform into working assets whatever crippling liabilities may be associated with that identity.

Silberman, Kardiner, Ovesey, and many others have neglected that special domain of Negro culture wherein black men have proved and preserved their humanity. This domain or sphere of interest may be broadly defined as entertainment from the white or public point of view and as ritual, drama, or dialectical catharsis from the Negro or theoretical standpoint. By this I mean only that certain Negro per-formances, called "entertaining" by Negroes and whites alike, have an added but usually unconscious ritual significance for Negroes. The ritualists I have in mind are singers, musicians, preachers, comedians, disc jockeys, some athletes,[25] and perhaps a few Negro novelists as well. These entertainers are the ablest representatives of a long cul-tural tradition—what might be called the soul tradition—and they are all identity experts, so to speak, specialists in changing the joke and slipping the yoke. An analysis of the Negro's situation in America today, if it is to be thorough and constructive, must take these strategic figures into account.[26]

The entertainment component of Negro culture is significant in at least four basic respects. First, it is the one area in Negro life that was clearly not stripped away or obliterated by slavery—the rituals I speak of have an indisputable West African foundation. Second, un-like the immigrant cultural traditions which have been either diluted or dissolved almost completely in the American context, this important cultural legacy linking American Negroes to Africa has not only survived but has thrived on adversity and grown stronger through the years. Third, it is now a full-fledged tradition in its own right. One does not have to be a specialist in African cultures ever on the alert for Africanisms or a psychologist of race relations studiously attuned to the marks of oppression in order to understand a performance by B. B. King, a sermon by the Reverend C. L. Franklin, a Moms Mabley comedy routine, or a John Coltrane saxophone solo. Familiarity (preferably intimate) with contemporary Negro culture and some sensitivity to the particular form of expression in question—music, rhetoric, choreography—are the only basic analytic prerequisites. Finally, and most important, the entertainers are masters of sound, movement, timing, the spoken word. One can therefore find in their performances the essentials and defining features—the very core in fact—of Negro culture as a whole.

The unique and full status of Negro culture is only partly dependent on the basic institutional elements, such as Church and family, that do not fit white American specifications. On another and perhaps more fundamental level, the shared sensibilities and common understandings of the Negro ghetto, its modes of perception and expression, its channels of communication, are predominantly auditory and tactile rather than visual and literate.[27] Sensibilities are of course matters of degree, and the sense ratio or "ratio-nality" of a particular culture can't be measured precisely. Nevertheless, the prominence of aural perception, oral expression, and kinesic codes or body movement in Negro life—its sound and feel—sharply demarcate the culture from the irrational white world outside the ghetto.[28] Negro and white Americans share the same general language (superficially a good argument for those who would relegate the Negro to a subcultural corner in homogenized America),[29] but their attitudes toward that language are polarized. In white America, the printed word—the literary tradition—and its attendant values, are revered. In the Negro community, more power resides in the spoken word and oral tradition—good talkers abound and the best gain power and prestige, but good writers are scarce.[30] It is no accident that much of America's slang is provided by Negro culture.[31] Nor is it strange that Negro music and dance have become America's music and dance, a process discussed in the following chapter.

What I have found initially mysterious, however, is the almost universal disregard for the cultural framework that has fostered these forms of expression. Writers, including writers on Negro life, have a vested interest in literacy and the visual world view, to be sure, and some may simply be deaf to the pervasive aural-oral qualities of Negro culture. Then too, real rhetoric and ritual, the pattern and form, heart and soul of Negro expression, are largely unknown in white America.[32] Indeed, the words themselves have taken on decidedly negative connotations—rhetoric: bombastic oratory, trickery, meaningless word play; ritual: dry formality, perfunctory action, unthinking and meaningless behavior. In the literary or typographic world, the labels mere rhetoric and ritualistic are the kiss of death. From this perspective, Negro culture heroes must appear as entertainers at best or at worst as clowns. Finally, a substantial number of influential Americans (politicians, white liberals, the Negro middle class) see Negro culture as a threat, if they can see it at all, for it is bound to make a mockery of hastily legislated integration.[33]

At this point let us look again to the literature on the Negro.

Two studies of the urban Negro have appeared in paperback form recently: *Black Metropolis*, by Cayton and Drake,[34] and *The Eighth Generation Grows Up*, by Rohrer and Edmonson.[35] Both offer a great deal of information on ghetto life in Chicago and New Orleans that the reader may find useful in evaluating and contextualizing the chapters which follow. These studies place justifiably strong emphasis on the cultural difference between lower-, middle-, and upper-class Negroes. The analytic theme of *Black Metropolis* is socio-economic; *The Eighth Generation Grows Up*, following an earlier work, *Children of Bondage*,[36] uses culture and personality as frames of reference. The two studies complement each other closely. *Black Metropolis* contains an excellent chapter on "The World of the Lower Class" devoted almost entirely to religious activities and attendant values.[37] The case histories presented in *The Eighth Generation Grows Up*, aided by generational time depth and an interdisciplinary approach, are much superior to those found in *Mark of Oppression*, particularly the biographies in which the ramifications of mother-centeredness are elaborated. Again, however, both books treat the entertainment world as peripheral. Drake and Cayton persistently talk about good-timing and pleasure-seeking in the Chicago Negro community, but view such behavior as escapist and nothing more. Rohrer and Edmonson include a ludicrous appendix reporting the statistical frequency of certain psychological variables in a sample of "authentically New Orleanian jazz songs" and "creole folk songs" (no further stylistic specification or sampling criteria given) that must rate as a small but classic example of sterile statistical significance in social science.[38] Nevertheless, these books are indispensable reading for those who want a more complete picture of the existence that nurtures the urban blues.

Rohrer and Edmonson make a sharp distinction between lower-class Negro culture[39] and two shadow cultures: the entertainment world and the underworld. Cayton and Drake are somewhat closer to reality, I think, when they distinguish three extensively overlapping groups within the Negro lower class: "a large group of disorganized and broken families"; "church folk" trying to be respectable; and "denizens of the underworld." "The lines separating these three basic groups are fluid and shifting, and a given household may incorporate individuals of all three types."[40] On the basis of my own limited research into lower-class life, I would go further, suggesting that the hustler (or underworld denizen) and the entertainer are ideal types representing two important value orientations for the lower-class Negro and need not be distinguished from the lower class as a whole. Both the hustler and the entertainer are seen as men who are clever and talented enough to be financially well off without working. In this sense, a good preacher can be both a hustler and an entertainer in the eyes of his parishioners and the Negro community at large.

Most ways of making good money without working are illegal, and Henry Williamson has explored many of these ways in *The Hustler.*[41] The most striking thing about his autobiography is not the thoroughly criminal character of his life, from the white American point of view, but that within his culture he is very well adapted, successful (when out of jail), and even enjoys "doin' wrong." Most important, perhaps, "Henry's account is surprisingly free of any signs of racial strife. He wears his Negro image comfortably—neither disgruntled nor proud."[42] Aside from hustlers, entertainers, and rare individuals like Malcolm X (who began his career as hustler) or Reinhardt (the archetypal preacher-hustler in Ellison's *Invisible Man*), few Negroes wear their image in real comfort. Those black men who are comfortable in this sense become logical career models for those who aren't. If we are ever to understand what urban Negro culture is all about, we had best view entertainers and hustlers as culture heroes—integral parts of the whole—rather than as deviants or shadow figures.

Roger Abrahams' aims and techniques in studying Negro folklore are similar to my own in approaching the blues, and, as might be expected, I admire his work immensely.[43] He has managed to specify many of the cultural pressures and personal needs that illuminate a limited range of stylized speech forms in a specific community, in this case a Negro neighborhood in Philadelphia. This is a rare achievement and a definite break from the dry and crusty tradition of folk-lore scholarship. Abrahams persists in yanking texts out of their social context and compiling them, but he for the most part abjures the dissection of archaic forms, and he does concentrate upon cultural processes in his discussion chapters. He lived in the neighborhood, and this fact alone accounts for many of the book's rare qualities.

Abrahams interprets most of the lore he has gathered in terms of the matrifocal complex, the battle of the sexes, and the plight of the disadvantaged, dispossessed Negro male.[44] He argues convincingly that verbal contest skills, good-talking, and word control in general enable a man to play out some of his aggressions and "achieve a kind of precarious masculine identity for himself and his group in a basically hostile environment."[45] Since manhood and the related themes of sex, aggression, control, and identity are basic to any consideration of the blues, the notion of "a kind of precarious masculine identity" and the reasoning behind it deserve close scrutiny.

Much Freudian and neo-Freudian psychological theory has been applied to the predicament of the Negro male. I feel that these applications have suffered from oversimplification and ethnocentrism. Although I do not have much new data to contribute or a full alternative theory with which to subvert the prevailing interpretation of Negro masculinity, I would like to question some of the basic tenets of this interpretation.

Parts of Abrahams' exposition are fairly typical:

Growing up in this matrifocal system, the boys receive little guidance from older males. There are few figures about during childhood through which the boys can achieve any sort of positive ego identity. Thus their ideas of masculinity are slow to appear under the tutelage of their mothers, and sometimes never do emerge.[46]

Women, then, are not only the dispensers of love and care but also of discipline and authority.[47]

He might, and does to some degree, react against his mother as the authority. But he is emotionally attached to his mother as a source of love and security. This attraction-repulsion paradox is further complicated by the fact that the trauma of rejection is persistently re-enacted for him. He sees his mother sharing herself not only with other children, but also often with numerous men. Finally, rejection comes completely when the boy begins to become the man, and the mother rejects him as a member of that other group.[48]

Having been denied a natural development of his sense of manness, he must constantly prove to himself that he is a man. Throughout most of the rest of his life this will be his major preoccupation, his "fixation."[49]

The spirit of contest . . . is exhibited in nearly every visible facet of the life of the Negro, from gang play to interplay between the sexes to clothes and choice of employment. And through it all the contests are self-defeating because they are never able to give the men a sense of their own identity. They remain throughout most of their lives men *manque*.[50]

These observations have a certain logical coherence and theoretical validity. Absent or disreputable fathers and loving but authoritarian mothers would seem to foster a formidable set of Oedipal and identity complexities. Indeed, Abrahams' statements are easily related to the aggression and adolescent sexuality that percolate through much of the folklore he gathered.[51] But I take strong exception to the view that lower-class Negro life style and its characteristic rituals and expressive roles are the products of overcompensation for masculine self-doubt. This is simply not true.

To begin with, it is entirely possible that "the Oedipal problem of managing and diverting aggression against the father"[52] may be easily resolved, mitigated, or avoided altogether in families in which the father is absent or weak and where a number of mothering women (grandmothers, aunts) are in or near the household. Even a large set of siblings and a string of visiting "uncles" do not compete for a mother's attention as a potent and omnipresent father might. The "uncles" and other males in the vicinity certainly offer some identity models to a young man growing up, but his sexual development is relatively unimpeded by them.

There is also some evidence which suggests that many Negro mothers do an excellent job of inculcating a strong masculine identity in their little boys at an early age. Esther Newton reports that mothers frequently vilify all those "no-good men" and conclude their indictment with the assertion that they are saving all their love and affection for "my little man right here, he's going to grow up and be a real lady killer," in other words, a no-good man.[53] Will Mama reject him when he attains that status, as Abrahams insists? I doubt it. Rather, she will take vicarious satisfaction from the fact that he exploits and mistreats the girls while retaining a basic loyalty to Mama.

The hustling career of "Edward Dodge: Nameless Con," chronicled with wonder and consternation by Rohrer and Edmonson in *The Eighth Generation Grows Up*[54] undermines the logic and theory of those who worry excessively about Negro masculinity. I would like to include the whole case history here, but a brief summary and a few excerpts must suffice. Edward grew up under classic matrifocal conditions; his mother was on her sixth official husband—a traveling preacher—at the time of the study. She seems to have loved, neglected, and disciplined Edward in random fashion during his formative years. He ran with a gang, spent time in reform school. "At 13 he was having sexual relations 'often' with little girls at school. He started 'doing it,' he says, when he was eight." At maturity, he is a typical hustler, pushing narcotics and apparently using them off and on, in and out of jail, separated from his wife, still living at his mother's flat, leading the fast life.

The authors find him a hopeless case, manifesting masculine insecurity in the worst way:

> Edward has fears about his manliness that seem to be altogether unconscious. Crude defensive methods, such as his beard and the tattoo of a girl's bosom on his chest, are evidences of his conflict about this.

> ... he sees himself unconsciously as weak and defenseless. He never admits this to himself; rather he idealizes himself as a powerful but misunderstood and mistreated man. He thinks he is a great lover, and even a proper family man, and he maintains this rationalization despite overwhelming evidence to the contrary.

> His morality is external. If he can get away with it, he does it. He is a hedonistic, impulsive man in conflict with a depriving world. He does not understand why this world should not grant him his infantile wishes for a stable of women, a fancy car, and a hundred suits.

> Despite his bravado and assertive masculinity, Edward has never been able to leave his mother, and he has long since internalized her ambivalence towards crime.... In his heart of hearts, Edward knows himself to be a failure—weak, nameless, and criminal, and he is unhappy.

Edward's mother, however, sees things very differently:

> Mrs. Burton blames Edward's trouble on bad company and women, explaining that he had to obtain lots of money to be able to entertain his girl friends. She thinks of herself as an exceptionally fine mother, and claims to be proud of her son, but her pride is inconsistent. She praises Edward's accomplishments as a swimmer and boxer, as well

as his abilities at outwitting the police, but . . . comments that "jail is just what he needs to straighten him out. . . ." Despite her conviction that women are the cause of Edward's troubles, his mother is exceedingly proud of his prowess as a lover, and delights in pointing out the number of good-looking girls he has had.

The extent of his promiscuous activities can be gauged by the frequent references made to them by his mother and by the pictures of numerous girls in his mother's house. His expensive shirts and suits were proudly displayed to one interviewer by Mrs. Burton. . . .

Edward's mother assures us that he has spent vast sums on whiskey and dope and good times. She is very proud of the fact that he was greatly sought after by the young men and women in the community. Men thought of him as a leader: women were proud to be seen with him.

One incident in particular gives the game away:

His relation to his current girl friend is similarly structured, and similarly obscure. She also is a nurse, and also proved loyal to him when he was jailed. To some extent, in fact, this girl was able to enlist the cooperation of both Edward's wife and mother in her efforts on his behalf, and remarkably she and his wife shared his attention on visiting days at the jail more or less amicably. Edward expressed no emotion about this girl in any of his interviews, and indicated that he had no expectation that she would be faithful to him during his prison term. Yet he clearly has some genuine success with women. An even more casual girl friend who worked as a barmaid near his mother's home also tried to help raise money to get him out on bail before his trial.

I don't think there can be any reasonable doubt that Edward's mother, wife, mistress, and assorted girl friends feel that he is a man, and a fairly impressive man at that. Edward thinks so too. Some white middle-class social scientists, enchanted with psychoanalytic theory, disagree. Whose word are we to believe on the matter? Clearly, lower-class Negro culture includes a concept of manhood that differs in kind from the white middle-class definition of a man as a head of a household, who holds down a steady job and sends his kids to college. Measured against this standard, Edward may well be a pathological, amoral deviant with profound psychological problems; but as far as he and his women are concerned, he spends his money freely, dresses well, and is great in bed. That's just the way he is—*a man*—and they like him that way, despite the fact that he's obviously "no good."

Abrahams, like Rohrer and Edmonson, conveniently ignores the culture, and is led to equally disastrous conclusions by the same theory of "masculine self-doubt and ambivalence."

> The love-hate ambivalence [toward mother and women generally], on the other hand, is undoubtedly responsible for many of the apparent effeminate traits of this otherwise masculine group. "Don Juanism," the method of hair grooming reminiscent of the handkerchief tying of Southern "Mammies," the importance of falsetto voices in quartet singing, the high prevalence of lisping, the whole "dandy" feeling of dress and walk—all are explicable because of this ambivalence. The "ego ideal" of these men is a confused one; though rejecting women they have accepted unconsciously certain symbols and actions of females.[55]

All "the apparent effeminate traits" that Abrahams notes are largely figments of his psychoanalytic imagination.

My impression is that those entertainers and hustlers who might be described as Don Juans are simply using their cash and prestige to enjoy a wide variety of women. Although most bluesmen of my acquaintance don't qualify for the supposedly monogamous middle class, they have formed lasting attachments and relationships with their wives; they like to "play around" whenever they can, but are hardly the victims of an insatiable desire to conquer every woman in sight.

The hair-processing techniques that Abrahams finds "reminiscent of the handkerchief tying of Southern "Mammies" are designed to heighten masculinity. Backstage at the Regal Theatre in Chicago "process rags" are everywhere in evidence among the male performers, the same performers who put the women in the audience into states that border on the ecstatic. Prettiness (wavy hair, manicured nails, frilly shirts, flashy jackets) plus strength, tender but tough—this is the style that many Negro women find irresistible. A blues singer is not unconsciously mimicking Elvis Presley's hairdo (the opposite may be true) or Aunt Jemima's when he straightens his hair and keeps it in place with a kerchief. He is enhancing his sex appeal—nothing more.

Falsetto singing comes directly from Africa, where it is considered to be the very essence of masculine expression. The smallest and highest-pitched drum in a West African percussion ensemble or "family" is designated the male drum because its tone is piercing and the role it plays is colorful, dynamic, and dominant. The falsetto techniques of a West African cabaret singer are sometimes indistinguishable from those employed so effectively by Ray Charles, B. B. King, or the lead voice in a gospel quartet.[56]

I have seen no evidence whatever for a "high prevalence of lisping" but "the whole 'dandy' feeling of dress and walk" is again more easily explained in terms of a distinctive masculine style, culturally defined. I see no reason for attributing such behavior to an underlying love-hate ambivalence toward women, even if this ambivalence can be shown to be an important factor in other areas of Negro life. Any sound analysis of Negro masculinity should first deal with the statements and responses of Negro women, the conscious motives of the men themselves, and the Negro cultural tradition. Applied in this setting, psychological theory may then be able to provide important new insights in place of basic and unfortunate distortions.

This is not to say that there are no ambivalent men in the Negro community or that Negro homosexuality shouldn't be studied[57]— quite the contrary. But there is an even more pressing need for a thorough, extensive, and intimate study of "normal" lower-class Negroes in a typical slum neighborhood. Most studies have focused upon abnormal Negroes out of context: those who found their way to the analyst's couch, or those who were willing to cooperate with inquisitive social scientists, most of whom were white. It is significant in this regard that Rohrer, Edmonson, and a large Negro and white staff found it extremely difficult to get any information from Edward Dodge, and most of his women and all his male cronies remained completely inaccessible. James Baldwin's *Go Tell It on the Mountain*[58] reminds us that some families are male-authoritarian rather than matrifocal, and undoubtedly many lower-class households do not fit easily into either category. The monumental works of Frazier[59] and Myrdal[60] (which need updating) and certain vivid slices of slum life included in *Black Metropolis* and *The Eighth Generation Grows Up* give further indications that the full range, variety, and complexity of day-to-day existence in America's black belts have yet to be fully revealed. It is only when more comprehensive studies of urban lower classes in other countries become available that we will be able to establish more effectively the parts that class, caste, urbanism, and ethnicity have played in shaping Negro culture and the diversity of individuals who are struggling to find identities within it.

Regardless of the forces which have shaped Negro culture, it exists, and within this culture a number of individuals have already found viable identities as men and women. In this respect, the entertainers in general and today's bluesmen in particular are outstanding —they take a firm stance at the center of contemporary Negro culture. If black Americans are to be free and if white Americans are to learn something essential concerning themselves from the Negro's effort to identify himself, a good beginning can be made by attempting to find out what the urban blues are all about.

NOTES

1. Some of the implications of urbanism and poverty are spelled out by Louis Wirth, "Urbanism as a Way of Life," *American Journal of Sociology* XLIV (1938), and by Michael Harrington, *The Other America* (New York, 1963).
2. Ralph Ellison, *Shadow and Act* (New York, 1964), p. 262.
3. Melville J. Herskovits, *The Myth of the Negro Past* (Boston, 1958), p. 2. Much of the myopic ignorance concerning Negro culture and styles that Nat Hentoff and I find so lamentable derives from the premature resolution of a debate between E. Franklin Frazier and Melville J. Herskovits (*The Negro in the United States,* rev. ed., New York, 1957). In his book, Herskovits attempted a thorough comparative study of African-derived cultures in the New World for the insights such a study might provide *vis a vis* "the American dilemma." Unfortunately, Herskovits overstated his case in the area of social organization when he insisted that the matrifocal family, economic independence of women, sexual attitudes, extended kinship patterns, and so on that are found in both contemporary West African cultures and American Negro communities can be seen as evidence of a tenacious, if somewhat generalized, set of familial values that were retained despite slavery. Frazier disagreed completely with this interpretation of the data, and I agree with him in this particular dispute. Slavery, as practiced in the United States at least, obliterated all but the faintest traces of African political, economic, and familial institutions. These aspects of life were rigidly controlled by the white slave masters. On the other hand, basic African predispositions governing religion and esthetics not only survived slavery, but were reshaped, nurtured, and magnified in response to slavery and post-slavery conditions. The facts that support this statement are available in abundance to anyone who will read *The Myth of the Negro Past.* Journalists and social scientists writing about the Negro in the past decade or so have invariably accepted Frazier's refutation of Herskovits' familial theories and have then proceeded to dismiss the rest of Herskovits' painstaking scholarship as well. Therefore, many writers have not even bothered to consult Herskovits' book before labeling the Negro traditionless, cultureless, and made in America.

4. No one can deny these two brute facts of ghetto life, but it is possible to show how a few Negroes have managed to survive and transcend them. I would also like to suggest that affluent white America suffers from spiritual impoverishment and that the suburban child is just as culturally deprived as his urban counterpart. Considering the white anxieties triggered by those unpredictable black forces penned up in the centers of American cities, contemplating the fifty billion dollars poured annually into that monument to terror, the Pentagon, and noting with alarm the growing generation of snipers, bombers, Minute Men, Birchers, and Klansmen, it also seems clear where the designation "culture of fear" belongs.

5. *The Village Voice*, Jan. 7, 1965, pp. 5, 16.

6. *Shadow and Act*, p. 263.

7. *Ibid.*, p. 262.

8. The Negro middle and upper classes form a special and rather "sick" American subculture according to two highly critical "participant observers." E. Franklin Frazier's *Black Bourgeoisie* (Glencoe, 1957) and Nathan Hare's recent vendetta *The Black Anglo-Saxons* (New York, 1965) do little more than ridicule the middle class as hopelessly trapped and deluded. A more sympathetic and constructive analysis of the difficulties faced by "newly arrived" Negroes, leavened perhaps with some humor, would be helpful and most refreshing at this point, it seems to me.

9. Weston LaBarre, *They Shall Take Up Serpents* (Minneapolis, 1962).

10. *The Eighth Generation Grows Up*, John H. Rohrer and Munro S. Edmonson, eds., p. 129. Copyright © 1960 by Harper & Row, Publishers, Incorporated. Reprinted by permission of Harper & Row, Publishers.

11. For a full and excellent discussion of sex role definitions and finance-romance relationships in the Negro community, see Esther Newton's "Men, Women and Status in the Negro Family" (unpublished Master's Thesis, University of Chicago, 1964).

12. *Advertisements for Myself* (New York, 1960), pp. 302–21.

13. Oscar Lewis, *The Children of Sanchez* (New York, 1963).

14. Compare Lewis' account of the Sanchez family in Mexico with the picture of Rio de Janeiro slums given in *Child of the Dark: The Diary of Carolina María de Jesús* (New York, 1962).

15. Stanley M. Elkins, *Slavery: A Problem in American Institutional and Intellectual Life* (Chicago, 1959).

16. The problem of distinguishing the skillful "put-on" from sincere "wishful thinking" is as important as it is complicated. In either, recited values often conflict with actual behavior. Do the reciters wish to be acceptable citizens, or do they want to push off (put on) agents of welfare colonialism and the white status quo so as to maintain their own way of life undisturbed? I suspect that most urban Negroes have both

goals—white acceptance and Negro identity—dimly in view. Question: are these goals incompatible or complementary?

17. © 1964 by Random House, Inc., New York.
18. From *The Mark of Oppression* by Abram Kardiner, M.D., and Lionel Ovesey, M.D. Copyright © 1951 by Abram Kardiner and Lionel Ovesey. Published by arrangement with The World Publishing Company, Cleveland and New York. A Meridian Book.
19. *Ibid.,* p. 384.
20. *Ibid.,* p. 385.
21. *Ibid.,* p. 340.
22. *Ibid.,* p. 341.
23. Silberman, *op. cit.,* p. 109.
24. *Ibid.,* p. 166.
25. I would not contest the usual argument that entertainment channels, broadly speaking, have been the only ones consistently open to Negroes in American society. It is important to note, however, that these ritualized forms developed within Negro culture and were only secondarily, if at all, patronized and appropriated by the American majority. Even when Negroes have contributed to established white American entertainment forms (sports, for example), a distinctively Negro style often shapes or accompanies that contribution. The nothing ball and sucker ball as pitched by Satchel Paige, the base as stolen by Maury Wills, the basket catches of Willie Mays, the antics of the Harlem Globetrotters, the beautiful ritualization of an ugly sport by Sonny Liston and Muhammad Ali —a full list of the symbolic transformations accomplished by Negro magicians in the sporting world would be most impressive.
26. This entertainment-ritual tradition probably does not provide, in itself, a satisfactory solution to the identity problem, and Silberman is quite correct in stressing the impact of emerging Africa on the Negro's self esteem. But identification with contemporary Africa and the African past must be consciously sought, indeed, created for the most part, whereas the soul tradition is home-grown (with African seeds), already created, and ready to be used. A mixture of indigenous soul and restored ties to West African cultural and historical traditions may ultimately resolve the identity confusion (see Appendix A).
27. To appreciate the many ramifications and implications of this statement, see Marshall McLuhan's fascinating study of print technology's impact on the Western world, *The Gutenberg Galaxy.* If McLuhan's thesis is correct, the electronic or post-literate age and its high powered auditory forces that are now upon us ought to give Negro culture a big technological boost.
28. An essay I have written, "Motion and Feeling through Music," *Journal of Aesthetics* (Spring, 1966), considers the kinesic aspect of music and adds a few pieces to McLuhan's "simultaneous mosaic."

29. Englishmen and Americans use the same language, yet references to the American subculture are rare, even in the English anthropological literature.
30. The two writers who have merited most acclaim both served sound apprenticeships: James Baldwin as a preacher, Ralph Ellison as a musician.
31. Approximately 90 per cent of the words that appear in the Sunday supplement slang glossaries can be traced to Negro culture. See also the dialogue in Clayton Riley's "Now That Henry Is Gone," *Liberator* V (July, 1965).
32. A thorough revamping of slum schools along ritualized and rhetorical lines (using the Lancasterian system as a starting point) would do far more to increase student motivation than all the Negro history, Negro contribution, and higher horizon courses combined. What is being taught to Negro children is certainly demoralizing enough, but the typographic manner in which it is being taught is even more destructive. A high degree of literacy should be one goal among many.
33. For the humor involved, listen to Moms Mabley's "Little Cindy Ella" monologue (Mercury LP, MG-20889). Moms' recorded works (at least eight albums) are a singularly rich reservoir of Negro oral expression. When folklorists finally wake up to the fact that the electronic media are making folk of us all, I'm sure this repository of lore will receive the volumes of analysis it deserves.
34. Rev. ed., Vols. I and II (New York, 1962).
35. New York, 1964.
36. Allison Davis and John Dollard (Washington, 1940).
37. The quality of this chapter was an important factor in my decision not to explore the intimate relationship between sacred and secular roles in greater detail.
38. For a book-length classic in the same vein, see Neil Leonard's *Jazz and the White Americans* (Chicago, 1962).
39. Within the lower-class culture they articulate very clearly the opposing value orientations of the matriarchy and the gang.
40. *Op. cit.,* p. 600.
41. This is the autobiography of Henry Williamson, edited by R. Lincoln Kaiser, with a commentary by Paul Bohannan (New York, 1965).
42. Bohannan in *ibid.,* p. 215.
43. Roger D. Abrahams, *Deep Down in the Jungle ... Negro Narrative Folklore from the Streets of Philadelphia* (Hatboro, Pa.: Folklore Associates, 1964).
44. I might add that all the materials were collected from a few men, since the author found the barrier between men and women and the boundaries of alien neighborhoods insurmountable.
45. *Ibid.,* p. 63.

46. *Ibid.,* p. 31.
47. *Ibid.*
48. *Ibid.,* p. 32.
49. *Ibid.,* p. 34.
50. *Ibid.,* p. 38.
51. And most of the lore seems to have been gathered from adolescents.
52. Erik Erikson, "Ego Development and Historical Change" in *Psychological Issues,* George S. Klein, ed. (New York, 1959), p. 29.
53. Personal communication.
54. All the following citations are from pp. 168–85.
55. Abrahams, *op. cit.,* p. 33.
56. I should like to stress again, however, that an Africanism argument may be both relevant and interesting, but it is not necessary to establish this point. If Negro women jump and shout when B. B. King cuts loose with a high falsetto, that is really all we need to know.
57. The nature of Negro homosexuality is a problem that needs to be explored in depth. A typology of faggots and Lesbians, coupled with the types of familial organization that tend to promote deviance, might go far in clearing the haze of illusion and controversy that surrounds Negro sexuality. I suspect that a surprising number of lower-class Negro men and women are ambisexual, homo-, or hetero- according to circumstances. I might add that I have noticed a high tolerance of sexual deviancy in some Chicago blues bars. I would also agree with Gershon Legman (in Abrahams, *op. cit.,* p. 29) that matrifocality probably produces more deviancy among daughters than sons. But all these issues need further study before suspicions will give way to reasonable interpretations.
58. New York, 1953.
59. E. Franklin Frazier, *The Negro Family in the United States* (Chicago, 1939).
60. Gunnar Myrdal, *An American Dilemma: The Negro Problem and Modern Democracy* (New York, 1944).

BLACK FATHERS*

Robert Coles

We have heard so much, and properly so, about the difficulty that black men have obtaining work, hence becoming good providers for their families. Needless to say, a man who cannot bring home money gets discouraged and bitter. Nor can we forget that, until recently, in many cities and counties families became eligible for welfare only when the father was dead or disabled or no longer at home. In thousands of instances, men have left their families for just that purpose. They sneak away when the welfare worker is expected, and return in-between her visits. Or go away and stay away. In Roxbury and Harlem and the Hough section of Cleveland and Chicago's West Side I have over and over again encountered families headed by mothers; and often the various children have different fathers. I have met up also, however, with sturdy, tough, outspoken black fathers, men of astonishing independence and vitality and resourcefulness, for all the burdens they bear, and doubts they have, the fears they fight every day. Somehow, those fathers are less apparent to the outsider than fatherless families, however careful and curious the observer may be. For one thing, they are working, or trying to find work, or off in some corner talking with a friend or two about how hard it is to get a good job and keep it. For another, they frequently are quiet, unassuming, quick to retreat when the children burst forth with remarks or the wife speaks out. But that is not to say a modest and reticent black man (worker, husband, father) needs to be labeled "weak" or "submissive"

*From Robert Coles, *The South Goes North,* © 1971, pp. 155–72. Reprinted with permission of Little, Brown and Company.

or "passive" or "dominated" by some "matriarch," some black virago who need only raise her eyebrow to have her way.

During the years that have gone into the work I am trying to report upon here, no individuals have confounded me so persistently as the "black fathers" I have met and spoken with and listened to and for long stretches of time, I believe, sorely misunderstood. Not that I understand black women all that clearly, but I have often found that black mothers can somehow find words for a passionate voice, a cry of mixed despair and hope. I once asked a black mother in Roxbury where, just where, she learned how to give forth so, assert herself, make her wishes and fears so vividly, compellingly known. She had a little trouble putting into words that particular answer, but soon one was forthcoming: "I'm not talking for myself. I'm speaking for Joseph and Sally and Harry and Stevie and Benjie and Mary. I'm speaking for them, and they push on me until I get the words out, that's what I believe. Because if ever I have trouble saying something, I look at my boys and my girls and the words come to my mouth."

One has to ask how black fathers can talk the way so many of them do, with their own kind of cleverness, guile, humor, sarcasm, exuberance, and often, in spite of everything, a certain guarded confidence. For instance, Henry R. Rollins speaks like this: "I'm poor, and I'll never be anything else. I don't care, because I'm rich, too. I have five children, four sons and a daughter, and they're the most wonderful people in the whole, big, wide world. I don't do right by them, I know. I don't bring home the money they all need. All the work I can get I do. I'm a janitor, and I keep on trying to take care of more buildings and more. I wouldn't mind taking care of every building in Roxbury, I'll tell you that, if it meant that my children had a little more. I'm their father and I owe them three meals, the best we can afford, and a good place to live. I'd like them to have more clothes. I wish I could get them a lot of toys. My oldest boy wants a baseball bat so bad that it hurts me to think about it, and he wants a glove, too. But there's no money for that. I took him aside and I told him. I said, 'Look here, son. I know, I know how bad you want it, the bat and glove, but we can't, we just can't go and get them.' Well, he said that he understood, and he won't tell me he doesn't still want them, but he was all the way with me, and he wished he was old enough to be working like I do, so there'd be a little more money for all of us."

Mr. Rollins's oldest son is nine, and if he is obviously close to his mother, and after a fashion a father to his younger brothers and sister, he is also close to Henry R. Rollins, though in more subtle ways. He does not stand next to his father, as he does with his mother, when a visitor comes. He does not give his father the intense and serious glances he casts toward his mother. He does not ask his father the questions he asks his mother: what to do and when and how. His mother affects him more, moves him and the other children emotionally, generates in them joy or disenchantment, the anticipation of pleasure or the expectation of those seemingly inevitable disappointments that come and come and come. But his father has his own kind of influence on the eldest son, and all the other children as well. The boys imitate him without being aware that they do: the way he puts his hands in his dungarees; the way he walks; the way he sighs about once every sentence spoken; the way he gazes off sometimes and seems utterly inaccessible, even though he is there, right there, and ready to respond, given a raised voice, a repeated request, a tap on his shoulder, or merely an impatient but persistent spell of silence which will cause him suddenly to come out of his thoughts and look sheepish and apologetic and faintly amused, as if to say: I just have to do that every once in a while, and I am grateful to you for being courteous enough not to hurry me along with remarks and shouts and a push or two.

All day long the man cleans out buildings, chases rats and mice, tries to keep hallways clear and reasonably well lighted, and responds to urgent pleas for help with a cautious and sincere interest, but by no means with promises of immediate action. He has so many buildings to oversee, and his employers, members of a large real estate company, have no great desire to keep the property in the very best of condition. Mr. Rollins is loyal to them, however—if that is the word. He has heard "the bosses" complain about their problems so often that he at least can make a pretense of sympathizing with them, and certainly he can imitate them. He can insist upon the rising cost of taxes, and the pressures upon owners of property not to raise rents, and the high price of all repair work. He can even talk this way about "the people," the families in those buildings: "It's hard keeping a place clean when you have everyone making a mess. They throw garbage right out the windows, a few of them do. The kids kick at the walls and write things and throw rocks at the light bulbs. What can you do? The owners say that they could go broke keeping up with the kids, and maybe it would take away from their profits."

That last phrase is very much Mr. Rollins's style: he can be truthful, ironic, sarcastic and utterly sincere and polite, all in a few words. He knows how to understate things. He has a smoldering sense of humor; even when he is sad and downcast he can find something to smile about, if not laugh at. He is tentative and almost self-effacing, yet he manages to say something that catches his listener's ear and isn't easily forgotten. He is an undramatic person, but he can readily summon the attention of his wife, his children, his neighbors. He can speak up, or simply move nearer and nearer without saying a word, all the while looking right into one's eyes. Here, for example, is what the man can say when he wants to say something: "I don't like to talk very much. I find that the more I get talking with the tenants, the less I can do, and the more fights I have. They want to blame someone, and I don't blame them for that; and I'm right here, around every day, so they blame me. They shout at me, and I nod to them and tell them that they're right. I promise I'll go tell the bosses, and maybe they'll come around and see for themselves. A tenant doesn't like to hear that, though. They want their satisfaction. They want something done. I'll be telling them that maybe something will happen in a few weeks or a few months, and they'll be registering in their minds that I'm *really* telling them I can't do a single thing. Then they get real mad at *me*. They want to know how I can work in a job like I have. They say I'm as bad as the white man, the owners of the buildings, and I'm an Uncle Tom and I'm a slave and—well, there isn't much I'm not called by the time the week has run out, I'll tell you.

"One woman keeps on telling me I should be shining the shoes of the owners. She says I'm the errand boy. I smile when she tells me that. What else can you do? Then she tells me to go look at my smile in the mirror, and I'll see what a nice yes-man I am, the worst Uncle Tom she's ever seen. I asked her what her husband did to earn a living. She shut the door in my face without telling me; she just pushed me out and slammed that door—and the next thing I knew she was complaining that the lock was broken and thieves will be opening up the door and stealing her property. Well, I fixed her door, and I found out from her neighbor about the husband. He doesn't have a job, no job at all. He shoots horse. She's telling me I'm no good and an Uncle Tom, and meanwhile her husband is an addict and he doesn't bring in a cent and he's never around! I went home and told my kids the story. I want them to know what's going on in the world. That's what a father can do for his kids. He's out in the world, and he finds out what is happening, and he can go back and make sure the wife and kids get to know."

He does more than that. He lifts his children up in the air and holds them there and tells them that one of these days—years from now, true, but *one of these days*—things will be different and they as grown-ups will be better off and higher up in the world, way higher up. Then, to make certain they get his point, feel its thrust, he gently bumps the child's head on the ceiling of the room. He also watches television with them. He doesn't say much, but he will smile, and upon occasion say "hah!" when he wants to underscore a particular thing said or shown. The children of course hear him when he shouts or mumbles his "hah!" or murmurs some indefinable phrase, but they also uncannily know when he is smiling, but making no sound at all. They look at him, immediately smile in response to his smile, then try to figure out what it was that occasioned his amusement in the first place.

And one more thing he does: he says good-night to his children. No matter how busy he is, and unless there is an emergency in one of the buildings he has to oversee, at bedtime he is there to kiss his children and tell them "good-bye, spend a good night sleeping, and come back to us all fresh and good in the morning." He is, again, not passionate and outspoken like his wife can be, or their minister, but he does have his stories to tell. Often those stories are about the South. Whereas Mrs. Rollins talks about the South moodily, nostalgically, bitterly, wistfully, Mr. Rollins has concrete stories to tell: "I like my kids to know that there once was a place where the black man lived different than up here. When I was their age I was down there, living in that cabin we had in Tunica County. Mississippi is a bad state for the black man; but my brother and I, we managed to squeeze some laughing out of our life down there. We had to go help our daddy, and we had to wash the bossman's cars. He had three of them, one for himself and one for his wife and one for his daughter. That was a lot of cars for someone to have in those days. We don't have a car even now, but today people who have money, I mean ordinary people making a good salary, they have two cars, I believe. Well, back in Tunica County the bossman's wife, she never wanted those cars to get dust on them. She'd go out for a drive after we worked on her car, and then she'd come home and we had to hose the car down again and polish it again. She was the neatest woman you'll ever meet. She was always complaining that her furniture got so dirty. She said the best colors are green and brown and black, because they don't show dirt and the worst are white and yellow and pink. My daddy used to say she should have been born black, and then her skin could hide dirt better, and she'd be happier.

"But I'll tell you, we kept those cars clean. As fast as anyone brought them back from a drive, we'd be at the garage, and we had the hose and the soap and we worked. Then she would come out and give my brother and me a lollipop. Sometimes she'd run out and she'd give us some sugar instead. I used to love sugar then. Now I can't bear to look at it, I mean the kind that's in those squares. 'Here's a cube of sugar for you, Henry,' she'd say, and I'd come running fast. The other day I saw a woman in one of the buildings lift one of those cubes out of a cup and put it in her mouth, and I thought I was going to pass right out. She asked me what was wrong, and I said, 'I don't know.' She said I didn't look too good. I didn't say anything, and I was just about recovered, when all of a sudden I heard her chewing on the sugar, and cutting it up with her teeth, the way I used to do, and I had to excuse myself real fast. I got out into the hall, and it was like I was back in Tunica County and I was eating the sugar, except my stomach was hurting. That used to happen sometimes. My daddy would say it was from eating the sugar too fast, and once I told the bossman's wife, and she said, 'Poor child, sugar probably brings on worms.' I told my daddy that, and he said not to believe her, but say yes to everything she says, no matter what it is. In the hall of the building I thought of the bossman and his wife and my daddy and those worms she told me I could get. I used to see a worm in the ground, wriggling and moving along, and I'd think to myself: is one of them inside me? In the hall I thought I should go and tell the woman not to take sugar that way, not to *eat* it, not to *chew* on it. But caught myself and I said, Henry, you're thinking the wrong thing, and stop. Instead I went back and knocked on the door and told her that I'd go and find a bulb, if I could, and put it in the hall so she wouldn't be stumbling all over the place. Being old, it's dangerous for her to fall, and if she can live to be as old as she has and eat those cubes then I thought: how could they be so bad for you? She doesn't look as if the worms have gotten much to eat from her. She's fat and she likes her food and, like I said, she's over seventy, she told me. That's not a bad age to pile up."

Not everyone can get to be seventy, he says rather more often than one might expect from a man in his early thirties. He has one ambition in life, and if he can realize it he will die happy. He wants his children to live elsewhere, to have jobs, to be better off than he is—which means he wants them, first, to stay in school and graduate from high school, and, second, to keep a safe distance from some of the things that go on near at hand: gambling, drinking, the use of drugs, prostitution and gang warfare. It is easy, all too easy, for someone like me to highlight those elements of Roxbury's life, or Harlem's. Again and again one hears about how awful it is in our ghettos, how mean and vicious and degrading life is there; and there's no doubt it is for some children and some grown men and women. Yet, a lot more goes on than often gets told, reported, described; and I fear that these days it is more than likely that observers like me will fail to take note of what is strong and balanced and growing and settled and utterly impressive about many, many so-called "ghetto families." And if we do so, if we try to convey the self-confidence and dignity and adroitness and moral sensibility and thoughtfulness of a Henry R. Rollins—poor and uneducated, upon occasion worried and fearful and at a loss to know what his future and his children's future will be—if we try to indicate the dimensions of Mr. Rollins's character, the range of his experience, the spread of attitudes and loyalties and commitments to be found in him, the possibilities he himself takes note of, the ambiguities he every day struggles to comprehend and contend with; if we attempt to do all that—even so we will have to remind ourselves that no life can ever be fully approximated by any observer, however bent he is on suggesting nuances and highlighting a person's vitality as well as his or her shortcomings.

We "observers" often fail to insist upon a complexity that gets more intricate the longer we look. I suppose we want to simplify and take a firm, clear-cut "stand" on some side, any side—and in so doing I fear we cannot do justice to the life of a man like Henry R. Rollins in our written descriptions. Ironically, I believe Mr. Rollins himself knows that people like to come upon conclusions and findings and discoveries that fit their own preconceptions. He knows that to be poor and black can often enough mean, among other things, to be misheard, misinterpreted, misunderstood—sometimes by people who loudly proclaim their good faith, their compassion, their benevolence: "I keep quiet a lot. I let the landlord have his say; then he goes away and I do what I do. You don't argue when it won't do any good. I come home and I'm tired. I'm glad to be able to sit down and listen to the kids make noise. My wife doesn't ask me to do things for her. She says there has to be *one* tenant who doesn't complain all the time to me! I hear white people talking, and black people. I have to take care of some stores as well as apartment buildings. I hear the police talking, and the real estate people, all kinds of people. Then I come home and I'll see my kids, and they'll go to bed, and next thing there's someone on television talking about the poor black man and all his troubles—you know, on the news and late at night on those programs. I fall asleep in my clothes early, then my wife wakes me up and I have some cookies and we watch television a little and we go to sleep. That's like having two nights of sleep in one!

"Why does everyone want to feel so sorry for us? Why do they all talk about us as though we're the worst-off people in the world? I'm a poor man, I know it; and I'm black, or a Negro, I don't care which it is they go and call me. But to Hell with being called every-thing under the sun! I'm Henry Rollins, that's my name and that's who I am. 'You black people,' I heard a cop shout at a friend of mine the other day, and my friend didn't say anything. Maybe I'd have been scared, too. But I'd *like* to say this to a cop: mister, what is your name? Then, if he told me, I'd say thank you, thank you very much, and *my* name is Henry R. Rollins and that's who I am. See what I mean? I bet he'd understand me. If you keep reminding people, they'll remem-ber after a while. I told my boss that I'll take care of his buildings, and I'll never do a thing wrong if I can help it. I told him I'd like to prove I can be my own boss. He said that was fine, but he hoped I'd be true to my word. I said I would be. If he heard some of the people talking about us on television, I can see why he'd think I'm no good. I could see why he wouldn't trust me. I don't think a lot of white people know us; that's what I believe. I don't even think one black man knows another. I hear people talking. I hear my own neighbors talking. Everyone has *ideas* about us, *opinions* about us. Who is 'us'? I'm me! I think they ought to leave the black man alone; I mean, I'm just trying to be myself, and it's like I'd tell the cop if I didn't think he'd pull a gun on me: I'm Henry Rollins, and that's all I can say.

"My kids tell me they're glad I'm their dad. To my kids I'm a father, not a black man. Yesterday I was telling their mother about the big signs that say YOU ARE BLACK: ACT IT! I can't even figure out what those signs mean. I read them and then I read them again, and then I say to myself: that's just no good, that message. What am I supposed to do? I can only act myself. I can't go acting the color of my skin. The color of my skin is me; yes, sure it is. But I'll be truth-ful: I don't have the time to be thinking of all that. When I come home I want to be my kids' daddy. How can I "act black," when I'm trying to be their *daddy*? It's a lot of talk, if you ask me."

We get further into the issue, though. I once tried to paraphrase as fairly as I know how the reply he would hear from the man who made up the slogan he happened to read, posted as it was in the window of a store he takes care of. He listened and he said yes, and he added some comments of his own, and he insisted that he quite understood what the man was getting at. Nevertheless, he had to make clear his amusement and surprise and mild annoyance, and he had to make clear that he was not to be confused in anyone's mind with any particular notion of how a person acts or should act or might someday come to act: "Like I said, I'm me—period. I don't know how to act, except to act like I do. I may be wrong about a lot of things, but I try to keep my head, I try to do my work. I try to tell my kids that they should respect their mother and respect me, and they should think for themselves and not let everyone they meet and play with tell them what is right and wrong. I want my kids to be as good as my grandfather was. That's right! He was called a 'big black buck' by some of the white people back in Mississippi. Yes, that's what my daddy told me. My grandfather was tall and heavy, and he was as strong as a man could be. There was a doctor there in Tunica County, and he told the bossman that my granddaddy was 'superior': he could lift things and break things and do anything, it seemed. They called him a 'smart nigger,' too. That's what my daddy told me. He had a big, deep voice, and you could hear him all the way across the field. He sang songs. He shouted. He marched down the road and white people would go by and turn around and stare, and the black folks just said: that's our Robbie. That's what he was called, Robbie.

"I was saying I'd like my kids to be like my grandfather. I mean, I'd like them to feel as big as he was and be as smart as he was. I don't care how they act, so long as it's like him. I try to think how he'd act if he'd have come up North, but there's no telling. He might have been pretty low. He might have decided to go back as fast as he could to Mississippi. He got the white people down there to be a little careful about him, and he got our own people to look up to him, and that's all anyone in Tunica County could have done, anyone who picked cotton! So, I'm not ashamed of him. He couldn't read and he couldn't write, but I'm glad he was my grandfather. I can recall him a little. He took me on his knee and said to me that I should never forget that God gave me good strong arms and legs, and He gave me ears and eyes and my head to use. He said if I learned to use my arms and legs as best I could, and if I used my head all the time and didn't get tricked and fooled, then I'd be a real big success in my life. He told me I was going to have a better life than he did, he believed that, but he wanted me to know something very important, in case he should die: never forget that he was glad he'd been born and he was proud of what he'd done in his life and he didn't feel he'd done a bad job, no. He kept on repeating himself. He said he was doing it because later on a lot of people were going to try to convince me that I was no good and he was no good and my daddy was no good, and if only we were different—if only we were white!—*then* we'd be good. Don't you believe that, he told me. Believe in yourself, he told me. I told him my daddy would say the same thing, and then he said *good, real good* and he put me down from his knee and gave me some gum.

"I'm sure my grandfather had a lot to learn. I'm sure he was wrong a lot of the time. But I'm proud of him when I think about him. He was a real good man, a mighty good one. It's too bad my kids never will see him. All I can do is talk about him to them—and I can try to be like him. I know it's different up here, and I can't be the cotton picker he was, or go do all those jobs they had him do in Tunica County. But I can show my kids, like he did, that they've got me here as their daddy, and I put in my time on the job, and I can honestly say: I got this far; now you go and do the same, and do more, and go even further. That was something else my granddaddy used to say. He'd say: I'm walking down the road as far as I can, and your daddy, he's walking along, and he'll get farther along than me, and you, I'll be hoping you go farther along than both of us. I tell that to my kids. I tell them they've got to keep walking and it won't be long before they're way out ahead of me; and their mother and I, we'll be pleased to be looking at them, out there in front of us."

When black families are discussed, such a father has to be thought about; he also is part of a particular race, and he also has behind him a particular cultural tradition. He cannot be dismissed as rare or unusual, or for that matter "atypical" and "unrepresentative." Once he made me smile by laughing out loud and saying this: "You'll probably find what you're looking for. I believe that." He was answering two questions I put to him: "Do you think there are many others who think like you? Do you think I'll find other fathers who are like you?" After he had been laconic and cryptic and a touch sarcastic, he decided to expand his remarks. He mentioned one man's name after another. He insisted that of course he was no rare bird. He let me know that nothing was more appalling to him than the misconceptions he in his own way has noted that millions of people like me have about people like him. He told me that a "plain, ordinary guy" like himself is to be found in apartment after apartment, in one street after another. Yes, there are all sorts of hurt, wretched, tormented people nearby—and far away, too: across town, across the tracks, among white people. But why is it, he both pleaded and asked, *why, oh why*, is it that a man like him, and all the other men he knows to be basically and at heart and in essence and fundamentally like him, never seem to catch the eye of people who talk about the black man and say "all those things about us?"

He is sure, he is very sure, that the various commentators and critics and scholars and writers are right and well intentioned and careful; and certainly they know much more than he ever will. Still, there is this to say: "I hear a man talking on television. He says he knows what we want, the black people. He says he knows us. He says he's black. Or if he's white he says he's looked into us. Then he says what the 'truth' is, and I've got my ears wide wide, open, and I'm listening, I'm really tuned in. But a lot of the time, I say: Hell, he's not talking about me; I'm Henry Rollins, and he hasn't told what goes through my mind. And a lot of other men I don't know, I'll bet he hasn't told what they're like, either."

Indeed there are men he does not know, men he might actually want to know, men both like him and unlike him, men whose roots are in, say, North Carolina and not Mississippi, who live in, perhaps, Cleveland and not Boston. One such man is Ray Phillips, a cabdriver, a black cabdriver. He says that, calls himself "a black cabdriver." He still remembers when many white people wouldn't take a cab driven by a black man, and when blacks took cabs far less frequently than they do today, and when white cabdrivers bumped him with their cabs and swore at him, and when the police were constantly asking him to identify himself and show cause why he should not be called a liar, a crook, a pretender, a public nuisance or menace. Now, at forty-eight, he is a father, a grandfather, a fairly good wage earner and, most important, he emphasizes, a husband: "I love my children, but most of all I love my wife. We've been married for thirty years. Yes, that's right: I was eighteen and so was she when we got married. The minister told us no, because our parents told us no, but then I got my dad to say yes, and pretty soon we were in the church there, swearing we'd stand by each other until the end of our lives. Thank God we *did* get married; a year or so later I was in the Army, the Second World War. My son was born when I was out in California and then I was sent to the Pacific and I didn't see him until he was five, I think it was. I'm getting hazy about all that. He's got two of his own children now. After the war we had a girl, then another girl, and then I said the time has come to stop. I'm no millionaire, and three kids is enough. Sometimes I think: I grew up and there were six of us, and maybe it would have been better with more children. But I'm glad we stayed at three. My wife would look a lot older than she does if she'd have had three or four more kids pulling on her and taking it out of her. A man doesn't know what his wife goes through all day. All he knows is his own troubles. He forgets what it means to bring up kids—and I mean *bring* them up, not drag them up.

"I'll be driving a customer someplace in the city, and if he's a nice, friendly guy he'll start telling me about all his troubles. He'll tell me his business is good, but it could be better, then he'll tell me some other worry he has. Then I'll try to change the subject. I ask if he's married. Yes, he says. Children? Yes, he says. How's the wife find *her* work, I say. Oh, fine, fine—that's what they'll say, unless they come at you with: *what* work? A lot of husbands just don't know what their wives do all day. I'm the kind of husband who does. I've tried to pitch in and help my wife every way I can. I've tried to be around my kids, too. I was a real father to them, not a man they called father. And I'm a good grandfather, I believe, a very good one. That means I spoil them the way someone should!"

The more he talks the more one forgets that he is anything but an American taxi driver who doesn't make a huge amount of money, who hustles (he puts it) for what he does make, who happens to know just about every street, or so it seems, in Cleveland, Ohio, and who happens also to be close to his wife, devoted to his children, and anxious to be a grandfather about nine or ten times, he says. He never finished high school. He was born in eastern North Carolina, but was brought to Cleveland at age three. His parents were not members of the "black bourgeoisie." His father left North Carolina because he told a white man to go to Hell and was promptly arrested. He escaped from jail, though Ray Phillips was told that the escape was permitted by a deputy sheriff who disliked the man who was insulted and who caused the black man's arrest. How, then, did Ray Phillips manage to do so well, become a successful cabdriver, be so good a husband and father?

Perhaps he has a right to ask me why I have to ask such a question, though God knows even more insulting and patronizing questions are asked these days. However, because Mr. Phillips has a radio in his car and hears a lot of "talk shows" and "call-in" programs, and because he also reads the papers regularly, and because he watches television documentaries, he is prepared for the likes of such questions: "Everyone is looking at the black man today and saying: who is he, and what's on his mind? I know. I flip from one station to another, or I'll meet a real honest fare and he'll say to me: come on, level with me and tell me what you think of all our race problems. Well, I do tell him, even if he's a big, fat white businessman. I say: mister, I'm a citizen of this country, just like you. I was over in the Pacific, fighting to beat Japan and win. I was under MacArthur. I've seen other parts of the world, and I'm glad to be living right here. If the white people would only get off our backs and leave us alone, we'd be the best citizens this country has, and everyone could relax and stop being so damn nervous. That's what I tell people. Sometimes they listen, and sometimes they don't. I can tell. If they want to hear more, I've got through to them. If they shut up and don't say another word, I know I haven't; and I know I'll be getting a real small tip—if I get *any* tip."

The more he talks the more he decides to call himself a teacher. He is only being half humorous. He sees a lot of people in the course of a day, a week, a year; and he tries to get the word across, spell out a certain message that he believes, that he considers just and sensible, and that he wants others to hear. He doesn't have the same words for each person. He realizes that many hear nothing, that many are hopeless causes, are unapproachable. He is an observant and intuitive man, a person who can sense what other people are like, can quietly and without a lot of trial-and-error exchanges decide who might and who might not want to hear some of his ideas. And as he gives expression to those ideas, he rather often hears in the casual atmosphere of his cab much the same kind of question I more formally have had in mind over the years, and indeed have just set down above: how is it that this man has become—well, "just like anyone else"? That is the way he finds a lot of white men putting it—tactfully, they believe. He does not get excited or angry with them. He smiles and brings out into the open what they "really" want to say, and thus helps them along, shows them how categorical and indiscriminate they have been: "I say, look: you've met me. Think of the thousands and thousands of guys you haven't met who would talk to you like me, if they had the chance. I happen to like to talk. I've been a cabdriver all these years, and it's an education, and you get to feel comfortable with people, so I can speak up. But I'm just one of about twenty million Negroes. Call me black, call me colored, call me a Negro. I don't care, so long as you see that I'm Ray Phillips—you hear?—and I have my wife and my kids and my grandchildren and I watch the same television shows everyone else does, and when the President said we've got to protect the country from Hitler and the emperor of Japan, he got me to go fight along with everyone else.

"They begin to think by then—the customers who have some sense in them to start with, I guess. You're right, you're right they'll say. Then I look at them through my mirror and I can tell by the look on their face that they *still* think I'm someone special. He's different, their face says. He's a real smart one, they seem to be saying. That's why I can't let it drop there. I have to work. I even have to knock myself a few pegs down. I have to convince them that for every me, there's another me—a million other me's. I have to tell them that my dad was a guy on the run, a 'fugitive from justice,' they called him. I have to let them know that I was born poor and if I'm not poor now, I'm sure a lot poorer than *they* are. Otherwise I keep hearing: you're exceptional, you're an unusual guy. When you hear that you know what that means: he thinks everyone else black is no goddam good. I'm supposed to feel big when someone says to me I'm the greatest person he's met, but I could take the guy to the building we live in and the one next door, and all up and down the street, and there would be men just like me: they're not rich; they work hard and they get by, they *just* get by, and sometimes they *don't*, I'll tell you, with prices going up, up; but most of all, they're like other people in this country. I mean, they try to do the best they can by their wives and their kids, and if they can only come home and be with them, they're willing to work hard, plenty hard, and be glad to have the work. If they don't find work, then that's another story. But so long as a man can get a job, and if he's honest and he's not crazy because of drugs or liquor, then he'll be fine, and if his wife is a good woman, he'll stand by her, I believe, and he'll stand by his children."

Of course, there are exceptions, he reminds himself and me. White fathers betray their children, and so do black fathers. Individual men can be fickle, unreliable, devious, awful examples to their children and harsh and callous men to their wives. Moreover, he repeatedly takes pains to remind me that it is "another story" when a man has no job, or has one but then is laid off and cannot find another one, or finds one but gets little pay and works under demeaning circumstances—all of which causes in husbands and fathers a kind of fearfulness and resentment which wives and children do indeed come to experience. I suppose, in sum, Ray Phillips has this to say: There are plenty of aimless, wandering dazed and ruined black men, even as in America white men by the thousands are alcoholics or philanderers or crook or loafers or clock-watchers or slowpokes or sleepy-heads. Yet, there are among black America's people many millions of men who are faithful husbands, devoted fathers and hard workers. By and large those men are not as well off as their white counterparts, do not have access to jobs many whites can either take for granted or obtain with relative ease if they so desire. Yet, despite such "facts of life," black men in street after street of our northern cities struggle to find what work they can, and struggle also to maintain intact homes in which children grow up with a sense of continuity and stability in their lives.

None of what I have just written is extraordinary or surprising, but I fear it is quite necessary to bring before the reader men like Henry Rollins and Ray Phillips, men who head black families, workingmen who are very much their children's father. No doubt about it, many black children (and many white children) don't have fathers like Henry Rollins and Ray Phillips, but many, many do—and in this last third of the twentieth century, when one slogan after another is fastened upon over twenty million American citizens, it is well to keep a janitor here, a taxi driver there, in mind as we go rushing on to the next moment of panic and despair.

We Are Black, Too

The so-called "black bourgeoisie" was often mentioned long before "black power" became (from 1965 on) a rallying cry, first for disappointed and embittered civil rights activists, and then for black people all over America. I remember well the mixed feelings many young black organizers in the rural South had toward black ministers, doctors, lawyers, storekeepers, insurance agents, funeral directors, postal clerks, real estate men and schoolteachers. Here is one member of SNCC speaking, in 1963, when the fight was most intense, but when the morale of the fighters was high indeed: "I hate them; they're as much the enemy as any lousy, rotten segregationist. They exploit their own people. They lick the boots of the white man. They're the white man's agents. They work for the white man. They do his bidding. They run the Negro community and make sure everyone stays in line, and they hand out little token rewards—just enough to keep people nice and quiet. I'll tell you: *they* are the enemy. If we could get rid of them, we'd have our own people much more up in arms. It would be easier to organize. This way, I have to try and persuade extremely poor people to fight not only the white world, the sheriffs and judges and state police, but the black leaders, our so-called black bourgeoisie."

Yet, at another time he could feel different. He could smile and be more historical, more reflective, less outraged: "It's a tough business. You want to *activate* people. You want them to begin standing up. You want them to say: go to Hell, goddam white man. That means saying: to Hell with you, all you Uncle Toms and all you bowing and scraping niggers; to Hell with saying 'yes suh' to whites, then bleeding your own people of the little they have. But I know it's more complicated than that. People need their self-respect. They need to feel they can produce doctors and lawyers and teachers and the rest. They need to feel that even if *they* can't make it, there are other black men who have. That's why they love Joe Louis and Louis Armstrong and Lena Horne. We may think the average man should be more political, but let's face it, in this country it's hard to get any large number of people to think in a highly political way.

"I go from door to door, and I'll hear these very poor mothers and fathers talking. They want their kids to study and graduate from school and get good jobs and become like so-and-so, who is a businessman or a lawyer. Now, I happen to know how he works and how crooked he is, so-and-so, but what can I do? I can't just knock him down. I can't tell those people—they've barely opened their door to me and the more they hear of my ideas, the more they're ready to close the door shut on me—I can't say: to Hell with the black middle class, because they're pathetic, man, just a big laugh. I've tried that, and people get really put out. They say in so many words: to Hell with *you*, brother. We want our kids to rise up and be somebody. We'd love our kids to be doctors and lawyers and ministers and all the rest. Don't go and take away our local heroes. We need more than a hero up in New York or over in Atlanta. We need our own people nearby, who look and dress and act respectable and nice and are an example to us and make us feel better about what is possible for a Negro in this country. The people I visit don't even have to say something like that; they feel it, and they let you know with a look on their faces that they do. And it takes someone like me a lot of time to realize how a person feels and to learn how to get around the problem. You learn that you have to go along with things to some extent. You pay your respect to Dr. X and you say sure, lawyer Y is a great guy, and that fellow Z, who is principal of the school—and owns three blocks of slum shacks —he's wonderful, and so is the Reverend Jones, who shouts and screams about God coming to separate the sheep from the goats, while he cheats on his wife and splits the profits with the undertaker—and on and on. Then you try to make a point or two by commenting on how few of those people we have, how the white community controls them, and how much more we need in the Negro community: hospitals and schools and legal aid and all the rest."

SOCIAL AND PSYCHOLOGICAL DIMENSIONS OF THE FAMILY ROLE PERFORMANCE OF THE NEGRO MALE*

*Seymour Parker and Robert J. Kleiner***

This paper was stimulated by the controversy that has developed over the Moynihan Report and the question of the extent to which the Negro family represents an institutionalization of culturally "deviant" norms. In order to probe this question further, an attempt was made to determine some of the concomitants of discrepancies between the subjectively perceived actual and ideal family role behavior of a sample of Negro males. The results indicate that such discrepancies in family role performance are related to relatively low evaluations of one's own achievements and probability of success in goal striving, as well as relatively higher discrepancies between achievement and aspiration. These findings point to the fact that discrepancies in family role performance of the Negro male are part of a more encompassing perception of failure in the larger arena of goal-striving behavior.

*Supported by Research Grant Number HM-10690. National Institutes of Health, Public Health Service, Bethesda, Maryland. The community survey was conducted by National Analysts, Inc., Philadelphia, Pennsylvania. The data were gathered in 1961.

*From the *Journal of Marriage and the Family* (August, 1969), pp. 500–506. Reprinted with permission of the authors and the National Council on Family Relations.

**Seymour Parker, Ph.D., is Professor and Chairman of the Department of Anthropology, University of Utah. Robert J. Kleiner, Ph.D., is Professor of Sociology at Temple University, Philadelphia, Pennsylvania.

The Negro family has in recent years become a subject not only of academic speculation and research, but also of political debate and invective. The Department of Labor publication on the Negro family,[1] sometimes referred to as the "Moynihan Report," has drawn attention to the disorganization of the Negro family and regards it as a source of many of the social problems currently experienced by the Negro people. In this and a more recent publication by Moynihan,[2] there is an *implicit* argument that although the Negro family has been—and continues to be—adversely affected by discrimination, semicaste position, unemployment, etc., it has become in recent years a self-perpetuating subculture propelled and sustained, to a considerable degree, by its own internal dynamics of family role deviancy.[3] A further implication of this argument is the idea that the problems of the Negro family can be explained not only as the result of overt behavioral family role deviance and as a direct response to external societal pressures, but also as an institutionalization of a *"deviant" normative* family role system—a distinct subculture within the larger society. This position is by no means confined to the Department of Labor publication and is said to characterize the Negro lower-status group, where unemployment and job instability is common, and not the middle-class family. Recent published analyses[4,5] of the 1960 Census data indicated that social status was inversely related to marital instability in the Negro population. However, at every status level, marital instability among Negroes exceeded that of whites. The authors conclude therefore that cultural factors must be introduced to explain fully white-Negro differences. Thus, social structural and normative values have been implicated in the idea of the institutionalization of Negro family deviance.

This position and the arguments that have ensued from it revolve mainly around the question of the extent to which deviant role performance in the Negro family can be explained as a painful adjustment to social conditions of discrimination and a high probability of failure, as against the view that it represents a normative conformity to a subculturally distinct family situation. Although it is dangerous to infer norms directly from overt behavior, this is frequently done. In spite of its manifest importance and policy implications, there is surprisingly little current empirical research relevant to this issue. The study of the Negro family by Frazier[6] pertains to the prewar period, while Moynihan's work depends largely on statistical analyses of census data that document the disorganization of the Negro family. Since the latter is not based on an actual study of the family, its conclusions concerning the issues raised above are largely inferential. Moynihan himself recognizes this and laments the fact that:

> the relation between economic phenomena, such as employment, and social phenomena, such as family structure, has hardly begun to be traced in the United States.[7]

The relevant recent empirical data we do have emerge from studies by Bell,[8] Blood and Wolfe,[9] Rainwater,[10] and Liebow.[11] Bell's data indicate that Negro lower-class females hold marital norms differing considerably from those in a white population. On the other hand, Blood and Wolfe document the fact that Negro women, compared to whites at the same economic levels, are consciously dissatisfied with important aspects of their married life. In a similar vein, after studying a number of Negro families in depth, Rainwater addresses himself to this issue directly:

> It is important to recognize that lower class Negroes know that their particular family forms are different from those of the rest of society and that, though they often see these forms as representing the only ways of behaving, given their circumstances, they also think of the more stable forms of the working class as more desirable. That is, lower class Negroes know what the "normal American family" is supposed to be like and they consider a stable family-centered way of life superior to the conjugal and familiar situations in which they find themselves. ... The existence of such ideas about normal family life represents a recurrent source of stress within families as individuals become aware that they are failing to measure up to the ideals.

Liebow's study is unique insofar as he used the participant-observer technique to study intensively a group of lower-class Negro males in Washington, D.C. This was a long-term study, and the author was able to establish an intimate relationship with some of the subjects. Liebow states unequivocally that the Negro lower-class male is not psychologically isolated from white middle-class family norms; he has not created a distinct family subculture (of illegitimacy and serial monogamy) that is perpetuated by cultural transmission. He learns to resort to unstable family behavior as a direct response to the failures (unemployment, low income, uninteresting jobs, discrimination, etc.) that he meets in life. With the exception of Bell's findings, the conclusions of Blood and Wolfe, Rainwater, and Liebow are clearly not in accord with the assumptions of a true subcultural difference.

The two different theoretical positions about the Negro family yield alternative hypotheses about family role performance. If one accepts the idea of an institutionalized normative subculture of deviance, then it follows that the family norms of lower-class Negroes should differ markedly from those of either stable white or Negro middle-class families. A second prediction would be that family role deviation among Negroes is associated with little psychological discomfort or stress. On the other hand, if one does *not* assume the existence of such a subculture, then there should be no status-linked differences in family norms, and deviation from middle-class standards would be accompanied by feelings of psychological stress. We will attempt to see if such perceived discrepancies are correlated with a number of social-psychological factors assumed to be stressful. In a previous study of a Negro population, the authors[12] of this paper found these factors to be associated with psychopathology. They consist of perception of one's social status position, estimates of the level of one's achievements, discrepancy between one's achievements and aspirations, and one's estimates of the probability of achieving valued goals. We hypothesize in the present study that these factors will also be capable of ordering the data on perceived discrepancy in family role performance; i.e., these variables will be prevalent in a population of Negro males who perceive discrepancies in their family role performance more than in a relatively non-discrepant population. This prediction is based on the assumption that unstable family behavior among Negro males is not normative. Rather, the disadvantaged position of many Negro males results in experiences of frustration in striving for valued goals, feelings of failure, and hopelessness, which are associated with family role deviancy. We assume that if what is commonly regarded as deviant family behavior is actually *normative* for Negro males, there would be little or no relationship between general feelings of failure and perceived discrepancies in family role performance. Since we wish to explore the generality of these stress variables in predicting various forms of deviant behavior, we shall also note the degree of their association with mental disorder.[13]

In summary, we shall first attempt to explore the idea of a distinct family subculture among lower-class Negro males by determining if various measures of status position can order the data concerning either norms of family role performance or perceived discrepancies in such role behavior.

Finally, we shall try to determine if various social-psychological factors associated with goal-striving stress, feelings of relative failure, and hopelessness are associated with perceived discrepancies in family role performance and mental disorder, i.e., two forms of social deviance.

PROCEDURE

The data reported in this paper are based on a subsample of interviews with a representative sample of the Philadelphia Negro community between 20 and 60 years of age (N=1,489) and a representative group of diagnosed mentally ill Negroes in the same age range and from the same city (N=1,423).[14] The latter sample consisted of "new cases" admitted to public and private, in-patient and out-patient treatment facilities (including private psychiatric practice and penal institutions) in the city during a specified time period; thus we were investigating incidence rather than prevalence. The interviews took place during 1960. The responses of married males in the community sample (N=455) and in the mentally ill sample (N=290) were selected for analysis.

To contrast the family role behavior of our groups, we selected four paired items from a larger battery of 17 paired statements designed to obtain a measure of the *perceived* discrepancy between actual performance and ideal role performance. Two of these paired items were applicable to the spouse role and two to the parental role. The format used to elicit these discrepancies was as follows: individuals were presented with a series of descriptions of role behavior all preceded by the statement "I am a person who. . . ." They were then asked to select one of the following precoded responses considered to be most applicable: "almost never," "occasionally," "usually," and "almost always." The four items in question were:

1. Makes the decisions on money and other important family matters.
2. Shares responsibility of financially supporting the household with my wife.
3. Shares the responsibility of training my children.
4. Talks to my wife about the things that bother me.

After completing these questions, the interviewer turned to other areas of behavior and did not obtain the "ideal" responses until about 20 minutes later. This procedure was followed to minimize the influence of response set. The ideal role descriptions and the precoded response categories corresponded to the previous set, but were preceded by the statement, "I would like to be a person who. . . ." The precoded categories for both the actual and ideal responses were numbered from one to four. The numerical difference between an individual's selections represented his actual-ideal role discrepancy. For purposes of these analyses, the "almost never" and "occasionally" responses were grouped together, as were the "usually" and "almost always" choices. Thus, a person was considered to be discrepant in the particular role only if his perception of his actual behavior and his stated ideal, respectively, fell into these different paired categories. This increased the possibilities that discrepancies were more than mere semantic artifacts.

We turn now to the operational measures of the four social-psychological variables referred to above that may provoke psychological discomfort or stress. Three were defined in terms of a *self-anchored striving scale* described by Cantril.[15] Respondents were presented with a card on which was drawn a series of ten steps. The top step (Number Ten) was labeled "the best possible way of life," and the bottom step (Number One) was labeled "the worst possible way of life." They were asked to "anchor" these steps by describing the things that occurred to them when they thought of their "best" and their "worst" way of life, respectively. They were then requested to select the step (from one to ten) that "best describes where you are now." The step selected represents the respondents' "perceived achievement," the first social psychological stress factor. Low perceived achievement was taken as an index of stress and dissatisfaction. They were then asked to select the step that "best describes where you would like to be a few years from now," i.e., level of aspiration. The second stress variable consisted of the numerical discrepancy between the perceived achievement and the aspiration level—or "perceived discrepancy." Finally, they were asked to estimate, numerically, their chances of reaching their aspiration level—called their "subjective probability of success." We assume that a low probability of success associated with a valued goal will result in a higher level of stress than if the probability estimate is high. The fourth variable, subjective class position, was derived by asking the respondent to judge whether he was above, at, or below average in terms of his own stated criteria of social status position. Those who evaluated themselves as below average were assumed to be experiencing stress. The hypothesized relationships between these social-psychological factors and the three population groups to be compared in this study will be specified in the following section.

The social-structural variables of interest in this paper include: *educational status, occupational status, income status, educational mobility,* and *occupational mobility.* The reasons for our inclusion of these variables are twofold. First, we have shown in a previous study that these variables were related to mental disorder, representing one form of deviant behavior.[16] We wish here to determine the usefulness of these variables in explaining deviant behavior in the area of family life. In addition, this question has relevance for the common allegation that the status position of the Negro male in our society is closely associated with his failure in family role performance. *Educational status* was categorized as follows: up to eight years of education, nine to 11 years of education, and 12 or more years of education. *Occupational status* was considered in terms of unskilled, semi-skilled, and skilled-white-collar groupings. *Income status* was also subdivided into three groups: yearly income less than $2,000, incomes between $2,000 and $4,000, and incomes over $4,000. Both *educational* and *occupational mobility* were defined in terms of the respondent's status achievement relative to that of his parents. Thus, those who achieved more education or higher-level occupations than their parents were regarded as "upwardly mobile." Those whose educational or occupational achievement fell below that of their parents were categorized as "downwardly mobile," and those whose status achievement did not differ from that of their parents were classified as "non-mobile."

RESULTS

Before presenting the findings relevant to the central issues of this study, we wish to compare the responses of the mentally ill and overall community samples. First, it is important to note that about 90 percent of the community respondents and only a slightly smaller percentage of the mentally ill said that they "usually" or "almost always" would like to be a person who (a) makes the decisions on money and other important family matters; (b) shares the responsibility of financially supporting the household with his wife; (c) shares the responsibility of training his children; and (d) talks to his wife about the things that bother him.[17] The uniformly high occurrence of these responses supports the idea that the family norms held by married Negro males[18] do not (as measured by the above items) differ markedly from those assumed to be associated with a stable family life. In spite of the uniformity of "ideal" responses, the reported discrepancies for each of the paired items were significantly[19] higher for the mentally ill than for the community sample. The percentages of discrepant responses for the two populations are, respectively, 33 and 17, 17 and 10, 15 and five, and 34 and 13.[20]

Since the "ideal" responses of the sample populations do not differ significantly, while their perceived discrepancies do, it is clear that the major differences between them is accounted for mainly by perceptions of actual role behavior. In this regard, the mentally ill are significantly higher than the community respondents in the "almost never" and "occasionally" category, e.g., 42 to 17 percent, 20 to ten percent, ten to five percent, and 40 to 18 percent, respectively. Thus, it is the perception of actual role behavior, not norms, that accounts for the major differences between the community and the mentally ill populations.

To what extent do measures of social status order the data on family role behavior among Negro males? Dividing the total community sample by status measures of income, occupation, and education (three status levels in each hierarchy), we find that none of the three measures of status are significantly related to perception of actual behavior, statement of ideals, or discrepancy between actual and ideal family behavior. Despite this lack of statistical significance, there was an inverse relationship between income status and discrepancy between the actual and the ideal behavior. In addition, neither occupational nor educational mobility (from the baseline of parental achievement) was found to order significantly these responses to family behavior.

The failure of status or mobility measures to order this data led us to probe the issue in greater detail. Turning to the self-anchored striving scale, we selected those respondents who spontaneously mentioned "family relationships" in specifying their "best" or "worst" way of life, and attempted to determine if their distribution by status position differed. Although none of these analyses were statistically significant, we did find that income was again inversely related to the tendency to mention family relationships in characterizing their best or worst way of life. In addition, of those who did spontaneously mention family relationships, the degree of importance attributed to goal-achievement in this area was not related to any status measure. Thus, our data do not support the idea of a "culture of poverty" as applied to lower-class Negro family life; the family ideals of the lower-status males (within the framework of the research operations employed) do not differ significantly from those of higher-status groups. In view of the fact that objective indices of family organization (such as desertion of the male) are more prevalent among lower-status Negroes than others, it is somewhat surprising to find no significant status dif-

TABLE 1-2 PERCEIVED ACHIEVEMENT AND FAMILY ROLE DISCREPANCY

Family Role Item	Population Group	Position on Self-Anchored Striving Scale %		
		Low-Medium	High	N
1[1]*	Mentally Ill	67	33	(290)
	Discrepant	40	60	(75)
	Non-Discrepant	36	64	(375)
2[2]	Mentally Ill	68	32	(291)
	Discrepant	47	53	(45)
	Non-Discrepant	35	65	(404)
3[3]	Mentally Ill	68	32	(276)
	Discrepant	40	60	(20)
	Non-Discrepant	34	66	(379)
4[4]	Mentally Ill	68	32	(277)
	Discrepant	40	60	(58)
	Non-Discrepant	36	64	(388)

[1] Makes the decisions on money and other important family matters.
[2] Shares the responsibility of financially supporting the household.
[3] Shares the responsibility of training my children.
[4] Talks to my wife about the things that bother me.
*By Chi-square each of the four analyses was significant, p < .001.

ferences in regard to *perceived* discrepancies in family role performance in this population. Although the relevant research reported in the literature is rather scant, Rainwater's study of family life[21] does support this finding. He reports that there are no differences in the percentage of Negro husbands in the lower-lower class and in the upper-lower class with respect to their perceived shortcomings as husbands. It would be interesting to explore further the reasons underlying this lack of status differences among Negro males, in view of prevailing assumptions about the relationship between status and norms.

We now are prepared to probe the question of whether perceived differences in family role performance among Negro males can be ordered by the social-psychological variables discussed above.

A. Family Role Discrepancy and Perceived
Achievement on the Self-Anchored Striving Scale

The position chosen on the striving scale can be considered to represent feelings of achievement or failure with respect to one's valued goals. This measure is closely related to self-esteem. We hypothesize that the choice of high positions will be least frequent among the mentally ill, most frequent among the non-discrepant individuals, and of intermediate frequency among those who show family role discrepancy. The results of this analysis, shown in Table 1, indicate that, for each of the four family roles, the data support the predictions; in each case the differences between the three population groups were significant. However, the differences between the discrepant and the non-discrepant groups in the community, although always going in the predicted direction, were not significant.

B. Family Role Discrepancy and Discrepancy
(Between Achievement and Aspiration) on the
Self-Anchored Striving Scale

This discrepancy measure derived from the striving scale was assumed to represent the degree of goal-striving frustration experienced by the individual. Here we hypothesize that the mentally ill will have the highest discrepancy, the non-discrepant will have the lowest goal-striving discrepancy, and the role-discrepant group will occupy an intermediate position. The results shown in Table 2 are in the predicted direction and are statistically significant for all four family role areas. Excluding the mentally ill, we find that all differences between the discrepant and non-discrepant groups go in the predicted direction but are not significant.

C. Family Role Discrepancy and Probability
of Success on the Self-Anchored Striving Scale

It will be recalled that after the respondent selected the step representing his aspiration level on the self-anchored striving scale, he was asked to estimate his chances of reaching his aspiration level from precoded choices ranging from one out of ten, to ten chances out of ten. This was regarded as a measure of hope-hopelessness. Consis-

TABLE 1-3 PERCEIVED DISCREPANCY (ASPIRATION-ACHIEVEMENT)
AND FAMILY ROLE DISCREPANCY

Family Role Item[1]	Population Group	Discrepancy Between Achievement and Aspiration on Striving Scale %		
		Low-Medium	High	N
1*	Mentally Ill	38	62	(290)
	Discrepant	72	28	(75)
	Non-Discrepant	73	27	(379)
2	Mentally Ill	38	62	(290)
	Discrepant	69	31	(45)
	Non-Discrepant	74	26	(403)
3	Mentally Ill	37	63	(272)
	Discrepant	75	25	(20)
	Non-Discrepant	76	24	(378)
4	Mentally Ill	38	62	(289)
	Discrepant	62	38	(48)
	Non-Discrepant	74	26	(387)

[1] Individual family role items defined in order given in legend of Table 1.
*By Chi-square each of the four analyses was significant, $p < .001$.

tent with our previous expressed rationale, we predict that the mentally ill will have the lowest probability of success estimate, the nondiscrepant group the highest, and those who are discrepant will occupy an intermediate position. Table 3 indicates that three of the four analyses, i.e., the first, second, and fourth, are in the predicted direction and are statistically significant. Considering only the two community groups, the differences between the discrepant and nondiscrepant individuals are all in the predicted direction and are all statistically significant.

D. Family Role Discrepancy and Subjective Social Class Position

The findings in our previous study,[22] concerning the association between this social-psychological stress variable and mental disorder, indicated that the mentally ill sample contained proportionately more individuals who considered themselves to be either "below average" or "above average" in social class position. Relatively few of them considered themselves to be "average." There is a consider-

TABLE 1-4 SUBJECTIVE PROBABILITY OF SUCCESS
AND FAMILY ROLE DISCREPANCY

Family Role Item[1]	Population Group	Probability of Success on Striving Scale %		
		Low-Medium	High	N
1*	Mentally Ill	44	56	(232)
	Discrepant	33	67	(75)
	Non-Discrepant	19	81	(374)
2	Mentally Ill	37	63	(282)
	Discrepant	34	66	(44)
	Non-Discrepant	20	80	(404)
3	Mentally Ill	37	63	(264)
	Discrepant	47	53	(17)
	Non-Discrepant	20	80	(378)
4	Mentally Ill	36	64	(280)
	Discrepant	34	66	(58)
	Non-Discrepant	20	80	(387)

[1] Individual family role items defined in order given in legend of Table 1.
*By Chi-square each of the four analyses was significant, $p < .001$.

able evidence in the literature of experimental social psychology that a population of individuals experiencing high levels of stress will exhibit a tendency toward polarization of its goal-striving behavior. As a defense mechanism, to bolster self-esteem, some will rigidly maintain unrealistically high goals (or in the present case, reference groups at high-status positions). Still others will psychologically "give up" and drop their aspirational levels drastically in order to relieve the pressures and anxieties associated with achievement striving and frustration.[23] Using this same rationale, we predict that the mentally ill will have proportionally the fewest "average" choices, the non-discrepant community group will have the highest percentage of "average" choices, and the role discrepant group will occupy an intermediate position. Table 4 indicates that for all four role items, the direction of the analyses emerges as predicted—three of these were significant. When we considered only the two community groups, the differences between the discrepant and the non-discrepant groups reached significance in one case, approached significance in another instance (i.e., p=.10), and were not significant in the remaining two cases.

Table 1-5   Subjective Class Position and Mental Illness
and Family Role Discrepancy

Family Role Item[1]	Population Group	Subjective Class Position %		
		Above Average	Average	Below Average
1*	Mentally Ill (n = 298)	20	47	33
	Discrepant (n = 73)	6	51	43
	Non-Discrepant (n = 369)	16	65	19
2**	Mentally Ill (n = 290)	22	46	32
	Discrepant (n = 42)	17	57	26
	Non-Discrepant (n = 397)	16	63	21
3	Mentally Ill (n = 272)	21	47	32
	Discrepant (n = 20)	10	50	40
	Non-Discrepant (n = 272)	21	53	26
4**	Mentally Ill (n = 289)	22	45	33
	Discrepant (n = 57)	19	51	30
	Non-Discrepant (n = 365)	15	64	21

[1] Individual family role items defined in order given in legend of Table 1.
*By Chi-square, $p < .01$.
**By Chi-square, $p < .001$.

In summary, of the 16 analyses including the mentally ill, 15 were in the predicted direction, and all of these were statistically significant. When one considers only the two community groups of Negro males, those who perceived discrepancies in their family role behavior differed from the non-discrepant, in the predicted direction, in all 16 comparisons—five of these differences were significant and two approached significance.

CONCLUSIONS

Our findings indicate that social structural factors such as status position and status mobility are not related to any perceived differences in the aspects of family role behavior dealt with in this study. The fact that ideals relevant to parental and spouse roles did not differ by status position argues against clear status-linked subcultural differences. Following these findings we turned our attention to the question of whether four social-psychological variables relating to degree of perceived success in life, and hope for the future, could order the data on family role discrepancies. It was assumed that if deviance in Negro male family role performance is actually normative, then conscious dissatisfaction with family role performance, i.e., discrepancies, would not be related particularly to generalized feelings of failure and hopelessness. The fact that such a relationship did exist leads to the possible conclusion that those Negro males who perceive themselves as relative failures, i.e., low achievers, with little hope of success, are also more prone to feel that they are failing in their family role performance. These findings cast further doubt on the idea that "deviant" family behavior among Negro males is a reflection of a distinct subculture. A more adequate interpretation of these data would involve the hypothesis that the problems encountered by the Negro male in the areas of employment, housing, and general social discrimination result in feelings of failure and inadequacy and an inability to perform his family role adequately.

NOTES

1. Office of Policy Planning and Research, United States Department of Labor, *The Negro Family,* March, 1965.
2. Daniel P. Moynihan, "Employment, Income, and the Ordeal of the Negro Family," in Talcott Parsons and Kenneth Clark, *The American Negro,* Boston: Houghton Mifflin Co., 1966, pp. 134–159.
3. In order to clarify our position and to avoid being unfair to Moynihan, we wish to emphasize that in his writings this position does not emerge explicitly and clearly. It is quite possible that Moynihan himself would not agree with it. However, we feel that this implicit assumption underlies his arguments and has important bearing on both academic and public policy issues. This conclusion is based on the following quotations from Moynihan. "The cumulative result of unemployment and low income and probably also of excessive dependence upon the income of

women, has produced an unmistakable crisis in the Negro family, and raises the serious question of whether or not this crisis is beginning to create conditions which tend to reinforce the cycle that produced it in the first instance." *Ibid.* "A more sophisticated but not less pressing question is whether the impact of economic disadvantage on the Negro community has gone on so long that genuine structural damage has occurred, so that a reversal in the course of economic events will no longer produce the expected response in social areas." *Ibid.* "For generations, Negroes have labored under the attribution of genetic inferiority; to raise the question of a 'deviant subculture' is to invite the charge of raising the same old canard of innate differences in a more respectable guise." *Commentary* (February, 1967), pp. 31–45.

4. J. Richard Udry, "Marital Instability by Race, Sex, Education, and Occupation Using 1960 Census Data," *American Journal of Sociology,* 72 (September, 1966), pp. 203–209.

5. Jessie Bernard, "Marital Stability and Patterns of Status in Negro-White and White-Negro Marriages," *Journal of Marriage and the Family,* 28:3 (November, 1966), pp. 274– 276.

6. E. Franklin Frazier, *The Negro Family in the United States,* New York: Dryden, rev. ed., 1948.

7. Moynihan, *Commentary, op. cit.*

8. Robert Bell, "The Relative Importance of Mother and Wife Roles Among Negro Lower Class Women," paper presented at the Groves Conference on Marriage and the Family, San Juan, Puerto Rico, April, 1967.

9. Robert O. Blood, Jr. and Donald M. Wolfe, *Husbands and Wives,* Glencoe: Free Press of Glencoe, 1960.

10. Lee Rainwater, "Crucible of Identity: The Negro Lower-Class Family," in Parsons and Clark, *op. cit.,* pp. 160–204.

11. Elliot Liebow, *Tally's Corner,* Boston: Little, Brown & Co., 1967.

12. Seymour Parker and Robert J. Kleiner, *Mental Illness in the Urban Negro Community,* New York: The Free Press, 1966.

13. We make no assumption here that family role discrepancy among Negroes is synonymous with or results from mental disorder. As stated, we merely wish to explore further the relationship of these stress factors with various forms of deviant behavior.

14. A detailed report of the sampling procedure can be found in Parker and Kleiner, *op, cit.,* pp. 30–38.

15. Hadley Cantril, *Patterns of Human Concern,* New Brunswick, New Jersey: Rutgers University Press, 1965.

16. Parker and Kleiner, *op. cit.*

17. The order of subsequent analyses of the items employed in this study will correspond to the order followed here.

18. In separate analyses we found that approximately the same percentages of unmarried Negro males report that they held these norms.

19. As used in this paper, comparisons will be regarded as "significant" if differences reach the .05 level of probability (Chi-square method).

20. The considerable item variation of the percentages of discrepant responses within each of the two populations argues against the possibility of response stereotypy.

21. Lee Rainwater, *Family Design,* Chicago: Aldine Publishing Co., 1965, p. 306.

22. Parker and Kleiner, *op. cit.,* pp. 150–153.

23. K. Lewin, T. Dembo, L. Festinger, and P. S. Sears, "Levels of Aspiration," in *Personality and Behavior Disorders: A Handbook Based on Experimental and Clinical Research,* ed. by J. McHunt, Vol. 1, New York: The Ronald Press Co., 1944, pp. 333–378; L. Festinger, "A Theory of Social Comparison Processes," *Human Relations,* 7 (1954), pp. 117–140; J. W. Atkinson, "Motivational Determinants of Risk-Taking Behavior," *Psychological Review,* 64 (1957), pp. 359–372.

2

STIGMATIZATION: SYSTEMATIC BRANDING

Doris Y. Wilkinson

Stigmatization is evaluated extensively in the Wilkinson selection on the belief network and psycho-political functions of discrediting actions. Stigmatizing behaviors directed toward blacks are viewed as patterned and designed processes which have had a measurable impact on the black male's psychology. Management of a stigmatized identity assumes a variety of forms ranging from the exaggerated use of fads and fashions to intra-group homicide. There are socioeconomic variations in the management of systematic negative labelling or branding. Moreover, variable response reactions to labelling exist indicating that there is not a monolithic personality configuration among black males although each shares experiences correlated with stigmatization.

Stigmas and stereotypes about the black male are diffused in American racial mythology by means of cultural indoctrination or socialization. Thus blacks and whites learn and internalize myths about themselves. Every society creates such beliefs which are functional as explanatory and validating stories regarding the origins of a people, their culture, customs, and destinies. The truth or falsity of a myth is not important for measuring the effect it has on the consciousness of members of a group. Myths are a fundamental part of all ritualization processes. Any traditional or legendary story or idea which functions to sustain existing ideologies or to validate social arrangements falls within the category of myths. The *Random House Dictionary of the English Language* defines a myth as:

> "an unproved collective belief that is accepted uncritically and used to justify a social institution, as in the belief in the biological inferiority of slaves used in support of slave societies."

This definition is directly applicable to this section which structures myths within the context of stigmatization.

Turner feels that mythology, symbolism, and folklore play a significant part in cultures and that reality is conceptualized within the framework of myths. Myths enable humans to categorize and codify infinite amounts of data. Specifically folklore and traditional tales about black-white relations have come to represent the objectively measurable dimensions of such relations. Coinciding with legends about black males have been pervasive stereotypical images now being exploited in television and the movie industry. Turner indicates that characters such as Wright's Bigger and Hughes' Simple are referents for real men; they reflect the reality.

Two key mythical notions are examined in Staples' critical dissection of the stigmatizing folklore about black males: the matriarchical figure story and the impotence idea. As a consequence of denying black males an opportunity for certain types of gainful employment, Staples contends that the African American woman has been thrown into the role of family provider. In this connection, "the myth of the black matriarchy is accompanied by the falsehood that the model black father has abdicated his paternal responsibilities." Such stigmatization has placed the black male in a tenuous position which has made it difficult for him to actualize manhood. In "The Myth of the Impotent Black Male," Staples emphasizes that stereotypes of the black male as psychologically impotent have not only been perpetuated through mass media but through social and behavior science as well. Predictably, these branding images have been accepted by blacks and whites alike.

A series of interrelated myths and labels have been assigned to the African American man. Among these are that he has been and is still childlike and as such is a source of amusement. He has also been seen as contented with enslavement and described in folklore as a docile and happy slave. In addition to these, before and after his emancipation, he was viewed as "different" in mind and body. Emphasis was placed on the latter in terms of ascribing to him physical attributes primarily. With respect to this, Edwards examines the myth of black superiority in athletics. He contends that many black males feel a constant struggle to win on the sports field—to beat "whitey." Inadvertently and understandably some blacks add credence to the myth of physical superiority. Whenever the black male is involved, physical athletic capabilities are viewed as racially determined. Edwards states that: "the myth of the black male's racially determined, inherent physical and athletic superiority over the white male rivals the myth of black sexual superiority." There is an obvious reluctance by whites to assign intellectual capabilities to blacks. As a consequence of this, even on the sports' field, blacks have been denied the opportunity to hold "thinking" positions.

The systematic purposive discrediting of the black male has represented the essence of America's racial *Weltanschauung.* Each of the myths and the body of folklore containing stigmatized images has been perpetuated throughout American history. A legendary notion such as the matriarchy has been incorporated in the behavioral and social sciences and documented in political annals. Staples indicates that this fallacious idea has resulted in the following additive myths: 1) pathologies within the family are cused by a matriarchal figure; 2) black men hate their mothers; 3) a matriarchal structure exploits black males; and 4) this matriarchal power arrangement is responsible for low educational aspirations and achievement of men reared under it. With this process of systematic stigmatization of the black male, the African American woman has also been stereotyped. Each of the myths examined here indicates their functional utility in the psychological and political process of stigmatization which results in keeping a people subjugated, powerless, and fragmented.

MYTHS AND STEREOTYPES:
THE AFRICAN MAN
IN AMERICA

William H. Turner *

The idea of myths and stereotypes pertaining to black men in America is not new. Folklore, mythology, symbolism, and stereotypes play an important part in cultures. Reality itself is often defined within the context of the myths and the stereotypes developed to account for it.[1] Thus, we begin this essay on the myths and stereotypes pertaining to black men with the proviso that we are "working toward a definition of *other* reality" away from the agreed-upon myths and stereotypes that constitute the reality historically known as black men. In that context, then, the point we reach about black men may be judged to be as mythological and as stereotypical as the point from which we are beginning. Our debunking and demythologizing a few ideas about black men gives these myths a certain legitimacy and reality which they'd not enjoy were they not accepted as *real*; thus, we are dealing with real-life entities (not myths and stereotypes).

Myths and stereotypes serve many culturally important functions: for one, they serve to lessen the cognitive-load of modern man inasmuch as we must codify and categorize the infinite amount of information on which reality itself is based. Thus, as a function of our socialization, we develop the tendency to classify objects and events into categories; it makes the world a lot simpler! This categorical atti-

*William H. Turner is Chairman of the Department of Social Science, University of Maryland, Eastern Shore. This is an original article written for this volume.

tude which we develop enables us (a) to note similarities in objects that are separate, (b) to group these objects into types, (c) to give names to the types, and (d) to generalize from there. Since man rarely reacts to an object or event in isolation, this process is presumably imbedded in man's use of symbols as part of a total system of classification. Stereotypes, however, constitute a special part of the categorical attitude developed in early life—often a negative part.[2]

Stereotyping is usually unfavorable, exceedingly exaggerated, and, to say the least, oversimplified. Moreover, stereotyping goes *beyond* the facts about the characteristics of the members of the category; and the essential point of this paper is to show that the *facts* pertaining to exactly "what black men are" have not been discovered nor developed *positively* in Western literature, or in the case where the facts are *known* and accepted, those facts have been manipulated and modified to perpetuate the myths and stereotypes. The originating question is: "What are the 'facts' pertaining to black men in America that provide the springboard for the myths and stereotypes which have been developed?"

ORIGINS OF THE HISTORICAL DEFINITIONS OF BLACK MEN IN AMERICA

Some of the beliefs that animate modern world racism are embodied in the works of Tacitus (circa. 98). It was he who started the belief that Germans were the original embodiment of "what *man* is." To Tacitus, Germans, or what we know as Nordic myth, are/were virtuous, individualistic, freedom-loving, and jealous of their racial purity. Physically these people are conceived as tall, blond, brave and tough; they live frugally, and are adventurous rather than toilsome. Further along in Western intellectual history, Count de Gobineau in his *Essay on the Inequality of Races*, developed a notion on "special race-characteristics, blood mixture and social decadence." By using the basic three anthropological divisions of races, de Gobineau reasoned that whites possessed all the noble qualities of manhood, i.e., leadership, energy, and intellectual superiority. To yellow people, he ascribed stability and fertility. The black he endowed with sensuality and the artistic impulse. For him, civilization only arrived with the mixing of races; but civilization leads to more and more mixing of inferior blood with that of the noble castes, so that the "great white race" becomes inevitably bastardized and decadent. We infer that he put a convex lens on the Darwinian scope which viewed man as "not coming *from* the ape, but moving toward it."[3]

Herbert Spencer and his contemporaries literally took up where de Gobineau stopped. They reasoned judiciously that races represented different stages of the evolutionary scale with the white race at the top. Accordingly, any given society represented the power and influence of its various racial stocks and the amount and quality of the intermixture among them. Heredity was considered immensely more important than environment in conditioning the development of societies; and, to many, heredity was synonymous with race. Africans, at this point, had never been studied extensively; thus, the "facts" of their lives were developed within the context of broadly based generalizations about Africa itself—the Dark Continent.

As *sub specie aeternitatis*, African personality was judged by Europeans with considerable misunderstanding and falsification, especially since the parties to the discussions were bent on world-expansion and the "burden of white men" to civilize people who were considered members of pagan social structures. Hence, the dramatic issue in Western intellectual activity became that of generalizing about the "others" known first as Africans, and later as slaves to the expanded (white) Western world. We then pick up this matter on myths and stereotypes of black men at the point of slavery.

Stereotypes and Realities

Psychological anthropology gives us the origins of many myths and stereotypes about black men in America. The main point we take for our purposes here is that groups of people personify traits; and, these collections of traits (or in this case stereotypes) come to be called the "personality of the so-and-so," even though no individual member of the "so-and-so" perfectly portrays them all. A variety of terms have been developed by psychological anthropologists to describe this fact; but the most popular ones are (a) modal personality, (b) national character, and (c) social personality. What that means is that any culturally distinctive aggregate of individuals, if categorically studied, can be made to reveal a fairly general system of overt and covert behavior—a group personality. Rutienbeek did this very thing long ago in his study of the Periclean Greeks. Hippocrates supposedly did such an analysis in attempting to understand the temperament of different races; and the Muslim scholar of the 12th century, Ibn Khaldun, wrote on this very issue in his essay, *Katib Al-Ibar*.[4] Thus, the concept known as "collective consciousness," popularized by Durkheim is based on the idea of personality characteristics found in social aggregates, nothing more.

At the heart of the Hegelian and Fanonian conception of the master-slave ethic is the master's definition of the slave's self—his essential being, his world, his worth in (his) the world, his everything. Furthermore, at the core of the master-slave status relationship is the language which the slave internalizes; a language which is *unlike* his own in the first place, but in this case, one already steeped in the history of European (English) expansionism which bespoke the virtual destruction of African civilization. Thus, the psycho-linguistic stage was *set* by the time one generation of slaves had reproduced in the New World.[5]

The folklore and tradition of black-white relations in the antebellum South is written many places. These forms came to stand literally (and figuratively) as the "realities." Thus, Elkins could develop his well-regarded treatise on "Sambo" as a proper personification of the black man in America at the height of slavery:

> Sambo, the typical plantation slave, was
> docile but irresponsible, loyal but lazy,
> humble but chronically given to lying and
> stealing; his behavior was full of infantile
> silliness and his talk inflated with childish
> exaggeration. His relationship with his master
> was one of utter dependence and childlike attach-
> ment; it was indeed this childlike quality that
> was the very key to his being. Although the
> merest hint to Sambo's manhood might fill
> the Southern breast with scorn, the child in
> his place could be both exasperating and kind.[6]

Elkins asks next: "Was (Sambo) real or unreal?" For most Europeans in the 1800's, Sambo was not *only* real, but his characteristics were the product of racial inheritance. In fact, many historians suggest that the slave agreed with this definition of reality; inasmuch as maximum rewards to him rested upon the legitimacy of Sambo. Some historians, however, like Morrison and Commager, took it the other way around, by assuming that blacks *accepted* the prevailing conditions just because they *acted* that way. Washington's Atlanta expository may be viewed as one black man's approach to maximizing rewards to his people by "shaming the legitimate myths."

Further along in American history, Simple and Bigger Thomas came to typify the stereotyped black man caught in the web of urbanization. They, unlike Sambo, were developed as "social protest mouthpieces," even though both were the stereotyped myths of the black man working out his confusion for identity, wrangling with impotence, powerlessness and namelessness. More recently, Liebow's *Tally* is taken as a legitimate incarnation of the modern-day "myth of the black man."[7]

Such figures as Elkin's *Sambo*, Hughes' *Simple*, Wright's *Bigger*, and Liebow's *Tally* are *out there*. They are defined as legitimate images of black men in America. As such, the *definition* of reality is the same as reality, particularly in the literary and scientific worlds. Most social research and non-black literature, therefore, came to develop models and images of black reality within the context of socially and culturally agreed-upon myths. The "myths" and the *separate* "realities" of black men, then, are possibly different aspects of one struggle for black men, ". . . the longing to attain self conscious manhood, to merge his double self into a better and truer self. In this longing he wishes neither of his older selves to be lost." Thus spoke DuBois on the question of "always looking at one's self through the eyes of others that look on in amused contempt and pity." Thus, Herskovits' *Myth of the Negro Past* may just as well be taken as a less figurative title![8]

BEHAVIORAL SCIENCE PARADIGMS: ONE-DIMENSIONAL MAN

Kuhn's *The Structure of Scientific Revolution* may have other worthy purposes, but it can be used well by students interested in the development and reinterpretation of social myths.[9] It is used here with emphasis on the replacement of one set of scientific and literary theories/images by another. Also it serves well as we shall begin to look at certain contemporary myths about black men as "social protest mouthpieces." Some works by Baraka and Fanon, when coupled with Kuhn's thesis give us the basis for asserting that behavioral science models of black men are themselves crumbling under the (scientific) revolution.

Kuhn looks at science and its use of "models and paradigms" as these explain and predict social phenomena. As his thesis goes, science "has at its hand models (paradigms) of their portions of the universe (which are) adequate to explain the phenomena considered of key importance." As our thesis goes, the content of many social science models concerning black men in America are inundated with the historical mythology discussed above. More than sufficient data have accumulated which historically negate the authenticity of the models and the myths. As a result, social science models about black men have lost their legitimacy, their predictability, and their "press" upon the reality of black men in America. That is due to the fact that black men throughout history have portrayed "enough significant anomalies and discrepancies" to render the myths and academic modeling impotent. In fact, Billingsley's work has provided significant input to establish that European scholars have always portrayed black families in negativistic and distorted fashions. Ladner's latest title, *The Death of White Sociology*, is critically important since it too deals directly with the "scientific revolution" regarding social science research on people of African descent.[10]

Attendant with the abandonment of Euro-centric myths, stereotypes, paradigms and models about African personality is the fact that no *single* new ones have won the approval of the majority of practicing scientists. Thus, as Kuhn has pointed out, "the situation is fluid, and numerous theoretical innovations/images will be propounded, and their various adherents will be in competition with each other in proselytizing to secure the allegiance of the remainder of the scientific community." The question of which image/model/stereotype of black men shall prevail is a major one. For one thing, as we know, modern science and academe in general have a fixed criterion for choosing between rival paradigms; and, theoreticians developing positive models about black reality—unlike their detractors—are encumbered when their works are unacceptable to the politically dominant economic groups such as the (hostile) universities, social critics, publishing company executives, etc. A cold fact of history is that the development and expansion of Euro-American hegemony has depended upon (a) the depopulation of Africa, (b) the social, political, and cultural emasculation of Africans born in the diaspora, and (c) the "dehumanization" of a large segment of the human race. This was in the *interest* of Europeans; thus it becomes understandable in an existential sense. As materialists though, we must understand the price to be paid (for a moment in history) when Africans begin to develop ideas about physical reality in *their interests*. Thus, when scientists and scholars of African descent begin to interpret reality in the *interest of their people*, they will necessarily work against the interest of much of European scholarship, to which many have emotional connections. This decision, among other things, is a political one; and must be made within the context of a proper ideological frame of reference.

Negation and Redefinitions

Ideology, after all, is a set of expressive symbols, and the values and beliefs embedded therein have much utility in providing meaning to individuals in this rapidly changing world. Therefore, the "cultural approach to ideology," focuses upon the process of symbolic (re) formulation. People of all races use the expressive symbols embodied in ideologies to perceive and understand the world. This, according to Touré, is extremely important in times of rapid social change, when old symbols/images/stereotypes seem to obstruct society's techno-social development. This is the situation confronting Africans in America as well as on the African continent. Many are conceptually confused given the illegitimacy ,of the regimes and intellectual paradigms on which colonial life was based. Turning here to the substance and reality of two popular new images regarding black men in America, let us affirm our need to synthesize the reality of black men in America with an ideological élan which protects us against popular disillusionment with ourselves.[11]

In addition to the blues idiom,[12] a major contribution of black men to American culture is language usage. Rapping, shucking, jiving, running-it-down, gripping, copping a plea, whuppin' a game, signifying, and sounding are manifestations of the black man's insult and suffering. Boastful or meek, these performances are attempts by black men to actualize control in some situation; it is based on the realization that their powerlessness is relative to an ability to pretend. *Sweet, Sweetback* provides one image of the modern-day Bigger Thomas— a personified myth of the black man in America. His is the stud image of black manhood, the incarnation of the impotent black male, and that black male personality (whether fancied or real) which drew the outrage of blacks who found him morally, socially, and culturally reprehensible. When placed in proper ideological context, Sweetback was/is a positive "myth" inasmuch as he used obscenities against the source of his (black men's) insult and suffering; thereby rendering it powerless with a greater insult.[13]

In this context, the "obscene, verbose, and niggardly" black man is a political weapon in America without comparable retaliation.

> Obscenities are not officially co-opted and sanctioned by the spoken and written professionals of the powers that be; their usage breaks the false ideological language and invalidates its definition.[14]

The obscenities used by Sweetback pertain to sex. This is no coincidence in that the Puritan ethos of American beginnings renders sex taboo. By making sex a moral issue, the American ethic has associated shame and guilt with an interpersonal relationship while it relieves impersonal activities which cause suffering and death as *beyond* the moral sphere.

In the film, *Sweet Sweetback's BaadAss Song*, we are confronted with an obscene situation. The obscenity does not manifest itself in the seduction of a young boy by a prostitute, or in the perversity of a sex orgy. We, as an extension of the involvement of the protagonist, are drawn into and affected by the brutal and impersonal beating which two white policemen give a captured suspect. *Their* act is the obscenity! Since the protagonist, Sweetback, is defined as the "sexual obscene," he can respond with a greater violence to the *unsexual,* but morally obscene beating of another black man. For his act of retaliatory obscenity, Sweetback becomes a fugitive deserving of retribution. His ensuing escape toward freedom is a manipulation of his environment to satisfy his own needs. That freedom takes precedence over any other needs. All his actions, therefore, are sublimated to this end.

As a powerless, nameless, and meaningless pimp, the instrument of his occupation is his sexual organ. Logically therefore our pristine association of (black) sex with morality makes Sweetback obscene. But, in terms of his material ends, this obscenity becomes a liberating factor. That film, and the myth/image it portends regarding black men, is a proper metaphoric description of man liberating himself from an ethic that defines him as obscene by utilizing that obscenity to free himself from a greater obscenity—the cause and perpetuation of black suffering in America. Sweetback transcends morality by removing sex from the moral sphere and by substituting in its place a goal of physical and mental liberation. This is the very dialectic in black life that many moralists and commentators (such as Cohen) overlook in their accounts of delinquency among blacks. Thus, within the context of a positive black aesthetic, we must, as Sekou Touré once said, "... understand both the language of Africans and its true contents, we must seek to find in their words, expressions, and formulations, not the abstract character of a dialectic, but the substance and reality of the life they express."[15]

There is also the need to deal substantially with Sweetback's mythical "opposite"—the black male intellectual. At a point in history when an "intellectual class" is emerging in America, we must come to grips with the role of the black intellectual class and the revolutionary movements of African peoples. For this paper, the "myths" surrounding the African intelligentsia cannot be gainsaid.

Historically, the African intelligentsia and elite has been divided into two basic groups, (1) those who are integrationist/accomodationist, who want to become an integral part of the colonial/slave system, and (2) those who are nationalist/revolutionary intellectuals who want to assist in the liberation of Africa. Generally, on this point, it cannot be reasonably denied that the former group, because they accept as valid the implicit ideology of Western scholarship, have greater visibility and clout as "carrier/interpreters" of black reality. Frazier's classic work, *Black Bourgeoisie*, documents all the reasons. The incarnate myth of this group accounts for much of the distrust that the black masses have for educated members of the race; to wit, it was they who offered much of the resistance to black nationalists such as Garvey and Paul Robeson.[16] The myth, then, of the black intellectual evolved around those who fought to remain a part of the system that oppressed them—to change their status in relationship to, but remain a part of, the Euro-centric intellectual world. In fact, the history of black social change in America shows very clearly that such change *only* followed the transfer of the allegiance of the black intellectuals. For it is they, the authors, editors, lecturers, artists, teachers, and preachers, whose function it is to form and guide mass opinion. It is when they become infested with the discontent of the repressed that social change (until then disorganized and dispersed) becomes purposive and coherent.

Intellectuals, as we know, serve a social function.[17] Each society, beyond the stages of primitive communalism, becomes composed of three classes of people: exploiters, nonproductive laborers, and productive laborers. Exploiters are those who control, direct, and live by the labor of others, "without giving," as Marxists claim, "any equivalent labor in return." Productive laborers are those who do the work necessary to maintain the society at a given level of culture. The nonproductive laborers (intellectuals) are the intermediate class whose work consists very largely in maintaining and transmitting the system intact to future generations. In any society, like this one, where there exists even a vague sense of repression, the small minority of exploiters (repressors) can maintain the system only so long as they have the willing support of the publicists (the intellectuals). The repressed masses, in terms of sheer physical numbers, can overcome both of the other classes whenever they become sufficiently class conscious and sufficiently organized to act collectively. Thus, the position of both repressors and publicists is precarious unless the publicists maintain sufficient confidence of the masses in the existing regime that they will continue to give it their support and loyalty. What has happened, essentially, is that the black intellectuals (publicists) have "acted-out" the myth of their own deluded sense of belongingness.

Given the transfer of allegiance of the black intellectuals in America, we envision, (especially after the generation of students from the black power/black studies days of the late 60's) a breaking-down of the myth of black intellectual impotence. The resurgent interest in black intellectuals such as Du Bois, Nkrumah, Touré, Fanon, Russworm and others is ample evidence that African American intellectuals clearly understand their relationship to Europe, its people and black interests, and Africa, its people and its interests. I suspect that black publicists will attack theories, myths, paradigms, and institutions with a zeal proportionate to their anger at having been deluded. The hallmark of that internal crisis for black intellectuals has its greatest expression in the myth of the "neutrality" of education:

> The man who has had a Western education, whether in his native country or in Europe or America, is inevitably separated from the uneducated man in outlook and mode of life. Western education introduces him to new styles of dress, speech, behavior, and opinion; it teaches him the value of Western culture, and, by implication, the worthlessness of tribal life and primitive custom. His reference group tends to become not his kin and the people of his native region; but the community of the educated people by whose standards he has been taught to live. He tends to be cut off also from indigenous religious and intellectual traditions, to be critical of traditional sources of authority, and to become oriented to the secular, industrial, urbane, and international culture of the west.[18]

Consequently, Black intellectuals "serve the myth" when they become deluded, self-indulgent, and confused. Understandably when they write about black people, the myth believed makes a myth!

SYNTHESIS AND CONCLUSION

We have attempted to trace the intellectual origins, the historical bases, the scientific modeling, and the negation and reformulation of myths about black men in America. It is hoped that the facts presented have shed light on the Euro-American intellectual approach to reality which places greater reliance on an over-socialized conception of the black man, rather than upon a conception that man can *will* to transform the status quo—in spite of prevailing myths and their press upon man's actions.

Finally, we have offered a view of the black man's transformation of myths about himself from the negative to positive; moving toward his interests rather than against himself. And, we have done that within the ideological context of Pan-African thinking, that positive mythology and symbolism will effect qualitative change and will contribute to cultural progress.

NOTES

1. Karl Mannheim, *Ideology and Utopia* (New York: Harvest Books, 1936), p. 90.
2. Robert Manners and David Kaplan, *Theory in Anthropology* (Chicago: Aldine Publishers, 1968), p. 21.
3. Charles Marden and Gladys Meyer, *Minorities in American Society* (New York: American Book Company, 1968), p. 64.
4. Manners and Kaplan, Ibid.
5. Frantz Fanon, *The Wretched of the Earth,* trans. by Maspero (New York: Grove Press, 1963), pp. 165–77.
6. Stanley Elkins, *Slavery: A Problem in American Institutional and Intellectual Life* (New York: The Universal Library, 1959).
7. Charles Watkins, "Simple: The Alter Ego of Langston Hughes," in *Black Scholar* 2, no. 10 (June, 1971): 19–27.
8. W. E. B. Du Bois, *The Souls of Black Folk* (New York: Fawcett Books, 1938).
9. Thomas Kuhn, *The Structure of Scientific Revolution* (Chicago: University of Chicago Press, 1964).
10. Joyce Ladner, *The Death of White Sociology* (New York: Vintage Books, 1973).
11. Sekou Touré, "A Dialectical Approach to Culture," in *Black Scholar* 1, no. 1 (November, 1969): 11–19.
12. Charles Keil, *Urban Blues* (Chicago: University of Chicago Press, 1966).
13. Sharon Stockard Martin, "Sweet SweetBack's BaadAss Song" (unpublished manuscript, Baton Rouge: Southern University, 1971).
14. Herbert Marcuse, *Essay on Liberation* (Boston: Beacon Press, 1969), pp. 8–11.
15. Albert Cohen, *Delinquency and Control* (Englewood Cliffs, N.J.: Prentice-Hall, 1966), p. 6.
16. E. Franklin Frazier, *Black Bourgeoisie,* New York: Collier Books, 1957).
17. Lyford Edwards, *The Natural History of Revolution* (Chicago: University of Chicago Press, 1927).
18. Edward Halsey, "Sociology of Education," in *Sociology* (Salt Lake City: Wiley, 1973) by Smelser (ed.), pp. 372–74.

THE MYTH OF THE IMPOTENT BLACK MALE*

Robert Staples

In white America there is a cultural belief that the Black community is dominated by its female members, its men having been emasculated by the historical vicissitudes of slavery and contemporary economic forces. This cultural belief contains a duality of meaning: that black men have been deprived of their masculinity and that black women participated in the emasculinization process. The myth of the black matriarchy has been exploded elsewhere.[1] Black female dominance is a cultural illusion that disguises the triple oppression of black women in this society. They are discriminated against on the basis of their sex role affiliation, their race and their location in the working class strata of this upper-class dominated country.

The assumption that black men have been socially castrated has yet to be challenged. Before examining the fallacies of black male castration, it is important to understand the function of these cultural images of black men and women for maintaining the staus quo level of black deprivation and white privilege. Most of these theories of black life come from the field of social science, a discipline, ostensibly dedicated to the pursuit of truth. It would be more realistic to view social science research as a form of ideology, a propaganda apparatus which serves to justify racist institutions and practices. Social science as ideology is a means of social control exercised by white America to retain its privileges in a society partially sustained by this ideology. As one observer noted:

*From *The Black Scholar* 2, no. 10 (June, 1971): 2–9. Reprinted with permission.

Social scientists and journalists in America generally operate under an ideology-laden code of professional conduct that requires objectivity . . . But this objectivity is in effect a commitment to the ruling class.[2]

Stereotypes of the black male as psychologically impotent and castrated have been perpetuated not only by social scientists but through the mass media and accepted by both blacks and whites alike. This assault on black masculinity is made *precisely because black males are men;* not because they are impotent and that is an important distinction to make. As one sociologist candidly admits, "Negro men have been more feared, sexually and occupationally, than Negro women."[3] She further admits that the Negro man had to be destroyed as a man to "protect" the white world.[4] It should be added that the attempt to destroy him failed but the myth of his demasculinization lingers on. One can see in this myth an unmitigated fear of black male power, an unrelenting determination on the part of white America to create in fiction what it has been unable to accomplish in the empirical world.

From a historical perspective, the black male's role has changed as he has traversed from the African continent to the shores of North America. This span of time has introduced the forces of slavery, racism and wage exploitation in the determination of his masculine expressions. In Africa, he resided in a male-dominated society. Although women had an important place in African society, most important decisions were made by male members of the community.[5]

Taken forcibly from his African roots, the black man experienced radical changes in his status. In the beginning of the period of slavery, black men greatly outnumbered black women. It was not until 1840 that there was an equal sex ratio among blacks.[6] As a result of this low sex ratio, there were numerous cases of sex relations between black slaves and indentured white women. The intermarriage rate between black men and white women increased to the extent that interracial marriages were prohibited. Previously, black men were encouraged to marry white women in order to augment the human capital of the slave-owning class.[7]

After black women were brought over to the New World, they served as breeders of children, who were treated as property, and as the gratifiers of the carnal desires of white plantation owners. More importantly, they became the central figure in black family life. The black man's only crucial function within the family was that of siring the children. The mother's role was far more important than the father's. She cleaned the house, prepared the food, made clothes and raised the children. The husband was at most his wife's assistant, her companion and her sex partner. He was often thought of as her possession, as was the cabin in which they lived. It was common for a mother and her children to be considered a family without reference to the father.[8]

Under slavery the role of father was, in essence, institutionally obliterated. Not only was the slave father deprived of his sociological and economic functions in the family but the very etiquette of plantation life eliminated even the honorific attributes of fatherhood from the black male, who was addressed as boy—until, when the vigorous years of his prime were past, he was permitted to assume the title of uncle. If he lived with a woman, "married," he was known as her husband (e.g. Sally's John), again denying him a position as head of the household.[9]

That black men were reduced to a subordinate status in the family is quite true. That they abdicated their responsibility to their families probably highlights the unusual—not the prosaic behavior of black men. Although somewhat unusual, for example, there was the case of a black slave who, when his wife complained of the beating she had taken from the overseer, took her to a cave away from harm. He fixed it up for her to live in, he brought her food; he protected her. Three children were born in the cave and only with emancipation did the family come out to join him.[10]

There are those who say that slavery prevented black men from coming to emotional maturity, that they were childlike, docile creatures who were viewed not as objects of fear or hatred but as a source of amusement.[11] In conflict with this view is the observation that:

> In spite of all attempts to crush it, the slave had a will of his own, which was actively, as well as passively, opposed to the master's. And it is this stubborn and rebellious will—tragic, heroic, defeated or triumphant—that, more than all else . . . haunted the master, frustrating his designs by a ceaseless though perhaps invisible countermining . . . The slave expresses his hatred of enslavement and his contempt for his enslaver in less subtle and more open ways, such as taking what belonged to him, escaping or assisting others to escape, secretly learning or teaching others to read and write, secret meetings, suicide, infanticide, homicide, and the like.[12]

In addition to this covert resistance the so-called "docile" slave put together a number of elaborate conspiracies and insurrections.

According to Aptheker, over 250 slave revolts were planned.[13] After slavery, however, the black male continued to encounter assaults on his manhood. In every aspect of his life, white America has tried to subjugate him. The historical literature, for instance, suggests that Jim Crow was directed more at the black male than the black female.[14] Black women, in a very limited way, were allowed more freedom, suffered less discrimination and provided more opportunities than black men.

The structural barriers to black manhood were great. In a capitalistic society, being able to provide basic life satisfactions is inextricably interwoven with manhood. It is the opportunity to provide for his family, both individually and collectively, which has been denied the black man. After emancipation, the economic role of the black woman was strengthened as blacks left the rural areas and migrated to the cities where it was difficult for black men to obtain employment. Although they had previously held jobs as skilled craftsmen, carpenters, etc., they were forced out of these occupations by a coalition of white workers and capitalists. In some instances they found employment only as strikebreakers.[15]

Through this systematic denial of an opportunity to work for black men, white America thrust the black woman into the role of family provider. This pattern of female headed families was reinforced by the marginal economic position of the black male. The jobs available to him lacked the security and level of income necessary to maintain a household and in some cases were simply not available. Additionally, certain jobs performed by black men (*e.g.* waiter, cook, dishwasher, teacher, social worker etc.) often carry a connotation in American society as being woman's work.[16]

Economically destitute black families may be forced into a welfare system where it makes "sense" in terms of daily economic security for black men to leave their families. An example is this black woman who refused to permit her husband back into the family after he got a job. She said:

> Not me! With him away I've got security. I know when my welfare check is coming and I know I can take him to court if he doesn't pay me child support. But as soon as he comes back in, then I don't know if he's going to keep his job; or if he's going to start acting up and staying out drinking and spending his pay away from home. This way I might be poor, but at least I know how much I got.[17]

White society has placed the black man in a tenuous position where manhood has been difficult to achieve. Black men have been lynched and brutalized in their attempts to retain their manhood. They have suffered from the cruelest assault on mankind that the world has ever known. For black men in this society it is not so much a matter of acquiring manhood as a struggle to feel it their own. As a pair of black psychiatrists comment:

> Whereas the white man regards his manhood as an ordained right, the Black man is engaged in a never ending battle for its possession. For the Black man, attaining any portion of manhood is an active process. He must penetrate barriers and overcome opposition in order to assume a masculine posture. For the inner psychological obstacles to manhood are never so formidable as the impediments woven into American society.[18]

After placing these obstacles to manhood in the black man's way, white America then has its ideological bearers, the social scientists, falsely indict him for his lack of manhood. There are various sociological and psychological studies which purport to show how black males are de-masculinized, in fact may be latent homosexuals. The reason they cite is that black males reared in female-centered households are more likely to acquire feminine characteristics because there is no consistent adult male model or image to shape their personalities.[19] One sociologist stated that since black males are unable to enact the masculine role, they tend to cultivate their personalities. In this respect they resemble women who use their personalities to compensate for their inferior status in relation to men.[20]

If the above reasoning seems weak and unsubstantiated, the other studies of black emasculation are equally feeble. Much of this supposition of the effeminate character of black men is based on their scores on the Minnesota Multiphasic Inventory Test (MMPI), a psychological instrument that asks the subject the applicability to himself of over five hundred simple statements. Black males score higher than white males on a measure of femininity. As an indicator of their femininity, the researchers cite the fact that black men more often agreed with such feminine choices as "I would like to be a singer" and "I think I feel more intensely than most people do."[21]

This is the kind of evidence that white society has marshalled to prove the feminization of the black male. The only thing this demonstrates is that white standards can not always be used in evaluating black behavior. Black people live in another environment, with different ways of thinking, acting and believing than in the white, middle-class world. Singers such as James Brown and others represent successful role models in the black community. Black male youth aspire to be singers because this appears to be an observable means for obtaining success in this country—not because they are more feminine than white males. Additionally, music is an integral part of black culture.

One can easily challenge the theory that black males can not learn the masculine role in father-absent homes. Black people are aware—if whites are not—that in female-headed households in the black community, there is seldom one where adult males are totally absent. A man of some kind is usually around. He may be a boyfriend, an uncle or just the neighborhood bookie. Even if these men do not assume a central family role, the black child may use them as source material for the identification of masculine behavior.[22]

Furthermore, men are not the only ones who teach boys about masculinity. Sex roles can also be learned by internalizing the culturally determined expectations of these roles. Consequently, black mothers can spell out the role requirements for their fatherless sons. She can symbolically communicate to him the way that men act. He will be showed the way men cross their legs, how they carry their books, the way they walk, etc. Through the culture's highly developed system of rewards for typical male behavior and punishment for signs of femininity, the black male child learns to identify with the culturally defined, stereotyped role of male.[23]

Black males are put in the psychological trick-bag of being "damned if they do, damned if they don't." If they acted effeminate they would be considered effeminate. Because they act like real men, they are charged with an exaggeration of normal masculine behavior to compensate for, or disguise, their femininity. The psychologists ignore one of their own tenets in this case: if men define situations as real, then they are real in their consequences.[24] If men define their behavior as masculine, for all practical purposes it becomes masculine to them. For black men, masculinity is the way they act. White America's definition of masculinity is of little importance, or validity, to them.

The myth of the black matriarchy is accompanied by the falsehood that the model black father has abdicated his paternal responsibilities. That this is untrue is confirmed in a study by Schulz which found that most black men assume a very responsible quasi-father role vis-a-vis their women and her children. Black men, however, have to spend a large part of their lives bargaining for a familial relationship, the major impediment being a limited income that cannot equal the combined resources of their present job plus their woman's welfare check. These men, who are not officially father or husband, play a more supportive role than is generally acknowledged.[25]

While some black men, obviously, relinquish their paternal role functions, most black men perform ably in that role considering the circumstances under which black families must live. Typical of the black father's concern for his children is this man's statement:

> My youngest boy is seven. All my kids are in school. I try to instill in their minds that the only sound way to succeed is by laying a good foundation of learning and then to get actual experience. I hope to be able to see them all through college. I own property where I live and have a few dollars in the bank. I own a car, too. My greatest ambition is to see my children come along and keep this cleaning and pressing business of mine going, or else get into something they like better.[26]

That many black fathers never realize their aspirations for their children can be attributed to America's racist social structure. Instead, black women are charged with complicity with white men to subordinate the black male to his lowly position. Contrary to this assumption, one finds that when the Afro-American male was subjected to such abject oppression, the black woman was left without protection and was used —and is still being used—as a scapegoat for all the oppression that the system of white racism has perpetrated on black men. The system found it functional to enslave and exploit them and did so without the consent, tacit or otherwise, of black women. Moreover, while black men may be subjected to all sorts of dehumanizing practices, they still have someone who is below them—black women.[27]

Nevertheless, black women have had a variety of responses to the plight of black men. Some black women accepted the prevailing image of manhood and womanhood that depicted black men as shiftless and lazy if they did not secure employment and support their families as they ought to. There are reported instances of the black male ceasing to provide any economic support for the family and having his wife withdraw her commitment from him and from the marriage.[28] Other black women have ambivalent feelings about black men and remember painful experiences with them. They believe that black men do not fully appreciate the role of black women in the survival of the black race. Some even internalize white society's low regard for black men but are bothered by their appraisals.[29]

These attitudes on the part of black women are understandable. There are many black male-female conflicts which are a result of the psychological problems generated by their oppressed condition. Under a system of domestic colonialism, the oppressed peoples turn their frustrations, their wrath, toward each other rather than their oppressor.[30] Being constantly confronted with problems of survival, blacks become more psychologically abusive toward their spouses than perhaps they would under other circumstances.

On the other hand some black women are very supportive of their men. As Hare notes, black women realize that they must encourage the black man and lay as much groundwork for black liberation as he will let her. She realizes that it is necessary to be patient with black men whenever they engage in symbolic assertions of manliness. Her role is to assist strongly but not dominate.[31] Black women, however, may not realize the contradiction between their desire for a comfortable standard of living and wanting the black man to exercise his masculinity. The expression of black masculinity can frequently be met with the harshest punishment white society can muster. Physical punishment, and economic deprivation, are frequently the white response to expressions of black manliness.

Whatever the role of the black woman, she realizes that the mythical castrated black male can rarely be dominated. In the dating situation, he has the upper hand because of the shortage of black men in the society. Black women, if they want a black man, frequently have to accept the relationship on male terms. If she does not give into his demands, there are always other women who will. The henpecked black husband is usually a mythical figure. The fact that black wives carry a slightly larger share of the housework than white wives[32]—while not a particularly desirable situation—effectively dispels any notion of the black husband in the role of a domestic servant.

It was mentioned earlier that the attempt to emasculate the black male was motivated by the fear of his sexual power. As Bernard has stated, "the white world's insistence on keeping Negro men walled up in the 'concentration camp' was motivated in large part by its fear of their sexuality."[33] One needs a deep understanding of the importance of sex in the United States in order to see the interrelationship of sex and racism in American society. In a society where white sexuality has been repressed, the imagined sexual power of the black male poses a serious threat. According to Hernton:

> There is in the psyche of the racist an inordinate disposition for sexual atrocity. He sees in the Negro the essence of his own sexuality, that is, those qualities that he wishes for but fears he does not possess. Symbolically, the Negro at once affirms and negates the white man's sense of sexual security . . . Contrary to what is claimed, it is not the white woman who is dear to the racist. It is not even the black woman toward whom his real sexual rage is directed. It is the black man who is sacred to the racist. And this is why he must castrate him.[34]

Whether the white woman is dear to the racist is debatable. It certainly appears that he is concerned about preserving the purity of white womanhood. Since 1698 social censure and severe penalties were reserved for the association of black men and white women.[35] The evidence for these suppositions is voluminous, ranging from the accusations by lynch mobs that the black man raped or threatened to rape the white woman, the white South's obsession with the purity of white womanhood, the literal castration of black men for centuries, and in the death of an Emmet Till, who was killed for looking at a white woman. As Fanon comments, the white man fears that the black man will "introduce his daughter into a sexual universe for which the father does not have the key, the weapons, or the attributes."[36]

The question might be posed: what is the empirical basis of black male sexual superiority? Contrary to prevailing folklore, it is not the size of his genitalia. According to the Kinsey Institute, the majority of both white and black penises measured in their sample were less than or equal to four and a half inches in the flaccid state and less than or equal to seven inches in their erect state.[37] However, three times as many black males had penises larger than seven inches in length. The Masters and Johnson Report indicates no particular relationship between penis size and sexual satisfaction except that induced by the psychological state of the female.[38]

What, then, can be said about the sexual abilities of white men and black men? First, it must be acknowledged that sexual attitudes and behavior are culturally determined—not inherent traits of a particular group. But—sex relations have a different nature and meaning to black people. Their sexual expression derives from the emphasis in the black culture on feeling, of releasing the natural functions of the body without artificiality or mechanical movements. In some circles this is called "soul" and may be found among peoples of African descent throughout the world.

In a concrete sense, this means that black men do not moderate their enthusiasm for sex relations as white men do. They do not have a history of suppressing the sexual expression of the majority of their women while singling out a segment of the female population for pre-marital and extramarital adventures. This lack of a double standard of sexual conduct has also unleashed the sexual expression of black women. Those black women who have sexual hangups acquired them by their acculturation of the puritanical moral values of white society.

The difference between black men and white men in sexual responses may be explained by realizing that for white men sex has to be fitted into time not devoted to building the technological society, whereas for black men it is a natural function, a way of life. An example of this is that white men when confronted with their woman's state of sexual readiness may say business first, pleasure later. The black man when shown the black woman's state of sexual excitation manages to take care of both the business and pleasure task. If one task is left unfinished, it is unlikely that the black woman is left wanting.

It is this trait of the black male that white society would prefer to label sexual immorality. The historical evidence reveals, however, that the white man's moral code has seldom been consistent with his actual behavior. The real issue here is one of power. In a society where women are regarded as a kind of sexual property, the white male tries to insure that he will not have to compete with black men on an equal basis for any woman. Not only may the white male experience guilt over his possession of black womanhood but he fears that as the black man attains a bedroom equality he will gain a political and economic equality as well.

Sexual fears, however, do not totally explain the attempted castration of black men. White society realizes quite well that it is the men of an oppressed group that form the vanguard, the bulwark, of any liberation struggle. By perpetrating the myth of the impotent black male on the consciousness of black and white people, they are engaging in wishful thinking. It is patently clear that men such as Nat Turner, Denmark Vesey, Frederick Douglass and Malcolm X were not impotent eunuchs. The task of black liberation has been carried out by black men from time immemorial. While black women have been magnificently supportive, it is black men who have joined the battle.

White America will continue to perpetuate the myth of the impotent black male as long as it serves their purpose. Meanwhile, the task of black liberation is at hand. It will continue to be in the hands of black men. While racists fantasize about the impotency of the black man, his childlike status, the liberation struggle will proceed, with one uncompromising goal: total freedom for all black people, men and women alike.

NOTES

1. Robert Staples, "The Myth of the Black Matriarchy," *The Black Scholar,* February, 1970, pp. 9–16.
2. William Ellis, *White Ethics and Black Power,* Chicago: Aldine Publishing Company, 1969, p. xiii.
3. Jessie Bernard, *Marriage and Family Among Negroes,* Englewood Cliffs, New Jersey: Prentice-Hall, Inc., 1966, p. 69.
4. *Ibid.,* p. 73.
5. John Hope Franklin, *From Slavery to Freedom,* New York: Random House, 1947.
6. *Ibid.*
7. E. Franklin Frazier, *The Negro Family in the United States,* Chicago: University of Chicago Press, 1939.
8. Maurice Davie, *Negroes in American Society,* New York: McGraw-Hill, 1949, p. 207.
9. Stanley M. Elkins, *Slavery: A Problem in American Institutional and Intellectual Life,* New York: Grosset and Dunlap, Inc., 1963, p. 130.
10. B. A. Botkin, *Lay My Burden Down,* Chicago: The University of Chicago Press, 1945, pp. 179–80.
11. Elkins, *op. cit.,* p. 128.
12. Botkin, *op. cit.,* pp. 137–38.
13. Herbert Aptheker, *American Negro Slave Revolts,* New York: International Publishers, 1963.
14. C. Vann Woodward, *The Strange Career of Jim Crow,* New York: Oxford University Press, 1966.
15. C. F. Pierre Van Der Berghe, *Race and Racism,* New York: John Wiley, 1967.
16. Harold Proshansky and Peggy Newton, "The Nature and Meaning of Negro Self-Identity," in *Social Class, Race and Psychological Development,* Martin Deutsch, *et al.,* eds., New York: Holt, Rinehart and Winston, 1968.
17. William Yancey, Vanderbilt University, personal communication 1971.
18. William H. Grier and Price M. Cobbs, *Black Rage,* New York: Basic Books, 1968, p. 49.
19. Thomas Pettigrew, *A Profile of the Negro American,* Princeton, New Jersey: D. Van Nostrand Company, 1964, pp. 17–22.

20. E: Franklin Frazier, *Black Bourgeoisie,* New York: Crowell-Collier Publishing Co., 1962, p. 182.
21. J. E. Hollanson and G. Calder, "Negro-White Differences on the MMPI," *Journal of Chemical Psychology,* 1960, pp. 32–33.
22. Ulf Hannerz, "The Roots of Black Manhood," *Transaction,* October, 1969, p. 16.
23. David Lynn, "The Process of Learning Parental and Sex Role Identification," *Marriage and Family Living,* 28, November, 1966, pp. 466–570.
24. C. F. W. I. Thomas and Florence Znaniecki, *The Polish Peasant in Europe and America,* New York: Alfred A. Knopf, 1927.
25. David Schulz, "The Role of the Boyfriend in Lower Class Negro Life," *The Family Life of Black People,* Charles V. Willie, ed., Columbus, Ohio: Charles E. Merrill, 1970, pp. 231–246.
26. St. Clair Drake and Horace Cayton, *Black Metropolis,* Chicago: University of Chicago Press, 1945, p. 665.
27. Frances Beal, "Double Jeopardy: To Be Black and Female," *New Generation,* 51, Fall 1969, pp. 23–28.
28. Lee Rainwater, "Crucible of Identity: The Negro Lower Class Family," *Daedalus,* 95, Winter 1966, pp. 251–255.
29. Nathan and Julia Hare, "Black Women 1970," *Transaction,* 8, November, 1970, pp. 66–67.
30. C. F. Frantz Fanon, *The Wretched of the Earth,* New York: Grove Press, 1966.
31. Hare, *Loc. cit.*
32. Robert O. Blood, Jr. and Donald M. Wofe, "Negro-White Difference in Blue Collar Marriages in a Northern Metropolis," *Social Forces,* 48, September, 1969, pp. 59–63.
33. Bernard, *op. cit.,* p. 75.
34. Calvin Hernton, *Sex and Racism in America,* Garden City, New York: Doubleday, 1965, pp. 111–112.
35. Frazier, *The Negro Family in the United States, op. cit.,* pp. 50–51.
36. Frantz Fanon, *Black Skin, White Masks,* New York: Grove Press, 1967, p. 163.
37. Allan Bell, *Black Sexuality, Fact and Fancy,* a paper, Black America Series, Indiana University, Bloomington, Indiana, 1968.
38. William Masters and Virginia Johnson, *Human Sexual Response,* Boston: Little, Brown and Co., 1966.

THE STIGMATIZATION PROCESS:
THE POLITICIZATION OF
THE BLACK MALE'S IDENTITY

Doris Y. Wilkinson

This discussion offers a brief theoretical interpretation of racial discrediting in terms of the socially and economically instrumental psycho-political process—stigmatization. It is based on observable behaviors and empirically verifiable premises. Whereas Goffman in his classical analysis of stigmas focused on the discredited and potentially discreditable and how a stigmatized individual manages his or her identity, the concentration of this analysis is on the stigmatizing *process* and the *experience*. Goffman correctly indicates that debased individuals are defined as subhuman and that this definition results in the stigmatized being discriminated against. Those who brand others develop a belief system—"a stigma theory"[1]—to explain the discredited's "inferiorized"[2] position. It is this belief system and its behavioral consequences which are of concern here.

Representing an interface between structure, ideology, and subsequent behavior, stigmatization is conceptualized as purposive conscious individual or collective actions involving assigning a defect to, reproaching, scapegoating, and maligning another individual or group. Stigmatizing experiences involve being a victim of such customs. Intricately interwoven with the evolution of the division of labor and the color-status hierarchy, and validating their composition and mode of operation, the psycho-political process of stigmatizing the black male incorporates a calculated orientation to lowering his self conceptions and restricting his potentially productive performance. This systematized pattern of defaming has been geometric in its form and influences throughout the history of American society. Each successive

145

series of interactional encounters and confrontations between the two polarized color groups has been characterized by an exponentiated growth of designs for subjugating black males. Operating as a ritualistic vilification network, stigmatization incorporates a configuration of aggressive debasing behaviors and practices interconnected by the sacred ideology of white supremacy.[3] A stigmatizing encounter means that the target of such ritualized acts experiences inner feelings of being discredited. Both polar collectivities have developed levels of consciousness related to these conditions. Rooted in the psychogenesis of meanings assigned to physical distinctions, biological differences have taken on a political character.

Two questions are addressed in this conceptualization of the dynamics characterizing the behavioral event of engaging in the *act of discrediting others* and *experiencing being discredited.* (1 How does the stigmatization process function for whites? (2 In what ways does the discrediting experience affect the identities of black males? At the socio-analytic level, stigmatization represents a goal oriented psycho-political process directed toward others outside one's identification reference group. It comprises intentional organized actions which reaffirm the social and material order—the restriction of opportunities for productive activity, effective role enactment, and the acquisition of crystallized identities of blacks in all social spheres. Even whites who do not profit directly from the byproducts of these outcomes behave as if they do thus enacting an adherence "to a racial ideology shaped by the interests of earlier generations of whites."[4]

The locus and forms of the stigmatization process are multi-faceted. In science,[5] literature,[6] sports,[7] the health area,[8] children's play objects,[9] and in every single institutional configuration as well as in the language system itself,[10] repetitive discrediting of the African American male pervades. Genetic fallacies[11] which posit the assumption that the black male is biologically inferior are part of the stigma doctrine which assigns a defect to his color. Matriarchy myths[12] which promulgate the belief that the black male is irresponsible, shiftless, and lazy, are incorporated in the gestalten of stigma dogma. Theories of limited cognitive and intellectual growth,[13] postulating that the black male's intelligence is genetically determined and that his potential for abstract reasoning and creative accomplishments is restricted by his biology, converge with and maintain the higher level process of "inferiorization."[14] Psychiatric diagnoses[15] that consistently label the black male as prone to aggressive emotional and other serious disorders are measurable indicators of the implications of stigmatization. Social and behavioral science deprivation postulates and deviance theorems sustain the prevailing color related status system. Designed to contribute to the belief that black males, as well as females, are culturally disadvantaged, linguistically deprived, engage in more criminality than whites, such social science misconceptions are all part of the stigmatizing process system.[16] In the present era of mass electronic teaching via television, regularized cross-national socialization to caricatures of black males also occurs through comedy characters and programs such as "Geraldine Jones," "The Jeffersons," "That's My Mama" and a host of others found in fiction[17] and non-fiction. Numerous films present negative portrayals of black males primarily.[18] And throughout the nineteenth and middle twentieth centuries, repulsive images of the black male as "Jolly Nigger," "Dancing Coon," and "Mammy's black-faced boy" were implanted in the imaginations of children via play objects.[19]

Stigmatization thus functions to maintain existing relations between blacks and whites. It validates the political order and is politically, socially, economically, and psychologically functional for whites. "The racist restrictions that strike at people of color in America result in a system of special privilege for the white majority."[20] Over a decade ago, one sociological analysis of 1960 census data on Urbanized Areas, exploring probable benefits incurred from the structural arrangement of blacks and whites, showed that "many whites in Southern Urbanized Areas benefit occupationally and economically from the presence and subordination of a large disadvantaged Negro population."[21] White employees in the higher status occupations—managerial, proprietary, upper-level manual and sales positions—were the major beneficiaries. Support for the consistent observation that whites receive occupational and income gains from black subordination[22] and, by logical inference its validating process of stigmatization, is provided in more recent census data. Table 1 shows that a significant discrepancy existed in the distribution of employment between the combined racial category of "Negro and other races" and whites in 1972. The most notable differences occurred between the lower and higher level occupations. With the exception of clerical positions, twice the proportion of white males than blacks, and similarly situated racial groupings, were employed in the white collar jobs. The opposite relationship is shown for operatives, transport equipment operatives, nonfarm laborers, and service workers. Thus an unequal division of labor on the basis of color is structured in the fabric of the stratification system. The stigmatization complex which embodies the racist orthodoxy that

blacks are not qualified for higher level positions reinforces and justifies this occupational disparity. Moreover in the economic structure,

TABLE 2-1   PERCENT DISTRIBUTION OF EMPLOYED MALE WORKERS,
BY OCCUPATION: 1972

Occupation	Negro and other races Male	White Male
Total employed ....thousands....	4,861	45,769
Percent	100.0	100.0
White-collar workers	22.2	41.7
Professional and technical workers	8.2	14.3
Managers and administrators, except farm	4.3	14.0
Sales workers	1.8	6.6
Clerical workers	7.4	6.8
Blue-collar workers	57.5	45.9
Craftsmen and kindred workers	14.7	21.2
Operatives, except transport	16.5	12.1
Transport equipment operatives	9.5	5.7
Nonfarm laborers	16.8	6.3
Service workers	15.8	7.3
Private household	0.2	0.1
Other	15.6	7.3
Farm workers	4.5	5.0

SOURCE: U.S. Department of Labor, Bureau of Labor Statistics. *The Social and
Economic Status of the Black Population in the United States,* 1972. Current Population Reports, Series P-23, No. 46, table 38, p. 50.

according to sociologist Blackwell,[23] black Americans at all occupational levels earn much less than whites. Table 2 shows median earnings of year round full-time wage and salary workers by occupation
group, labor union membership, and race. For black and other males
classified in the same racial category, their 1970 annual earnings were
significantly less than those of white males regardless of labor union
membership. Although the ratio of nonwhite to white earnings was
larger for union than for nonunion workers, the pattern prevails. Consequently the normative action of defining the value of labor and income worth in terms of color is reflected in this economic matrix. The
maintenance of income disparities between white and black male
workers primarily is one of the measurable benefits incurred from
black stigmatization.

Sociological analyses of the interrelations between the various
measures of social status tend to consistently demonstrate a correlation
between income and educational attainment. But, in view of this dis-

cussion, any relationships ascertained between the two variables must be considered within the context of the color stratified system and its concomitant supporting beliefs and processes. Table 3 shows median earnings for black and white males in the 25 to 34 year old age group who worked year round in 1969. Although median earnings rose with increased educational attainment, at all educational levels black males earn less than white males in each region of the country. The economic system is thus stratified on the basis of color and receives its justification via discrediting process.

TABLE 2-2   MEDIAN EARNINGS OF YEAR ROUND, FULL-TIME MALE WAGE
AND SALARY WORKERS BY OCCUPATION GROUP AND LABOR UNION
MEMBERSHIP: MARCH 1970

Occupation group of longest job held in 1970	Male		
	Negro and other races	White	Ratio: Negro and other races to white
IN LABOR UNIONS			
All occupations[1]	$7,732	$9,285	0.83
White-collar workers	8,883	9,923	0.90
Blue-collar workers	7,772	9,175	0.85
Service workers	6,335	8,682	0.73
NOT IN LABOR UNIONS			
All occupations[1]	5,906	9,478	0.62
White-collar workers	8,330	11,542	0.72
Blue-collar workers	5,469	7,802	0.70
Service workers	5,319	6,929	0.77
RATIO: MEDIAN EARNINGS OF UNION TO NONUNION WORKERS			
All occupations[1]	1.31	0.98	(X)
White-collar workers	1.07	0.86	(X)
Blue-collar workers	1.42	1.18	(X)
Service workers	1.19	1.25	(X)

X Not applicable.
[1] Includes farm workers not shown separately.
SOURCE: U.S. Department of Labor, Bureau of Labor Statistics. *The Social and Economic Status of the Black Population in the United States,* 1972. Current Population Reports, Series P-23, No. 46, table 43, p. 55.

There is also a bio-social purpose to defaming the black male. Discrediting his identity and character serves to superiorize the social situations of whites. This function is not unique to the United States and has its roots in the evolution of meanings assigned to physical dif-

TABLE 2-3   MEDIAN EARNINGS IN 1969 AND EDUCATIONAL
ATTAINMENT OF MALES 25 TO 34 YEARS OLD, WHO WORKED YEAR ROUND
IN 1969, BY REGION: 1970

	Male		
Area and education	Negro	White	Ratio: Negro to white
UNITED STATES			
Total	$6,346	$8,839	0.72
Elementary: 8 years or less	4,743	6,618	0.72
High school: 1 to 3 years	5,749	7,910	0.73
4 years	6,789	8,613	0.79
College: 1 to 3 years	7,699	9,190	0.84
4 years	8,715	11,212	0.78
5 years or more	9,955	11,808	0.84
NORTH AND WEST			
Total	$7,478	$9,127	0.82
Elementary: 8 years or less	6,314	7,278	0.87
High school: 1 to 3 years	6,737	8,319	0.81
4 years	7,650	8,838	0.87
College: 1 to 3 years	8,233	9,383	0.88
4 years	9,747	11,394	0.86
5 years or more	11,099	11,927	0.93
SOUTH			
Total	$5,226	$8,090	0.65
Elementary: 8 years or less	4,220	5,782	0.73
High school: 1 to 3 years	4,872	6,928	0.70
4 years	5,783	7,987	0.72
College: 1 to 3 years	6,525	8,669	0.75
4 years	7,372	10,738	0.69
5 years or more	8,784	11,439	0.77

NOTE: Data are for persons in experienced civilian labor force who worked 50
to 52 weeks in 1969 and had earnings.
SOURCE: U.S. Department of Commerce, Social and Economics Statistics Administra-
tion, Bureau of the Census. *The Social and Economic Status of the Black
Population in the United States,* 1972. Current Population Reports, Series
P-23, No. 46, table 15, p. 25.

ferences and the accompanying consciousness and self-consciousness
of these distinctions. Yet there is considerable historical documenta-
tion for the assumption that the stigmatization process directed against
blacks has maintained its present form since the inception of slavery
in America.[24] In the 18th century, the liberal statesman Thomas Jeffer-

son crystallized the dynamics of the process by reasserting biogenetic views held of black males.

> They seem to require less sleep. A black after hard labour through the day, will be induced by the slightest amusements to sit up till midnight or later, though knowing he must be out with the first dawn of the morning. . . . They are more ardent after their female: but love seems with them to be more an eager desire, than a tender delicate mixture of sentiment and sensation. Their griefs are transient . . . In general, their existence appears to participate more of sensation than reflection . . . Their love is ardent, but it kindles the senses only, not the imagination . . . I advance it therefore as a suspicion only, that the blacks, whether originally a distinct race, or made distinct by time and circumstances, are inferior to the whites in the endowments both of body and mind.[25]

A cursory content analysis of this passage reveals that every dimension of the black male's identity is maligned: his fundamental biological needs, emotional system, intellectual and cognitive abilities, capability for expressing human feelings, orientation toward black women, use of leisure time, in short the totality of his existential and biological self. Each of Jefferson's claims had as its intended purpose and ultimate consequence that of subjugating the African male while simultaneously superiorizing the identity and status of the European American male. Through the language of stigmatization during the era of slavery, perpetual vilification became intricately interwoven with all other values, customs, and behaviors deemed essential to maintaining the positions of white males in the existing political and cultural milieu. The language of stigmatization thus represented a significant type of "practical consciousness"[26] as evidenced by its psycholinguistic content and economic consequences.

With respect to the black male–white male interactional arena, for white males, there are ego fulfilling benefits gained from black male stigmatization. Jefferson Davis once said that it exalts and dignifies every white man to have a lower race present in his midst.[27] This stigma orientation is deeply rooted in America's racist ideology and in turn provides a validation for it. In this connection, racism as a psycho-biological explanatory system has been defined by one psychiatrist as "a low-level defense and adjustment mechanism utilized by groups to deal with psychological and social insecurities."[28] With respect to this clarification, the ideology of racism and its accompanying process of stigmatization thus enable persons who have insecurities, defects, or low self esteem to feel good about themselves. Vilification, shaming, and scapegoating others assists one's own psychological adjustment.[29] Another psychiatrist, analyzing the psychoanalytic functions of racism, posits the assumption that "in the majority of instances any neurotic drive for superiority and supremacy is usually founded upon a deep and pervading sense of inadequacy and inferiority."[30] Stigmatization of others therefore operates as a defense mechanism which aids individuals not functioning well in having high self esteem. Such a psychological strategy, oriented to coping with personal inadequacies, results in a failure to recognize one's own limitations. Any ego bolstering strategem can be used in this manner.

While white males from all socio-economic strata have traditionally defined the black male's nature in terms of bio-genetic dimensions, the African male has sought to conquer deep-seated anxieties stemming from the reduction of his social self to a physical entity. Although the effects and manifestations of this are variable depending on one's position in the economic sphere, cultural backgrounds, and existing self conceptions, those affected significantly employ a diversity of management techniques to minimize the impact of the stigmatizing encounter. But regardless of the methods devised for managing a discredited identity, all black males are exposed to the stigmatizing experience. One mode of adapting to an identity maligned by the dominant sector is through marriage to a white female.[31] This adaptation has been referred to as the politics of the black male-white female union.[32] Preoccupation with the threat of such marriages, on the part of white males, occurred early in the history of America. One of the first laws prohibiting marriage between white women and black men was enacted in the state of Maryland in 1664. Less than thirty years later in Virginia, the class of free Africans became a source of fear with respect to the possibility of black male-white female marriages. A law enacted, similar to many others across the country, stipulated that "any white woman in Virginia marrying a Negro or mulatto, bond or free" was to be banished.[33] Throughout the 17th, 18th, 19th, and 20th centuries, similar legislation prevailed. It was not until 1968 that the Supreme Court ruled on the unconstitutionality of anti-black-white marriage regulations. Although most black men marry black women, in the 1960s available records showed that nearly 17,000 black men married white women. A marked increase in such marriages was noted in the 1970 census. The irony of interracial marriage as a stigma reduction coping mechanism is that the white female lacks the social power to formulate decisions which would alter the ascribed positions of black men. Instead, in an interracial union she undergoes the discrediting experience. In spite of the legality of and increase in such marriages, she carries a "stigma symbol,"[34] that is, she is discredited.

Another psychological strategy for handling the stigmatizing experience is through the creation and acceptance of an exaggerated role model—the authentic ghetto-dwelling male.[35] Labeled a "cool dude" and assumed to have been invented by blacks, the role enactor of the model is perceived as a symbolic summation of manhood indigenous to African American culture. The developmental life cycle of this role archetype, found primarily in the ghetto, is spent in the street culture vernacular "playing it cool," "pimping," and "ragging and rapping."[36] Taking on the attitudes and behaviors of this significant-other prototype reflects valued social customs. The reference model and associated conduct represent highly functional adaptations which have resulted in a unique range of behaviors for males in the lower socio-economic strata who are black in America.[37] Ironically, although blacks may consider the dude concept and character part of their unparalleled situational language system and indigenous role sets, the label was once used to describe a toy manufactured to entertain white children.[38]

Malcolm X, a probing and perceptive social thinker, critically evaluated an earlier romanticized prototype for the contemporary "superfly" character—the ghetto hustler. In examining the psycho-social dynamics of this exemplary model for young males, he stated: "What makes the ghetto hustler yet more dangerous is his 'glamor' image to the school drop-out youth in the ghetto ... ghetto youth become attracted to the hustler worlds of dope, thievery, prostitution, and general crime, and immorality."[39] However each of these outcomes mirrors the subjugating and stigmatizing experiences.

The discrediting effect also manifests itself in excessive use of stigma reduction material objects such as expensive and elaborate cars, jewelry, furnishings, dwellings, and clothing. An examination of material possessions of those in the entertainment world provides supportive data for this assertion. For innumerable black males, ornate clothing, for example, has become a key medium to convey a glamorized sense of masculine identity. Presumably symbolizing what is in vogue, recently "super-fly" fashions have mushroomed. Observable dress styles and fashion magazine advertisements indicate that black males wear this type of clothing with a much greater frequency than males of other racial and ethnic groupings. Paradoxically, while such attire provides a sense of visible masculinity, elaborately styled pants, blouses, multicolored platform shoes, and pocket books simultaneously emit a feminized appearance. It is highly probable that at the psycho-social level of coping with subordination and the stigmatizing experience, flamboyantly designed fashions enable black males who wear them to acquire a sense of identity crystallization and masculine self feelings. Operating in this manner clothes thus have clinical value for those who wear them.[40]

Because patriarchy or male domination over the political and economic life of a society is basically a universal phenomenon resulting in collective bonds of solidarity among men,[41] a constant "inferiorization"-stigmatizing encounter is much more precarious for males than it is for females. This does not mean that the denial of human attributes and accompanying deprivation of opportunity for productive survival of the black female is not injurious. Such psychopolitical practices are critically damaging to their life chances. But pertinent data indicate that black males tend to display in a much more measurably intense way, than females, the negative impact of the white racism ideology. Restricting opportunities and life chances, along with historically systematized discrediting, have had a profound effect on the black male's self conceptions, his psychology, his relationship with black women, his relationship with other black men, especially in the confines of the ghetto, and his interactions with whites of both sexes. For the process of stigmatization has been targeted primarily at him, his family, his offspring. One extreme indicator of the effect of the reduction of black males to maligned status-role occupants and hence the fragmentation of their reference group identity is detected in mortality rates resulting from black men killing each other. The rate of intra-group homicide among blacks is increasing and the major victims are young males between 15 and 24.[42]

An underlying contention of this discussion has been that discrediting actions are deeply ingrained in the collective historical behavioral practices and cosmological labyrinth of Euro-Americans. With respect to this verified assumption based on observable behavior, one white male psychiatrist recently stated:

> Nothing so demonstrates the oddity of the West's attitude toward property as the manner in which Western man enslaved black Africans ... For the American slaver did not simply own the body of his black slave ... he first reduced the human self of his black slave to a body and then reduced the body to a thing; he dehumanized his slave.[43]

Thus simultaneously with the seizure of the labor of Africans in America and the resulting ascription of positions in the economic and property hierarchy, a purposive ostracism format, a cult of stigmatization developed which permeated the intrapsychic structure of white and black Americans. It was rooted in a configuration of racist beliefs and political values. Although presently prevalent as a world wide doctrine, the economic and political ramifications of racism are more readily observed in the United States, Rhodesia, and the Republic of South Africa. Throughout the evolution of the territorial, cultural and technological organization of the American social system, the stigmatization complex has supported a stratified milieu based primarily on meanings assigned to color. It has sustained and legitimized segregation, disenfranchisement, restriction of opportunities, and spatial isolation of descendants of slaves.[44] The position of African slaves was consciously and deliberately structured to reduce black males to what one perceptive psychiatrist labels "functional inferiors."[45] A stigmatizing policy emerged simultaneously as an intricate set of explanatory and validating beliefs and practices oriented to perpetuation of the color status hierarchy.[46] Stigmatization, as a psycho-political process, has served to reaffirm the historically designed racial ordering of the society—the differential allocation of social privileges and economic rewards. While politicizing the identities of each racial sector in the society, it has superiorized the self images and positions of whites and blemished perhaps permanently, the identities of innumerable black males.

NOTES

1. Erving Goffman, *Stigma: Notes on the Management of A Spoiled Identity* (Englewood Cliffs, New Jersey: Prentice-Hall, Inc., 1963), p. 51.
2. Frances Cress Welsing, "The 'Conspiracy' To Make Blacks Inferior," *Ebony* 29 (September, 1974): 85,88,92. See also the analysis of the cult of "cultural inferiority" in Kenneth B. Clark, *Dark Ghetto* (New York: Harper & Row, 1965).
3. Doris Y. Wilkinson, "Coming of Age in a Racist Society: The Whitening of America," *Youth and Society* 3 (Sept., 1971): 100–18. Also see: James W. Vander Zanden, "The Ideology of White Supremacy," in Barry N. Schwartz and Robert Disch, eds., *White Racism: Its History, Pathology and Practice* (New York: Dell Publishing Co., 1970), pp. 121–139.
4. Norval D. Glenn, "White Gains from Negro Subordination," *Social Problems* 14 (Fall, 1966): 178.
5. Alexander Thomas and Samuel Sillen, *Racism and Psychiatry* (New York: Brunner/Mazel, Publishers, 1972).

6. See: P. C. Deane, "The Persistence of Uncle Tom: An Examination of the Image of the Negro in Children's Fiction Series," *Journal of Negro Education* 37 (Spring, 1968) : 140–45. Sterling A. Brown, "Negro Characters as Seen by White Authors," *Journal of Negro Education* 2 (April, 1933) : 179–203.

7. Harry Edwards, "The Sources of the Black Athlete's Superiority," *The Black Scholar* 3 (November, 1971) : 32–41. Also see: Harry Edwards, "The Black Athlete: 20th Century Gladiators for White America," *Psychology Today* 7 (November, 1973) : 43–47, 50, 52.

8. I. A. Newby, "White Supremacy," in *Black Carolinians: A History of Blacks in South Carolina from 1895 to 1968* (Columbia, South Carolina: University of South Carolina Press, 1973) .

9. Doris Y. Wilkinson, "Racial Socialization Through Children's Toys: A Sociohistorical Examination," *Journal of Black Studies* 5 (September, 1974) : 96–109.

10. David R. Burgest, "The Racist Use of the English Language," *The Black Scholar* 5 (September, 1973) : 37–45.

11. Frances C. Welsing, "On 'Black Genetic Inferiority'," *Ebony* 29 (July, 1974) : 104–5.

12. Robert Staples, "The Myth of the Black Matriarchy," *The Black Scholar* 1 (January-February, 1970) : 8–16.

13. See: T. Dobzhansky, *Mankind Evolving: The Evolution of the Human Species* (New Haven: Yale University Press, 1962) ; M. H. Fried, "The Need to End the Pseudoscientific Investigation of Race," in Margaret Mead, et al, eds., *Science and the Concept of Race* (New York: Columbia University Press, 1968) .

14. Frances C. Welsing, "The 'Conspiracy' to Make Blacks Inferior," *Ebony* 29 (Sept., 1974) : 85, 88, 92.

15. Lloyd Brown, Psychoanalysis vs. the Negro People," *Masses and Mainstream* 4 (1951) : 16–24. K. Alan Wesson, "The Black Man's Burden: The White Clinician," *The Black Scholar* 6 (July-August, 1975) : 13–18. Janet Saxe, "A Review of Black Rage," *Black Scholar* 1 (March, 1970) : 58–62.

16. See: William Ryan, *Blaming the Victim* (New York: Pantheon, 1971) . Doris Y. Wilkinson, "Racism and American Sociology: The Myth of Scientific Objectivity," *Sociological Abstracts* 20 (December, 1972) : 1888.

17. Sterling A. Brown, "Negro Characters as Seen by White Authors," *Journal of Negro Education* 2 (April, 1933) : 179–203.

18. Thomas R. Cripps, "The Death of Rastus: Negroes in American Films Since 1945," *Phylon* 28 (Fall, 1967) : 267–75. See: Daniel J. Leab, *From Sambo to Superspade* (New York: Houghton Mifflin Co., 1975) .

19. Doris Y. Wilkinson, "Racial Socialization Through Children's Toys: A Sociohistorical Examination," *Journal ·of Black Studies* 5 (September, 1974) : 96–109.

20. Robert Blauner, *Racial Oppression in America* (New York: Harper & Row, Publishers, 1972), p. 22.

21. Glenn D. Norval, "White Gains from Negro Subordination," *Social Problems* 14 (Fall, 1966): 159–78.

22. John Dollard, *Class and Caste in a Southern Town* (New Haven: Yale University Press, 1937), chapter 6. Philips Cutright, "Negro Subordination and White Gains," *American Sociological Review* 30 (February, 1965): 110–12.

23. James E. Blackwell, *The Black Community: Diversity and Unity* (New York: Dodd, Mead & Company, 1975).

24. See: Frederick K. Douglass, *Narrative of the Life of Frederick Douglass: An American Slave* (New York: The New American Library, 1968). W. E. B. Du Bois, *Black Reconstruction* (New York: Harcourt, Brace & Co., 1935). John Hope Franklin, *From Slavery to Freedom* (New York: Alfred A. Knopf, Inc., 1948). Stokely Carmichael and Charles V. Hamilton, "White Power: The Colonial Situation," in *Black Power: The Politics of Liberation in America* by Stokely Carmichael and Charles V. Hamilton (New York: Random House, 1967).

25. Winthrop D. Jordan, "The Debate on the Negro's Nature, 1787–1809," in *The Negro Versus Equality, 1762–1826* (Chicago: Rand McNally & Company, 1969), pp. 19,20,22. Also see: Thomas Jefferson, *Notes on the State of Virginia* (Philadelphia, 1787), pp. 61–66, 146–54. See also: Carlyle C. Douglas, "The Dilemma of Thomas Jefferson," *Ebony* 30 (August, 1975): 60–66.

26. Karl Marx and Friedrich Engels, *The German Ideology,* Parts I and II. Edited by R. Pascal. (New York: International Publishers, 1947), pp. 14–22.

27. Michael Banton, *Race Relations* (New York: Basic Books, 1967), p. 117. Cited in Blauner, Ibid., p. 27.

28. James P. Comer, "White Racism: Its Root, Form, and Function," *American Journal of Psychiatry* 126 (1969): 802–6.

29. See: Nevitt Sanford, "The Roots of Prejudice: Emotional Dynamics," in Peter Watson, ed., *Psychology and Race* (Chicago: Aldine Publishing Company, 1973), pp. 57–75.

30. Frances Cress Welsing, "The Cress Theory of Color-Confrontation," *The Black Scholar* 5 (May, 1974): 32–40.

31. Doris Y. Wilkinson, "Sociological Research on Interracial Marriage," in Doris Y. Wilkinson, ed., *Black Male/White Female* (Cambridge: Schenkman Publishing Co., 1975), pp. 7–8.

32. William Turner, "Black Men-White Women: A Philosophical View," in Doris Y. Wilkinson, ed., *Black Male/White Female* (Cambridge, Mass.: Schenkman Publishing Co., 1975), pp. 170–74.

33. Peter M. Bergman, *The Chronological History of the Negro in America* (New York: Harper & Row, Publishers, 1969), p. 21.

34. See: Goffman, Ibid., pp. 43–44.

35. Doris Y. Wilkinson, "Black Youth," in *Youth 1975* (Chicago: The National Society for the Study of Education, 1975), pp. 291–93.

36. John Horton, "Time and Cool People," *Trans-action* 4 (April, 1967): 5–12. Thomas Kochman, " 'Rapping' in the Black Ghetto," *Trans-action* 6 (February, 1969): 26–34. Thomas Sewell, "Radical Chic is Vicious," *Psychology Today*, February, 1973, pp. 41–44.

37. See: Ulf Hannerz, *Soulside: Inquiries into Ghetto Culture and Community* (New York: Columbia University Press, 1969).

38. Doris Y. Wilkinson, "Racial Socialization Through Children's Toys: A Sociohistorical Examination," *Journal of Black Studies* 5 (Sept., 1974).

39. Malcom X (with Alex Haley), *The Autobiography of Malcom X* (New York: Grove Press, Inc., 1966), pp. 276–311.

40. Goffman discusses the wearing of "visible signs" to advertise failure. Goffman, Ibid., pp. 100.

41. Lionel Tiger, *Men in Groups* (New York: Vintage, 1970).

42. Hamilton Bims, "Why Black Men Die Younger," *Ebony* 30 (December, 1974): 44–52. Poussaint, Alvin F., *Why Blacks Kill Blacks* (New York: Emerson Hall Publishers, Inc., 1972).

43. Joel Kovel, *White Racism: A Psychohistory* (New York: Pantheon Books, 1970), 17–18.

44. St. George Tucker, *A Dissertation on Slavery: With a Proposal for the Gradual Abolition of It in the State of Virginia* (Philadelphia, 1796), pp. 76–98, in Winthrop D. Jordan, *The Negro Versus Equality, 1762–1826* (Chicago: Rand McNally & Co., 1969), pp. 54–55.

45. Frances Cress Welsing, "The Cress Theory of Color Confrontation," *The Black Scholar* 5 (May, 1974): 32–40.

46. " 'Separate but Equal' 1896: A Shocking Decision," *Life: The 100 Events That Shaped America* (Bicentennial Issue, 1975), pp. 48, 49, 53.

THE SOURCES OF THE BLACK ATHLETE'S SUPERIORITY*

Harry Edwards

In 1967 and 1968, America was shocked into a new consciousness regarding the totality of black people's commitment to achieving liberation from racism, injustice, and inhumanity. During a sixteen month period ending in October of 1968 at the Olympic Game in Mexico City, a number of dedicated black athletes had taken the struggle of human dignity into the sacred empire of American sports, shattering long-standing myths, exposing countless hypocrisies, and laying bare the fact that the sports establishment is nothing more nor less than racist, authoritarian, vulturistic, white America functioning in microcosm. Not since the days of Paul Leroy Robeson (the Rutgers University All-American who turned his back on the recognition derived from playing the role of the "responsible Negro athlete") has white society in general and the sports world in particular, exhibited such anger over the refusal of black men to entertain a decadent social order by performing as uni-dimensional Twentieth Century gladiators.

Since 1968, the countless rebellions, boycotts, and strikes carried out by black athletes and others have made it quite clear that the revolt in sports is a good deal more than a passing fad or political gesture. It has even spread to the ranks of white athletes, a fact attested to in recent books by Dave Meggesy and Jim Bouton who point out and denounce numerous characteristic examples of racism, facism, and inhumane exploitation in both amateur and professional athletics.

Since the onset of the revolt of the black athlete there have

*From *The Black Scholar* 3 (November, 1971): 32–41. Reprinted with permission of the editors and author.

been numerous occurrences which many interpret as indicative of improvement in the overall racial situation in the sports arena:

1. The hiring of unprecedented numbers of black coaches and administrative assistants at predominantly white educational institutions which have traditionally depended heavily upon black athletic talent for sports success;
2. The naming of a black manager to a minor league or farm club subsidiary of a major league professional baseball team;
3. The naming of three black player-coaches in the National Basketball Association;
4. The establishment of athletic boards and committees at many institutions to handle the grievances of black athletes;
5. The nomination of pre-1947 baseball stars to a "special" baseball hall of fame roster;
6. A highly visible increase in the number of black athletes doing paid television commercials.

There have also been several positive intangibles which have emerged from the black revolt in sports. One of the most important of these has been the development of a heightened consciousness among actual and aspiring black athletes as to their political responsibilities and potentials in the worldwide black liberation struggle. Another intangible result has been a partial dissolution of the black athlete's image as the purely physical and apolitical automation, the unquestioningly obedient Uncle Tom. These were images well-established and legitimated by a long line of Negroes who were only too happy to fulfill their assigned roles for money, a few sports trinkets, or a few sentences in the newspaper.

Finally, there is the fact that the black athlete has achieved new prestige and respect among the black masses, not because of his athletic excellence, but because, despite his relatively high status, he has at long last begun to speak out on the social and political issues affecting the lives and destinies of all Afro-American athletes and non-athletes alike. Only time will disclose whether or not these accomplishments of the revolt will have any impact toward positively altering the oppressed and degrading conditions of black people, inside and outside the sports world.

Wide-spread publicity in recent months has been given yet another "accomplishment." Many view it as a concession by the white-controlled sports world—unrecognition of the new spirit of pride, political awareness, and cultural identity among black athletes. This would-be accomplishment is embodied in the fact that diverse and highly influential persons and publications (usually considered part of the "sports establishment" in America) have finally admitted what every objective observer of the sports scene already knew—to wit, that the performance of black athletes, on the average, is significantly superior to that of whites in all sports participated in by both groups in numbers. This admission has not been put forth grudgingly; rather it has been enthusiastically presented and echoed, even by sports commentators and coaches, usually considered conservative or right-wing in their orientation toward the thrust for black dignity in sports.

While there can be little argument with the obvious fact that black performances in sports have been and continue to be superior on the whole, to those of whites, there is room for considerable debate over the identity and character of the factors which have determined that superiority and contributed to its perpetuation.

The world of the athlete is one dominated by competition, where the value of one's performance is never absolute but always relative to both the past and the present performances of others. In his newly established role as one of the most visible manifestations of black pride and competence, the black athlete often feels increased pressures to conquer "whitey" in the sports arena. Thus, in their hasty grasp for long-overdue recognition of the general superiority of blacks over whites in athletics, it was perhaps to be expected that many well-meaning black athletes would inadvertently substantiate not only the fact of that superiority itself but also the prevailing arguments put forth regarding the casual factors underlying that situation. Apparently, few paused before making their comments to give serious consideration to the broader implications of these arguments for either black athletes or the black population at large.

The central concern of this essay is to analyze these arguments and their implications. Further, what is considered here to be a more scientifically defensible postulation of the causal factors underlying black athletic superiority will be presented.

The myth of the black male's racially determined, inherent physical and athletic superiority over the white male, rivals the myth of black sexual superiority in antiquity. While both are well fixed in the Negrolore and folk-beliefs of American society, in recent years the former has been subject to increasing emphasis due to the overwhelmingly disproportionate representation of black athletes on all-star rosters, on Olympic teams, in the various "most valuable player" categories, and due to the black athlete's overall domination of the highly publicized or so-called "major sports"—basketball, football, baseball, track and field. But seldom in recent times has the myth of racially-linked black athletic prowess been subject to so explicit a formulation and presentation as in the January 18, 1971 issue of *Sports Illustrated* magazine. In an article entitled "An Assessment of 'Black is Best'" by Martin Kane, one of the magazine's senior editors, several arguments are detailed, discussed, and affirmed by a number of widely known medical scientists, athletic researchers, coaches, and black athletes. In essence, the article constitutes an attempt to develop a logical and scientifically defensible foundation for the assertion that black athletic superiority in sports is due to racial characteristics indigenous to the black population in America but not generally found within the white population.

Kane cites the following as evidence of the black athlete's superior abilities:

1. In basketball three of the five players named to the 1969–1970 all NBA team were black, as were all five of the athletes named to the all-rookie team. Blacks have won the league's Most Valuable Player award twelve times in the past thirteen seasons;
2. In professional football, all four of the 1969 Rookie of the Year awards for the offense and defense were won by blacks;
3. In baseball, black men have won the National League's Most Valuable Player awards sixteen times in the past twenty-two seasons;
4. Today there are 150 blacks out of 600 players in major league baseball, 330 blacks out of 1,040 athletes in professional football, and 153 players out of 280 in basketball are black. Of the athletes in professional sports in 1969–70 All-Star teams, 36% in baseball were black, 44% in football were black, and blacks comprised 63% of the All-Star talent in basketball.

Clearly there is no argument that black society is contributing more than its 11% share of athletes and star-status performers to professional sports. And where blatant racism and discrimination do not keep blacks from participation almost completely—such as in the Southeastern conference—a similar pattern of black domination prevails in colleges and at other amateur levels where major sports endeavors are pursued.

Attempting to explain this disproportionate representation, Kane mentions, almost in passing, the probable influences of contemporary societal conditions and then launches into a delineation and discussion of the major factors giving rise to black athletic superiority. They are as follows:

Racially Linked Physical and Psychological Characteristics

1. Proportionately longer leg lengths, narrower hips, wider calf bones, and greater arm circumference among black athletes than among whites.
2. A greater ratio of tendon to muscle among blacks, giving rise to a condition typically termed "double jointedness," a relatively dense bone structure.
3. A basically elongated body structure among black athletes enabling them to function as more efficient heat dissipators relative to whites.

Race Related Psychological Factors

1. The black athlete's greater capacity for relaxation under pressure relative to the capacity of the white athlete.

Racially Specific Historical Occurrences

1. The selectivity of American slavery in weeding out the hereditarily and congenitally weak from among those who came to be the forebears of today's black population.

Let us now turn to a general consideration of these major factors.

RACIALLY-LINKED PHYSICAL AND PHYSIOLOGICAL CHARACTERISTICS

Kane's attempt to establish the legitimacy of this category of factors as major contributions to the emergence of black athletic superiority suffers from two basic maladies—one methodological, the other arising from a dependence upon scientifically debatable assumptions and presumptions concerning differences between the "races" of men and the impact of these differences upon capacity for physical achievement.

Simply stated, one grossly indefensible methodological tactic is obvious in virtually every case of "scientific" evidence presented in support of a physical or physiological basis for black athletic superiority. *In no case was the evidence presented gathered from a random sample of subjects selected from the black population at large in America.* Thus, supporting data, for the most part, was taken from black athletes of already proven excellence or from blacks who were available due to other circumstances reflective of some degree of uncontrolled social, political, or otherwise continued selectivity. Therefore, the generalization of the research findings on these subjects to the black population as a whole—even assuming the findings to be valid—constitutes a scientific blunder of the highest magnitude and invalidates the would-be scientific foundations of this component of the author's argument.

But there are still other considerations which doubt as to the credibility of Kane's presentation. There is first of all, the problem of justifying the posing of his argument within a context which assumes the biological and genetic validity of delineating human populations into "races." The use of such an approach in an attempt to discover athletically meaningful patterns of differences between the defined groups, does not take complete consideration of the fact that human breeding populations are determined to a great extent by cultural circumstances, and social and political conditions, as well as the factors of opportunity, propinquity, and convenience, not merely by the factor of similarity in morphological characteristics. Thus, to assume a biological and genetic validity to the concept of race implies that, as a population, Afro-Americans have bred endogamously and have maintained their original genotypical and anatomical traits—excepting for an occasional mutation brought about by natural or environmental selectivity.

This of course is nonsense. Virtually every attempt to define or pose problems within a context which either assumes or explicitly postulates the validity of a biological and/or genetic concept of race, has resulted in a troublesome issue of defensibility for the scientist involved, not to speak of the social and political problems that have emerged. This accounts for such widespread disagreement among human biologists and anthropologists concerning the definitions of race and the identification of the races of man. These definitions range all the way from the denial that genetically and biologically discernible races exist at all to those which delineate specific "races" of man numbering from two or three categories to classifications totaling in the hundreds. Invariably, once a biologist or anthropologist has settled upon a definition which suits him, he discovers there is little that he can do with his "races" other than list them. For typically they have defied any effort at deriving consistent patterns of valid relationships between racial heritage and meaningful social, intellectual, or physical capabilities. Hence, Kane treads upon ground of dubious solidity from the moment he couches his argument within the assumption that scientifically valid delineations of racial groupings exit at all.

A more specific analysis of the major points incorporated into this aspect of the author's overall argument only furthers the above assertions. With regard to the alleged physical traits supposedly characteristic of black athletes, the question can justifiably be posed, "what two outstanding black athletes look alike or have identical build?" One of Kane's resource persons answers this question:

"Floyd C. 'Bud' Winter makes it quite obvious that black athletes differ from each other physically quite as much as whites do. He notes that Ray Norton, a sprinter, was tall and slender with scarcely discernible hips, that Bobby Painter, a sprinter, was squat and dumpy with a sway back and a big butt, that Denis Johnson was short and wiry, that Tommy Smith was tall and wiry and so on." Further evidence is plentiful: "What physical characteristics does Lew Alcindor have in common with Elgin Baylor, or Wilt Chamberlain with Al Attles, etc? The point is simply that Wilt Chamberlain and Lew Alcindor have more in common physically with Mel Counts and Henry Finkel, two seven-foot white athletes, than with most of their fellow black athletes."

Even excepting the hyperbolic illustrations just documented, what emerges from any objective analysis of supposed physical differences between so-called races is the undeniable fact that there exist more differences between individual members of any one racial group than between any two groups as a whole. So, a fabricated "average" of the differences between racial groupings, even if it is scientifically generated, may serve certain heuristic purposes but provides a woefully inadequate basis for explaining specific cases of athletic excellence or superior ability. No black athlete conforms to that artificial average. As a matter of scientific fact, black athletes, as is true with the black population as a whole, manifest a wide range of physical builds, body proportions, and other highly diverse anatomical, physiological, and biological features, as do other groups including the so-called white race.

Recognition of this essential fact precludes the type of incredible qualification that Kane is forced to make when faced with exceptions which do not fit the framework which he has developed. A case in point is his assertion that the physical differences between white and black racial groupings predisposes blacks to dominate the sports requiring speed and strength while whites, due to racially-linked physical traits, are predestined to prevail in those sporting events requiring endurance. When confronted with the fact that black Kenyans won distance races and defeated highly touted and capable whites in the 1968 Olympic Games, the author makes the ridiculous posthoc assertion that (the Kenyans) Keino and Bikila have black skin but many white features.

Directly pertinent to Kane's presentation of would-be evidence that physiological differences underly black athletic superiority are the facts concerning efficient heat dissipation. In essence, the author attempts to present a case for the notion that due to an elongation of the body, black athletes are more efficient heat dissipators than are whites and thus, excel over whites in sports. First of all, either tall or short individuals may have body builds which enable them to function as relatively efficient heat dissipators. The efficiency with whirh one's body dissipates heat is only incidentally related to the factor of height; it is directly related to the rate of body surface to body mass. Therefore, one way to maximize heat dissipating efficiency is to present a proportionately greater amount of body surface to the air by stretching a given body mass into an elongated shape. Another way of changing the gross mass to surface ratio is to change the overall size of the body. Hence, a decrease in size will decrease the mass (proportional to the cube root of any linear dimension) in relation to the surface area, the end product being the accomplishment of the same thing that body elongation can do.

Substantiation for the accuracy of this formulation is evidenced simply by the Nilotic African or Watusi who is normal in body mass but elongated in shape. Thus, the factor of elongated body proportions becomes neutralized by the fact that a small white athlete could be as efficient a heat dissipator as an elongated black athlete. In sports where the small athlete can function effectively against other athletes, one would expect at least occasionally to see small and elongated black and white athletes performing at comparable levels of excellence. Evidence of the invalidity of Kane's argument in this regard is the fact that black athletes of a variety of sizes and shapes have dominated sports such as track and field over white athletes who themselves embodied a variety of shapes and sizes and thus body mass to body surface ratio. One last point: given the complexity of variables which determine athletic excellence, even where physical differences exist between individuals, one proceeds on dangerous grounds when he assumes that these observable or discernable differences are the major factors determining differences in demonstrated athletic excellence.

RACE-RELATED PSYCHOLOGICAL FACTORS

Here, the incredibility of Kane's presentation and the supporting statements of those who attempt to substantiate it are almost beyond belief. The academic belief in the existence of a national or a racial "character" was supposedly disposed of by scholars decades ago. Their persistence among the ranks of coaches and other segments of the American population only indicates the difficulty with which racial stereotypes and caricatures are destroyed or altered to comply with prevailing knowledge. Kane and his resource persons, mostly coaches, recreate a portrait of the black athlete as the happy-go-lucky, casual, "what—me worry?" Negro made so familiar to Americans through history books, Stepin Fetchit movies, and other societal outlets. But beside the fact that the overall portrayal itself is inappropriate, not even the specific psychological traits attributed to black athletes are substantiated by contemporary knowledge.

Kane quotes Lloyd C. Winter, former coach of a long line of successful black track and field athletes as stating: "A limber athlete has body control, and body control is part of skill. It is obvious that many black people have some sort of head-start motor in them, but for now I can only theorize that their great advantage is relaxation under stress. As a class, the black athletes who have trained under me are far ahead of whites in that one factor—relaxation under pressure. It's their secret."

In data collected by Bruce C. Ogolvie and Thomas A. Tutko, two athletic psychologists whose work was ironically featured in the same issue of *Sports Illustrated* in which Kane's article appears, a strong case is made for the fact that black athletes are significantly less relaxed than white athletes in the competitive situation. (I am intimately familiar with these data as a result of my Ph.D. dissertation.) Using a test which has been found to have a high degree of reliability in both cross-cultural and simple comparative investigations, the following findings emerged when the psychological orientations of successful black and white athletes were compared:

1. On the I.P.A.T., successful black athletes showed themselves to be considerably more serious, concerned and "uptight" than their white counterparts as indicated by their relative scores on the item "Sober—happy-go-lucky." Blacks had a mean stern score of 5.1 as compared to a mean score for whites of 5.5 (level of significance of differences is .01; N = 396 whites, 136 blacks).
2. On the I.P.A.T. item of "Casual-Controlled" successful black ath-

letes, indicating a more controlled orientation. Blacks had a mean stern score of 6.6 as compared with the whites' mean score of 6.2 (level of significance of differences is .01; N = 396 whites, 136 blacks).

Sociologically, this pattern of differences given black athletes is expected, as they are aware that they operate at a decided disadvantage competing against whites for highly valued positions and rewards in an admittedly white racist society. Furthermore, sports hold the only promise of escape from the material degradation of oppressed black society. Thus, the assertion that black athletes are more "relaxed" than whites not only lacks scientific validation but is ludicrous as even a common sense assumption.

RACIALLY SPECIFIC HISTORICAL OCCURRENCES

This is perhaps the most odious part of Kane's presentation, perhaps because he enlists the opinions of undoubtedly well-meaning but uninformed and unthinking black athletes to support his assertions. Kane cites the remarks of Yale University graduate Calvin Hill who now plays football for the Washington Redskins professional football team:

> I have a theory about why so many pro stars are black. I think it boils down to the survival of the fittest. Think of what the African slaves were forced to endure in this country merely to survive. Well, black athletes are their descendants. They are the offspring of those who are physically and mentally tough enough to survive.... We were simply bred for physical qualities.

Continuing, Kane himself states that "it might be that without special breeding the African has a superior physique." The statements of Kane and his resource persons evidence confusion as to the scope of characteristics involved in the selectivity process as it has affected mankind. Natural selection or "the survival of the fittest" has been predicated upon relative strength and physical attributes to a lesser degree in mankind than in any other form of animal life. This has been due largely to man's tremendously developed mental capabilities. The same would have held for the slave. While some may have survived as a result of greater physical strength and toughness, many undoubtedly also survived due to their shrewdness and thinking abilities.

Secondly, Kane and his informants speak as if blacks in American society have somehow remained "pure" as a racial stock. The fact of the matter is that our best sociological, genetic, and demographical knowledge indicates that the genetic make-up of blacks in America is at least 35%white, not counting genetic influences from various other so-called racial groupings. Therefore, to assert that Afro-Americans are superior athletes due to the genetic make-up or physical prowess of the original slaves would be naive and ridiculous.

Finally, Kane's argument is that for blacks, demonstration of physical ability alone is all that is required to become a successful athlete. Anyone who is even vaguely familiar with the internal dynamics of organized sports at either the amateur or professional levels in America, knows that physical ability will *maybe* open that door, but before one reaches the level of a Bill Russell or a Gayle Sayers there are a great number of political, psychological, and racial hurdles to conquer. Hence, perhaps the most vaguely related influence on the determination of black athletic superiority is the genetic or biological heritage of the black population as a racial group. Undoubtedly of much more importance as a determining factor is the facility with which the black athlete surmounts arbitrary political, psychological, and racial barriers, reflective of the contemporary sickness of American society. For the black athlete, the implications of Kane's article and similiar perspectives on black athletic superiority are the following:

1. These arguments imply that the accomplishments of the black athlete in sports are as natural to him as flight is to an eagle, and thus the facts of a lifetime of dedication, effort, sweat, blood, and tears are ignored. What Kane is essentially telling black athletes is that "you would have been a superior athlete despite yourself." Perhaps it is coincidental but such a stance allows racist whites in American society to affirm the undeniable superiority of the black athlete on the one hand and maintain their definitions of black people as lazy, shiftless, and irresponsible on the other.

2. The notion that black athletes are by racial heritage physically superior to white athletes provides a basis for maintaining a white monopoly on certain key positions in sports which ostensibly require greater thinking and organizational ability—e.g., quarterback in football, manager in baseball, and head coach in most sports. Thus, no matter how excellent an athlete a black player might be, a white player always gets the nod over him for these "intellectual" positions since the black athlete excels on inborn physical superiority alone. Since the white athlete, under these conditions, would have to work harder toward mastering any given sport, he would probably know the dynamics of the sport better

than the black athlete who "naturally" sails through the requirements of the endeavor and, hence, the white athlete would make a better coach or manager.

The major implication of Kane's argument for the black population at large is that it opens the door for at least an informal acceptance of the idea that whites are *intellectually* superior to blacks. Blacks, whether athletes or non-athletes, must not give even passing credence to the possibility of white intellectual superiority. By a tempered or even enthusiastic admission of black physical superiority, the white population of this racist society loses nothing. For it is a simple fact that a multitude of even lower animals are physically superior, not only to whites, but to mankind as a whole: gorillas are physically superior to whites, leopards are physically superior to whites, as are lions, walruses, and elephants. So by asserting that blacks are physically superior, whites at best reinforce some old stereotypes long held about Afro-Americans—to wit, that they are little removed from the apes in their evolutionary development.

On the other hand, intellectual capability is the highest priced commodity on the world market today. If in a fit of black identity or simple stupidity, we accept the myth of innate black physical superiority, we could be inadvertently recognizing and accepting an ideology which has been used as the justification for black slavery, segregation, and general oppression. Further, it was just such an ideology which led to genocide against native Americans in this country and against the Jews in Nazi Germany.

To those black athletes who have spoken out in support of the ideas expressed in Kane's article, I say only that it is a wise warrior who proceeds with caution and discretion when an enemy tosses bouquets in his direction. The argument that blacks are physically superior to whites as athletes or as a people is merely a racist ideology camouflaged to appeal to the ignorant, the unthinking, and the unaware in a period heightened by black identity. If it is accepted by blacks, whites will be released from the pressure to come up with a white hope in sports, year after year, and they can also maintain their gut beliefs in white supremacy—unchallenged. The sacrifice of black human dignity and respect, born of almost 400 years of struggle and despair, is too high a price to pay for white recognition of black athletic prowess. The black athlete has worked hard and diligently to achieve his present status in the athletic world—perhaps harder than his white counterpart, who has fewer numbers of obstacles facing him.

What then are the major factors underlying black athletic superiority? The factors underlying black athletic superiority emerge from a complex of societal conditions. These conditions instill a heightened motivation among black male youths to achieve success in sports; thus, they channel a proportionately greater number of talented black people than whites into sports participation. Our best sociological evidence indicates that capacity for physical achievement (like other common human traits such as intelligence, artistic ability, etc.) are evenly distributed throughout any population. Thus, it cuts across class, religious, and, more particularly, racial lines. For race, like class and religion, is primarily a culturally determined classification. *The simple fact of the matter is that the scientific concept of race has no proven biological or genetic validity.* As a cultural delineation, however, it does have a social and political reality. This social and political reality of race is the primary basis of stratification in this society and the key means of determining the priority of who shall have access to means—valued goods and services.

Blacks are relegates in this country, having the lowest priority to claiming valued goods and services. This fact, however, does not negate the equal and proportionate distribution of talent across both black and white populations. Hence, a situation arises wherein whites, being the dominant group in the society, have access to *all* means toward achieving desirable valuables defined by the society. Blacks on the other hand are channeled into the one or two endeavors open to them—sports, and to a lesser degree—entertainment.

Bill Russell once stated that he had to work as hard to achieve his status as the greatest basketball player of the last decade, as the president of General Motors had to work to achieve his position. The evidence tends to indicate that Russell is quite correct. In short, it takes just as much talent, perseverance, dedication, and earnest effort to succeed in sports as to become a leading financier, business executive, attorney or doctor. Few occupations (music and art being perhaps the exceptions) demand more time and dedication than sports. A world-class athlete will usually have spent a good deal of his youth practicing the skills and techniques of his chosen sports endeavor.

The competition for the few positions is extremely keen and if he is fortunate he will survive in that competition long enough to become a professional athlete or an outstanding figure in one of the amateur sports. For as he moves up through the various levels of competition, fewer and fewer slots or positions are available and the competition for these becomes increasingly intense because the rewards are greater. (Since the talents of 25 million Afro-Americans have a disproportionately higher concentration in sports, the number of highly gifted whites in sports is proportionately less than the number of blacks.) Under such circumstances, black athletes naturally predominate. Further, the white athletes who do participate in sports operate at a psychological disadvantage (relative to their black counterparts) because they believe blacks to be inherently superior as athletes. Thus, the white man has become the chief victim of his own lie.

Therefore, white racism in American society seems to be responsible for black athletic superiority to whites. That being the case, the real question is perhaps not "why is the number of black athletes so disproportionately high?" The basic factor determining that the number of blacks in sports does not soar still higher is white racism in the sports sphere itself. Sports aggregations at all levels of athletic participation operate under informal quotas as to the number of blacks allowed to make the roster. This is particularly true in the college and professional ranks where the rewards of participation are relatively higher. Also, as was mentioned earlier, certain positions in sports—such as quarterback—are the monopoly of white players.

Each year white America publicizes a "white hope" in sports: in 1968, it was Jim Ryun at the Olympic games; in 1970 it was Jerry Quarry in his fight against Muhammed Ali; in 1971 it was Pete Maravich. If this society is ever to realize its fondest dream in the sports realm—the development of at least relative parity between black and white athletes with regard to sports excellence—it must give Afro-Americans an opportunity for achievement in high status endeavors outside of sports participation.

It is well known that all the great quarterbacks are white because blacks have never, en masse, had an opportunity to play that position. All the great professional football coaches and baseball managers are white because blacks have never had an opportunity to be professional head football coaches or major league baseball managers. So even these "great" white sports figures are contrived phonies, as are the so-called greats in the many other sports closed to blacks. This is due to racism which leads to a de facto denial of opportunity to blacks who have potential for excellence in these activities. The latter is particularly true of sports such as golf, tennis, swimming and auto racing.

The necessity for white America to generate a white hope year after year, and to attempt to justify far-flung and irrational myths (as postulated in Kane's article), will all decrease proportionately to the degree that American society divests itself of the racist restrictions that limit opportunity for blacks across the occupational spectrum. As long as sports provide the only visible, high-status, occupational role model for the masses of black male youths, black superiority over whites shall go unchallenged.

THE MYTH OF THE BLACK MATRIARCHY*

Robert Staples

In dealing with the question of the role of the black woman in the black struggle one must ultimately encounter the assertion that the black community is organized along matriarchal lines, that the domineering black female has been placed in a superordinate position in the family by the historical vicissitudes of slavery, and that her ascendency to power has resulted in the psychological castration of the black male and produced a host of other negative results that include low educational achievement, personality disorders, juvenile delinquency, etc. One of the solutions to the "Negro" question we hear is that black males divest themselves of this female control of black society and reorganize it along patriarchal lines which will eventually solve the problem created by black female dominance.

And one can easily understand how the typical black female would react when told that the problem of black liberation lies on her shoulders, that by renouncing her control over the black male, their other common problems such as inadequate education, chronic unemployment and other pathologies will dissipate into a dim memory.

The myth of a black matriarchy is a cruel hoax.

It is adding insult to injury to black liberation. For the black female, her objective reality is a society where she is economically exploited because she is both female and black; she must face the in-

*Reprinted from *The Black Scholar* 1 (January-February, 1970): 8–16. Copyright © 1970 by *The Black Scholar*.

evitable situation of a shortage of black males because they have been taken out of circulation by America's neo-colonialist wars, railroaded into prisons, or killed off early by the effects of ghetto living conditions. To label her a matriarch is a classical example of what Malcolm X called making the victim the criminal.[1]

To explode this myth of a black female matriarchy, one must understand the historical role of the black woman and the development of that role as it was influenced by the political and economic organization of American society. Like most myths, the one of a black matriarchy contains some elements of truth. Black women have not been passive objects who were satisfied with watching their menfolk make history. If they had been contented to accept the passive role ascribed to the female gender, then the travail of the past four centuries might have found the black race just as extinct as the dinosaur. It is a poor tribute to their historical deeds to characterize them as "sapphires," an opprobrious term that belies their real contribution to the black struggle.

Referring to black women as matriarchs is not only in contra-distinction to the empirical reality of their status but also is replete with historical and semantic inaccuracies. It was in the study by J. J. Bachofen[2] that the term matriarchy was first employed. He was attempting to present a case for the high position of women in ancient society. His conclusion was that since free sexual relations had prevailed during that time and the fathers of the children were unknown, this gave women their leading status in the period he called "mother-right."

A matriarchy is a society in which some, if not all, of the legal powers relating to the ordering and governing of the family-power over property, over inheritance, over marriage, over the house—are lodged in women rather than men.[3] If one accepts this formal definition, the consensus of most historians is that "men reign dominant in all societies; no matriarchy (*i.e.,* a society ruled by women) is known to exist."[4]

From a historical perspective, the black woman has always occupied a highly esteemed place in black culture. The African woman who first reached the shores of the American continent was already part and parcel of the fabric of history. She was descended from women who had birthed some of the great militarists of antiquity and from whose number had come some of the most famous queens to sit upon the thrones of ancient Egypt and Ethiopia. Her exploits and beauty were remembered by Semitic writers and fused into Greek mythology.[5]

Despite her important historical role, there is little doubt about the respective authority patterns in the black family of the pre-slave period of African civilization. There, the family organization was patriarchal in character and was a stable and secure institution. E. Franklin Frazier described the African patriarchal family this way:

> His wife and children gathered around him, and served him with as much respect as the best drilled domestics serve their masters; and if it was a fete day or Sunday, his sons-in-law and daughters did not fail to be present, and bring him some small gifts. They formed a circle about him, and conversed with him while he was eating. When he had finished, his pipe was brought to him, and then he bade them eat. They paid him their reverences, and passed into another room, where they all ate together with their mother.[6]

The ordeal of slavery wrought many changes in the family life of Afro-Americans, including the male and female roles. Family life of the African model was an impossibility when the slave's existence had to be devoted primarily to the cultivation and manufacture of tobacco and cotton. The buying and selling of slaves involved the splitting up of families, while the maintenance of discipline on the plantation prevented the husband and father from protecting his wife and children against his white masters and other more favored slaves. The financial value set on slave children and the rewards given to successful motherhood in cash, kind, and promotion from field slave to house slave gave an especially high status to the mother, a status which the father could only enjoy if placed in a position akin to that of a stud animal, this leading to a breaking of family ties and the degradation of family life still further.

Under the conditions of slavery, the American black father was forcefully deprived of the responsibilities and privileges of fatherhood. The black family's desire to remain together was subordinated to the economic interests of the slave-owning class. Only the mother-child bond continually resisted the disruptive effect of economic interests that dictated the sale of fathers away from their families. Not only did the practice of selling away fathers leave the black mother as the prime authority in the household but whenever the black male was present, he was not allowed to play the normal masculine role in American culture. Davie reports that:

> In the plantation domestic establishment, the woman's role was more

important than that of her husband. The cabin was hers and rations of corn and salt pork were issued to her. She cooked the meals, tended the vegetable patch, and often raised chickens to supplement the rations. If there was a surplus to sell, the money was hers. She made the clothes and reared the children. If the family received any special favors it was generally through her efforts.[7]

Just as in the society at large, power relationships in the family are aligned along economic lines. The power base of the patriarchal family is, in large part, based on the economic dependence of the female member. In the black slave family, the black woman was independent of the black male for support and assumed a type of leadership in her famliy life not found in the patriarchal family. At the same time, white society continued to deny black males the opportunity to obtain the economic wherewithal to assume leadership in the family constellation.

The reasons for this suppression of the black male are found in both the economic imperatives of slavery and the sexual value system of white America. In the early period of colonial America, the white family was strongly patriarchal and many of the income and property rights enjoyed by women and children were those 'given' to them by the husband or father. White women had primarily a chattel status, particularly in the Southern part of the country. They were expected to remain chaste until marriage while white Southern males were permitted, or often encouraged, to sow their wild oats before, during and after marriage.[8]

A double standard of sexual behavior allowing premarital sex for men while denying it to women, always poses the problem of what females will provide the source of sexual gratification for bachelor males. There is adequate historical evidence that black slave women were forced into various sexual associations with white males because of their captive status. That physical compulsion was necessary to secure compliance on the part of black women is documented by Frazier, in relating this young man's story:

> Approximately a century and a quarter ago, a group of slaves were picking cotton on a plantation near where Troy, Alabama, is now located. Among them was a Negro woman, who despite her position, carried herself like a queen and was tall and stately. The overseer (who was the plantation owner's son) sent her to the house on some errand. It was necessary to pass through a wooded pasture to reach the house and the overseer intercepted her in the woods and forced her to put

her head between the rails in an old stake and rider fence, and there in that position my great-great-grandfather was conceived.[9]

Thus, the double-standard of premarital sexual behavior allowed the Southern white woman to remain "pure" and the bodies of the captive female slaves became the objects of their ruler's sexual passion. Consequently, black males had to be suppressed to prevent them from daring to defend the black woman's honor. For those black males who would not accept their suppression passively, the consequences were severe. As one person reports the story of his father's defense of his mother:

> His right ear had been cut off close to his head, and he had received a hundred lashes on his back. He had beaten the overseer for a brutal assault on my mother, and this was his punishment. Furious at such treatment, my father became a different man, and was so morose, disobedient, and intractable, that Mr. N. decided to sell him. He accordingly parted with him, not long after, to his son, who lived in Alabama; and neither mother nor I ever heard from him again.[10]

During the period of slavery, the physical resistance of black males to the rape of their women was met with all the brutal punishment white society could muster. That they were not totally successful in their efforts to crush the black man is evidenced in the heroic deeds of Denmark Vesey, Nat Turner, Frederick Douglass, David Walker and others. The acts of these black males are sometimes played down in favor of the efforts of Harriet Tubman, Sojourner Truth and other black females in securing the slave's freedom. Such favoritism can be expected of a racist society bent on perpetuating the myth of a black female matriarchy, with males pictured as ineffective husbands and fathers who are mere caricatures of real men. The literary castration of the black male is illustrated by the best selling novel, *The Confessions of Nat Turner*,[11] which generated much heat and little light, in terms of understanding one of the most important black revolutionists of his time.

The cultural stereotype of the domineering black woman belies the existence of the masses of black women who constituted a defenseless group against the onslaught of white racism in its most virulent sexual and economic manifestations. That black women are still involuntarily subjected to the white male's lust is reflected in the revelations of a white employer to John Howard Griffin, as reported in his book, *Black Like Me*:

He told me how all of the white men in the region crave colored girls. He said he hired a lot of them both for housework and in his business. "And I guarantee you, I've had it in every one of them before they ever get on the payroll."

"Surely some refuse," I suggested cautiously.
"Not if they want to eat—or feed their kids," he snorted. "If they don't put out, they don't get the job."[12]

Black women have frequently been slandered by the cultural folklore that the only free people in the South were the white man and the black woman. While there have been a few black women who have gained material rewards and status through the dispensation of their sexual favors to white men, the massive indictment of all black women for the acts of a few only creates unnecessary intra-group antagonisms and impedes the struggle for black self-determination.

Many proponents of the black matriarchy philosophy assert that the black female gained ascendency in black society through her economic support of the family. Although the unemployment rate of black males is disproportionately higher than that of white males, only a very small minority of black families with both parents present are dependent on the mother for their maintenance. It is a rather curious use of logic to assume that black females, who in 1960 earned an annual wage of $2,372 a year as compared to the annual wage of $3,410 for white women and $3,789 for black men,[13] have an economic advantage over any group in this society.

However, what semblance of black female dominance that is found in our society can be traced to the persistent rate of high unemployment among black males which prevents them from becoming the major economic support of their family. The economic causes of female dominance are manifest. For instance, the percentage of black women in the labor market declines as the percentage of black males employed in manufacturing and mechanical industries is increasing. The effect of higher black male employment is the male's added responsibility for his family's support; the authority of the wife declines and that of the husband increases.

Many black men have not been permitted to become the kings of their castles. If black women wanted to work, there was always employment for them—even during depressions. Sometimes it was even a higher kind of work than that available to black men. Historically, black males have suffered from irregularity of employment more than any other segment of the American proletariat. Thus, they have been placed in a weak economic position which prevents them from becoming steady providers for their families. Any inordinate power that black women possess, they owe to white America's racist employment barriers. The net effect of this phenomenon is, in reality, not black female dominance but greater economic deprivation for families deprived of the father's income.

The myth of a black matriarchy was strengthened by the Moynihan Report released in 1965.[14] Moynihan's central thesis was that the black family was crumbling and that a major part of the blame lay with the black matriarchy extant in the black community. Some of the evidence cited would lack credibility to all but a group bent on making the victim responsible for the crimes of the criminal. Such sources of proof as the higher educational level of black females vis-à-vis black males conveniently overlook the alternative possibility—that many black males are forced to terminate their formal education early in order to help support their family. Instead, they cite the wholly unsupported statement by a "Negro" expert that, "Historically, in the matriarchal society, mothers made sure that if one of their children had a chance for higher education the daughter was the one to pursue it."[15] In a society where men are expected to have a greater amount of education and earn a higher income, it is difficult to imagine black women celebrating the fact that over 60 percent of the college degrees awarded American blacks are received by women. The end result of this disparity, according to one study, is that almost 50 percent of black female college graduates are married to men employed at a lower socio-economic level than their wives.[16]

Moreover, according to Moynihan and his cohorts, the black matriarchy is responsible for the low educational achievements of black males. In marshalling this arsenal of evidence, Moynihan was apparently unable to find any likelihood that the racist educational system, with its concomitant racist teachers, bore any responsibility for the failure of black males to reach acceptable educational levels by white standards. In the criminalization of the victim, countervailing evidence is dismissed out of hand. The fact that black schools are more likely to be housed in inadequate buildings, with inferior facilities, staffed by inexperienced and racist teachers and overcrowded,[17] only confuses the issue, especially when there is a matriarchal structure that is more handily blamed.

According to the "experts" on the black family, the black male is harshly exploited by the black matriarchy. Many black mothers, they report, express an open preference for girls.[18] This charge is confirmed by a white psychologist, described by a major magazine as devoid of any racism, who states that black males have an inordinate hatred for their mothers.[19] Although there are research studies that reveal no sex-role preference on the part of black mothers,[20] it appears that the practitioners of white social science have not been content with pitting husband against wife but also wish to turn sons against mothers, brothers against sisters. The evidence for these assumptions is not only flimsy, but in some cases also non-existent. If the research is similar to other psychological studies, they have probably used a sample of ten blacks, who, on the verge of a psychotic breakup, wandered into their mental clinic.

These charges of black men hating their mothers must be very puzzling to the black mothers aware of them. They would be puzzled because they realize that if a preference is shown for any sex-role in the black family, it would more likely be expressed in favor of the male child. The problems of raising a black male child in a racist society have been great. Many black mothers out of fear—real or fancied —repressed the aggressive tendencies of their sons in order to save them from the white man's chopping block. For to act as a man in a society which feared his masculinity, the black male was subject to the force of brutal white retaliation. The black mother had to constantly live with the realization that her son might be killed for exercising the prerogatives of manhood. For those black mothers who exorcised their son's aggressive drives out of concern for their safety, hatred seems to be an inappropriate, and most improbable, response.

In addition to the host of pathologies putatively generated by the black matriarchy, the familiar theory of a relationship between fatherless homes and juvenile delinquency is brought up again. While there is nothing inherently wrong with a woman heading a family, the problem arises when she tries to compete in a society which promotes, expects and rewards male leadership. Consequently, she is unable to bring to her family the share of the social and economic rewards received by father-headed households. It is this very factor that probably accounts for any discernible correlation between mother-headed households and juvenile delinquency. The children in a fatherless home are frequently relegated to the lowest living standards in our society. The problems facing husbandless women with children are compounded by the inequities in American society based on sex role ascriptions.

It is impossible to state that the black woman is just like the women of other races. Her history is different from that of the prototypical white woman and her present-day behavioral patterns have evolved out of her historical experiences. In general, she is more aggressive and independent than white women. There are studies that show that black females are more non-conforming than white females as early as age ten. The reason for her greater self-reliance is that it has been a necessary trait in order for her and her children to survive in a racist and hostile society. Moreover, the society has permitted her more self-assertion than the white female.

Among male chauvinists, aggressiveness per se may be considered an undesirable trait in women and should be restricted to the male species. But this is all part of the age-old myth about the inherent nature of woman as a passive creature. More often than not, it has served as a subterfuge for the exploitation of women for the psychological and material gain of the male species. Black women lose nothing by their greater tenacity. That tenacity has, historically, been a source of strength in the black community. While white women have entered the history books for making flags and engaging in social work, black women have participated in the total black liberation struggle.

While recognizing these differences, the question before us now is how much power do black women really have and how is it exercised? Power is commonly defined as the ability to dominate men, to compel their action even against their wishes.[21]

The black woman has often been characterized as a more powerful figure in the family because she participates more in making decisions about what kind of car to buy, where to go on a vacation, etc.[22] In certain cases, she is the only one to make major decisions. A closer inspection of her decision-making powers often reveals that she does not make decisions counter to husband's wishes, but renders them because he fails to do so. The reason he defers to her in certain decisions is simply because she is better equipped to make them. Usually, she has more formal education than her mate and in matters relating to the white society, she knows her way around better. She is more familiar with the machinations of white bureaucracies since contacts with the white world have been more available to black women than to black men.

Making decisions that black men cannot, or will not, make is a poor measure of the power a black woman has in the family. The chances are good that no decisions are made which he actively opposes. The power of black women is much like American democracy—it is more apparent than real. Power alignments are frequently based on the alternatives an individual has in a situation where there is a conflict of interests. It is here where the black male achieves the upper level of the power dimension.

Whenever a black man and black woman find themselves in objective and irremediable conflict, the best solution is to find another mate. The objective reality of black women is that black men are scarcer than hen's teeth. For a variety of reasons, there is an extremely low sex ratio in the black community, especially during the marriageable years—18 to 45 years.[23] This means that black women must compete for a relatively scarce commodity when they look forward to marriage. They are buyers in a seller's market. Black women, like all women, have their affectional and sexual needs. Many a black male's shortcomings must be tolerated for the sake of affection and companionship. In a sense, many black women have to take love on male terms.

The low sex ratio hardly allows black women to exercise any meaningful control over black men. In fact, as one black woman states:

> As long as she is confined to an area in which she must compete fiercely for a mate, she remains the object of sexual exploitation and the victim of all the social evils which such exploitation involves.

> In the Negro population, the excess of girls is greatest in the fifteen-to-forty-four age group which covers the college years and the age when most marriages occur ... the explosive social implications of an excess of more than half a million Negro girls and women over fourteen years of age are obvious. ... How much of the tensions and conflicts traditionally associated with the matriarchal framework of Negro society are in reality due to this imbalance and the pressures it generates.[24]

Another index of the matriarchy is simply the percentage of female-headed households in the black community. The Moynihan theory of the black matriarchy derives from his findings that 25 percent of all black families have a female head. This "proof" of a matriarchal family structure brings up many interesting questions, not excluding the important one: over whom do these women have control?

Logically, the only power they have is to face a super-exploitation by the system of white racism that bi-parental black families do not encounter to the same degree.

The matriarchal myth is not always applied to only black families. A number of social scientists claim that suburban white families are matriarchal. They point out that the commuting father's disappearance during the day leaves the mother in charge of the home and children. As a result, the father's power is reduced in these areas, and he is relegated to enacting the "feminine" role of handyman.[25] This observation has prompted one person to suggest that exhorting black slum dwellers to emulate the presumably more stable white middle-class, restore father to his rightful place, and build a more durable family life will subsequently expose them to the threat of the suburban matriarchy.[26]

Any profound analysis of the black matriarchy proposition should reveal its fallacious underpinnings. Recognition of this fact raises the crucial question as to why white society continues to impose this myth on the consciousness of black people. This writer submits that it has been functional for the white ruling class, through its ideological apparatus, to create internal antagonisms in the black community between black men and black women to divide them and to ward off effective attacks on the external system of white racism. It is a mere manifestation of the divide-and-conquer strategy, used by most ruling classes through the annals of man, to continue the exploitation of an oppressed group.

In the colonial period of Algeria, the same situation existed wherein the colonists attempted to use the female population to continue their colonial rule. Fanon reports that the colonial administration devised a political doctrine for destroying the structure of Algerian society. By encouraging Algerian women to break the bonds of male domination in their society—setting male against female—the colonialists hoped to dilute the Algerian capacity for resistance. According to Fanon, it was:

> the woman who was given the historic mission of shaking up the Algerian man. Converting the woman, winning her over to the foreign values, wrenching her free from her status, was at the same time achieving a real power over the man and attaining a practical, effective means of destroying Algerian culture.[27]

In contemporary America, a female liberation movement is beginning to gain impetus.[28] This movement is presently dominated by white women seeking to break out of the centuries-old bondage imposed upon them by the male chauvinists of the ruling class. Whether black women should participate in such a movement is questionable. Hatred of a social curse which is part and parcel of an exploitative society that discriminates not only against blacks but also women should not be confused with hatred of men. The adversary is not one sex or the other—it is the racist, capitalist system which needs, breeds and preys upon oppressions of all types.

Any movement that augments the sex-role antagonisms extant in the black community will only sow the seed of disunity and hinder the liberation struggle. Whether black women will participate in a female liberation movement is, of course, up to them. One, however, must be cognizant of the need to avoid a diffusion of energy devoted to the liberation struggle lest it dilute the over-all effectiveness of the movement. Black women cannot be free *qua* women until all blacks attain their liberation.

The role of the black woman in the black liberation struggle is an important one and cannot be forgotten. From her womb have come the revolutionary warriors of our time.[29] The revolutionary vanguard has a male leadership but the black woman has stepped beside her man engaged in struggle and given him her total faith and commitment. She has thrust herself into the life or death struggle to destroy the last vestige of racism and exploitation in the American social structure. In the process of continuing her life-long fight against racist oppression, the myth of her matriarchal nature will soon join the death agony of America's racist empire. Until that time arrives, the black woman should be revered and celebrated—not only for her historical deeds in the building of African civilization, in the struggle to maintain the black peoples of America as a viable entity—but for her contemporary role in enabling black people to forge ahead in their efforts to achieve a black nationhood.

NOTES

1. George Breitman, *Malcolm X Speaks*. New York: Merit Publishers, 1965.
2. J. J. Bachofen, *Das Mutterrecht*, Stuttgart, 1861.
3. Margaret Mead, *Male and Female*, New York: William Morrow and Company, 1949, p. 301.
4. William Goode, *The Family*, Englewood Cliffs, New Jersey: Prentice-Hall, Inc., 1964, p. 14.

5. John Hope Franklin, *From Slavery to Freedom,* New York: Random House, 1947.

6. E. Franklin Frazier, *The Negro Family in the United States,* Chicago: University of Chicago Press, 1939, p. 7.

7. Maurice Davie, *Negroes in American Society,* New York: McGraw-Hill, 1949, p. 207.

8. Arthur W. Calhoun, *A Social History of the American Family,* New York: Barnes and Noble, 1919.

9. E. F. Frazier, *op. cit.,* p. 53.

10. *Ibid.,* p. 48.

11. William Styron, *The Confessions of Nat Turner,* New York: Random House, 1967.

12. John Howard Griffin, *Black Like Me,* New York: Signet, 1963.

13. *United States Census of Population Report,* 1960.

14. *The Negro Family: The Case for National Action,* United States Department of Labor, 1965.

15. Whitney Young, *To Be Equal,* New York: McGraw-Hill, 1964, p. 25.

16. Jean Noble, *The Negro Woman College Graduate,* New York: Columbia University Press, 1956, p. 64.

17. *Equality of Educational Opportunity,* United States Department of Health, Education and Welfare, Office of Education, 1966.

18. Thomas F. Pettigrew, *A Profile of the Negro American,* Princeton, New Jersey: D. Van Nostrand, 1964, p. 16.

19. The particular psychologist in question, Herbert Hendin, was quoted in *Newsweek,* November 17, 1966, pp. 119–120.

20. Robert Bell, *The One-Parent Mother in the Negro Lower Class,* Unpublished paper presented to the Eastern Sociological Society, 1965.

21. Henry P. Fairchild, *Dictionary of Sociology and Related Sciences,* Totowa, N.J.: Littlefield, Adams and Co., 1965, p. 227.

22. Robert O. Blood, Jr., and Donald Wolfe, *Husbands and Wives,* New York: The Free Press, 1960.

23. In New York City, for instance, there are only 75 black men for every 100 black women in about this same age range.

24. Paula Murray, *The Negro Woman in the Quest for Equality,* paper presented at Leadership Conference, National Council of Negro Women (Washington, D.C., November 1963), pp. 11–12, 12–18.

25. Ernest W. Burgess and Harvey J. Locke, *The Family,* New York: American Book Co., 1960, p. 112.

26. Eric Josephson. "The Matriarchy: Myth and Reality," *The Family Coordinator,* 1969, pp. 18, 268–276.

27. Frantz Fanon, *A Dying Colonialism,* tr. by Haakon Chevalier, New York: Grove Press, 1967, p. 39.

28. See Evelyn Reed, *Problems of Women's Liberation,* New York: Merit

Publishers, 1969, for one white radical's approach to the matriarchal origin of society question.

29. It is interesting to note that, despite unfounded rumors about the emasculation of the black male, the thrust of the black liberation struggle has been provided almost exclusively by a black male leadership. In selecting leaders of black organizations, black females inevitably defer to some competent black male, an act which shows how much they really prefer the dominating position they supposedly have in black society.

3

THE ISSUE OF INTERRACIAL MATING

Doris Y. Wilkinson

Since the earliest beginnings of slavery in European colonial America, color and sex have been intricately interwoven in the definitions and social fabric of all interracial relationships. The juxtaposition of these two status attributes, which has taken on deeply rooted cultural, psychological, and political meaning, has resulted in relatively standardized behavioral patterns between males and females legally or customarily defined as racially different. The idea of selecting mates from racial groups other than one's own is accompanied by predictable responses acquired through a long period of indoctrination to America's color ideology. Myths, stigmas, and culturally induced fears, ingrained in the society's normative ideology, engulf interracial unions—especially the most frequent trans-color matching, the black male-white female dyadic unit. Yet the distinct character of this partnership, whatever its historical and symbolic dimensions, reflects a unique arrangement of color-sex role relationships in the universe of male-female interactions and mate selection.

The mating process can be examined from a number of differ-

189

ent levels of analysis. To mate at the social psychological level of usage simply means to associate with as a counterpart or as members of an affectional pair. In this connection a mate may be an habitual role partner of equal or unequal rank, or a tentative counter-role performer in a transient interpersonal encounter. Sociologically, mating, if it assumes the quality of relative permanence, refers to the establishment of a family nucleus or at least the formation of prolonged associational ties. With respect to bio-genetics, it may be thought of primarily in terms of the propagation of offspring. Operating as a functional prerequisite for a society's survival, mating represents a natural process of biological matching or breeding for the purpose of perpetuating a species, although it may serendipitously eliminate another. Serendipitous population elimination refers to the unanticipated and unplanned consequences of racial intermixing. It results in genotypic and phenotypic hybrids.

In her work on the *Sexual Life Between Blacks and Whites,* Beth Day probes hidden fears permeating potential black male-white female mating. She scrutinizes the range of emotions which exist in America toward black-white dyadic relationships in general. The various psycho-social states establish predispositions which elicit diverse individual and collective responses ranging from mild hate stares to violent crime, to the enactment of legislation for the prevention of cross color bonding. According to Day, at one time in our recent history forty of the fifty states had regulations prohibiting marriage outside one's color category, and as late as 1968 a number of Southern and border states carried the negatively labeled "miscegenation" laws. Only in the past decade have large numbers of states begun to remove anti-trans-color mating and marriage statutes from their records. Although a spectacular growth in the rate of black-white marriages is not envisioned, Day predicts a lessening in alleged sexual fears of whites toward color mixed unions.

Despite prohibitive mating bond norms, black male-white female marital pairs have, according to recent census data and research, increased. In evaluating the legal and social aspects of interracial alliances, Blackwell points out that the actual numbers of white males taking black wives dropped from 25,913 in 1960 to 23,566 in 1970, but the numbers of black men marrying white women showed an upsurge from slightly over 25,000 to over 41,000. Downs contends, in the selection on "Black/White Dating," that the dramatic growth in the frequency of inter-ethnic and trans-color contact leading to dating and marriage began in the politically liberal decade of the 60's. Yet in spite of that activist, consciousness raising milieu and the formation of greater numbers of interracial liasons, negative stereotypes and degrading stigmas remain intact.

With the evolution of "black awareness," and a shared mood of anticipated ideological solidarity, black males were criticized by their community constituents for crossing color boundaries in marrying white women. Their actions were viewed as violating intragroup rules of racial distance. Black females argued that any black male who selects a white female for a partner lacks the political consciousness necessary for the establishment of black unification. Controversy exists regarding the political nature of such mating bonds, although Hernton indicates that many black males have used the "negritude" concept to exploit white women. My own selection on the social psychological aspects of expectations and salience in interracial encounters suggests that the perception of the meaning of "negritude" serves to heighten the psycho-sexual imagery of a black male. Such themes add an intensity to the expectations for a black male's role behavior.

Moreover, Downs observes that young white college women frequently have heard about or experienced the well rehearsed "Black Rap" during their freshman years. At the social interactional level, the "Black Rap" communication format represents a masking game involving mutual pseudo-deception in which a white female either permits or is deceived by a black male's playing at an idolized and symbolic masculine role. At the same time, many young black female college students have been left on the periphery of social circles with relatively limited options, and far fewer of them mate across color lines.

Frequent association and cultural exchange are viewed as significant catalysts in increasing inter-color mating. However, to date, this contact and interaction have had no measurable impact on the reduction of racist myths. Color exogamy has not decreased institutionalized white racism. Numerous personal problems still confront those who intermarry. These range from the future of the partnership in a social order which stigmatizes the relationship, to how to rear children in a contradictory familial milieu, to what labels should be used in defining the identity of offspring. America's color conscious legislative history has established various labels: mulattoes, octoroons, quadroons.

A 1971 Harris poll identified significant and prevailing

historically-based, anti-cross color mating attitudes. Forty percent of those questioned agreed with the view that, "it seems to violate God's law for people of different races to marry and produce mixed-blood children." Half of those polled expressed verbally that, "any white girl who goes out with a black man is going to ruin her reputation." Yet in spite of these prevailing, historically-rooted sentiments and the sustaining normative prohibitions, interracial dating and marriage continue.

Hernton describes the African American male's preoccupation with the white female in terms of prolonged idolization and tabus surrounding her. From his perspective, such customs have produced a socio-sexuality which induces a predisposition toward white women in large numbers of black males. He observes that no white American can grasp the nature of socialization for the black male growing up in the South. Paradoxically, according to Hernton, the white female symbolizes both freedom and bondage in the mind and life of the Southern black male. While emphasis is placed on socialization in Southern culture, Hernton evaluates the pervasiveness of this psychological state nationally and how it permeates bi-racial mating bonds, particularly the cultural linkage between a white female and a black male. To what extent Hernton's general social psychological thesis will be confirmed or negated in the 1980's and throughout the remainder of this century will depend on how black males, especially those who have acquired the requisite analytic tools for comprehending their political history in a racist society, enact their cultural biographies.

THE HIDDEN FEAR*

Beth Day

> *It has been suggested that "sex" is at the*
> *root of many problems in the racial field*
> JOHN DOLLARD

In March 1965 a white matron, Viola Liuzzo, was shot and killed in Alabama by a white man unknown to her when he saw her driving her car with a black male passenger sitting beside her.

A scant two years later, in September 1967, Peggy Rusk, daughter of the then U.S. Secretary of State Dean Rusk, married her girlhood black sweetheart, Guy Smith, in a formal church ceremony that was attended by both sets of parents. Apart from an insignificant handful of crank letters received by the State Department and a few tasteless jokes, the interracial marriage was handled, received, and reported with quiet dignity.

The range of emotion displayed here, from the violent hatred expressed in the Liuzzo murder to the calm acceptance of the Rusk-Smith marriage, reflects the ambivalance that exists in this country toward black/white couples. Whereas blacks have long been aware that one of the most virulent, emotion-packed bases that supports our racial caste system is sexual fear and hatred, all but a handful of whites have chosen to ignore it, or stubbornly deny it. When Norman Mailer suggested (in an article in *The Independent* in 1957) that resistance to school integration in the South lay primarily in white sex fears, he

*From *Sexual Life Between Blacks and Whites* by Beth Day, © 1972, pp. 1-17. Reprinted with permission from Thomas Y. Crowell Company, Inc., New York.

was roundly chided on all sides—a remonstrance that included a lady-like sniff of "horrible" from Eleanor Roosevelt. When Mailer later expounded the interracial sexual theme in *The White Negro*, equating the American black with sexual forces that were compelling to the white hipster who was trying to disengage himself from conventional society, he again drew the wrath of his readers, including that of black essayist and novelist James Baldwin who accused Mailer of further festering race relations with his stereotype of black as sex.

Societal rage falls with catholic impartiality in anyone, black or white, who persists in bringing up the interracial sexual theme. Baldwin himself, long acclaimed by whites, was temporarily out of favor because of production of his stinging play *Blues for Mister Charlie*. Loosely based on the case of the fourteen-year-old Chicago black Emmett Till, who was murdered in Mississippi for whistling at a white woman, the play dramatically illustrated the white male sex fear of blacks, and showed also that, far from being an innocent child, Till himself was a sexually mature teen-ager who bragged about his white conquests and taunted his murderer. The play was received with a mixture of embarrassment, confusion, and distress. The one reviewer —Tom Driver, then drama critic of *The Reporter*—who spelled out the sexual-racial theme of the play had his review canceled and eventually resigned over the incident. The review—which Max Ascoli, the liberal founder and editor of *The Reporter*, called "rabble-rousing" —later appeared in *The Village Voice*.

William Bradford Huie, who researched and reported the Till case, first for *Look* magazine and then at greater length in book form, showed in his re-creation of the crime and record of the subsequent trial that Till's real sin was his bullheaded persistence in behaving like a man. His abductors, the husband of the offended woman and the husband's half brother, had actually first thought only to scare the boy and "chase his black ass back to Chicago." But their young victim refused to cry out when they beat him, or to show fear, grovel, or plead for mercy. "What else could we do?" the brother, Ben Milam, explained helplessly to the court, "except kill him?"

Whenever an American black male attempts publicly to assert his manhood—by such traditionally masculine behavior as acting aggressively or competitively toward other males, or fighting for what he believes are his rights—white society is apt to react with a psychopathic display of fear and rage that spills over into such apparently unrelated areas as education, housing, employment, voting rights, and welfare. Black males are allowed to participate in American society and to reap some of its rewards provided that they fall into one of three categories that are comfortable for the white male's view of himself:

1. *The Bright Child.* This includes all blacks under the age of eight, most actors, comedians, and musicians. A black male may remain a Bright Child until any chronological age provided that he does not threaten the status quo. (An example of the Bright Child is the late Louis Armstrong.)
2. *The Black Egghead.* These are the seemingly sexless, totally cerebral, nonthreatening black scholars, educators, judges, and some ministers (not Adam Clayton Powell) —men whose public appearance and behavior are godlike and dignified, such as Ralph Bunche or Thurgood Marshall.
3. *The Black Jocks.* The "all brawn and no brains" athletes. It is acceptable, apparently, for a black male to be an animal provided that he is all animal. One of the best comments on this arbitrary dichotomy is recorded in Jim Toback's book *Jim*, on black athlete-cum-actor-cum-businessman Jim Brown, when Brown told Toback, "I'm supposed to be an animal . . . a big bad evil spook who can't think and talk. I'm supposed to rely on my size and strength. . . . That's bullshit. . . . All real victories are psychological."

Probably no single man ever enraged so many people as prize-fighter Jack Johnson, who persisted in defeating white challengers and marrying white women (he had four white wives). Laws were created to stop him; a white champion, Jess Willard, was enticed out of retirement to fight (and hopefully kill) him. Johnson was exiled, chased with writs and subpoenas. He was dragged into court on the Mann Act (for traveling across a state line with a known prostitute). He was called a brute for sleeping with a white woman, who announced publicly that he was the best lover she had ever had. That the venom against Johnson obtains to this day was attested when white actress Jane Alexander, who starred with James Earl Jones in the Howard Sackler play about Johnson (*The Great White Hope*), was showered with hate mail and obscenities when the play opened.

On a lesser but nonetheless indicative level, we find the recent federal harassment of Muhammed Ali (Cassius Clay) over his religious convictions, which the Supreme Court chose first of all to deny could be sincere, although they later reversed themselves; and FBI director J. Edgar Hoover's use of Martin Luther King's extramarital activities as a lever to silence his criticism of the FBI.

Throughout history men have always sought out others they

could feel superior to. In America's case, the black man furnished a convenient subject for inferior status by virtue of his slavery. Unfortunately, following the abolition of slavery, the black man was not able to work up out of his caste position because of the stigmata of color. Unlike the later arriving immigrants—the Irish, Italians, and Jews—the black has never been able to achieve upward mobility into the power class simply by disappearing into the mass of society (except for those light-skinned enough to "pass"). Black is always visible. No matter what the black achieves in this country, he remains a victim of caste.

There is a story that blacks tell about the white mother and the black mother in a maternity ward. The white mother looks at her son proudly and murmurs, "Who knows? Someday you may be president!" and the black mother gazes sadly at her baby and says, "Son, forgive me for what I've done!"

A white male born in this country qualifies for American manhood when he is born with a white skin. What he does with his life depends to a large extent upon his individual abilities and limitations. The black male has no such clear options open to him. No matter how intelligent he is or how much he may aspire to achieve, there is no guarantee that any amount of effort on his part will earn him the rewards of status, identity, or power that the democratic system promises. And as for his manhood, he will probably have to battle for its recognition throughout the course of his life.

Locked into a psychologically confusing position—with the democratic promise of a free competitive society on the one hand and societal pressure to keep him down to a caste level from which, with his black skin, he cannot hope to escape, on the other—the black male is severely handicapped in attaining masculine identity and status. He may go through the long medical school grind and not find a hospital where he can practice or take his patients; he may achieve a master's degree in education or psychology only to discover that the sole job open to him is sorting mail at the post office. He can make a million dollars and not be eligible to buy a house in the suburbs that is available to a white prostitute or to a member of the Mafia. If he does manage to complete a college degree he can be assured that he will receive an income thirty percent less than that of a white male with similar qualifications. He also will die seven years sooner.

The black psychiatrists, such as William Grier, Price Cobbs, and Alvin Poussaint, who deal firsthand with the psychic problems of black alienation, have charted the psychic and physical damage done to the male who is not allowed to compete successfully as an adult. The results are professional anxiety, early failure, escape into the addictions of alcohol and drugs. Physical manifestations include a higher incidence of hypertension than that suffered by white males, and, for urban males between the ages of twenty and thirty-five, a higher rate of suicide.

Ironically, the one area in which the black male can compete successfully with the white male is in bed. Within this single human activity the black man can know he is equal to the white man. Sexually, outside of dangerous pockets in the Deep South, he is a free agent. Moreover, the white man has told him that sexually he is superior. In slave days, when white slaveowners enjoyed black slave women clandestinely, they needed to set up some barrier between their white women and black men so that the white women would not do likewise. Mulatto babies, who usually stayed with the black mother, took her status as slave, and posed no threat to the white power structure. But mulatto babies at the breasts of white mothers posed quite another problem. If the white mother had kept the baby and persisted in giving him such white advantages as education, this hybrid child might threaten white power. To insure against such a threatening possibility, a white myth about black men emerged, designed to keep white women away from them.

Without any anatomy books around to dispute them, the white men said that a black man is sexually dangerous for a white woman. It'll hurt, they warned the women (that is, the black penis is bigger). Your babies will be sickly, inferior mongrels (black and white races can't mix—a rather peculiar theory in the light of all those pretty, healthy mulatto babies running around the slave quarters).

The man in Alabama who shot Viola Liuzzo was echoing the white southern edict: We told you to stay away from black men. You didn't take our warning. You didn't accept our protection. So—there's nothing for it but to kill you.

One of the sad features about that theory is that the white women never did ask to be protected from those black men. It was their fathers', husbands', and brothers' idea. So far as the controls went that were used to keep everyone in his prescribed place during the feudal slave society, white women were as much victims of the system as black men. They were allowed no sexual freedom of choice. The very sound reason behind that was that white men, who were so powerfully attracted to black women, were afraid that their own upper-caste women might prove equally attracted to black men. Such a turn of events would have been disastrous to the social order.

They were, of course, correct. Both men and women have been crossing racial lines sexually ever since Moses was chided for his preference for an Ethiopian woman. Romans—apparently both male and female—enjoyed black lovers, as did Arabs, Turks, Persians, and Hindus. (The mother of the present king of Morocco [Hassan II] was his father's favorite black concubine.) That peripatetic Victorian, Sir Richard Burton, noted that most wealthy Near Eastern white males kept black concubines, and those black eunuchs who were so fortunate as to have had their penises left intact were favorite sexual partners for the sultan's harem (detesticled, they never ejaculated, never tired). More recently, white South Africans have flooded into Swaziland in such numbers seeking black sex that in January 1972 Swaziland considered enacting its own restricting law—not against intermarriage but against interracial sex, to try to cut down on its unwanted white guests.

As thousands of adult black African males were separated from their own culture and brought as slaves into this country, repressive controls, through myth and eventually law, quickly evolved to keep these displaced men away from sexual contact with white women (it was not until the 1840s that there were as many black women as men). To justify the enslavement of other men in a so-called democratic society, it was, first of all, necessary for whites to believe that black men were not human beings. So they convinced themselves that blacks were not men at all—they were merely beasts of labor, without minds or souls. And as mindless beasts their only mission in life was physical toil and the procreation of more slaves. So far as sexual contact with white women was concerned, these black men were to be feared and shunned.

While the fantasy of black beasts with bull-sized genitals may have caused gently reared antebellum southern ladies to faint, or project their sublimated sexual drive onto the black man with hysterical cries of "Rape," it had a different effect in recent times on more liberated women. One of the ironies of the myth of black supersexuality is that it drove so many carnally curious white women in hot pursuit of black men.

The sexual myth has backfired badly in all ways. The white man invented it to frighten white women away from black men. But when he fears that it may, indeed, be true, he becomes neurotically concerned with his own sexual performance. Also, by the persistent social emasculation of black males, white males inadvertently created a situation in which sex is the one area where a black man can successfully compete with his rival and enemy, the white man.

The racial battle being waged today in America is for blacks to have access to the same freedoms and status that whites enjoy. But since the white man remains so reluctant to share the power structure, the black man's main successful area of competition is still sexual. It is not surprising that even the coolest and most cerebral black man may feel compelled to channel his aspiration for status into sexual detours, substituting sexual prowess for professional success. Both he and his oppressor have become unwitting partners in perpetuating the myth of black sexuality, participating in a sexual contest that is doing untold damage to the human relationships between all blacks and whites.

The desire for the black man to prove himself sexually with a white partner has provoked a bitter conflict between black males and black females, just at a time when they most need to consolidate their ranks in their joint struggle for freedom. With fewer black males than black females in number and fewer black males than black females with higher education, the black/black marriage market is difficult at best. Observing many of the best educated, most advantaged of the "brothers" taking their detour to maturity via the white woman's bed is a sore point with many black women.

The competition for black men has also succeeded in building a wall of distrust and anger between black women and white women, when cooperation could be valuable in breaking down the barriers of discriminatory employment practices and in pressing for more female political power.

The myth of black supersexuality also puts the white woman who is genuinely attracted to a black man in the potential position of being sexually exploited—a pawn in the revenge that the black male seeks to wreak on the white male for his history of oppression.

For many years the liberal view in America held, in the interests of good racial relations, that sex fears and fantasies were not a basis of racism, and that interracial sex was the very "last thing on the list" for aspiring blacks. Gunnar Myrdal had shown the desire for interracial marriage ranking seventh on the list of things blacks wanted (in precisely the reverse order to what whites feared). And in one profound sense the liberal view was correct. Blacks certainly needed freedom more than they needed interracial sex. But by the unfortunate fluke of white sexual mythology coupled with the white caste system, sex was to become the principal social activity available to the black, and the black man's desire to share a piece of the power pie often became subverted to sexual drive. An interracial sexual encounter became almost a ritual experience for the young black male in search of his masculine identity. Black males migrating to the northern cities from southern states in the great migrations of World War I and World War II traditionally celebrated their arrival with a white sex partner. Once the black male had proved himself a man by sleeping with "The Ogre" (as Eldridge Cleaver calls the white woman), he could then get on with other more important business.

In a similar vein, black GIs and travelers abroad often made it part of their personal odyssey to sleep with a nonblack woman. Each black man who arrived by boat train to that black Eden, Paris, during the black exodus to France in the twenties and thirties, promptly shacked up with a French girl. It did not really matter whether she was a countess or prostitute—it was a rite of black manhood. Black GIs all over the world practiced the same tradition, which accounts for the thousands of mixed-race children in Germany, England, and Vietnam. What was originally intended as a means of keeping the black man in his place served in the long run to provoke him into becoming an international sexual athlete. And so long as white society persists in denying him other avenues of masculine aggression, many a black man will go on getting his revenge in bed.

Despite all the societal and psychological obstacles, both temporary and permanent interracial relationships continue to increase. As to precisely how many people this involves, it is impossible to say. On the marriage level, the known interracial couples represent only about one-half of one percent of all marriages, affecting roughly no more than two percent of the total black population, and an infinitesimal percentage of whites.

There are no accurate statistics on interracial marriage. The 1960 census reported a known 51,000 black/white married couples, and it is estimated that about 2,400 marry each year. The latest published census (1969) has even less specific information. Eleven states were not included because they have no statewide file on marriage certificates, and of the thirty-six reporting states (which represented only around fifty percent of all marriages) an increasing number are no longer requiring information on the race of the applicants. (New

York, California, and Michigan have deleted "race" from marriage certificates.) The census did show some black/white marriage for nearly every one of the seventeen states that still carry miscegenation statutes, but there was no spectacular rise, nor is any expected. Economist Eli Ginzberg, who has made a study of racial economics, predicts no more than a "modest rise" in black/white intermarriage. "Probably not more than one percent of the Negroes who marry in the next generation," he says, "will marry whites."

None of these statistics or projections, however, includes the unknown numbers of people with black ancestry who "pass" over into the white world each year. Andrew D. Weinberger, a New York attorney and a director of the National Association for the Advancement of Colored People (NAACP), has made a study of miscegenation laws and come up with quite a different picture. Using the passing rate developed by Stuckert in his 1941–1950 study, Weinberger estimated in 1966 that 23,000 people with some black ancestry were passing each year. Even allowing a ten-percent discount for those who might not marry (based on the national percentage) and another ten percent for those who might marry others who had passed, Weinberger arrived at a figure of 550,000 who would probably marry a white partner, bringing the number of mixed couples in the United States up to 600,000 as opposed to the 51,000 couples reported by the Bureau of the Census. Based on the same system, that would mean the current (1971–1972) figure is actually around one million.

In what is probably the last such study possible (made between the time when the miscegenation law was struck down in California and the race of the applicant was deleted from marriage applications), John H. Burma discovered certain trends in mixed marriages in Los Angeles County from 1948 to 1959 that may prove indicative for the rest of the country. Although there was no rush on the marriage bureau immediately after the law against mixed marriage was rescinded (which happened in 1948), there was a gradual, steady increase in mixed marriage, and in the final two years of the study—1957 to 1959 —the intermarriage rate more than doubled. White males proved least likely to out marry, although they accounted for thirty-five percent of the partners. Black females proved more likely to out marry than white females, but less likely to do so than the black males, who out marry in proportionately greater numbers than any other group. (In Los Angeles they represented only seven percent of the population, yet accounted for twenty-seven percent of the mixed marriages.)

As to interracial dating and affairs, there are no estimates available. Most college students live off campus these days, and university deans' offices keep no score on interracial dating. Faculty and students can tell only what they observe. Black/white couples are reported on every integrated campus in the northern, eastern, and western states—and as far south as the University of Texas. In Georgia, Charlayne Hunter, the first black coed to graduate from the University of Georgia, married a white journalism student whom she met there—thus confirming white southern fears that educational propinquity may, indeed, lead to matrimony.

A study of foreign and interracial college dating and marriage conducted in 1966 by Harrop and Ruth Freeman of the Cornell University law department showed that although most campus interracial affairs tended not to culminate in marriage, the percentage of those that did exceeded the national rate of increase in interracial marriage.

Of all civil rights, the right to interracial sex and marriage proved the most incendiary—and the very last to receive national legal sanction. As to whether individual black/white couples chose to marry was actually of little importance to the overall civil rights struggle, and couples could always cross state lines and marry where it was legal. But so long as individuals did not have the freedom to marry the partner of their choice, everyone's civil rights remained in jeopardy.

Yet because the subject was so sensitive, the Supreme Court dragged its heels for nearly a decade after other rights had been assured. At one time forty of the fifty states had statutes against interracial marriage (the offspring of interracial marriage were also considered illegitimate). The issue of miscegenation was presented directly to the Supreme Court in 1954 and again in 1956, but the court ducked a decision by declining jurisdiction, despite its 1954 reading of the Fourteenth Amendment's guarantee of equal rights and equal opportunity to include all citizens "regardless of color."

By 1964 seventeen southern and border states still carried miscegenation laws. That year the court had an opportunity to strike a decisive legal blow to end the states' ban against interracial relationships in the *McLaughlin* v. *Florida* decision. The case concerned a black Honduran hotel worker named McLaughlin who was found to be living with a white waitress. They were arrested for interracial cohabitation and were convicted. There was actually no law against cohabitation in Florida, but there was a law against interracial marriage and against a male and female of different races occupying the same room at night. When the appeal case was heard before the court, James G. Mahorner, an assistant attorney general of the state of Florida, presented the state's case, basing his argument on a particular (and peculiar) reading of the Fourteenth Amendment. The state of Florida claimed that the congressional framers of the amendment really had no intention of upsetting the established laws against miscegenation.

Chief Justice Earl Warren asked Mahorner whether it then followed that a state could constitutionally prohibit marriage between Jews and gentiles.

"No, sir," the attorney answered.

"Why not?" Warren wanted to know.

"We say the intention was expressed as to Negroes and whites," the Floridian explained. He then went on to argue that a state had the right to exert power over marriage and sexual relationships because of the state's responsibility for the welfare of children—that is, the children of a mixed marriage would be at a disadvantage and therefore should not be born (the shaky and uncharitable premise on which most miscegenation laws are based).

The court struck down the Florida ban on interracial cohabitation, but refrained from taking a stand against the ban on marriage.

Three years later, another case involving an interracial relationship appeared before the court. This time there was no avoiding the issue of interracial marriage. A white Virginian, Percy Loving, had married a part-black, part-Indian woman from his home county. They had gone to Washington, D.C., to get married because they could not do so in Virginia, but then had returned to Virginia to live. They were arrested for living together illegally in the state. They pleaded guilty and were offered a curious choice: they could serve a year in jail or be banished from the state, "not to return for twenty-five years." Instead, Loving hid out his family in a rented farm in the friendly community where he and his wife had both been born and reared, then commuted to a job in Washington, D.C., by car. The couple was never seen publicly together. But Loving wanted more than that for his wife and family. In Washington, he appealed to Robert Kennedy, who was then attorney general, and was referred to the American Civil Liberties Union (ACLU), which carried the case through to the Supreme Court. Nine years and three children after his marriage, Loving was at long last, as he proudly put it, able "to put my arm around my wife in the state of Virginia."

This time the case was clearly and simply the right of a black and white to marry, and the court could delay a decision on miscegenation no longer. It struck down Virginia's miscegenation law. In presenting the decision, Chief Justice Warren stated: "Miscegenation statutes adopted by Virginia to prevent marriages between persons solely on the basis of racial classification violate the equal protection and due process clauses of the Fourteenth Amendment." This time there was no doubt how the Fourteenth Amendment was to be read.

With the states' bans struck down once and for all, today's barriers against interracial marriage are social and psychological rather than legal. Perhaps to many segregationists' surprise, now that there are no valid laws against intermarriage, there has been no great run on the marriage market. All those dire prophecies of racial apocalypse that had been shouted from pulpits and state senate floors for a hundred years predicting that if the barriers were ever lifted blacks would stampede for white partners, simply did not materialize. In the four years since the miscegenation law was struck down, there has been no large-scale interracial mixing in the states that had miscegenation laws at the time of the court decision. In a survey made through the facilities of the ACLU during the preparation of this book, it was found that only a scattering of marriages have taken place. Mississippi celebrated its first legal mixed marriage in August 1970 when a white civil rights worker married a black woman in Jackson. In Louisiana, where a mixed couple had been refused a marriage license and had appealed through ACLU when the decision on the Loving case was pending, the federal judge simply postponed his ruling until the Supreme Court handed down its decision, and then ruled in their favor. In two more recent cases, one in Alabama and one in Georgia, applicants who were refused marriage licenses appealed to the Justice Department, which filed against the individual states, overturning their laws. Apart from some isolated reports of harassment from individuals, there has not been much evidence of difficulty.

In the three cases in which state laws have been tested and overturned, the couples involved consisted of white servicemen stationed in the South and their black fiancées. These couples illustrate a strong but little-recognized trend in mixed marriages today in which black women in small communities and rural and farm areas marry white men. Since these couples are seldom visible in urban centers (such as the Los Angeles area, where the Burma study was made) and on college campuses where so many black man/white woman couples are commonly seen, it is erroneously assumed that most interracial dating and marriage is between black men and white women. This idea, first put forward by anthropologist Kingsley Davis, has become so firmly fixed in the public mind that it has regularly been carried unquestioned in articles and even textbooks dealing with interracial marriage. In 1968 an alert sociologist, Lewis F. Carter, decided to investigate the validity of this common assumption and came up with evidence that it may indeed be a full-scale myth. The Bureau of the Census figures of the 51,000 known interracial marriages actually reflect a ratio of one-to-one, hypergamy to hypogamy. Carter projects the theory that the one-to-one ratio may prove valid for all interracial marriages, reported and unreported, as the marriages of black women to white husbands pass relatively unnoted because they are much more apt to occur in rural settings, such as in the landmark Loving case and the servicemen's marriages that tested the state laws. Black women are apt to marry their white husbands at a later age (twenty-six plus), and are likely to meet them either in a job situation, through social work, civil rights organizations or on farms. In support of Carter's thesis of "visibility," three of the four black wife/white husband couples interviewed in the New York area were found to be living outside of the city itself, in suburban or rural communities. In Paris, where the black wife/white husband couple is highly visible as they tend to live within the city for economic reasons, eight out of the ten mixed couples interviewed consisted of a white male (French or American) married to a black female (American or West Indian).

There are more people involved in interracial dating than in marriage, and here, too, we encounter a new trend. Twenty years ago mixed couples were most likely to meet at work, and they both usually lived at a low income level, often being employed in domestic service. Many of the white spouses were foreign-born. Today's young blacks and whites who mix and sometimes marry are most often native-born Americans who usually meet on college campuses or in pursuit of their careers. They are middle rather than lower class, and they both have at least high school education. Of those who do go on and marry, it is likely to be a second marriage for one or both partners; the partners are older than those that marry within their own race and, contrasted to the high percentage of childless mixed couples of a generation ago, the couples will probably have children.

The public attitude toward mixed couples has also changed in recent years. Although few white American parents are as yet prepared to "let their daughter marry one," they are more inclined not to kick and scream and throw rocks if their neighbor's daughter, or son, does. In national polls conducted six years apart, in 1965 and again in 1971, the years had wrought a surprising change in attitude. In the 1965 poll, nearly half of the respondents favored making interracial marriage a crime. But by 1971 a Harris Poll commissioned by *Life* magazine in connection with a study of interracial dating found a general acceptance of both interracial dating and marriage, although considerable concern and pessimism about the possible success of such relationships. The black/white marriage is apparently now considered inevitable and on the increase, and the majority of those polled agreed that eventually interracial couples will probably become both commonplace and accepted. This softening of attitude toward interracial dating and marriage on the part of whites is not currently reflected in the black community, where the popular view is separatist. Yet individual blacks, even among the most vocally militant, keep slipping, romantically, across the color line.

For those couples brave enough to face the hostility of both sides many of the cliché problems still obtain, despite today's changing attitudes. White males, and some females—especially southern-born— still swallow hard and may even physically strike out at the vision of the little blonde girl cuddled up against that big black stud. A UCLA coed who had married a black schoolmate and later separated from him confessed that she had simply not been able to take the public stares and public pressure. "When we walked down the street together, there was always some wise guy—a cop or just a pedestrian—who would stop and ask if that man was molesting me. It made me sick to have to keep trying to explain to people that he was my husband."

Of sterner stuff was the white girl on the arm of her black boyfriend in New York City who, when a well-meaning Texas lady asked her if she was "awright, or do you need he'p, honey?" laughed in her face.

The current ambivalence and confusion surrounding interracial sexual relationships date back to our peculiar form of slavery. Of all slave societies the world has known, America was the most modern, and thus the very worst.

BLACK/WHITE DATING*

Joan Downs

They are almost lost in the noon spill of students emptying onto the Minnesota mall, a lean dark man and a shy pretty girl with soft swinging hair. Ten years ago Faye Becker and Dexter Clarke, a white woman and a black man, would have risked almost certain ostracism for dating each other. Today, with increased exposure between blacks and whites—in the classroom, on the job, in the armed forces—individuals in growing numbers are moving past old racial barriers.

But the change creates a whole new series of personal dilemmas: how, in a time of deeply troubled black/white relations, does one reconcile group loyalty with friendship—even love—across the color line? On both sides, feelings run deep. Two elements emerge with particular force: the initiative in interracial pairing no longer belongs only to whites; and the black who decides to go out with a white must face the censure of his own people.

The current upsurge in interracial contact began in the '60s and gained impetus from the civil rights movement, the Peace Corps and Vista, all of which provided broader opportunity for the races to meet and to mix. It is still not a stampede. Mixed couples may not be so rare a sight in public today, but they are not entirely accepted, either. Where once those who dated and married interracially could be most often found among the intellectuals, the hip, and the fringes of society, racial interaction now occurs in the middle class as well.

In 1965 nearly half of the respondents to a national poll favored making interracial marriage a crime. This spring *Life* commissioned Louis Harris and Associates to conduct a much broader poll investigating public attitudes toward interracial dating and marriage. The returns reveal a growing tolerance of racial mixing—and a great many residual doubts.

In examining the pitfalls of social relationships between young blacks and whites, *Life* interviewed 60 interracial couples and many more individuals, as well as sociologists, psychologists and educators at 28 colleges across the country. Some are crusaders, some are adventurers off on sexual excursions. Most interracial couples, however, consist of a boy and a girl who like each other and incidently have different color skin. "He's just like any other guy I've ever dated, only his skin is black. I've never felt self-conscious with him." Faye Becker, 20, grew up in Benson, Minn. She had never met a Negro until she came to Minneapolis and her roommate arranged a date with Dexter Clarke, who is 21. "He's a good conversationalist and we always have fun, going to shows or just listening to records." A white boyfriend thoughtfully warned Faye that some blacks he had known in the army were "rotten." But when she told her parents she was dating a black, they said, "Go ahead, but date others too and don't let it get serious." She adheres to this policy, dating Dexter and others too, both black and white. The calm of the elder Beckers is not typical. At other households similar news often precipitates explosions and tears. After learning her daughter's date was black, a Philadelphia mother appeared at dinner in dark glasses that barely concealed the ravages of a tearful afternoon. Black families, if not enthusiastic, are generally more sympathetic. Some, like Dexter Clarke's parents, are even cordial. "They're used to a racial mix," Dexter says. "Mother runs an integrated day care center and Dad's a musician. Our friends have always been biracial." This works to Dexter's advantage and he realizes it. "I'm more at home in white groups than Faye, whose experience with blacks is limited, is in my world." He continues: "There has to be a certain amount of selection when you date the opposite race. A girl must be sensitive and able to handle herself." At one time a black man with a white woman was looked on with awe by other blacks—a taboo-defier, a player with lightning. Now, against the growth of black awareness, he is often criticized by his own race for making such a social choice. Some black men, like senior Cordell Pastel, believe that racial interaction helps destroy racism and is therefore justification enough for dating whites. For a good many other black men, interracial dating is a matter of crass, opportunistic economics. Black Pride can be profitable, and some men make a career of dating white girls.

"They pay for dates and give you money. I know one guy who even gets an allowance from his old lady." Donnie, a wide-featured heavy-set man, prefers women of his own race, but goes with a white girl, explaining: "To her it's a date, to me it's a job. I'd be with a sister but I'm poor. The time I put into her, I'd have to put into any job. If I lose this one I'll find another." He flashes a broad grin.

White parents eye black boyfriends warily for other reasons. Noel, a black man, complains: "Sandra's folks say they understand, but they were taught races shouldn't mix. They're afraid we'll get married."

What Sandra's parents fear almost as much as interracial marriage, of course, is interracial sex—Pill or no Pill. A white sorority girl comments: "Whenever people see a mixed couple, they immediately assume they're sleeping together. Nobody ever considers maybe they're just having a Coke or happen to dig Fellini films." The powerful myth of black sexual prowess continues to be perpetuated. Black men, well aware of the myth—and often embittered by its dehumanizing implications—regard middle-class white women as more permissive than middle-class black girls. On all campuses *Life* visited, black men are believed to expect their white dates to permit intimacy sooner than girls of their own race. One white freshman recalls telling her roommates that she had accepted a date with a handsome black football player: "They handed me three sex manuals."

Even interracial friendships between men do not escape the sexual factor. A black law student complains he has never had a white friend who inside of two weeks didn't ask if he'd ever had relations with a white girl. In fact there are some psychiatrists who believe a substantial amount of racial disharmony may be disguised sexual insecurity—*on both sides.*

In dingy student grills at scores of colleges across the country there is a familiar scene played with a cast of three: white woman, black man and, off to the side and crackling mad, the black woman. The dialogue sounds like this: "Baby, I've been digging you for a long time. I've been looking at you." He leans closer to the white girl. "And I called last night but there's never any answer." At a corner booth the black girl looks up. "But I was home studying for the Spanish quiz," the white girl says. He shrugs, reaching over to tease a stray wisp at her collar. "Maybe your phone doesn't work. You should have it checked." Ten minutes later they leave, a pale thin-faced blond girl and a haughty black man in neon orange and purple. "A dashiki, an

Afro, the clenched fist, but look what's on his arm," glowers the black girl and resumes drinking her coffee, alone.

Although there is little reason to believe that whites have accepted the new black/white relationship, the loudest voices raised in protest are black, especially black women. "What's wrong with me? There aren't enough black men to go around and *he's* messing with Charlie's daughter." Irene, 19, is a college freshman. Like many other black women she is acutely aware that there is a large national surplus of black women over black men. The numbers of white women preempting black men make her feel panicky. "If the white woman was in my position, she'd feel just as threatened. When your field of choice is wiped out, your world is torn apart." Ironically, the black woman is further disadvantaged when her traditionally greater education creates a gap between her and the black man. While she may improve her social and economic status, each year of school beyond the ninth grade actually reduces her chances of finding a suitable black marriage partner. "The educated black woman doesn't have anybody out there." Small wonder she views with rising concern the competition from white women.

On the streets, black girls stare malevolently at white girls clinging to black dates. In some cities they band together in clubs to "Save Our Men." On campus the sight of an interracial couple incites some black women to physical abuse. One white co-ed who dated black reports being shoved against a wall outside the gym by eight black girls, and given a bloody nose. "I thought my life was on the line, even though I tried to explain I had only wanted to learn how to dance." White girls hear stories of marauding bands of black girls stalking white "invaders." The reality of the rumors is usually quite low—but a biannual episode can sustain the legend. For his part, the black man can be equally intimidated. One recalls being surrounded by a group of black girls outside a lunchroom where he had been having coffee with a white girl. "They were like hornets, man."

"Black girls really mean business," observes a white junior. "Their grapevine is incredible. I dated a black guy one night. The next morning a black girl who lives on the floor below in my dorm came up and asked, 'How long have you been messing with David?' I never saw him again, but the day after summer vacation she wanted to know if I was still 'messing with David.'" Black men and women are quick to assert that in many instances it is the white woman who is the aggressor. Molly, a 25-year-old graduate student, complains: "If a black guy walks up to a group of black and white girls in a bar, the white chick makes her move before he can open his mouth. She monopolizes the conversation. What can you do—say, 'Hey, let me talk, too?' So you sit there awkwardly. At the end of the evening he says, 'What're you so quiet about?' Then he's out the door with the honky and you end up going home alone."

The white woman is not always the instigator. Before the end of their freshman year most white girls have heard about and some have been through what is called the Black Rap. Beginning with a ritual sermon on Black Power, the Rap eases into "I'm a human being, too." There is hardly a campus of any size that doesn't have one student hangout where a white girl can sit down and in ten minutes some black man wearing a tan leather trench coat and a real sincere smile will amble over to inquire, "Do you like black men, baby? Hey, have you ever gone out with one?" All she has to be is white and alone.

Especially if she's blond. Despite blistering Black Nationalist rhetoric, there are few black men who have not been influenced by the white aesthetic. To many, "Black is Beautiful" is no more than a catchy slogan. "There's that whole business of if you're yellow you're mellow," one black woman says sourly. "Any black who says it's dead is lying. You hear it in very subtle ways: 'Oh man, you know I saw a chick I could really dig. She was black, but man she was pretty.' It is there. Two dudes are waiting for a bus. A white girl goes by, the heads snap, the way they light up—it's all there."

White girls singled out by black men are often ultra-feminine in manner and appearance. They are the handful wearing skirts and pastel sweaters when other co-eds slump around in faded jeans. But, says a black woman who teaches Black Personality at a large Midwestern university, "I've never heard a black man say about a white woman, 'I love her,' even when she's his wife. Check it out. Sometimes I'll ask a brother who's been seen with a white girl, "Why're you doing that?' 'Well,' he'll say, 'she's got a car. She's got bread. If ever I need something, there's never a hassle.' The black man is drawn to the white woman for her convenience."

A certain amount of interracial dating can be accounted for on a sheer numerical basis. The increasing number of blacks on most college campuses makes it more likely that social interaction will occur.

Nevertheless, one crucial fact should not be obscured: young black men and women have a serious problem relating to one another, partly because black women are fatally ready to snipe at black men. The Black Personality professor acknowledges the problem: "Wow, our mouth. White girls have learned to capitalize on that. We'll use that tongue on you, cut you to pieces. We really will. At the same time we're digging you and loving you all the while." The new black man has little patience with his woman's scalding tongue. "I wouldn't go out with one of those nigger bitches for all the money in the world. They're mean, they're evil, they're hard to get along with," snarls a black graduate student who dates white women exclusively. Another says, "It's time black women were busted back where they belong." To many black men the dominant black woman is a symbol of a history he would really rather forget. On the brink of winning his manhood, he has no wish to be put down once again. So they stand apart, glaring at one another, the arrogant man and the proud, bristling woman.

Concealing her longing for appreciation in a cloak of independence, the black woman appears cold and unfriendly, although in isolated spots, such as the University of Minnesota, one black student felt he detected a recent change. "In 1967 when I came here—before Black Power and Black Is Beautiful—black girls were slobs. Then last year some of them underwent a terrific personality change. Now even when I'm with my white girl friend and I see a black girl, she says 'Hi!' It's kind of nice." The mysterious personality transformation may reflect the efforts of Maureen Wilson, a 24-year-old black graduate student and teacher. Last fall she and her friends mounted a quiet but intensive campaign to help black women reopen the lines of communication with black men. "When you see a brother with a white girl, don't ignore him. Speak to him, force him to speak to you," she urged. "You're not trying to catch him. You're just saying 'Hi, I'm here, I want you to know I'm here!'" Black men are not blameless. According to Maureen Wilson, "The guys here don't even speak to you. I bend over backwards to meet people, but you can walk down the hall, smile and say hello and they look the other way. Especially the ones who date white girls. They feel superior. Black guys outnumber black girls here three to one, but on weekends attractive black girls sit in their rooms with no place to go. Downstairs black guys wait in line to call up their white dates."

One solution proposed by black psychiatrist Kermit Mehlinger is that the women borrow a leaf from the men's book and date white. Although a few would be willing to "date a Caucasian if he sees me as a person," it is highly unlikely this suggestion will meet widespread acceptance. Most black women are solidly opposed to interracial dating, which they view as a contradiction for a true black person. "I don't want to date a white guy, and I have trouble understanding why black men want to date white women. Progress for us is going to have to start with the improvement of the black male-female relationship." Rose, a black college senior, is strikingly handsome. Her low voice dips almost to a whisper: "There's really no such thing as an individual when you're speaking of the black race. Before, I thought of me—what am I going to accomplish. Now I think what are *we* going to accomplish for the black race as a whole. To survive, the black community must remain unified. Only blacks understand what blacks have been through. I've been exposed to the white viewpoint for so long I'm very preoccupied with the way black people feel. We have a beautiful culture and I want it to get blacker. I want whites to stay white."

The ultimate and feared outcome of interracial dating is intermarriage. "We're just another couple," maintain Germaine and Walter Lide. Germaine Jones, small and fair with a wide grin, met Walter Lide, tall and reedy with an astonishing Bronx accent, three years ago when both were students at Minnesota. She held a liberal arts scholarship and he was majoring in psychology on the GI Bill. Eight months ago they married and are at the stage where many conversations begin, "Oh, Wally, can we please go to the movies?" and end, "Sure, Germ, sure." At first, they insist they have "no special problems." This denial is characteristic of mixed couples. Soon enough the problems pour out. Germaine winces when Walter reminds her of the letter from home after her family learned she was dating a black, "They called me a slut." For Walter, whose mother had told him never to bring home a white girl, things were not much easier. "I couldn't figure out how to tell her about Germaine. Finally one Sunday afternoon I called and asked her to give a friend the recipe for making collard greens. Now any black girl over ten knows how to cook collard greens. Then I put Germaine on the phone. Two days later I got a letter asking what the hell was going on."

Mixed couples must face some hard questions. One of the most difficult concerns the black's need to reconcile his choice of a white partner with his black identity. "At times I feel like a cop-out," Walter Lide admits. "Occasionally I wonder what I'm doing in this situation. Not very often... sometimes... in the middle of the night. Being married to Germaine will make certain things harder—above all for the children we hope to have. But Germaine understands me, I've never been able to talk as openly to anyone. After a while marriage was the only thing that made any sense. I'll be stuck with her for the rest of my life, but that's okay. I love her." But as the poll on the following pages indicates, their years ahead will not be made any easier by the attitudes of many of their fellow Americans.

The national poll conducted for *Life* by Louis Harris and Associates indicates that almost one American in five has had a date with someone outside his or her own race. (In the West and among young people age 21 to 25 across the nation, the figure rises to one in three. In the South it's less than one in ten.) Yet for most Americans, interracial dating remains something that is done by "other people," and in a fairly restricted circle. In fact, a substantial majority (55%) says it doesn't even *know* anyone who has dated interracially.

The responses to the Harris survey reveal an acceptance of the fact that increased black/white dating, like other contacts between the races, is inevitable. And most people—particularly the young, the affluent, the better educated—have no quarrel with the trend, at least in theory. But when the questions begin to touch on the actual problems of interracial pairing, the responses take on an ambivalence that occasionally amounts to outright self-contradiction. Thus the same person could agree with a statement that "if all men are created equal it shouldn't make any difference who goes out with whom," and in the next breath admit that "a white girl who dates a black man is going to ruin her reputation as far as I'm concerned." As Harris reports, "One cannot simply say that half the country is tolerant and the other half intolerant. The most overtly bigoted responses were few, but even among those who professed tolerance, doubts emerged."

The doubts grow larger as the questions hit closer to home. Only 3%, for instance, would actively encourage a member of their own family, male or female, to date someone of another race. Only 28% unreservedly approve such dating for their own children, and more than half would actively discourage it. (Among those who have dated interracially themselves, approval is much higher: 60%.) Two-thirds of those interviewed, including a majority of the well-educated, high-income group, believe that parents should impose at least some restrictions on interracial dating "until children are grown up enough to handle things themselves."

The whole question of how effectively parents can impose their will on their offspring is, to put it mildly, debatable. Nevertheless, for 25% of all parents, the desirable "restriction" is simple and draconic: forbid interracial dating altogether. Another 42% would allow the couple to go out in groups but not alone. About half also would have their child seek guidance first from a clergyman or a school official. The most popular response (72%) was characteristically ambivalent: parents should "discuss the dangers and disadvantages of interracial dating with the young people fully, then allow them to make up their own minds." Harris found an overwhelming feeling that a child's age was an important factor. Almost 80% of those interviewed believe that dating in general is okay at age 16 or younger, but only 11% would allow interracial dating at that age, and a majority disapproves of it for anyone under 21.

As to what kinds of people are most likely to date a member of another race, the most common opinion was "students and hippies," with "broad-minded people without prejudices or hang-ups about race" running a reasonably close second. Thoughts on the reasons why people of different races might want to go out together were fairly humdrum: the two enjoy each other's company, they have common interests, there is a physical attraction. Some 15%, however, believe the reason might be curiosity—the desire for a "different" experience. And 10% believe that people date interracially to shock other people and to get attention.

Though four people out of five have never dated interracially themselves, 42% say they have either seen or heard about an interracial couple having difficulties when they appear in public. When that happens,

57% say they feel sympathy for the couple,
20% believe the couple deserves the hostility,
23% feel no particular reaction either way.

But although they may sympathize with a couple under attack a large number (44%) contend that it is all right for anyone who honestly believes it's "wrong" to date interracially to express his opinions openly—*i.e.,* to give the couple a bad time. Just over half think that those opposed should mind their own business.

Accurately or not, most of those polled perceived a distinct generation gap in the acceptance of interracial dating. Asked "Do you think most *adults* get upset when they see an interracial couple?" 81% answered yes. "Does it upset young people?" No, 54%. In another touchy area—the question of which combination of sexes disturbs adults more —six times as many people said a black man with a white girl than the reverse.

The answers of blacks to the poll were very close to the total response—in which blacks were included as 11% of the population. Only one in four has ever dated interracially, fewer than half know anyone who has, and almost none would actively encourage it in their own families.

But in several areas, the black response was significantly different from the total. Asked whether they would approve of their children dating someone of a different race, 42% said they would—as opposed to only 28% of all respondents. And blacks are more sensitive than the average to interracial couples being subjected to public hostility. While 71% would feel sympathy for the couple, only 10% would think the hard time deserved. Interestingly, a majority of both blacks and whites believes that where resentment of interracial dating exists, it is shared by members of both races. The reasons offered most often for this are that:

1. Both races are equally prejudiced and neither wants intermingling.

2. Neither race wants intermarriage because of the problem of children.

The specter of interracial marriage lies at the root of many attitudes about dating, even though a majority says it is convinced that young people who date interracially are merely "going through a phase" and that most of them eventually will marry within their own race. The same majority senses that mixed marriages are increasing in number. But they are definitely not optimistic about the chances of a mixed marriage succeeding. Compared to a marriage between two people of the same race, a mixed marriage was rated by a two-thirds majority as less likely to succeed.

The reasons for this pessimism range from "lack of social acceptance" to "marriage has enough problems; mixed marriage just adds one more" and "it's hard on the children." More than 70% were convinced that children of a mixed marriage "face a life of prejudice and harassment."

For all their reservations, most Americans believe that interracial dating is inevitable, and they even foresee a day when mixed couples will be routinely accepted. However, two-thirds of the public thinks that that day is still a generation or more away. Another quarter thinks it will arrive in perhaps five or ten years. And two percent believe it is here now.

The Harris poll asked a nationwide cross section how they felt about a series of statements on interracial dating and marriage. The answers reveal not so much a split between the extremists on either end of the spectrum as an honest, even painful confusion over the many nuances of the problem. On the whole, the responses show a rising acceptance of the idea as a moral proposition. But that abstract acceptance conflicts with a residual distaste for the realities as each individual sees them. Black opinion, which often matches and occasionally contrasts with the total opinion, is shown separately.

The percentages indicate agreement with each of the following statements:

1. No matter what older people and parents say, young people of different races are going to see each other socially and we'd better get used to it.

   Total 77%   Blacks 82%

2. Whites and blacks who date each other are probably just as moral as anyone else.

   Total 68%   Blacks 78%

3. Any white girl who goes out with a black man is going to ruin her reputation as far as I'm concerned.

   Total 51%   Blacks 35%

4. There's nothing wrong with interracial dating in itself, but sex and marriage between races really bothers me.

   Total 47%   Blacks 34%

5. If all men are created equal, it shouldn't make any difference who goes out with whom.

   Total 51%   Blacks 78%

6. If black men had any pride, they'd stay with members of their own race. It's degrading for them to go chasing after white women.

   Total 51%   Blacks 40%

7. If parents would keep boys and girls apart at the time they're dating, they could stop interracial marriage at the source and it wouldn't get to be a problem.

   Total 32%   Blacks 26%

8. Whites who go out with blacks are interested in only one thing: sex.

Total 25% Blacks 25%

9. Young people of different races who date each other have a lot of courage and integrity.

Total 54% Blacks 63%

10. There is a real risk of being hurt emotionally when a person gets involved with someone of a different race.

Total 77% Blacks 61%

11. If two mature people really love each other, that will count more toward a successful marriage than any difference in race.

Total 62% Blacks 76%

12. Each couple should have the right to decide their own life without laws telling them they can't marry someone of another race.

Total 70% Blacks 81%

13. It just seems to violate God's law for people of different races to marry and produce mixed-blood children.

Total 40% Blacks 26%

SOCIAL AND LEGAL
DIMENSIONS OF
INTERRACIAL LIAISONS

*James E. Blackwell**

In this section, we call attention to several dimensions of interracial sexual liaisons. The term liaisons refers to close associations between male and female blacks and whites, usually involving sexual activity. The sexual aspect of the relationship may cover a wide range of activity including a simple kiss, heavy petting, sexual intercourse with or without mutual consent, and promiscuity. Sexual liaisons, whether legal or illicit, evoke a wide range of societal responses when the participants cross color lines. At various times, society may accept or condemn the relationships, depending upon their nature and upon who are the major participants. Sometimes, as was the case for most of the period between 1661 and 1967, legal barriers are promulgated to prevent interracial liaisons from occurring. Particularly in a highly technological, urbanized and impersonal society, such as the American society, responses to interracial liaisons range unevenly from social disapprobation to violence directed against participants.

The primary focus here is on the role of the black male in interracial liaisons. To place his role(s) in proper perspective, special attention will be given (1) to interracial liaisons during slavery and the impact of the institution of slavery on the formation of attitudes, belief systems and legal constraints designed to control the participation

*James E. Blackwell is chairman of the Department of Sociology at the University of Massachusetts-Boston. This is an original article written for this volume.

of the black male in interracial affairs, (2) to perceptions and stereotypes pertaining to black male sexuality, (3) to the sexual basis of Jim
Crow legislation, (4) to anti-miscegenation legislation in modern
times, (5) to contemporary patterns of mate selection and factors accounting for changes in these patterns, and (6) to the social costs of
interracial liaisons. Although our primary focus is on black-white relations in the United States, it should be stressed that inter-group liaisons are by no means unique to the United States; nor are they exclusively a phenomenon of race. Just as liaisons occur across racial, ethnic,
and social class lines in the United States so do they occur across these
same barriers in other parts of the world.

A THEORETICAL PERSPECTIVE

The theoretical basis for this analysis can be briefly summarized
as follows. Most marriages in the United States are endogamous. However, increases in out-group marriages, or exogamous marriages, have
been observed in recent years even though taboos or cacogamous attitudes still prevail. Exogamous marriages usually occur in one of two
identifiable patterns; that is, they are either hypergamous or hypogamous. Hypergamy refers to institutionalized or non-institutionalized
intermarriage patterns in which the female marries upward in a stratification system. Hypogamy denotes marriage by a female into a lower
social stratum.[1] Given the nature of the American social structure with
its traditional caste-like relationships between blacks and whites, it
is assumed that a white female who marries a black male marries a
person in a lower social stratum because of his unfavored position in
the larger social system. Thus, these marriages, black male-white female, the most common type of interracial marriages, are characteristically hypogamous. But, the very fact that racial intermarriages constitute such a small proportion of the total number of marriages in the
United States indicates the degree to which most people conform to
deeply imbedded social norms relative to mate selection. Thus, racial
endogamy is not unexpected since people are by and large governed
in their behavior by the normative structures dominant in their social
group. Similarly, "preferential class endogamy," as described by Barron,[2] occurs both within racial groups and, quite homogamously
(marriage among equals or near equals), across racial lines.

All things considered, endogamy is encouraged for many reasons,
explicit and implicit. It serves the function of increasing in-group solidarity. It is a powerful centripetal force which strengthens social cohe-

sion between members of a social group. Endogamy protects the power, authority and the structure of privilege developed over time against encroachments from outsiders. Not only does endogamy isolate members from other groups, it is, in general, an important mechanism of group exclusion. Thus, cacogamous or tabooed marriage represents a breach in the network of established social relations between super-ordinates and subordinates for it implies a degree of social equality not previously granted by the superordinate group.[3] Simultaneously, this structure of privilege, power and authority, and preferred status of the dominant group permits the white male to engage in sex relations with the black female on a more frequent basis than is the reverse situation. The white male may not out-marry as much as the white female, although he may more freely engage in sexual activity with non-white members, because of his rigid adherence to the rules of endogamy or because his marriages are, in Barron's term, more often agathogamous or norm-conforming. Again, disjunctions may exist between normative expectations regarding marriage, on the one hand, and general practice regarding sexual relations, on the other hand.

Whether black or white, according to Stuart's SVR Theory, mate selection "involves a series of sequential stages, . . . labeled stimulus, value, and role" (SVR). Moreover, the viability of the relationship between interracial partners is dependent upon the "equality of exchange" participants experience. Stimulus values refer to noninteractional cues, where interaction is free and open, that draw people toward each other, including "perceptions of physical, social, mental and reputational attributes." People get together because they are attracted to each other. This stimulus stage must precede the second stage of value comparison which occurs through verbal interaction. The interracial couple, who reaches this stage, makes comparisons of attitudes toward a number of things, including religion, politics, sex roles, sex, and life in general. Such comparisons may or may not enhance the desirability of the potential marriage partner. If the comparisons are positive, individuals may enter into the third and final stage, the role stage. Here they determine the degree to which role compatibility occurs between them and the extent to which their perceptions of husband-wife roles, for example, conflict. In terms of exchange, individuals assess cost factors as opposed to rewards to be accrued from the relationship. In a word, what are the assets and the liabilities of the relationship. It is, therefore, assumed that marriage follows successful traversing of the three stages of stimulus, value and role. With regard to interracial marriages, it is highly probable that individuals meet more often in a closed situation such as in a classroom where verbal communication is high. Thus, they either by-pass the stimulus stage or it is blended with the value orientation stage as they become mutually attracted because of verbal interaction.[4] However, it should be reiterated that where dominant group status with its attendant attributes of power and privilege maximizes advantages of its members, sexual relations with minority group members are often exploitative, especially if they occur outside the bond of marriage.

SEX AND RACISM IN THE UNITED STATES:
PRE-SLAVERY AND THE SLAVERY PERIOD

The Pre-Slavery Period: From the beginning, when they first met as a people, intimate associations developed between blacks and whites. Before slavery was formally introduced in America in the mid-seventeenth century, black indentured servants established intimate relations with whites, most of whom were indentured servants themselves. These relationships, which often included marriage, were conducted without fear of impositions of social restraints, ostracism, taboos or of physical abuse. In many instances, interracial affairs were between black men and white women. They fraternized and cohabited both in and outside the bonds of marriage. Their associations undoubtedly led to the first accounts of interracial marriage in the United States. Among the progeny of these early interracial marriages was Benjamin Banneker, a famous black astronomer and mathematician. Records indicate that Banneker was the grandson of a marriage between a white female formerly-indentured servant from England and a manumitted slave who had been freed by the woman who became his wife.[5] The example provided by Benjamin Banneker illustrates how men and women of both races did operationalize their rights to marry across color lines and to live relatively undisturbed lives. Some black men and white women, as well as white men and black women, lived in common-law marriage arrangements. Many married white males sought out black women as concubines or as mistresses with whom they maintained such illicit relationships for several years. Other white males, even in this pre-slavery period, had already begun the practice of sexually exploiting and abusing the black female indentured servant. These various patterns of interracial mingling were well underway before slavery was given statutory recognition in Virginia (1661) and in Maryland (1663).[6] An important issue for many whites was how to curtail what seemed to them the alarming proportions of interracial sexual affairs. Many white men viewed the black male, slave or free, as a serious threat to their own sexual prerogatives. Many white women not only believed themselves disgraced by the brazen affairs conducted by their husbands with black women but that their own social position and authority over the household were jeopardized by the extra-marital affairs of their husbands. Hence, both white men and women were convinced of the necessity to impose serious legal restraints to control, if not prevent, cohabitation across the color line.

Slavery: Interracial cohabitation undoubtedly began on African soil. It was started by slave merchants who continued their activities on the slave ships across the Atlantic and who helped develop interracial sex as a growing concern on the plantations.[7]

Early Anti-Miscegenation Legislation: The first major step to curtail interracial cohabitation was taken by the General Assembly of the Colony of Maryland. In 1661, Maryland enacted a statute which was directed specifically at the white female who showed a preference for black men. According to this statute, a white woman who married a black slave man was to be punished by serving the slave's master throughout the life of her slave husband. The statute also declared a slave status for all children resulting from such unions. This statute may have reduced the number of cacogamous or tabooed marriages but it did not stop cohabitation between black men and white women nor between white men and black women. However, where it was successful, it resulted in additional problems for many white slave masters and society in general because both were given the additional responsibility of providing for legitimate and illegitimate mulatto children.[8] So much was this a problem, in Maryland for example, that new legislation was promulgated which required violators of the earlier statute to reimburse masters for the maintenance of children resulting from the union of black slaves with white women.[9]

Unions, especially between black men, slave and free, with white women, as well as those between white men and black women, were not only defined as a social problem of major proportions in Maryland; similar perceptions were held in other colonies. Hence, several colonies followed the pattern initiated by Maryland for controlling what were becoming defined as both cacogamous and hypogamous relationships. Virginia followed Maryland in 1691 by restricting intermarriage. Then came Massachusetts (1705), North Carolina (1715),

South Carolina (1717), Delaware (1721), and Pennsylvania (1725). In varying degrees, these new laws could extend the period of servitude for white female indentured servants who either married black men or who bore children fathered by black men. These laws also levied sanctions against free white men and women who married blacks. They could be fined, imprisoned or reduced to a previous condition of servitude. Free blacks who violated the law could be reduced to slavery or they could be sold to another province as a way of dissolving the union and separating families. Some of the new laws also imposed severe sanctions upon ministers who performed interracial marriages.[10] The most common form of sanction was a heavy fine. In other instances, social ostracism, ridicule, floggings and whippings were employed as deterrents against sexual activity between blacks and whites.

Slavery: Even the institution of slavery and the harsh realities of its ubiquitous control of masters over the daily lives of slaves did not totally abolish either marriage or mating across the color lines. Lerone Bennett maintains that the innumerable divorce petitions in which the white male accused the black male of alienation of affection is sufficient evidence that black male-white female liaisons and common-law marriages persisted during the slave period. Similarly, divorce petitions by white wives who charged their husbands with adultery or concubinage with slave women provides further support for this view.[11]

Although the laws promulgated during slavery against miscegenation did not and could not prevent its occurrence, they did have another major, perhaps intended, consequence. The anti-miscegenation laws, as well as informal social sanctions, maximized the freedom of the white male to engage in sexual liaisons with black females by simultaneously restricting the freedom and access of both the black male and the white female with each other. Moreover, white men would violate the very laws they themselves created—a common practice among members of dominant groups who come to believe that they can bend the law to their advantage and for the disadvantage of subordinate groups. Thus, the most persistent pattern of miscegenation during the period of slavery would become liaisons between white men and black females. They would result from their close associations in the work situation and the ability of the white male to exercise his authority as a dominant group member by subjecting black women to his lasciviousness.

In some instances, slave masters lived in common-law arrangements with black women. Some white men and black women were mutually attracted to each other and engaged in sexual affairs of mutual free will. Many slave masters and overseers used persuasion, promises of better jobs and lighter work loads in exchange for sexual favors. Others forced black women to submit to their will under the threat of whippings, floggings or bodily mutilations. Some defenseless black women used their ability to permit sexual favors with white men as a bargaining mechanism for other rewards they sought. On many occasions, lustful white males literally raped black women because they believed it to be the master's right to which he was entitled as an owner of slaves. In capitalizing on his position of privilege and power in the American social structure, the white male began to carefully and systematically construct a new reality principle—the unchallenged superiority of the white population in the United States. This construction involved stringent requirements for endogamous marriage which, in turn, became intertwined with elaborate defenses of the racial caste system institutionalized particularly in the American South. The articulation of extensive stereotypes about the black male and the rise of the "white female on a pedestal" syndrome emerged as formidable components of the racial caste system.

Endogamy, or marriage within one's own group, as opposed to exogamy (or inter-group marriage), maintained white dominance and black subordination. In so doing, it was an effective instrument for denying social equality between the races. Obviously, uncontrolled intermarriage was an acknowledgement of social equality but this practice was inconsistent with notions of white superiority and had to be checked. Assuming that black men had strong desires for white women and that white women, in turn, would be receptive to proposals from black men, rigid enforcement of rules of endogamy could help accomplish the goal of racial separateness.[12] Moreover, rules of endogamy could conserve the white female, her virginity, her purity and her supposed superiority for a white husband. One of the major problems with this rule was that, in restricting sexual freedom for the white female and the black male, it created a double standard of morality which engendered special privilege for the white male. Therefore, if the basic function of the caste system was the ultimate protection of the entire white race or to retain its ritualistically sexual purity through rigid enforcement of rules of endogamy, it failed miserably. As will be explained in a following section, interracial cohabitation continued on such a wide scale that millions of Americans are today racially mixed. Some of them are unaware of the mixed nature of their ancestry and would be shocked to discover such knowledge about themselves.

In the process of strengthing a social caste system and in preventing intermingling between black men and white women, innumerable stereotypes about the black male were developed. Some of them persist into contemporary life.

Perceptions of the Black Male: The black male was variously described as a "walking phallus"; an animalistic satyr possessed with insatiable sexual appetites; a man endowed with exceptionally large genitalia and gifted with extraordinary sexual prowess; and a sexually uninhibited man preoccupied with sex. In contemporary vernacular, the black male was pictured as a "super-stud" whose outstanding sexual prowess evoked jealousies among white men and fantasies among white women. It was claimed that black men everywhere lusted after white women who in turn were everywhere endangered by possible attack by the black male.[13] Perhaps unintentionally, this belief system among whites made the black male what Alvin Poussaint called "America's fearsome sex symbol."[14]

There was, and is, of course, a certain amount of projection and fantasy in these perceptions of the black male. Perceptions of black men involve, to some extent, guilt among many white males emanating from centuries of sexual exploitation of defenseless black women; a bad conscience among many white men over the use of their power and privileged position to "manipulate powerless black women for sexual experimentation and gratification,"[15] and, among some whites, it involves an excessive "fascination with the black man's genitals."[16] These preoccupations do not necessarily deter black-white liaisons; in many instances, they have the unintended consequence of heightening curiosity and encouraging sexual liaisons across color lines by romanticizing the black male as the ultimate in sexual experience.

Another variance on this theme of uninhibited sexual cravings by the black male for the white female is that the black male is a violent aggressor, especially against white females, so intent upon achieving his goal that white women are in constant danger of rape. Evidence does not support this observation even though black men have historically been accused of raping white women, lynched, murdered, hanged, maimed and castrated because of such allegations whether true or not. By contrast, few white men have ever been convicted of raping black women and none sentenced to jail or condemned to die for "reckless eyeballing" or making sexual passes at black women.

Rapes tend to be intra-group rather than inter-group. Black females have an 18 to one chance of being victimized by rape and this is about nine times the potential rate for white females.[17] However, whenever rape is alleged to occur across color lines, especially in the case of a black male accused of raping a white female, punishment is likely to be quick and severe. Judge Joseph Howard of Baltimore documented the enormity of disparity in apprehension, conviction and punishment in rape cases involving blacks on whites in comparison to white on black and black on black. Howard found that in his examination of 750 rape cases alleged in Baltimore between 1962 and 1966, 505 of them were black on black incidents, 175 involved whites against whites, 61 were blacks against whites and 9 cases involved allegations of rape by white men against black women. Thus, a significant majority of the cases were intra-group, and the great majority of them involved black males accused of rape offenses against black women. Howard also found that indictment and conviction rates were higher when the black male was accused of rape offenses against white women than when accused of offenses against black women. His punishment was considerably more severe in the former instances than in the latter. By contrast, the courts appear to be much harder on the white male who is accused of rape offenses against white females than when he is accused of attacks against black females. For example, four-fifths of the black males indicted for rape offenses against white females were convicted and 92.3 percent of the convictions permitted the imposition of the death penalty at the discretion of the judge. However, no more than five of the nine cases involving white males accused of sexually assaulting or raping black women "ever reached the sentencing stage of the trial."[18]

Racial Mixture: Because neither laws nor social customs have succeeded in preventing interracial cohabitation in the United States, and because thousands of persons who would be legally defined as black despite their white physical features pass relatively unnoticed into the white race each year, a sizeable proportion of the American population is racially mixed. One of the more insightful studies which attempted to establish the degree to which the American population is racially mixed was conducted by Robert P. Stuckert and first reported in 1958.[19] Stuckert attempted to determine the validity of the belief that white Americans are "free of the taint" of black ancestry or "blood." After carefully constructing a genetic probability table and developing assumptions which enabled statistical estimations of the probability of black and non-black ancestry, Professor Stuckert reached some extremely interesting conclusions. His research led him to conclude that: (1) in 1790, although the persons classified as white having black ancestry was relatively small, the percentage of such persons climbed rapidly between 1790 and 1950; (2) with few exceptions in succeeding decennial years, the proportion of white Americans with black ancestry increased in each census year; (3) by 1960, the proportion of the white population with black ancestry had increased to 23 per cent; (4) among those persons classified as blacks in 1790, nineteen per cent had white ancestry; however, (5) the proportion of such persons in the total black population climbed steadily in each succeeding decennial year so that by 1960 almost seven-tenths (69.9 per cent) of the black population was reported to have some white ancestry. According to Stuckert, the 1960 figure represented a drop from 77.4 per cent of blacks with some degree of white ancestry in 1940. That drop may be explained partially by the number of legal blacks who "passed for white" to obtain jobs, a better economic life or an escape from oppressive racism during World War II. Hence, it is now estimated that more than thirty-six million white Americans have some degree of black ancestry and the overwhelming majority of black Americans have white ancestors. Therefore, interracial cohabitation has occurred on such a wide scale in the United States that notions of biological or racial purity are invalid.

Sex, Racism and Jim Crow Legislation: By 1870, cohabitation between blacks and whites had become such a part of the American social fabric that slightly less than two fifths (39.7 per cent) of persons classified as blacks and slightly less than one fifth (18 per cent) of those classified as whites were racially mixed. The percentages would rise in 1900 to 56.6 per cent and 19.5 per cent, respectively.[20] These changes undoubtedly reflected a relaxation in the rules of endogamy and the increased freedom to engage in sexual liaisons across the color line during the period of Reconstruction. One cannot assume, however, that the social etiquette which governed associations between blacks and whites during the period of slavery was completely abrogated. Although some of the previous social norms may not have been as rigidly enforced as they were during the periods of absolute white dominance over the black population, the norms of racial separateness were still practiced by a large segment of the population.

Reconstruction ended with the restoration of white rule in the South through the Compromise of 1877, and by the declaration of the United States Supreme Court in 1883 that the Civil Rights Act of 1875 was unconstitutional, and by the subsequent enactment of extensive Jim Crow legislation designed to separate the races. By virtue of changes following these events, white supremacy and racial apartheid once again became the established way of life in the United States. Especially through Jim Crow legislation, white America was free to extend the principle of dominant group advantage which is implicit in rules of endogamy, to other areas of daily life as a way of guaranteeing limited access of white women to black men and to protect the system of privilege and entitlements assumed to be prerogatives of the dominant white male. The races were separate but not equal in all institutions—in the church, the school, in recreation, in housing, in politics, occupations and the general economic sphere. Laws preventing racial amalgamation in those areas of daily life provided an effective boundary maintenance system for limiting black male-white female social interaction. However, primarily because of white privilege and the reduction of the black male to a dependent state in the economic structure, black women became increasingly accessible to white men. Once again, white men could take advantage of black women who worked as house servants or in their cotton fields and on their farms. Nevertheless, the fear that white women would continue to engage in sexual liaisons with black men was widespread. New social control mechanisms were devised. Thus, between 1884 and 1900, more than 2,500 lynchings occurred in the United States; the majority of the victims were southern blacks,[21] and it is safe to say that a sizeable number of the black victims were accused of some form of sexual transgression against white women. However, the evidence is muddled as to whether or not the majority of lynch victims were accused of sexual misconduct. Franklin observed that during the first fourteen years of the twentieth century 315 lynch victims were accused of rape or attempted rape but more than 500 lynch victims were accused of homicide.[22] These incidents occurred at the same time that many young white males were being socialized into the belief that their manhood and their rites of passage into sexual maturity could best be accomplished by cohabitation with black women. Thus, they could preserve the white female's purity and keep her on a pedestal while they sexually experimented with helpless, low status black females or sowed their wild oats with them as "preferred sex partners." Once again, a double standard of privilege and morality prevailed to the advantage of the white male.

Anti-Miscegenation Laws: Nevertheless, many states saw the necessity of enacting extensive laws and imposing numerous legal sanctions to prevent or curtail interracial cohabitation. Some states considered interracial cohabitation, particularly as permitted through intermarriage, so fundamental that prohibitions against intermarriage were incorporated in their state constitutions.[23] At the end of the 1940s, thirty-six states had enacted anti-miscegenation legislation.[24] There was little agreement among the states as to how much black blood was necessary in order to be defined as a black and thus to effect an interracial union. Arkansas, California, Delaware, Idaho, Kentucky and Louisiana made it illegal for a white person to marry a mulatto. Was a mulatto the offspring of an unmixed white with an unmixed black, as was assumed to be true by ethnologists? Or was a mulatto simply an offspring possessing a known trace of black blood or one sixty-fourth black ancestry? Definitions invariably were devised to suit the specific prejudices paramount at a particular time in a given state. [25] Thus, possessing one-eighth or more black blood could bar a marriage with a white person in such states as Alabama, Florida, Indiana, Maryland, Mississippi, Missouri, Nebraska, North Carolina, South Dakota, Tennessee, and Texas. In other states, such as Georgia, Montana, Oklahoma, and Virginia, even the remotest strain of black ancestry was sufficient to prevent interracial marriage. But in Oregon, a person with less than one-fourth black ancestry was declared white and could not, therefore, marry a quadroon or a mulatto.[26]

Just as laws varied from state to state regarding definitions of what constitutes membership in the black race and thus who is eligible to marry a white person, these laws altered such definitions over time. For example, many Virginians were forced to change their racial status or identification at least three times between 1866 and 1930. In 1866, a person was white if he or she had less than one-fourth black or Indian ancestry. The proportion of black or Indian ancestry was raised to one-sixteenth in 1910 to "no trace whatsoever" in 1924 to "no ascertainable Negro strain" in 1930. It is also interesting to note that under one Virginia law, an Indian became black once he left the reservation.[27] Colorado was at one time a mosaic of confusion regarding mixed marriages. That state permitted mixed marriages in its southern part primarily in deference to Spanish settlers but banned them in its northern half which was settled by Anglo-Saxons.[28]

Twenty-six states enacted legislation which declared intermarriage null and void. Most of them provided penalties against participants, including spouses and those who performed the marriage ceremony, which included fines and/or imprisonment.[29] In addition, pseudo-scientific arguments to the effect that interracial cohabitation leads inevitably to abnormalities in the offspring and to mongrelization, in general, were used as a deterrent against liaisons between the races. Since persons who sought to marry across the color line were often presumed to be mentally unbalanced, "mental tests" were sometimes used to establish the sanity of such couples, and, therefore, as deterrents against such marriages.

Quasi-legal sanctions and informal social taboos developed to prevent interracial liaisons, especially hypogamous marriage between black men and white women. Thus, the couple and their children were socially isolated, scorned, ridiculed and spatially confined largely to the black community. Children and their parents often were verbally abused and subjected to slurs and epithets.

In time, however, due to a number of factors and shifts in the American social structure, the right to marry, to cohabit, or to socialize across color barriers came under serious discussion. Some individuals who sought this right to marry a person of another race, for instance, carried their battles to state Supreme courts. Others carried their struggle to the United States Supreme Court. Thus, in 1948, in Perez v. California, the Supreme Court of California stated that bans against interracial marriages violated the guarantees of equal protection of the laws.[30] In McLaughlin v. Florida, the U.S. Supreme Court abrogated a Florida prohibition against black-white sexual relations. The Court failed, however, to rule on the Florida statute which forbade intermarriage.[31] It was not until 1967 in the case of Loving v. Virginia that the United States Supreme Court declared all bans against interracial marriage unconstitutional. The Supreme Court decision came at a time when the trend in most states was to abolish restrictive legislation against interracial unions. For example, by 1966, only two states outside the South (Indiana and Wyoming) in addition to seventeen southern states prohibited interracial marriages. Moreover, a discerni-

ble trend toward increasing marriages across color lines, although still
minimal, and increasing interracial dating, particularly among college
and high school students in integrated settings, was observed.

Trends in Interracial Liaisons: Using data covering a period
between 1948 and 1951, George Simpson and Milton Yinger reported
that black-white intermarriage rates in New York City, Boston, and
Los Angeles varied from one to five per cent of all marriages in which
blacks participated. In their view, black male-white female marriages
constituted the most common form of black-white intermarriage.[32]
In another major study, David Heer examined marriage records in
Hawaii, California and Michigan. He noted a trend toward increases
in black-white marriages. In California, for example, he observed that,
between 1955 and 1959, the proportion of whites marrying blacks increased from 0.14 per cent to 0.21 per cent. California had one of the
highest interracial marriage rates for whites of both sexes in 1959.
Heer also noted increases in white-black marriage rates in Michigan
between 1953 and 1962. He found that the proportion of white marrying blacks in Michigan increased from 0.07 per cent to 0.12 per cent.[33]
Although these increases may appear to be miniscule when compared
to the total number of marriages, which still tends to be endogamous,
Heer was able to demonstrate an upward trend in interracial unions.

According to Milton Barron[34] who used census data as the
basis for this observation, interracial marriages now occur two and
a half times more frequently than they did during the 1930's. The
51,409 black-white couples reported in the 1960 census represented
0.12 per cent of the total number of married couples in the United
States at that time. It is generally assumed that a greater tendency
exists among black men to marry white women than for white men
to marry black women. The 1950 census reports indicated that 44 per
cent of the husbands in interracial marriages were white;[35] however,
by 1960 this proportion of white husbands in interracial couples had
climbed to fifty per cent of all such marriages. This evidence would
seem to contradict claims of a predominance of black males in interracial marriages. But, when Irving R. Stuart examined some 19 studies
of interracial marriages, covering a period between 1874 and 1965, in
addition to an examination of census data, he found evidence to support his contention that white male-black female marriages are increasing even though the most frequent form of interracial marriage
remains that involving the black male and a white female.[36]

More recently, 1970 census data show a number of changes in

interracial marriages in the United States. A special census report on marriage revealed: (1) a sixty-three per cent increase in marriage between whites and non-whites during the nineteen sixties; (2) interracial marriages constituted 0.70 per cent of the total number of marriages recorded in 1970 or an increase from 0.44 per cent of the 1960 total to 0.70 per cent of the 1970 total; (3) the actual number of white men marrying black women declined from 25,913 in 1960 to 23,566 in 1970 while the number of black men taking white wives showed a dramatic increase in the same period from 25,496 to 41,223; and (4) provided empirical data to support the hypothesis that black-white marriages are not a phenomenon of the low-income groups. Thus, according to this report, the proportion of black men involved in black-white marriages who earn ten thousand dollars or more per year is double that of the number of such men who earn less than three thousand dollars per annum.[37] Inasmuch as educational attainment and income are often statistically associated, these findings lend support to earlier observations that interracial couples are likely to be better educated than married people in general. For example, Barron reported that the percentage of interracial couples possessing some college education is in excess of ten to fifteen times the proportion that existed in the 1920's. Further, he claimed that, when interracial couples in New York were studied, they were found to have a median of 16.5 years of schooling which was above the average for married couples.[38]

With regard to dating, Harris poll data showed that at least one of every five Americans has dated across racial lines. This same poll demonstrated significant variations in dating patterns from one region of the country to another. For example, the figure for interracial dating was one in three Americans under the age of twenty-five in the West but only one in ten in the South.[39] Although the black-white dating is on the increase and has a modest degree of acceptability across the nation, American social customs still regard interracial marriage as a form of deviant behavior.[40] Regardless of these attitudes, both interracial marriage and interracial dating are on the increase in the United States.

Factors Accounting for Increases in Interracial Liaisons: Attention should now be called to the many factors which account for the increases in out-group dating and marriages as well as for the increases in the phenomena we have observed.

Early in this century, Lester Frank Ward, a founder of American sociology, postulated "four laws of race mixing." Accordingly, (1) "the women of any race will freely accept the men of a race which they regard as higher than their own"; (2) "the women of any race will vehemently reject the men of a race which they regard as lower than their own"; (3) "the men of any race will greatly prefer the women of a race which they regard as higher than their own"; and (4) "the men of any race, in default of women of a higher race, will be content with women of a lower race."[41] According to J.A. Rogers' adaptation of Ward's four laws, when applied to black-white relationships, these laws mean that: (1) "Negro women will freely accept white men"; (2) "white women will vehemently reject Negro men"; (3) "Negro men will greatly prefer white women"; and (4) "Negro men, unable to get white women, will be content with Negro women."[42] Although the percentages of black-white marriages are increasing, and, despite the popularity of some of Ward's beliefs advanced more than three score years ago, there is reason to doubt the validity of his laws. The following discussion explains the dubious nature of Ward's position.

In more recent times, Simpson and Yinger maintained that four factors were responsible for racial and ethnic, as well as religious, minority group men to out-marry. They claimed that: (1) men have greater opportunities for meeting women of out-groups, moreso than women do; (2) minority group women are more often more strongly influenced by religious and other institutional controls than are minority group men; (3) men take the initiative in dating which inevitably leaves many minority group women among the under-chosen; and (4) minority group men, who marry a woman from the dominant group or a minority group woman whose physical appearance approximates that of dominant group female norms, has a symbolic success value and helps to assure prestige and social acceptance in the larger society.[43] There is evidence, however, that the factors which influence interracial dating and marriage are numerous and highly complex. They include demographic factors, sex ratios, numerical size of the group, conditions within the group, opportunities for social interaction between racial groups of both sexes as found, for instance, in the work place, residential propinquity, recreational sites, desegregated educational facilities, spatial and social mobility, the degree of cultural similarities between potential dating partners or marital mates, attitudes of significant others toward interracial associations, and the intensity of institutional controls over the individual's social life.[44] No research has clearly demonstrated that any one of these factors clearly exercises greater influence than all others in determining the decision to date or marry across racial lines. Research undertaken in New York City, Los Angeles, Burlington, New Haven and elsewhere suggests that an unbalanced sex ratio and numerically small representation are particularly influential factors. But, some writers claim that the factor of propinquity of individual participants, as related to place of residence, work and education, for example is a more important influence on the decision to date or marry across racial lines. Still, it is claimed that, if all other factors were equal, cultural similarity would be the dominant factor in this process.[45] Undoubtedly, cultural similarity is influenced by educational attainment and *opportunities for racial mixing* provided by desegregation in educational institutions which followed the major Supreme Court Decisions affecting higher education in the late forties and fifties. Moreover, especially as a result of the serious efforts by formerly all-white colleges and universities to increase minority group presence in their student bodies, the number of black students in predominantly white universities increased appreciably in the late sixties and early seventies. These events accentuated the propinquity factor as a major variable in influencing interracial social relations. Too, it must be assumed that higher educational attainment among black males gave rise to better economic benefits and occupational choices which, in turn, increased their eligibility for interracial marriage, for example. However, all those variables that fall under demographic characteristics are by and large evidence of opportunities for race mixing and do not necessarily address the normative elements in the social structure which influence such decisions.

Although institutional controls, such as religious bodies and the state, once coalesced as major deterrents against overt interracial liaisons, they no longer hold their formerly unchallenged power in the decision to date or marry across racial lines. Undoubtedly, attitudes of family members, peer groups, friendship cliques and the immediate public are more important in choices for mate selection. The decision of whites to marry blacks or even to date them may depend upon the availability of blacks in all spheres of life or upon the degree of social interaction provided by the social structure. On the other hand, the decision of blacks to marry whites may reflect the degree of black-white marriage acceptability in a given community.[46] Here, we are concerned about prevailing normative structures which facilitate or impede social interaction. These structures may also embrace attitudinal constructs of family members, friendship cliques, peer groups and the generalized immediate public.

What, then, are the types of attitudes one encounters when engaging in interracial dating and interracial marriage? Polls taken by Harris and Gallup have shown an increasing degree of acceptance by the public of interracial liaisons although relationships still meet with disapprobation among the majority of adult Americans. In 1965, for example, a Gallup Poll revealed that almost one-half (48 per cent) of all American adults approved criminal antimiscegenation laws. Significantly, however, 41 per cent of them disapproved of such legislation and the remaining six per cent had no opinion about such legislation. In 1966 the Louis Harris Poll showed that almost nine in ten adults (88 per cent) would disapprove of their teenage child dating a black and almost four fifths of them (79 per cent) would be upset if a close friend or relative married a black. Two years later, in 1968, Gallup reported that the proportion of adults who disapproved of interracial marriage had dropped to 72 per cent but at least twenty per cent stated outright approval of interracial marriages.[47] Thus, it is not unexpected that by 1973 at least one of every five Americans reported that they had dated across racial lines.[48] There may now, as in the past, be disjunctions between principles regarding interracial liaisons and practices in everyday life.

It is generally believed that blacks are particularly tolerant of interracial liaisons and that is the reason why black men with white women choose to live in predominantly black neighborhoods. A major study conducted by Donald Bogue and Jan Dizard in Chicago of 721 black families is instructive on this subject. They found that: (1) almost none of the black families would encourage their children to marry white persons; (2) almost four-fifths would permit marriage between their children and whites if they had become attached without their knowledge; (3) they were about evenly divided between those who would actively oppose interracial marriage and those who would tolerate it; and (4) there was no evidence of a strong desire among blacks for miscegenation except among a small group of individuals.[49]

Powerful negative sanctions are more often invoked against black male-white female unions, whether dating or marrying, than in other black-white relationships. At varying times, the black male, who dates or marries across color lines, sometimes is viewed by other blacks as having transgressed in-group solidarity, and may have been subjected to name-calling and physical violence.[50] Black nationalists claim that such black males have acted contrarily to principles of black ethnicity and have demeaned other blacks.[51] In some instances, even with increasing acceptance of black-white dating and marriage, these individuals are socially isolated, victims of insults, states of disapproval and institutional discrimination (e.g., housing, job promotion, and so forth). Not infrequently, black women more vehemently disapprove of black male affairs with white women than do black men. Their disapproval can be explained by a distorted sex ratio between black women and black men which reduces the number of available black men for dating and marriage. It may be further explained by their knowledge that the pool of highly educated black men compared to the number of educated black women is low. Also, the number of eligible black males is restricted by his impoverished economic conditions and the disproportionate number of black men in prisons. Thus, affairs between black men and white females further reduces the number of available black males. On predominantly white college campuses, where few black students are enrolled, this situation often reaches critical proportions and black female hostility against black male-white female affairs rises.[52] Thus, the black male is called upon to defend his decision to engage in social relations across the color line.

The social costs for interracial dating and interracial marriage by whites also vary immensely. The white female, as does the black female who wishes to date across the color line, must be conscious of possible damage to her reputation. This situation is exacerbated by the prevailing belief that interracial dating, for example, inevitably involves interracial sexual relations. Thus, the girl who interracially dates may be labeled sexually promiscuous or easy bait. However, it is not generally assumed that in-group dating automatically means sex relations or that the female is promiscuous. The morality of the female participant is rarely an issue in within-group dating or marriage. But, in many instances, a white female who dates a black male will later find that she is unacceptable as a dating partner for white males, except for older white men and less prejudiced men in her community.[53] Another view is that a white girl who has sexual relations with a black male has "been ruined by him" because of his presumed genitalia size and bestiality. This belief may once again be a projection of the white male's insecurity in competing as an equal to black men in terms of sexual prowess. Such taboos, pressures by the white

community against interracial dating and social ostracism of participants in interracial affairs, may be rationalizations for white community members' unwillingness to concede that a white female may be
genuinely attracted to a black male.[54]

Who marries or dates across the color line? This question has
been answered in many different ways. Some people dismissed such
interracial activity as whims of crazed individuals suffering from
deeply-rooted psychological problems and the socially deviant. Other
more sophisticated efforts have been made to establish social types
among those who intermarry, for instance. In one such study in Chicago, the intermarried were classified as (1) intellectuals or bohe-
mians; (2) religious and political radicals; (3) persons from the
"sporting" world; and (4) persons from the stable middle class. The
data supporting this typology seems scanty at best.[55]

In another study, unsupported by data, Robert K. Merton hypothesized that (1) lower-class black females and lower-class white
males marry with about the same frequency as lower-class black males
with lower-class white females, and (2) the most frequent type of
intermarriage occurs between lower-class white females and upper-
class black males.[56] These hypotheses seem consistent with Ward's
first and third Laws of Race Mixing mentioned above (i.e., "Negro
women will freely accept white men" and "Negro men will greatly
prefer white women") . But, holding the social class variable constant,
Merton's hypotheses would seem to reject Ward's Law that "white
women will vehemently reject Negro men." Nevertheless, it is this
view enunciated in Merton's second hypothesis that is traditional and
has enjoyed wide popularity; that white women tend to marry higher
status black males and black males, conversely, marry lower class white
females. It is generally assumed that an exchange principle is involved
in such marriages because the lower class female exchanges the prestige of being from the dominant group for the higher socio-economic
standing she obtains from marrying a higher status black male.[57] This
situation depicts a kind of reverse hypergamy, but it assumes that her
prestige, even though lower than the black male in social class, makes
her equal to him.

Merton's original hypotheses were carefully scrutinized by Irving Stuart in an examination of a series of studies conducted since
1950. Stuart claims that these studies do not support Merton's hypotheses. For example, evidence refutes the notion that lower-class black females and lower-class write males marry either about the same fre-

quency as lower-class black males and lower-class white females. The ratio between such marriages is approximately 1 to 3. With regard to the second hypothesis that the most frequent type of intermarriage occurs between lower-class white females and upper-class black males, subsequent findings lead to the conclusion that this type of intermarriage occurs with far less frequency than other types. Citing studies from both Philadelphia and Indiana, Stuart maintains that the principle of homogamy (i.e., marriage between equals or near equals) operates, at least in terms of occupations, between black males and white females who marry.[58]

A recent study conducted by Ernest Porterfield attempted to examine many of the questions and issues associated with interracial marriages by collecting and analysing data drawn from intensive interviews with twenty black-white couples in a midwestern city. He was particularly interested in understanding their motives for marrying interracially, the happiness and security of their marriage, the types of reactions they received from their families and friends, the impact of the marriage on their children in terms of their social and emotional development, and the pressures brought to bear on them from the outside community.[59] The interviews consisted of sixteen black male-white female marriages and four white male-black female marriages. Eighteen of the twenty couples were living together at the time of the study and about one-fourth of the total of forty respondents were then in their second marriage. This group had a mean age of 24.5 when they married. Twenty-five of the forty respondents indicated no religious preference; nine were Protestants and the remainder were unevenly distributed among Catholics, Bahai and Jews. More than half of them had received one or more years of college training and slightly more than a fourth were at least college graduates. In terms of occupations, not including eleven housewives, most of them were professional and technical workers while others were concentrated in the categories of clerical and sales workers, craftsmen and foreman.[60]

These couples reported a variety of motives for getting married but most of them expressed basically the same reasons as persons from the same race express for deciding to marry: love and compatibility; shared interests; ideas and values. In only one instance, which involved a white female, was pregnancy cited as the primary motive for getting married. Some black husbands expressed a resentment against dominant black women; thus, they sought out white partners to help restore their manhood. Moreover, to these men, white women were more understanding of their needs, more passive and more affectionate. In a few instances, racial motives were stated as a major motivating factor. For example, some black husbands stated that initially revenge against the white male motivated them to date white women. By dating white females, they were defying one of the most rigorous taboos of white society. In this sense, their subsequent marriage was cacogamous since it involved tabooed deviations from the norms governing mate selection. For some black men, dating and marrying a white female meant not only the acquisition of a highly prized status symbol but provided them with a sense of power since she preferred him to the white male.[61]

Vindictiveness against the white male is often the reason given by the black male for interracial dating. Other writers have commented that black male respondents rationalized interracial dating with the claim that white women were freer with their money; while others stated in rather blunt terms that their cohabitation with white women cures them of racism, and, thereby, helps black people. [62] Still others express a need to seduce a white female because she is and has been the forbidden fruit. For others interracial contact gives them a special sense of worth and virility. Obviously, there is a need for considerably more empirical data on the motives of black men and of white women who date interracially before any definitive answer can be provided to this question. It would appear, however, that Porterfield's observation, that the significant majority of blacks and whites who marry or date across the color lines do so for fundamentally the same reasons as persons who date and marry within their own race, is accurate.

In Porterfield's study, the security of the marriage was affected by the same types of situations and factors as one finds in any other marriage: ability to listen to each other and understand each other's feelings and moods and developing a sense of understanding regarding such issues as money matters, division of labor, and the disciplining of children. In a few instances, difficulties were experienced as a consequence of their ambiguity relative to black awareness. This problem seems to be resolved by a self-realization that marriage is a personal choice that does not necessarily mean that the individual is less committed to the goals of creating a just society for both black and white people.[63]

Among a majority of the couples studied, white parents and relatives opposed the marriage. In contrast to the twelve of sixteen white brides whose families opposed the marriage, only three of the sixteen black grooms reported initial parental opposition. Almost half of the white brides reported little or no contact with their families but all the families of black spouses gradually accepted the white mate. The effect of negative reactions from white parents caused trauma for most white brides. That fact, coupled with parental rejection of their children, was particularly devastating to white brides. This situation is partially offset by the minimal problems encountered by the children in this study. The couples were about evenly divided in terms of favorable and unfavorable experiences with the white community. Half of them reported rejection and ostracism by the white community whereas the remaining half reported either congenial relationships or no difficulty with the white community. Although the black community seemed apathetic or indifferent to interracial couples, white brides were somewhat more strongly opposed than a black bride of a white husband. Nevertheless, there appears to be a greater inclination by the black community to accept interracial couples than by the white community. Obviously, such couples must possess the inner strengths to make ordinary marriage work and even moreso when the marriage is compounded by race and color. One of the most significant findings in this study is the sentiment expressed by many couples that intermarriage is the only way that the American society can ameliorate the problem of prejudice and racism.[64]

In any event, as opportunities for equal status interaction between black and white people increase, and as people become less and less resistant to the idea itself, we can expect a continuing increase in black-white dating and marriage in the United States. The black male, like others, will be no exception to the rule that dating and marriage involve choices influenced by innumerable factors and those choices are highly personal in a democratic and open society.

NOTES

1. Milton Barron, *The Blending American* (Chicago: Quadrangle Books, 1972), p. 16.
2. Ibid., p. 20.
3. Ibid., p. 23.
4. Irving R. Stuart, *Interracial Marriage: Expectation and Realities* (New York: Grossman Publishers, 1973), pp. 23–31.
5. Lerone Bennett, Jr., *Before the Mayflower* (Chicago: Johnson Publishing Company, 1962), p. 66.

6. John Hope Franklin, *From Slavery to Freedom* (New York: Alfred Knopf, 1952), pp. 71–74, and 203–4.
7. Lerone Bennett, op. cit., pp. 243–44.
8. Ibid., p. 246.
9. Ibid.
10. Ibid., p. 247.
11. Ibid., pp. 86–87.
12. Arnold Rose, *The Negro In America* (New York: Harper & Row, 1964), p. 194.
13. J. R. Washington, *Marriage in Black and White* (Boston: Beacon Press, 1970), pp. 190–91.
14. Alvin Poussaint, M.D., "Sex and The Black Male," *Ebony* 27, no. 10 (August, 1972): 114.
15. J. R. Washington, op. cit., p. 190.
16. Ibid.
17. James E. Blackwell, *The Black Community: Diversity and Unity* (New York: Dodd, Mead & Company, Inc., 1975).
18. Joseph C. Howard, Sr., "The Administration of Rape Cases in the City of Baltimore and the State of Maryland," Baltimore: A Paper Prepared for the Monumental Bar Association, August, 1967.
19. Robert P. Stuckert, "African Ancestry of the White Population," *Ohio Journal of Science* 58 (1958): 155–60. Also see revised version which appears in Peter B. Hammond, ed., *Physical Anthropology and Archaeology* (New York: Macmillan Company, 1964), pp. 192–96.
20. Ibid., p. 195.
21. John Hope Franklin, op. cit., p. 431.
22. Ibid., p. 432.
23. Milton Barron, op cit., p. 78.
24. Ibid. Also see J. A. Rogers, *Sex and Race,* vol. 3 (New York: Helga M. Rogers Company, 1964), pp. 18–24.
25. J. A. Rogers, op. cit., p. 18.
26. Ibid., p. 19.
27. Ibid., p. 20.
28. Ibid., p. 21.
29. Milton Barron, op. cit., p. 81.
30. Robert Sickels, *Race, Marriage and the Law* (Alburquerque: University of New Mexico Press, 1972), p. 98.
31. Ibid., p. 100.
32. George E. Simpson and J. Milton Yinger, *Racial and Cultural Minorities* (New York: Harper & Row, 1953), pp. 371–72.
33. David Heer, "Recent Data on Negro-White Marriages in the United States," (this paper was first presented at the annual meetings of the American Sociological Association in Montreal, August, 1964), p. 1.

34. Milton Barron, op. cit., p. 114.
35. Ibid., p. 125.
36. Irving R. Stuart, op. cit., p. 152.
37. *Special Report on Marriage,* U.S. Bureau of Census, Department of Commerce (Washington, D.C.: U.S. Government Printing Office, 1972).
38. Milton Barron, op. cit., p. 125.
39. Irving R. Stuart, op. cit., p. 129.
40. Ernest Porterfield, "Mixed Marriage," *Psychology Today* 6 (January, 1973): 71.
41. Lester F. Ward, *Pure Sociology* (New York: Macmillan and Company, 1914), pp. 358–60.
42. J. A. Rogers, op. cit., p. 64.
43. Simpson and Yinger, op. cit., p. 373.
44. For a lengthy discussion of these factors, cf. Sickels, op. cit., pp. 254–55; J. R. Washington, op. cit., pp. 200–201; and Milton Barron, op. cit., pp. 7–8, 41–43, and 101–102.
45. J. R. Washington, op. cit., p. 201.
46. Ibid., p. 294.
47. Sickels, op. cit., p. 27.
48. Porterfield, op. cit., p. 71.
49. Donald Bogue and Jan Dizard (this research was reported in the *Washington Post,* May 25, 1964).
50. Irving R. Stuart, op. cit., p. 130.
51. J. R. Washington, op. cit., pp. 313–16.
52. Charles V. Willie and Joan D. Levy, "Black Is Lonely," *Psychology Today* 5 (March 1972): 50–52, and 76–80.
53. Irving R. Stuart, op. cit., p. 136.
54. Ibid.
55. Simpson and Yinger, op. cit., p. 378.
56. Robert K. Merton, "Intermarriage and the Social Structure: Facts and Theory," *Psychiatry* 4 (1941): 361–74.
57. Simpson and Yinger, op. cit., p. 373.
58. Irving R. Stuart, op. cit., pp. 157–158.
59. Ernest Porterfield, op. cit., p. 72.
60. Ibid., p. 74.
61. Ibid.
62. Alvin Poussaint, op. cit., p. 117.
63. Ernest Porterfield, op. cit., p. 76.
64. Ibid., p. 78.

THE NEGRO MALE*

Calvin Hernton

I am not absolutely certain at what age I became conscious of my color as a limitation on where I could go, sit, or with whom I could associate. I think it was during my seventh year, for that was when I received my first beating for associating with a white female.

I know I was quite young, because the incident occurred in connection with my long hikes from grammar school, which was about four miles from my house. After traveling half the distance the other Negro children would gradually break off and go their separate ways. I would walk the rest of the way to my house alone. One afternoon, I met another child who had books and was about my age, or at least my size. At first, we did not say anything. But as the days went on, we began to talk to each other, we became friends and made a habit of meeting at the intersection of our similar yet different routes home. Every afternoon we romped up and down the street. I think we argued once—about what I do not recall. I know I hit her because of the argument. She cried. I apologized. After that we became greater friends.

One day my grandmother appeared on the sidewalk before us. I did not know where she came from. She seemed just to *be* there, and, although I did not know what the trouble was, I sensed from the look on her face that something was terribly wrong. My grandmother, who was not yet fifty, caught me by the back of my collar, and literally dragged me all the way home. She did not speak a word. At home, she gave me the beating of my life. I yelled and kicked, and I did not know what I had done . . . yet, I think, on some level of consciousness,

*From Calvin Hernton, *Sex and Racism in America,* © 1965. Reprinted with permission from Doubleday & Co., Garden City, N.Y.

I knew that it had something to do with my friend. When Grandmother finished lashing my backside with her belt, bubbles of perspiration stood on her hot, black face. Then she began to lash me with her tongue.

"Boy, is you done gone clean out of your mind!" There was terror in her eyes, and I looked at her dumbly.

"Do you want to git yoself lynched! Messing round wit a *white* gurl! A little, trashy, white heifer. Do you want to git me kilt! Git all the colored folks slaughtered . . ."

On and on she went. Her words put a fear into me that I have never forgotten—the same fear that was instilled so deeply in her that, as she talked, her whole body trembled. I began to tremble also; for, I believe, at that moment I was awakened to a vital part of me that somehow I would have to kill. And it was then, only then, that I began to cry.

No white person knows, really knows, how it is to grow up as a Negro boy in the South. The taboo of the white woman eats into the psyche, erodes away significant portions of boyhood sexual development, alters the total concept of masculinity, and creates in the Negro male a hidden ambivalence towards all women, black as well as white.

I do not know if other black boys had the fear of the white woman instilled in their minds through as shocking an incident as I. I do know that they learned it. The particular incident may vary from Negro to Negro, but the lesson is the same: avoid the woman that is white, act as if she does not exist. I learned as a boy, and later as a man, to bow and avert my eyes whenever talking to a white woman. In the South a Negro never looks a white woman straight in the face, never marvels at her figure no matter how attractive she is. On buses, in stores, on crowded streets, the Negro, at all costs, must avoid physical contact with white flesh. In Mississippi and other places in the Deep South, it is reported jokingly that a Negro must step off the sidewalk when a white woman approaches. This is not far from the truth. I know for a fact that it is dangerous in the South for a Negro to be caught (arrested, for instance) with a photograph of a white female in his possession. It would take a lot of nerve for a Negro to express his admiration for a movie star (Marilyn Monroe, Sophia Loren, etc.) in the company of a southern white man. John Dollard, in *Caste and Class in a Southern Town*, tells of an incident where a Negro was afraid to receive a simple letter from a white woman. Even in the North, as I shall show in more detail later, the Negro's fear of the consequences of being familiar with a white woman is not unusual.

Because he must act like a eunuch when it comes to white women, there arises within the Negro an undefined sense of dread and self-mutilation. Psychologically he experiences himself as castrated.

If a Negro acts differently, he runs the risk of being jailed, beaten, or lynched. Nevertheless, many Negroes run this risk. In secrecy, among themselves in pool rooms, on street corners, late at night when no white person is around, you can hear Negro men and teen-agers whispering and sometimes talking aloud about their adventures with white women. Each man who tells a story is laughed at, rebuffed, and "put down." The talk swirls as in a childhood fantasy. Yet every man knows that not all of the stories are lies or pure wishful thinking. Too often the news leaks out about a chauffeur caught red-handed, a handyman escaped North, a teen-ager lynched or electro-cuted. Always the crime is "rape," but everybody, especially the white women, rich or "poor trash," knows better.

I do not propose to evaluate the singular, long-range effects of the beating my grandmother gave me as a result of associating with a white girl. How can I? So much has taken place since then, both *to* me and *in* me. I know this: had my grandmother not discovered my particular transgression against the ethics of segregation when she did, it would have been only a matter of time before someone else would have noticed, and the consequence might or might not have been as severe as a beating. What was important for me—as it is for every Negro boy in the South—was that I gradually learned to fear and hate white girls. My hatred was as immobile as my fear. I feared and hated without understanding. The thought as well as the sight of a white woman completely awed me, and since I knew the white woman was taboo, although not precisely why, an ominous gloom settled upon my mood and lingered throughout my early life.

I remember, during the Depression, standing with my grand-mother in long, endless lines with other black folks, waiting for hours, day in and day out, and never reaching the doors of the building in-side of which potatoes and fat-back meat were being issued. All the while the white women and their children were moving up and on-ward. When at last, after our legs and faces were frozen from stand-ing all day, and we were inside, the white women behind the counter (who were merely teen-age girls) would tell Grandmother that there was no food. They were arrogant, flippant, and would usher us back out in the cold, empty-handed. Tears would hang in Grandmother's eyes as she would begin to moan the old spiritual about being "A Stranger in Dis Land." And that would seem to comfort her. It did not comfort me.

I knew that my grandmother knew that those girls were lying. There was food, and it was being given to the white women who pushed and shoved us around. I knew Grandmother was a proud, self-willed woman, and I could not understand why she belittled herself before those nasty, lying white girls. I hated those girls. I hated all white women. More important, there arose in me an incipient resentment towards my grandmother, indeed, towards all black women—because I could not help but compare them with white women, and in all phases of public life it was the Negro female who bowed her head and tucked her tail between her legs like a little black puppy.

I think now—no, I *know* now—that this is one of the reasons Negro women encounter so much frustration with their men. Living in a society where the objective social position and the reputed virtues of white women smother whatever worth black women may have, the Negro male is put to judging his women by what he sees and imagines the white woman is. A common expression among Negro males when anything goes wrong between them and their women is to say that a white woman would act differently. Without ever having associated with, let alone having been married to, a white woman, the black man asserts, half-heartedly but significantly, that black women are hell to get along with! The fact that this may be said about all American women does little to alter the black man's depreciatory concept of Negro females. How can it? For the myth of white womanhood has soaked into the Negro's skin. In matters of beauty, manners, social graces, and womanly virtues, the white woman is elevated by American society to the status of a near goddess. Everywhere, the Negro hears about and sees these nymphlike creatures. The Negro's world is thoroughly invaded by the white woman—the mass media, newspapers, magazines, radio, and especially television, bring these lily sirens into the blackness of the Negro's home and mind. It becomes all but impossible for the black man to separate his view of the *ideal* woman from that of the *white* woman. He may do it intellectually, cognitively, but it is a far more difficult feat to achieve emotionally! This is the reason many Negro men feel an estranged resentment towards black women, although they have no alternative but to live with and try to love them.

The human ego is, in large part, a reflection of (or an internalization of) what happens when one person encounters another person. This is especially true when the encounter involves individuals of the opposite sex. Before Grandmother whipped me, a girl was just a girl. After the beating, all females took on a meaning beyond their sex, a meaning symbolized and defined by the color of their skins. And this meaning, this symbolization of pigment severely altered my developing concept of myself as a black boy—a Negro male—in a world of black and white creatures called women. Although I did not understand the ethics of southern Jim Crow, I adhered to them. As long as I attended that school I walked out of my way to avoid my white friend, and I have never seen her again. But in the dream world, in the world of fantasy and nightmare, I saw her—and have seen her—countless times. And this—the autistic, or vicarious, compensation for the injury one suffers in real life—does not make for therapy, but adds to the diseased way in which the Negro male conceives of himself, of white women, and of black women too.

For reasons I consider irrelevant here, I have always wanted a sister. The rest is not irrelevant. Shortly after my first "lesson" in Jim Crow, I began to dream that I had a sister. Sometimes my sister would be colored. Most of the time she would be white—and even the colored sister would be of such light skin that if she wanted to (or if *I* wanted her to) she could pass for white. In both cases, one of the functions of my imaginary sister was to introduce me to imaginary interracial couples. My sister was beautiful, you see, and, of course, not prejudiced. Most of all, she *loved* me. We, my sister, and our interracial friends would do all kinds of things that young people ordinarily do. We played, went to movies, went on bus outings, and so on. We would even fight, but only to make up and become greater comrades. When I say I had such dreams, I do not mean dreaming merely while asleep, I mean daydreaming, outright childhood fantasizing. I made the world *good*; I made black and white people—especially men and women—like and enjoy each other. And yet, there was always the "outside world," a hostile world of blacks and whites of whom we—I, my sister, and friends—had to be cautious. For instance, I fantasized a fabulous apartment left to us by our parents (*you see, our parents were dead*). And this was where we spent most of out time, hidden from the outside world. When *we* went somewhere in public, we acted in such a way that people could not really tell that we were together. Frequently my dreams assumed a deeper, perhaps more psychiatric, dimension. I would, with her consent, have sex with my sister, the colored one. And always she would turn into the white sister. I would begin to scream and run, thinking she was going to yell and bring down the white community on me and my grandmother. But she never did; instead, she would hold me and reassure me that no one would ever know. I always woke up in a cold sweat.

These dreams and fantasies persisted on an ever widening and deepening level throughout my teens—that is, until I finished high school. At that time I began to date rather seriously. My dates were always light-skinned Negro girls, never dark or black ones, no matter how pretty they might have been. For, I know now, my desire for a girl was affected by the myth and taboo of the white woman. I know now why I enjoyed the envy of other black boys—because I had a light-skinned girl friend. As we walked the streets, all eyes, black and white, would linger or flash quickly upon us. And I was proud. But not proud enough. I felt a partial fulfillment of my ego as a black boy, but it was only partial—because although my girl was very light with long black hair, she was still a Negro. She was, for that alone, not as good as a real white girl. I made up for this also by dreaming. Often while we sat cheek to cheek in the dark of a movie, I would look at her through the depraved eye of my mind and imagine her as white—and some- times I would even grow afraid to touch her face. At about that time the Negro press had made big headlines of an event in Georgia: a Negro had failed to help a desperate white woman escape from the flaming wreckage of an automobile, because he had been afraid of the consequences of laying his black hands on her flesh in order to pull her free. The woman had perished.

To every Negro boy who grows up in the South, the light-skinned Negro woman—the "high yellow," the mulatto—incites awe. The white woman incites even *more* awe. As a boy I was, to say the least, confused. As I grew older, the desire to see what it was that made white women so dear and angelic became a secret, grotesque burden to my psyche. It is that to almost all Negro men, no matter how suc- cessfully they hide and deny it. And for these reasons—the absurd idoli- zation of the white woman and the equal absurdity of the taboo sur- rounding her—there arises within almost all Negroes a sociosexually induced predisposition for white women. The fact that few Negroes will readily admit this is due more to their knowledge that black women and whites in general bitterly disapprove of it, than to their honesty. For if a situation occurs where a white woman makes herself accessible to a black man, the Negro usually takes her. However cautiously, he takes her at once like a grateful baby and like a savage monster. He suffers mixed emotions of triumph, fulfillment, and guilt. At eighteen I had an affair with a white girl in a small town in Alabama. She met me one night in an abandoned railroad yard. I was nervous and scared, not primarily that someone might discover us—although I was scared of that too—but mainly just because she was *white*. I kissed her mouth. I wanted to see if it was different, if it was better than a black mouth. I looked at her for the first time directly and long. It felt like magic—and yet why? Why! I was baffled over whatever white women were supposed to possess that made them objects of grave consequences. Why were they so important? I wondered about her anatomy. I ran my hands over her body. I wanted to know if it was different, if it felt better than black flesh. I kept wanting to find out what made white womanhood *white womanhood*; I wanted to unearth the quality that made her angelic and forbidden.

My search failed. There was nothing objectively or inherently emotional that was *that* different or angelic. Yet there was something —and it was distorted and horrible. There was all of the southern ideology of racism and sex that had been instilled in my mind, in my very skin, and no doubt in hers too. Cautiously, diligently, maddeningly I took her. I hated her for what she made me feel, for the good and bad that she inspired in me; for what she *reduced* me to. I loved her too! But somehow I could not purge myself of the feeling that it was wrong and perverse. I came away not knowing whether I felt elated or outraged.

When I was a student at a southern Negro college, one of the unexpected experiences I had was when I went to the library one day and pulled from the shelves a book which contained a collection of writings by Negroes. I opened the book and there on the first page was the title in large caps: WHAT THE NEGRO WANTS. Just below the title something had been scribbled and erased. But I could still discern what it had been; it was a "reply" to the title of the book, WHAT THE NEGRO WANTS: "Some white p — — — y."

The southern white man claims that Negroes are possessed by a savage urge to have sex with white women, or, more correctly, that Negroes want to rape white women. If there is truth in this claim, it is not because of any natural urge in the Negro. The desire to have sex with or to rape the white woman is a by-product of what racism,

Jim Crow, and prejudice have made of not only the Negro but everybody affected by American bigotry.

In the mind and the life of the Negro man the white woman symbolizes at once his freedom and his bondage. She is made into an object of temptation and repulsion, love and hate. It appears to me that the black man's sexual existence in the South is predicated upon the existence of the white woman who is inaccessible. A kind of reverse racism sets in. The Negro, like everyone else, hates what he cannot love; he wants what he cannot have; he degrades and mutilates that which humiliates and deranges him.

"Just look at all those proud, white asses shaking like jelly," said a friend of mine as we drove through the downtown section of Nashville, Tennessee. "I hate those white ugly bitches," he went on. "They think they own the world. And they do. Say, look at that one. What a fine dish! I'd like to rape her with a telegraph pole." He laughed. "No I wouldn't either. I'd use my own penis. Look at them, coming out of those offices, sitting on their fine asses all day, doing nothing. I could screw every one I see. Especially that one over there in the blue skirt. I bet I could make her moan and groan like no white man's ever done, make her *love* me. Damn!—the white man's got everything—money, jobs, even our own women—everything! And don't know what to do with any of it. Say, what you smiling at? What you thinking?" "Nothing," I lied. I was studying his face, the way it grew tight, tense, the way it lit up or flickered as he talked. There was hatred, envy, love, fear, impotence, desire, and the mixture of emotions that almost every Negro male learns to feel towards the white woman. I was thinking, Could this man actually commit rape? Was it possible that the white woman could have such an effect upon an otherwise bright and well-bred Negro?

I had known him for several years. We had come through college together at the head of our class. Another year in graduate school and he would be a chemist. He had already been offered a top position with a major chemical firm. I was pondering the nature of a way of life that could cripple a healthy individual to the point that the individual, black or white, could lose control and, if the situation occurred, become a rapist, heaving and ravishing like a wild animal. I am well aware that, like murder, rape has many motives. But when the motive for rape, however psychotic, is basically racial, that is a different matter. I know now that, at one time or another, in every

Negro who grows up in the South, there is a rapist, no matter how hidden. And that rapist has been conceived in the Negro by a system of morals based on guilt, hatred, and human denial.

My friend, the chemist, as far as I know, never raped a white woman. He did something better than that, or maybe worse. He married and divorced, and then remarried. His second marriage took place in California, to a white woman from Texas.

Not only are the customs, attitudes, and sentiments in America unequivocally against personal relationships between Negro men and white women, but the taboos against such relations are incorporated in the legal statutes of southern cities and states. In addition to this, the mere association of Negro men and white women in any manner whatever, except in the strictest formal or business sense, is a crime. In Selma, Alabama, for instance, a Negro can be arrested simply for talking to ("socializing with") a white woman in private or public surroundings. This means, as interpreted by local police, that a Negro can be jailed for walking too close to a white woman on the sidewalk!

In the North, unlike the South, there are very few laws prohibiting interracial relations between the sexes. It is not the law, then, that is being tested when an interracial couple marries or is seen on the streets north of the Mason-Dixon Line. What are being tested are the informal attitudes and disapprovals. It is axiomatic that the sentiments of an overwhelming majority of northern whites are against interracial couples, especially couples comprising Negro men and white women. More significant are the deeply embedded emotions of the Negro himself toward white women.

There is much truth in the adage that it is a relatively easy matter to take the boy out of the country, but one does not so easily take the country out of the boy. Those Negroes who have come from the South, but who still have the South in them, react in the North to the white woman in more or less the same pattern that they learned in the South. They may work beside and indulge in conversation with white women, but it is all on the up and up, strictly impersonal. By and large, one hears and sees in action in the North the same attitude of ambivalence and avoidance toward the white woman as one sees and hears in the South. This is especially true with older Negroes. Then, too, most Negroes in the North live, for one bad reason or another, in ghettos. They may work outside of the ghetto in an "integrated atmosphere," but they *live* in milieus that are difficult to distinguish from the ones in which Negroes live in the South. Not only does the "outer society" punish a Negro for associating with a white woman, his very own people extract an oath from him to associate exclusively with his own kind. The greatest pressure of this sort comes, understandably, from the Negro female, who feels that her chances of obtaining a man are lessened when she has to compete not only with females of her own race but with white women too.

At present, a Negro who marries or embarks on a personal relationship with a member of the white race, is ostracized and intimidated by such groups as the Black Nationalists and the Black Muslims. Basically, these groups, fanatic in zeal, employ in reverse the same arguments against race mixing as their white counterparts who are racists. They extol the "purity" of black womanhood, exalt the "superiority" of black people, and insist on thoroughly living up to the creed which says: "Buy Black, Think Black," and most of all, "Love Black!" During the Birmingham rallies that took place in Harlem, Eartha Kitt was booed and jeered off the rostrum by hundreds of Negroes because, among other things, she had married a white man. A brilliant young Negro was fired from his position with a now defunct organization because his wife, whose dedication to the Negro struggle is outmatched only by her beauty, is white. Pressure is also put on Negroes to love and marry black by a class of Negroes who otherwise go along with the integration and equality program. These Negroes claim that, since the sex issue is so explosive, and the segregationists use this issue to their advantage, Negroes should avoid intimacy with white women because it will "hurt the movement for civil rights." Always, the strongest pressure, on the part of both black and white, is not so much against Negro women marrying white men as against black men marrying white women.

Now, while I recognize the existence of these pressures from both the white and black communities in the North, I must give credence to the proposition that in the mind of the Negro the North consitutes the proving ground of his freedom. Coming North has always been, and still is, an experience of intense anticipation for the Negro. Among all of the things the Negro male looks forward to, encountering the white woman is definitely one of them. I recall when I was a youth living in the South, a certain young man went North. Upon his return all of the boys from the neighborhood gathered around him. Among the most important questions we asked was, "Did you meet any white girls, did you see any Negroes with white women? Are things really like they say they are up North?" When the young man, with obvious pride, pulled from his wallet a photograph of a beautiful white girl, we all sighed, and a great loneliness settled over us.

In matters such as housing, employment, civil rights, and so forth, the Negro in the North takes a positive position, even if he is disillusioned in the end. More often than not, he is. But in the presence of the white woman the Negro is not so sure of himself. He has heard stories about white women and Negro men in the North from (as indicated above) Negroes who came North and returned South. He realizes that bits of truth and bits of fantasy are interwoven in such tales. Because of the tremendous fear and trembling that has been shot into his brain while living in the South, the Negro, even in the North, cannot completely extricate himself from the cataclysm of emotions he has learned to feel toward the white woman. In her presence, he is in a quandary: Should he act like most Negroes, as if he were still down South? Should he be forthright but businesslike? Should he approach her in all his manliness as he would any other woman? Or should he strive for some kind of equilibrium or compromise between these attitudes? At first he does not know.

I recall when I first came North I got along fine. I sat anywhere I chose, ate anywhere, looked for a job anywhere. In all of this, however, I dreaded the white woman. I pretended otherwise, but I know now that I did. The first time a white woman sat down beside me on the subway, it was difficult for me to control myself. I stole glances at her out of the corner of my eye. I looked at others on the subway to check their reaction. I could smell her perfume, and I was relieved when she got off. I also remember making the rounds of employment agencies. Whenever the interviewer was a white female, I grew tense and my hands perspired. On one occasion I made the interview short and hurried out of the office. The young woman who was interviewing me appeared tender and fragile, yet she treated me as if I—the *real* I—did not exist. I was not ashamed of being a Negro, and I wanted her to recognize me as such and not treat me like some anonymous entity. I could tell she was conscious of my Negroness, while deliberately pretending she was not. I do not want anybody to love me simply because I am black. Neither do I want people to ignore me because of my color.

It seems to me that every Negro male who encounters a white woman in the North is subtly testing the degree to which he is accepted by the way the woman reacts toward the visual perception of his person as a black man. Much of this is due to plain curiosity. A sort of flirtation with the unknown, a desire for new experience, or simply a desire for a fuller, if not richer, life. And when, as is so often the case, the Negro is not accepted, he reverts back to the southern ethics of race relations. He rejects the white woman, he hates that which denies his existence, he stays his social and psychological distance, and he spouts the rhetoric of sour grapes.

On the other hand, one does not walk the streets of any major northern city without passing a few mixed couples here and there. For one reason or another, the various external pressures and overt social taboos are not severe enough in the North to prevent some black men from pursuing the white woman. In fact, it may be these very pressures and taboos that stimulate the Negro to pursue the white woman. Emphasizing the perils and sacrifices of associating with a white woman may tend to enhance her value in the eyes of the Negro. To such a Negro, the prize is worth the challenge. Indeed, it is this sort of spirit or "guts" that has made America a great nation. The rugged individualist, the man who transcends the chains of background and provincialism to surge ahead toward new frontiers is an American hero. For the contemporary Negro the white woman definitely represents a "new frontier."

In all "civilized" societies there seems to be something about men and women so that, from time to time, one finds various couples from diverse backgrounds falling in love and marrying, despite the taboos that may exist against these unions. I suspect, or at least hope, the same principle applies to some interracial love affairs and marriages.

However, I do not think that the personality forces that mobilize most Negroes who seek relations with white women are free of ulterior or psychiatric motives. I have in mind those Negroes, mostly youths, who journey from Harlem down to Greenwich Village every weekend with one purpose in mind—to "make some ofay chick." The Lower East Side of New York (the "East Village") is notorious for its interracial, bohemian-type weekend parties. White girls make themselves readily available to black boys, and black boys shuffle through the assortment of white flesh like fierce hunters on safari. As one goes from party to party, from one beatnik bar to the other, one becomes aware of a kind of mutual conspiracy between white women and black men. One of the features that characterizes the behavior of these Negroes is their attempt to intimidate the white male by making free play with his woman. At one of these parties I observed such a scene in action. There was a young, sandy-headed, timid-looking fellow standing in one corner of the room. On his arm was a shapely girl of about nineteen. A tall, black, mawkish but rather handsome Negro emerged in the center of the room. He was pretending to be drunker than he really was. He reeled and tottered, peered around. I watched him. Then he saw the couple. He staggered over to them, reached for the girl, caught her hand and muttered, "Le's do the thang." The girl followed him onto the floor and he danced her a vulgar whirl, no, *twirl* is the right word. He fondled her buttocks and breasts right there on the floor, and mumbled words into her mouth. All the while he was glancing over her head at the sandy-haired fellow in the corner, who was fuming but trying his best to ignore the scene. When the Negro had finished, he slapped the girl on her round, plump buttocks. Then he went over to the fellow in the corner and, with a smirk on his mouth, said, "Thank you, dad." It cut like a razor.

I know for certain—and I *must* say this—that white men in the North show more restraint and courtesy in their dealings with Negro women. Not once have I seen a white man insult or intimidate his black girl in mixed company. Maybe he is afraid, or perhaps he has no need for it.

In the confines of the hip, the beatniks, and the young liberals one learns that many Negroes exploit the exploitable. In the process, the Negroes exploit themselves. They parade and display their Negroness. No, no, it is the *nigger* in them that they display, the stereotype to which white women must respond in order to prove their liberalness or hiptitude. For these Negroes, "making the ofay chick" is at once an act or aggression against white society and against the girl herself.

In this connection it is well to mention a term that, with the rise of African nationalism, has become more and more a part of the Negro's vocabulary. The word is "negritude." From what I understand, this word is supposed to lend pride and even superiority to Negro characteristics, both physical and cultural, as opposed to the devaluation of these characteristics by the standards of the white world. While there is much validity to negritude, I suspect that many, too many, Negroes use negritude to exploit white women. In fact, this is their only appeal. Many such Negroes, for instance, will not comb their hair or take a bath, and they exaggerate their Negroness in order to obtain a white girl. And it is true that many white girls, who are trying so desperately to liberate themselves from prejudice and racial bias, respond, however painful it may be to do so, to this type of "negritude," this kind of vulgarization of the so-called "black mystique."

I think of a story told to me by a young Negro who had just moved into a new neighborhood. He inquired, among the Negroes who had been in the neighborhood for some time, as to the availability of girls. One Negro told him,

> Look man, you don't have to worry about getting a chick. You are *black;* all you have to do is walk into a party and act *black,* act mean.

A great many of these Negroes hate white women, and having sexual relations with them is one way of destroying or mutilating the enemy (ofay).

Surprisingly (or is it to be expected?), there are Negroes who are afflicted with the white man's mythological concept of Negro sexhood. Their behavior around white women is strictly sexual. They prance around, jump up and down, gyrate their pelvises, and nearly every word they speak has a sexual reference. It is not simply a matter of trying to exploit the white man's sex image of the Negro. No! Such Negroes would have us believe that they live entirely in their sex, and, like raving cripples, they do! These *Negroes* are *diseased* by the racist's grotesque sex image of them, which, after all, is nothing more than a myth. It is not uncommon to discover that many of the Negroes who constantly strive to project such mammoth sexuality around white women are lonely men. In fact, they are sexual failures with Negro women, if not repressed homosexuals. At the bottom of their hearts many of the Negroes who pursue or marry white women have the same concept of white women as do the white racists. This is understandable, for, *like the white racists, these Negroes are victims of the myth of sacred white womanhood.* For instance, a Negro writer admitted that his white wife was a "jewel, too lovely and delicate to make love to." The writer keeps his "jewel" in the house and seldom lets her go anywhere. She is his secret "prize." Meanwhile he "runs around" pursuing Negro women. On the other hand, some Negroes react in the opposite way—and here I have in mind those Negroes we see daily (in Greenwich Village, for instance) who make a public display of hugging and caressing their white women on the streets, in restaurants, and wherever there are people to watch. "It was my way of defying the society," stated an older Negro as he recalled that he used to do the same thing. He further stated:

It was my way of getting back at the white world. Even during inter-course, I was getting back at white folks for everything they inflicted upon me as a Negro. But that kind of thing wears lean after a while—when you get older I mean—and you settle down to love her and for-get about the white world; I mean, if you love her in the first place.

I might add that, it seems to me, many Negroes never get over "that kind of thing." None of their relationships with white women ever get over "that kind of thing." None of their relationships with white women ever progress beyond the state of "getting back at the white world" through sadistic treatment of white women. And to my mind, this seems as "sick and disgusting" as the sadistic treatment of Negro women in the South by white racists. And yet one gets the im-pression, deep behind the smoldering eyes (acting "mean"), that there is an intense desire on the part of many of these Negroes to really love the white woman. But because of the deranged emotional fabric with which racism in America has afflicted the majority of such Negroes, they are, alas, incapable of genuine love for *any* woman.

Again, in Greenwich Village, as in other parts of the North, one finds also the professional white-woman chaser, or more correctly, the white-woman seducer. Such Negroes earn their living—food, clothing, drink, rent—from white women who are starved for attention and af-fection. The Negro is not necessarily handsome; in fact, I think it is better for the woman if the Negro is unattractive, that is, by white standards. For the women who are susceptible to this kind of Negro are predominantly depraved women who despise themselves for one reason or another. The professional white-woman seducer is aware of this; he capitalizes on it. He does not love these women. He cannot love them. Like all pimps, the professional hustler of white women is beyond love, for he has come to believe that it is only for fools and babies.

In Baldwin's *Another Country*, the jazz musician, Rufus, who lives with a southern-born, socially defunct white woman, is the fic-tional image of the extremely paranoid Negro who marries or "shacks up" with a white woman. Rufus hated his white girl friend, he hated her very "whiteness." In and through her, he hated the whole society. Coupled with this, Rufus hated himself for being black. On both counts he loved and hated his white girl friend, the symbol of all that was good and evil in his life. Hate, sadistic love, and resentment won out. Rufus not only beat her unmercifully, he committed every atroc-ity a man can commit against a woman. In the end he drove her in-sane and himself to suicide.

In too many of the environments where interracial sex is sought, it is the Rufus type of syndrome—the hunger, the hatred, the love and resentment for white women—that one discerns smoldering beneath the eyes of black men. The would-be greats, the jazz musicians, the small-time hipsters, the disgruntled writers, poets, and painters, the marijuana smokers, the seekers of thrills and orgies, the misfits, the socially deformed, the outcasts—all are possessed by a design on the white woman which is chillingly similar to the white racist's design on the black woman. To the black man who is sexually sick, the white woman represents an object for symbolic mutilation as well as an escape from a despised self through the act of sexual intercourse. To the depraved Negro, every white woman is the living embodiment of the forces that have oppressed and crippled him.

The history of cults, movements, cultures, and cliques prove one thing, if nothing else. No ideology—political, national, religious, or otherwise—is strong enough to restrict an individual's preference for a certain approved group or class of females. Strangely enough, or perhaps it is altogether natural, young Africans in this country tend to avoid close ties with American Negroes, to snub them with superior airs. It is nothing, on the other hand, for these proud young Africans to date and cater to white women. I am certain that most American Negroes—especially the Black Muslims and Black Nationalists—would be shocked to know that the first and perhaps foremost American Negro leader, Frederick Douglass, married in 1884 a white woman, Helen Pitts, who was his secretary while he held the post of Recorder of Deeds for the District of Columbia. Negroes were "shocked and disappointed." Everyone, including Douglass's children and his long-trusted house servant, felt betrayed. Of late, a rather accomplished Negro man of letters has remarked that this marriage was the "most dramatic challenge to color prejudice in America."[1] Any oppressed group, when obtaining power, tends to acquire the females of the group which has been the oppressor.

Although racism of any sort is ideological in content, its effect upon the individual is psychopathic. As Sartre has brilliantly shown (*Portrait of an Anti-Semite*), a man prejudiced against Jews may either burst with pornographic sexual excitement or may become suddenly impotent when confronted by a woman who is Jewish. The same thing applies to both sides of the racial coin in the United States today.

In America, however, where the Negro is the underdog and the white woman is the great symbol of sexual purity and pride, the black man is often driven to pursue her *in lieu* of aggrandizing his lack of self-esteem. Having the white woman, who is the prize of our culture, is a way of triumphing over a society that denies the Negro his basic humanity. Going up the color ladder in America is one way of acquiring status. Within the Negro community, value is distributed on the basis of shades of pigment. A man who marries a light-skinned Negro woman has "achieved" more prestige through his marriage than one who marries a darker woman. Similarly, for many black men the white woman is the zenith of status symbols.

In one of Langston Hughes's poems, he writes about Negro babies in Alabama having white mammies who rocked them in their laps and nestled them close to their white breasts. There is straight psycho-analytical truth in his words. It seems altogether plausible that deep in the psyches of many Negroes there is the rejection of their black mothers, or, positively stated, there is the wish for a white mother. After all, if the Negro had a white mother, the chances are he would not be black. If the white racist has an incestuous urge for black women because of the infantile or boyhood memory of his black mammy who nursed and suckled him on her big, black breasts, I think it is reasonable to explore the possibility of some Negroes relating to white women on the same principle.

I know Negroes whose relationship with their white women approximates this type of situation. It is always embarrassing to visit their homes. The Negro is usually a steady drinker, he does very little around the apartment, he "writes" or engages in some other "artistic endeavor," but he very seldom produces. To show how unprejudiced he is, he never fails to bring up the race problem. He lies all over and fondles his wife deliberately in your presence. One thing is certain— without her he is nothing. Unless she needs this kind of neurotic behavior, the wife or lover has a very hard time with this type of Negro. Even if the woman is neurotic herself, sometimes the situation becomes so absurd and embarrassing that she will order her black husband to stop and sit down in an individual chair. On one occasion, a young woman burst into tears in my presence.

Some Negroes who seek out white women show a marked readiness for jealousy when they see a white man with a black woman (one of "ours"). They will try to intimidate the woman by making some kind of "smart" remark or by accusing her of "selling out the race." One Negro girl informed me that it is very common for a Negro, upon finding out that she is married to a white fellow, to walk up to her and whisper in her ear, "Are you being satisfied?" Such Negroes act and talk like schizophrenics. They preach "black pride" and exhibit "black jealousy," on the one hand, while on the other hand, they are constantly haunting interracial bars, parties, and so forth, always seeking to woo the white woman. They are afflicted with what I have termed elsewhere "the syndrome of blackness." Despising both races, they want to be white and black at the same time. They want to eat their color and have it too.[2]

With Negroes who *have* to marry white women, much more than status or an attempt to escape a despised self is involved. There is something metaphysical about their need for white women. I believe that this was the case with a famous Negro writer. He was great in his own person. He did not need a white woman to display to the world as a sign of his having "achieved." He needed—I mean *needed* —a white woman for something more urgent than this. Elsewhere I have written that, in the disposition of the deformed, there is the organic craving to be loved by those who have crippled them, to be redeemed by those who have damned them. The hero of Richard Wright's second major novel, *The Outsider*, is a young Negro named Cross Damon. In the course of the book he murders four people. Cross is a clever, intellectual, superbly self-controlled Negro, and no one can accuse him of the crimes. Although dread and guilt weigh heavily upon him, throughout the entire novel he never breaks down—except once. The occasion involves a white woman:

> "Have mercy on me," we hear Cross cry out to her, "Pity me; be my judge; tell me if I am to live or die."

He is on his knees, and he begs the white woman to *judge* him, to absolve him from his sins, from the guilt that floods his being. The woman sympathizes, but she really does not know what her black prince is talking about.

Because the Negro is hated, South and North, so deeply on the basis of his blackness, any black man who receives kind treatment from a white person is indeed grateful—and especially so if the white person is a female. After the depraved self-concept that centuries of racism has wrought within the Negro, a simple act of human kindness from a white female elicits the most extreme feelings of gratitude from the Negro. He wants to respond in the most tender way possible—sexually. Even a white man, John Griffin, who had dyed his skin and was pretending to be a Negro, felt gratitude when a southern white woman merely refrained from staring at him in the usual hateful manner. He writes:

> She merely looked at me and did not change her expression. My gratitude to her was so great it astonished me![3]

A very dark Negro who served as an informant for this book reported how he felt when he first experienced a white woman who said she loved him because he was black.

> Man, I felt like a king. And yet I felt humble like a baby. I didn't let her know it though. But hell, man, nobody has ever loved me because I was black—not even my own wife. It was the first time in my whole life that anybody ever made me feel proud of being black.

Precisely! Many Negro men who are black, and therefore "ugly" (by white standards), find it difficult to acquire a suitable Negro mate. Negro women tend to choose Negro men on one of two bases: 1) the Negro must *not* be "black and ugly"; or 2), if he is, he must then be a professional man such as a doctor, lawyer, or professor. A "black and ugly" man, if he is not rich or a professional, usually has to settle for any female he can get and from any sort of background. Even if the Negro is a professional and succeeds in getting a woman who is educated and more or less refined in manners and social outlook, her resentment for his blackness comes out sporadically, if not constantly, to plague his ego. For instance, one Negro who fits the above description reported the following about his "light-skinned," educated wife.

> I see her sometimes looking at me when I am naked or just when I am milling around the house—I see the resentment in her well-guarded eyes. Whenever I do something she doesn't like, she always calls me a black bastard. If she catches me in a lie, I'm not a lying bastard, I'm a *black* bastard. If I cheat on her, I'm not a cheating bastard, I'm a *black* bastard. No matter what it is she's mad at me about, I'm always a black bastard.

Anyone who is familiar with what happens between dark-skinned Negro men and women when they are arguing can bear witness to the racial epithets that the couple fling back and forth at one another. "Black bastard," "thick-lip bastard," "ugly nigger," "nappy-head bitch," "black dog," and so on. Such epithets, no matter how they are used, do considerable damage to the Negro's appreciation of himself.

Negroes have come to think of themselves in terms of white standards of beauty and attractiveness. This is what someone has called *the mark of oppression*. The point is, however, that many of the darker Negro men who pursue white mates do so because their own women have rejected them because they are "black and ugly." Whereas, white women, not having actually suffered the negative valuation accorded Negroid features, can live with a so-called "black and ugly" Negro without constantly making the Negro secretly despise himself for the way he happens to look. Because the white woman is not herself involved with all the ego effects of being black, it is even possible for her to look, if she will, at the Negro with fresh eyes and see him as some kind of "exotic beauty," which the Negro woman who is involved with being black herself cannot do. Thus, we hear some Negro men proclaiming that such and such a white woman treats them better than the females of their own race. (Needless to say, all of this applies to Negro women and white men also.)

Although the American Negro will quickly deny the assertion that he has a religious urge for the white woman, in a great number of instances the black man not only seeks aggression in taking the white woman's body, but through her flesh he renders himself up as if to God, praying that his sense of guilt for his blackness will be conjured away. For this kind of Negro, sex with the white woman is an exigency as holy as Communion. It is a matter of sin and absolution.

I have stated that the whole denial of the Negro's humanity, specifically his masculinity, is in large measure predicated upon the existence of the white world. The white world is virtuous, holy, chaste. The black world is dirty, savage, sinful. At the center of the clean world stands the white woman. To Negroes who feel and suffer the atrocities of racism and inhumanity with intensity, one of the necessary components for transcending or "cleansing" the sin of blackness from their beings is to possess the white woman. According to the myth of white supremacy, it is the white woman who is the "Immaculate Conception" of our civilization. Her body is a holy sacrament, her possession is a sort of ontological affirmation of the black man's being. Hatred, guilt, bitterness, love, and resentment are all involved, I suspect. But with men like Richard Wright, the magnitude of their commitment to truth and life—rather than to death and hate—makes their love and comradeship burn through. Few white women marry black men of this caliber. Those who do should count themselves among the fortunate.

NOTES

1. See Arna Bontemps, *100 Years of Negro Freedom* (New York: Dodd, Mead & Co., 1961), pp. 111–13.
2. See my article, "Black Muslims and White Liberals," *Negro Digest,* October 1963.
3. John Griffin, *Black Like Me* (New York: Signet Books, 1963), p. 117.

EXPECTATIONS AND SALIENCE IN WHITE FEMALE-AFRICAN MALE SELF-OTHER ROLE DEFINITIONS*

Doris Y. Wilkinson

The concepts of role and self are central to social psychological explanations of linkage patterns between structure and personality. They represent key variables in interpretations of situational interpersonal and collective relational processes. Conceptions and definitions of social roles permeate the human social universe, and all small-scale interpersonal encounters represent microcosms of the broader cultural milieu.[1] Particularly essential in the structural arrangement or organization of a society are self-role translations and uses of the bio-genetic status of an individual's sex.[2] Universally female and male status-role nuclei are related to expectations and behavioral enactments and to a division of labor system. Cross culturally, habituated custom; physical strength; functional necessity in terms of individual and collective needs; relationships to systems of production, distribution, and exchange are correlated with the anatomy of sex. The life cycle of a society revolves around sex-role definitions and expected behaviors. Cultural values and historical precedents transcend the bio-genetic essence of sex distinctions, for the former subsequently determine expectations for role enactments. In this connection, it has been aptly stated that "sexual identities are defined in social interaction" and that each soci-

*Doris Y. Wilkinson, Ph.D., is a professor in the Department of Sociology, Macalester College, Saint Paul, Minnesota. This is an original paper written for this volume.

ety "takes the basic biological differences between men and women and creates a special reality."[3]

Similarly in a society where variations in color are given meaning, a new reality is created. However, the substance, extent and intensity of the formation of an identity based on color designated rules for role behavior *and* the socialization to sex roles vary depending on which ascriptive qualities assume prominence or saliency. In the cultural history of America and in the contemporary setting, as in South Africa, color forms the foundation for stratification of peoples, related role definitions, and expected performances. And in any society where color becomes a central ingredient in social distinctions, a system of differential privileges, rewards, and expectations emerges which favors both the color and sex of the group holding a monopoly on the economic machinery and mechanisms for the acquisition and maintenance of mastery over all societal functionings. In such a network, sex differences, among economically powerless people of contrasting complexion, which are assigned meaning by the ruling strata, become blurred. To legitimize and maintain the positions of both groups, the ruling elite creates a color-sex ideology.

Of interest in this discussion, which incorporates a few pertinent concepts from role theory,[4] is the interweaving of color and sex in terms of the construction of a unique set of role expectations, definitions, and perceptions surrounding their unification. Specifically the focus is on the complementarity of expectations characterizing initial dating-mating encounters between an African American male and a white female. Regardless of the setting, whether a bar, church, academic institution, or civil rights organization, a reciprocity of signs and signals or symbols, based on mutually learned conceptions and expections, characterizes the encounter. The signs are typically conventional gestures used to communicate a feeling, mood, or an idea, such as in the "hate stare."[5] Closely interwoven with signs are actual signals[6]—behaviors which incite some complimentary actions. Both signs and signals carry an intrinsic value inseparable from that which they symbolize. This inseparability is vividly illustrated in an initial encounter between a black male and a white female. Whenever a social situation has the potential for a mating liaison, the relevance of cultural cues as keys to expectations and salience in self-other definitions is demonstrated. Salient aspects of roles based on color-directed definitions indicate a finite universe of signs and signals in a highly symbolic interactional arena. Any discussion of mating oriented signals and cultural cues in terms of color and sex logically centers on the black male-white female as a focal unit since it is the most frequent type of inter-color dyadic system. And because of the nature and impact of white racism on sex roles, the black male-white female union has the dimensions of status-role reversal which characterize no other ideal or normatively expected male-female relationship. Moreover the 1970 census showed a relative decrease in the absolute numbers of white male-black female marriages.[7]

When an individual holds a set of expectations for self and "significant" or "generalized" others, a collection of regulations and symbols for eliciting predictable behavior responses is in existence. To expect simply means to anticipate or believe on the basis of prior knowledge and experience, or inferences deducted from indoctrination in cultural rules, that certain types of events or behaviors will occur. When something is expected, it is regarded as likely to happen. There may also be a wish component connected with expectations wherein one hopes some event will take place. In the mathematical sense an expectation refers to the probability or the degree of likelihood of the occurrence of something. This conception is applicable to social anticipation. Surrounded by the appropriate cultural cues, all role definitions are composed of a series of interconnected expectations involving a probability or likelihood dimension. Simultaneously with an expectation is an alertness mental set—a condition of readiness to respond *first* with respect to the actualization of the expectation held, and secondly in terms of the degree of variance between the anticipation and the actual images or behaviors which occur. The greater the degree of convergence between an expectation and the enactment of the expected, the greater the degree of confidence one can have in future interactional milieux where similar anticipated images, role conceptions, and behaviors occur. Whenever there are a series of anticipatory wishes, wants, beliefs, not all of these will be equally prominent. Differential weighting enters into expectations. Some aspects of these varying expectations will be more desirable or important than others. When this is the case it means that the expectations for an event such as a new experience or repetition of a past rewarding experience will differ in the degree of their intensity and the likelihood of their occurrence.

Moreover, whenever a role component or self-other attribute is perceived as highly significant or salient, this selectivity in perception indicates that one role gestalten or feature of the focused role is more prominent, conspicuous, or striking than all others. Therefore in interactional encounters[8] in which cultural precedents have been established which reinforce and contribute to the saliency of selected aspects of a role definition and the expectations governing them, only the more prominent features will comprise the focus of attention. Even though occupying male status, for example, may characterize the most salient aspect of one's role interpretations in most social exchanges, in countries with racist ideologies, situational systems involving black males or black females demonstrate that sex as a status quality with role implications is reduced in its saliency. This is due to assigning color *relevancy* in the affairs of humans and giving it a higher order meaning than sexual status. In all social milieux in America, expectations surrounding color invariably result in this factor transcending the sex dimension of one's external characteristics.

Racial history and the present cultural matrix with its deeply ingrained ideology of "colorism" determine the prominent components of interpersonal exchange in black male/white female dating-mating confrontations. Whenever a white female and a black male enter into a potential dating-mating alliance with the previously designated cultural symbols and data which structure the meaning of the encounter, they bring with them a set of mutual expectations concerning images of each other and how each is to act in terms of the culturally perceived salient component of their self-other images-*color*. Since history has provided each with a configuration of guidelines for the other's responses and subsequent behavioral enactments based on a color-sex rank ordered combination, color projects itself as the focus of attention. The white female, for example, does not see a male as such, she sees a *black* with all the negative meanings assigned blackness in the white-ruled Western world's cosmology.[9] Reciprocating, the black male sees an image in which the "whiteness" attribute is most salient. Thus the two enter into a reciprocity of color-directed expectations. Even though the encounter involves a male and a female, the mutuality of perceptions and definitions reflects color saliency based on historical precepts.

Moreover there is a novel feature characterizing the white female-black male initial encounter: role reversal. Practically universally in male-female dating-mating arenas, the male has the cultural privilege by tradition and evolutionary practices to assume the initiative. By virtue of custom he also has the *freedom* to take the initiative. This, however, *is not* applicable in the same sense to the white female-black male encounter. Every African American male who meets a white female *in a potential dating-mating arrangement* is restricted in his choices of white females and in his behavioral responses toward her. In a sense, even though his role is a recipient-non-initiating one, he has only two options: compliance or rejection of the potential relation altogether. If he does not reject the association, he cannot by historical custom and prevailing definitions act as the dominant role initiator in interracial "partnering" despite his socio-economic status, degree of intelligence, talent, physical appearance, or personality. These variables are basically irrelevant since they do not comprise the normative expectations learned and internalized on the part of either party. The *white* female does not hold the view that the *black* male has a cultural right to initiate a relationship with her. Therefore in any interracial marriage involving them, this rite of passage merely indicates that the *black male has been married by a white female.* That black males in interracial dyads believe they have been free to choose which white women they wish to marry or even which to socialize with is an understandable myth—a functional imperative which permits a facade of masculine symmetry. In a social order where white beliefs form fundamental explanations of how individuals should enact their color-sex positions and associated role expectations, black males simply *do not,* regardless of their economic status or intellectual capabilities, have the cultural prerogative to take the initiative. White American male-defined history and psychology have given them no such privilege.

Unless one is totally ignorant of the cultural biographies of the black male and white female, one recognizes that the mere existence of the former designates a platform of expectations related to debasing sexual propaganda.[10] As a consequence of justifying enslavement and subsequent stigmatization[11] of the African American male, emphasis has been placed on the biofeedback of his color-sex ascription. Unified, these two dimensions have not only been deeply ingrained in habituated practices, they have functioned as politicized targets for legislation throughout American chronology. Of special importance in America's autobiographical legislative history has been the dreaded anticipation of white female/black male liaisons. Throughout the era of slavery in many states, whenever a free white woman married an African slave, she and her children were required by law to assume the status of slave. Some states like Virginia enacted legislation which declared that "any white woman in Virginia marrying a Negro or mulatto, bond or free"[12] was to be placed in exile. At the turn of the 18th century, a kind of mass panic permeated white male expectations since the number of states enacting laws forbidding marriage between African males and white women proliferated at a geometric rate. Northern states were not immune to this preoccupation with interracial marriages. In 1705 cross-color marriages were designated as illegal in Massachusetts.[13] Although cultural taboos had been in existence for some time, twenty years later Pennsylvania prohibited the mixture of races. Throughout the country, laws and sexual mores established a set of color-sex normative prescriptions. The color factor was given absolute and irrevocable saliency.[14] It was not until the twentieth century in 1967 that a test case was made of a black male-white female marriage in Tennessee. Earlier the U.S. Supreme Court invalidated a Florida statute making interracial mating a crime.[15] With the Tennessee case, the Court ruled that: "The 14th amendment requires that freedom of choice to marry not be restricted by invidious racial discrimination." It was a somewhat mythical declaration. Freedom of choice in such matters has never been a right for African Americans. Thus predictably in spite of the Supreme Court's proclamation, as in the case of school desegregation, custom has a survival character which transcends laws.[16] Sexual mores and taboos based on color have a measurable quality of permanence. For example, in 1968 a Gallup Poll disclosed the extent and perpetuation of anti-interracial marriage sentiments among white Americans. Seventy-one percent (71%) of the men and seventy-four percent (74%) of the women expressed disapproval of such marriages. In a 1972 survey, sixty-five percent of the whites expressed disapproval of black-white marriage. Males and females did not differ significantly in their responses.[17]

Given this sustained historically defined color conscious milieu, motivations for black male-white female mating unions are consequently based on the saliency of color. Regardless of the socioeconomic status of either partner, the political identities of either, the talents and intellectual capabilities, *the essence of all motivations for white women dating-mating black males revolves around the color-sex matrix.* Although Americans are socialized in a culture where the love ethic is predominant, it is an obvious and documented thesis that motivations underlying black male-white female mating unions are color-based. What each partner in the relationship expects, needs, or wants from the other cannot be measured in terms of the romantic mystique. Motivational forces operative in a white female's attraction to and seeking out a black male reflect customary evaluations of blackness as a salient component of one's attributes. "In fact, it is the racial meaning of Negro sexuality, in all of its pornography, that the white woman *expects* and *demands* when she becomes intimate with a Negro."[18] The principle of opposite color fixation in sexual terms adds a different dimension to the intensity and nature of expectations and the overall role gestalten. This principle refers to a constant preoccupation—an obsession with the sexual meaning of color. Color fixation, vividly illustrated in Cleaver's penetrating dissection,[19] means that the color-sex rank ordered combination becomes embedded in the mind, memory, and imagination of the person of the opposite color-sex combination. A white female's obsession or dating-mating directed interest is predictably based on the multiplicity of racialistically prescribed stimuli which bombard her when she meets the African American male. All of the historical and contemporarily reinforced interpretations of the animalistic features of his color-sex configuration permeate the fabric of her perceptive system and role expectancy network. Focus on the parameters of the black male's anatomy—not his talents, occupational status, his feelings, or his intellect—dominates the encounter. Some white females have stated that in potential mating situations, the white female justifies her sexual preoccupation in terms of feelings of guilt about how black people have been treated or how pathetic the black male appears to her. Many black males misread the latent *and* manifest motivations for the white female's advances. Or if they do read them, they think of themselves as one black male student in my classes recently stated: "the black male is the most desirable male universally." Tragically, the young have been thoroughly indoctrinated in the expectations which emphasize the black as a sexual creature. Historically assigned paramagnetic sexual qualities continue to permeate the sex role identity of the African American male. With the black male fragmentized and hence denied an opportunity to become a whole person or to actualize manhood, the expression of white male ascribed traits on the part of the black male converges with the expectations of the white female. Thus only the male's color is significant and salient.

Moreover, there exists a kaleidoscope of contradictory data about the black male. On one hand he is defined as having unrestrained libidinal impulses;[20] on the other he is depicted as feminized and over-mothered by a mythical matriarch. At times he is accused of being impotent;[21] on other occasions an opposite label is assigned him. Like women of all colors, the white female is thus bombarded with an extraordinary set of information regarding the black male's identity, his role imagery, and his behavioral responses. In spite of the seeming disparities existing in the information disseminated, there is a dominant theme in these contradictory debasing stigmas: the color-sex rank ordered mixture. Regardless of the inconsistencies, unceasing repetition of this sexually fixated imagery, with accompanying behavioral expectations, has resulted in the black male's extraordinary fascination for the white female, in particular. *Because he has been systematically sacrificed to biology, she can have no expectations of him other than those based on his historically ascribed physical magnetism.* The black male thus becomes a receptive prey,[22] an onlooker in a repetitive drama in which he is restricted in his choice of performances. Yet regardless of this, for black males, *being dated or married by a white female* provides a functional rite of passage. Basically this functionally deceptive transitional rite offers a perceived alteration of an historically restricted self conception with limited role outlets. To the black male, regardless of whether he is still hemmed in the walls of the ghetto or has escaped them symbolically, whether he is a part of the "superfly" culture or the bourgeoisie, or whether he is a writer or illiterate, a Richard Wright or a "Bigger Thomas," the "whiteness" of a female is a salient and psychologically functional quality. To the white female, the "racism of sex"[23] has created a set of anticipations about the black male as a configuration of attractive-repulsive stimuli—in short as a Black Taurus. Denied intellectual attributes, he has perpetually been defined as a surrealistic embodiment of masculinity. And this is precisely all a white female sees in her first culturally symbolic exchange involving the shared expectation that the encounter is potentially a dating-mating arena. Both victims and perpetuators of the "racism of sex" enter into a conversation of shared gestures and signals regarding the sexual meaning of the color attribute. This latter quality becomes the salient component of their conventionally defined positions and role conceptions. What makes the black male-white female dyadic network universally different in male dominated social systems is that it is only the *white* female who has the cultural right to establish the rules for the mating game, to initiate an exchange of self-other signs, signals, and expectations, or even to terminate the encounter. Because of the multi-dimensional ramifications and meanings of role reversal and status transition, the black male-white female unit respresents an insular behavioral configuration in the universe of male-female interactional transactions.

NOTES

1. Doris Y. Wilkinson and Judith Erickson, "Through the Looking Glass Self Darkly: A Glossary for the Profession," *Sociological Focus* 5 (September, 1972) : 67–78.
2. Margaret Mead, *Sex and Temperament in Three Primitive Societies* (New York: William Morrow and Company, 1935).
3. James Spradley and Brenda Mann, *The Cocktail Waitress: Woman's Work in a Man's World* (New York: John Wiley & Sons, Inc., 1975), pp. 148, 4.
4. B. J. Biddle and E. J. Thomas, eds., *Role Theory: Concepts and Research* (New York: John Wiley & Sons, 1966). See: Raymond G. Hunt, "Role and Role Conflict," in Edwin P. Hollander and Raymond G. Hunt, eds., *Current Perspectives in Social Psychology*, 2nd ed. (New York: Oxford University Press, 1967), pp. 259–65.
5. Doris Y. Wilkinson, "Status Differences and the Black Hate Stare: A Conversation of Gestures," *Phylon* 30 (Summer, 1969) : 191–96.
6. *The Random House Dictionary of the English Language*, unabridged edition (New York: Random House, 1967), pp. 1325, 1440.
7. "Black-White Marriage Ratio Rises," *Springfield Union* (Springfield, Mass., February 14, 1973). See: David Heer, "Negro-White Marriage in the United States," *Journal of Marriage and the Family* (August, 1966), pp. 262–273.
8. See: Erving Goffman, *Encounters: Two Studies in the Sociology of Interaction* (Indianapolis: Bobbs-Merrill, 1963). Also: Erving Goffman, *The Presentation of Self in Everyday Life* (New York: Doubleday, 1959); and especially: Erving Goffman, *Stigma: Notes on the Management of Spoiled Identity* (Englewood Cliffs, New Jersey: Prentice-Hall, 1963).
9. David R. Burgest, "The Racist Use of the English Language," *The Black Scholar* 5 (September, 1973): 37–45.
10. Selma Hirsch, "The Negro: Why Whites Fear Him," *Science Digest* (October, 1963), pp. 12–17.
11. Doris Y. Wilkinson, "The Stigmatization Process: The Politicization of the Black Male's Identity," in Doris Y. Wilkinson and Ronald L. Taylor, eds., *The Black Male in America: Perspectives on His Status in Contemporary Society* (Chicago: Nelson-Hall Inc., 1976, pp. 147–60.
12. Peter M. Bergman, *The Chronological History of the Negro in America* (New York: Harper & Row Publishers, 1969).
13. William D. Zabel, "Interracial Marriage and the Law," *Atlantic Monthly* 216 (October, 1965) : 75–79.
14. See August B. Hollingshead, "Cultural Factors in the Selection of Marriage Mates," in Marvin B. Sussman, ed., *Sourcebook in Marriage*

and the Family (Boston: Houghton Mifflin Company, 1963), pp. 101–8.

15. Zabel, *op. cit.,* p. 76.

16. William Graham Sumner, *Folkways* (Boston: Ginn, 1906).

17. American Institute of Public Opinion, *The Gallup Poll,* 1968, 1972. The sample size of each survey was at least 1500.

18. Calvin C. Hernton, *Sex and Racism* (London, England: Paladin, 1970), p. 51.

19. Eldridge Cleaver, *Soul on Ice* (New York: McGraw-Hill Book Co., 1968).

20. William Grier and Price Cobbs, *Black Rage* (New York: Basic Books, Inc., 1968), pp. 87–92.

21. Robert Staples, "The Myth of the Impotent Black Male," *The Black Scholar* 2 (June, 1971): 2–9.

22. See: Doris Y. Wilkinson, "Black Youth," in *Yearbook of the National Society for the Study of Education* (Chicago: University of Chicago Press, 1975), p. 303. Hugo G. Biegel, "Problems and Motives in Interracial Relationships," *Journal of Sex Research* 2 (November, 1966): 185–205. Robert K. Merton, "Intermarriage and the Social Structure," *Psychiatry* 4 (August, 1941): 361–74.

4

ROLES AND STATUSES IN POST-INDUSTRIAL SOCIETY

Ronald L. Taylor

During the third quarter of the twentieth century a score of social, economic, and political events supplied the impulse for fundamental revisions in the role and status of the black man in American society. The 1960's represent a watershed in the struggle for justice and self-determination. That decade saw significant improvements in education, employment, and overall economic conditions in the black community. The forces behind these changes were the Civil Rights Movement and violent eruptions in urban centers which enlisted the support and energies of countless thousands of black and white Americans, and focused national attention on the so-called "black problem," a problem in reality created and sustained by the white majority. The apparent success of the movement inspired a greater degree of self-consciousness among black Americans as to the palpable realities of their socioeconomic and political situation, while at the same time it encouraged the use of more drastic measures in pursuit of those rights and opportunities which abstractly belong to all American citizens. Supporters of the cause, particularly intellectuals, predicted that blacks would very shortly gain access to the portals of power and privilege to which they had long been entitled.

While attention was riveted on the "black revolt," another more insidious and consequential revolution was coming to maturity. The seeds of this revolution had already been sown before the dramatic events of the 60's, and were partly responsible for the growing insurgency of black Americans since the Second World War. It has been called "technological" by those who see it merely as a further extension of industrialization, and "post-industrial" by observers who perceive a fundamental shift in the social organization of industrial technology itself, suggesting major new alignments within the social and political systems. However writers may differ in their overall assessments of this phenomenon, there is considerable agreement on its economic imperatives. For example, just as the impact of automation eradicated the considerable gains made by blacks following World War II, the impact of the technological revolution threatens to eliminate a substantial number of black workers from the productive equation altogether. In view of these new realities, scholars who had earlier claimed rapid and inevitable progress for black Americans now seem less sanguine in their proclamations, if not totally pessimistic.

What are the implications of this movement for the black community in general and the black male in particular? For example, in light of the notable progress achieved on many fronts during the 1960's, can it be reasonably assumed that the impact of technological advance will be lessened as a consequence? More specifically, how might the projected changes in social structure be expected to affect black employment, political motivations, and general life styles? And what of the black family? Will the economics of technology generate a new dynamic through which roles and statuses in the family will be determined? Answers to these questions require acts of social forecasting that have yet to be initiated. However, the articles assembled here have been selected because of the contribution they make toward establishing a basis upon which reasoned inferences can be drawn regarding the probable consequences of large scale alterations in the social structure for black Americans, both male and female.

The impact of technological change is reflected first in the changing structure of the labor force—that is, in the characteristics of the social division of labor. In the selection "The Black Worker in 'Post-Industrial' Society," Taylor examines the current occupational distributions of the black labor force in order to arrive at some estimates of black occupational status and employment several decades hence. He finds that the bulk of the black labor force is still to be found in low paying, low status occupations, despite significant improvements that had occurred over the decade 1960–70. Thus he concludes that a "racial division of labor" can still be said to exist in the United States in 1975. Among the factors identified as contributing to the continuing differential occupational status between black and white workers are employment discrimination and long-term unemployment, particularly among young black workers in central cities. Further, the more rapid progress experienced by a small proportion of blacks, as against the larger proportion trapped in unattractive, unproductive jobs, is seen as contributing to the "deepening schism" which has become apparent in the black community in recent years, as reflected in increasing differentials in income, educational attainment, and employment opportunities. The social and political implications of these developments have yet to be determined, but would appear to be serious in their consequences.

Some sense of the political consequences of a serious deterioration in the overall economic status of blacks is conveyed in the article by Caplan. His review of more than a dozen recent empirical studies yields a profile of the black militant—the new ghetto man. Contrary to the commonly held notion that militancy is characteristic of only a small proportion of black residents, the data reviewed by the author show normative support for this position. The militant tends to be better educated, but under employed, is strongly committed to the Protestant ethic of hard work, but feels frustrated in achieving personal goals by social systemic constraints, and is intensely proud of being black, but is neither anti-white nor preoccupied by cross comparisons with whites. However, militants were found to be particularly sensitive to where they stood in relation to other blacks, and were especially concerned about what they perceived to be a widening gap between blacks at or near the top of the socioeconomic ladder and those at the bottom, a fact that further underscores the serious implication of the growing schism alluded to in the selection by Taylor. Caplan warns that an end to violent disruptions in urban centers should not be interpreted as signaling an end to black militancy or protest (indeed the "protest psychology" is very much alive among youthful elements in the black community). The potential for violence is ever present so long as the black's "political, social, and economic efficacy is not aligned with his new and increasing sense of personal potency."

In "Jobs and the Negro Family: An Appraisal," Harwood and

Hodge examine the evidence bearing on the question of the relative advantages of black males and females in the labor force. They argue that, contrary to the myth of the economically impotent black male, black men enjoy a clear economic superiority over black women, and evidence shows that this has been true in the past (at least since 1890), and is likely to remain so in the foreseeable future. These conclusions are derived from their analysis of census data which show a greater diversification of jobs among black men than black women for every decennial census since 1890. The concentration of black women in only a few occupational categories (e.g., household services, clerks, etc.) has often meant less work and lower wages in the course of a year, in contrast to black men who, when they are employed, do considerably better. The assumption of female economic superiority is, of course, intimately tied to the black matriarchy theory, but the data adduced by these authors would strongly urge a reconceptualization of this thesis. Indeed they argue that the black woman's handicaps in the job market may turn out to be more significantly related to the family patterns of urban blacks than the problems encountered by black males.

Technological change will undoubtedly have a differential impact on the general life styles and destinies of different classes of blacks. In the provocative selection, "The Black Family and Social Class," Willie presents a detailed analysis of nine black families representing a composite of three socioeconomic levels in the black community, in order to demonstrate similarities and differences in life styles. The observed differences, he contends, are not merely reaction-formations to various forms of discrimination to which these families are exposed, but represent creative innovations. Using Merton's well-known typology of individual adaptations to social organizations, Willie refers to the black middle-class as "affluent conformists," the working class as "innovative marginals," and the lower-class black family as the "struggling poor." These designations are based on his examination of family life and inter-personal relations, education, income, employment, community participation, and general orientation toward life, among these classes. His analysis raises a number of intriguing questions as to the nature of response that might be anticipated at each of the three class levels to a changing economic and labor market situation, given the current level of resources (both collective and personal) to be found within these three categories.

Black families not only differ at each class level but within each class as well. In the selection, "Variations in the Father Role in Complete Families of the Negro Lower Class," Schulz identifies at least three variations in the husband/father role among ten black families in a mid-western community. These variations were discerned on the basis of the "strength" of the marital bond, the extent of paternal support, and the father's relationship to the children in the family. The "indiscreet free-man," the "discreet free-man," and the "monogamous father," each claims authority in the family on somewhat different grounds, varying from a reliance on an ability to cope with the environment by means of manipulative strategies, to an ability to protect and adequately support the family. The variety of husband/father roles identified in this study may be found with increasing frequency as the employment problems of black males at the lower class level become more acute.

THE BLACK WORKER IN
"POST-INDUSTRIAL" SOCIETY*

Ronald L. Taylor

The term "post-industrial" society has become increasingly current as a concept denoting the transition from an industrial order to a new more complex set of socioeconomic and political arrangements. Daniel Bell's *The Coming of Post Industrial Society* (1973) is perhaps the single best known attempt to forecast the trajectory of change—to enunciate the essential dynamic of the new age toward which modern industrial societies are moving with implacable speed. In what is destined to become his magnum opus, Bell sets out in this volume to elaborate the "axial principles" of the new industrial order and to identify the common core of problems to which they will give rise. As he explains:

> The post industrial society . . . is primarily a change in the character of social structure—in a dimension, not the total configuration of society. It is an "ideal type" . . . In descriptive terms, there are three components: in the economic sector, it is a shift from manufacturing to services; in technology, it is the centrality of the new science based industries; in sociological terms, it is the rise of new technical elites and the advent of a new principle of stratification. (p. 487)

Bell envisages a steady diminution of the goods producing labor force and the rise of service workers and the white collar sector. However, services in post industrial society will consist of business, professional, and human services but do not encompass workers of the

*Original article prepared for this volume by Ronald L. Taylor, Assistant Professor, Department of Sociology, University of Connecticut, Storrs, Connecticut.

personal and household type. The new principle of stratification is to become technical skills and knowledge, and higher education the necessary means of obtaining these skills and knowledge.

Curiously missing from Bell's ambitious attempt at social forecasting is any substantive discussion of the role of the various so-called "subgroups" (e.g., racial and ethnic minorities) in the new industrial order. Are we to assume that the inexorable workings of the system will soon render such groups obsolete? Such a possibility is more or less implied but seems unlikely since the projected changes in social structure will more than likely generate new tensions between groups and raise de novo the issues of power, privilege, and participation. It is doubtful, then, that the advent of post-industrial society will see an end to group conflicts or competing interest groups; it may well intensify them.

How may blacks be expected to fare in the post-industrial society? The question, of course, is both intellectually and politically significant. Given their peculiar status in American society, blacks have enjoyed (or suffered) the continual scrutiny of the intellectual establishment, their socioeconomic status often serving as a measure of how well the society has progressed toward fulfilling its promise of equality of opportunity. Even so, blacks remain an intellectual enigma. As Lyman (1972) has observed, "nothing would seem more true about the black in America than the fact that his present is problematic, his past unknown, and his future uncertain" (p. 182). The status of blacks in American society, as well as the obstacles to their full participation, will no doubt continue to attract considerable intellectual interest. Moreover, the extent to which their socioeconomic status improves (or fails to improve) over the next several decades will have important political and social implications for the society at large. Substantial economic and social reversals may occasion a recrudescence of social and political turbulence reminiscent of the 1960's.

Recent accounts of the social and economic status of blacks would lead one to believe that they are moving with remarkable speed toward achieving parity with whites on nearly every front. Some observers predict that if the rate of progress achieved over the decade 1960–70 persists, disparities in income, education, and occupational distributions will soon disappear (cf. Wattenberg and Scammon, 1973; Moynihan, 1972). For example, during the decade 1960–70, black family income went up by 99.6 per cent, while white income rose by only 69 per cent. Moreover, the ratio of black to white family income increased from 53 per cent in 1961 to 61 per cent in 1971—a significant gain considering that during the previous decade no change occurred. When the data are broken down by age, family characteristics, and region, black gains over the decade would appear even more impressive. Excluding the South, young black families where both husband and wife worked had incomes *higher* than whites in 1970. In black families with heads under 35 years of age income was 104 per cent of whites; in families with heads under 25, black income was a surprising 113 per cent of whites! Even when all of the necessary qualifications are added and the effects of inflation are factored out, black gains in income would still appear to be substantial. This dramatic rise in income has led one well known observer to remark: "if the present income equality of these young black/white families holds up as they grow older, one of the fundamental correlates of race in the United States—inferior earning power—will disappear" (Moynihan, 1972, p. 11).

Along with higher incomes, blacks are reported to have made notable gains in education and employment. By 1970, 54 per cent of young black men (25–29) and 58 per cent of young black women had completed high school, as against 36 per cent and 41 per cent respectively, who had done so in 1960. Thus while in 1950 the gap between young blacks and whites in the number of years completed was 3.5 years, in 1970 the gap had been narrowed to only 4 months. At the college level, significant increases are also reported. From 1964 to 1970, total black college enrollment increased by 101 per cent (from 234,000 to 470,000). For young blacks aged 18–24, the per cent enrolled in college increased from 10 per cent in 1965 to 18 per cent in 1971. For whites in the same age range, the figures were 26 per cent and 27 per cent respectively. While there remains a significant percentage difference between blacks and whites (9 per cent), the gap has been reduced considerably.

In employment, notable improvements have occurred in professional, technical and kindred occupations; among clerical and kindred workers, in semi-skilled and factory jobs, and in nonhousehold services. The number of black managers, officials, and proprietors also increased during the decade, though at a slower rate than total black employment. The number of private household workers, farmers, and nonfarm laborers also declined significantly. Although the number of blacks in low skilled, low paying occupations remains substantial, the trend is generally said to be upward (Brimmer, 1972; Spratlen, 1974).

A more critical examination of these recent data, however, would indicate that some of the highly touted gains of blacks may only be temporary and superficial rather than long term and substantive. With reference to income gains, for example, a less sanguine view is warranted when it is considered that the ratio of black to white income was 57 per cent in 1945 and 61 per cent in 1971—a gain of 4 percentage points in 25 years! At this rate, blacks would achieve income parity around the year 2270. Moreover, the tendency to disregard the smaller proportion of blacks to which the more favorable data relates mask what Andrew Brimmer (1969) has referred to as the "deepening schism" in the black community:

> This deepening schism can be traced in a number of ways, including the substantial rise in the proportion of Negroes employed in professional and technical jobs—while the proportion in low-skilled occupations also edges upward; in the sizable decline in unemployment—while the share of Negroes among the long-term unemployed rises; in the persistence of inequality in income distribution within the black community—while a trend toward greater equality is evident among white families; above all in the dramatic deterioration in the position of Negro families headed by females.
>
> In my judgment, this deepening schism within the black community should interest us as much as the real progress that has been made by Negroes as a group. (Quoted in Moynihan, 1972, p. 13)

Differential educational progress within the black community helps to explain this deepening schism, but so too does the occupational distribution of the black labor force. The latter explains why blacks have higher rates of unemployment and lower incomes than whites. In fact, black occupational distributions are much responsible for the "up and down" pattern of change in their relative economic status (Glenn, 1963). A closer look at the employment situation and occupational distributions of the black labor force, together with the extent of labor force participation among young blacks, might offer some clues as to the role of blacks among the new cadre of "post-industrial" workers.

EMPLOYMENT AND OCCUPATIONAL DISTRIBUTIONS

As noted, blacks made significant gains during the last decade whether defined in terms of employment, changing occupational characteristics, education, or income. In 1973, there were 9.1 million black and other races in the labor force—a rise of about one third since 1960.[1] Black employment rose more rapidly than employment for all workers (by 32 per cent for the former compared with 26 per cent for the latter). However, trends in the level of labor force participation over the last 13 years have varied sharply between blacks and whites for most age and sex categories. For example, there has been a significant decline in the participation rate for black males in nearly every age group, while the rates have risen or remained stable for white males in the 16 to 44 age groups, and declined for men 45 years old and over. By contrast, labor force participation has increased sharply for black women 20 to 44 years old.

Occupational upgrading among blacks during the period 1960–1973 has resulted in a more equitable distribution of employment—though gross disparities in job patterns persist. In the ten broad occupational groups presented in Table 1, black and other races improved their job status considerably. As the figures show, the relative changes were greater for blacks than for whites. The largest increases have occurred in the four categories: professional, technical, and kindred workers—172 per cent for blacks and 52 per cent for whites; among clerical and kindred workers, 169 per cent for blacks and 42 per cent for whites; managers, officials, and proprietors, 110 per cent for blacks and 20 per cent for whites; and sales workers, 107 per cent for blacks and 26 per cent for whites. The number of craftsmen and kindred workers also increased by 95 per cent for black workers as compared with only 29 per cent for whites. Thus by 1973, blacks accounted for 6 per cent of the total employment for professional and technical workers; 3 per cent of all managers, officials, and proprietors; 6 per cent of all craftsmen and kindred workers; 8 per cent of clerical workers; and, 3 per cent of all sales workers. Moreover, blacks almost doubled their share of white collar jobs—from 15.3 per cent in 1963 to 29 per cent in 1973. Even so, the black participation rate for white collar employment averaged about 60 per cent in 1973. Expressed differently, the percentage of blacks in white collar occupations would have to be increased by almost 40 per cent in order for black and white distributions in this category to be the same.

By contrast, the proportion of blacks in lower-paying occupations declined markedly during the period 1960–1973. The number of black farmers and farm workers dropped by almost 70 per cent (to 255 thousand), compared with 36 per cent for whites. Blacks accounted for about 7 per cent of employment in agriculture in 1973 as compared with 16 per cent in 1960. A significant decline in private

TABLE 4-1 EMPLOYED PERSONS BY OCCUPATION, 1960 AND 1973 (NUMBERS IN THOUSANDS)

| | 1960 | | 1973 | | Change 1960 to 1973 | | | |
| | | | | | Number | | Percent | |
	White	Black & Other Races	White	Black & Other Races	White	Black & Other Races	White	Black & Other Races
Total Employed	58,850	6,927	75,278	9,131	16,428	2,204	27.9%	31.6%
Professional, technical and kindred workers	7,138	331	10,876	901	3,738	570	52.4%	172.2%
Managers, officials, & prop. (except farm)	6,889	178	8,270	374	1,381	196	20.0	110.1
Clerical & kindred workers	9,259	503	13,192	1,356	3,933	853	42.5	169.6
Sales workers	4,123	101	5,207	209	1,084	108	26.3	106.9
Craftsmen & kindred workers	8,139	415	10,479	809	2,340	394	28.8	94.9
Operatives, including transport	10,536	1,414	12,239	2,030	1,703	616	16.2	43.8
Nonfarm laborers	2,602	951	3,429	883	827	−68	31.8	−7.2
Service workers (except private household)	4,836	1,214	7,981	1,794	3,145	580	65.0	47.8
Farmers & farm workers	4,335	841	2,772	255	−1,563	−586	−36.1	−69.7
Private household workers	991	982	883	520	−158	−462	−15.9	−47.0

SOURCE: Data for 1960, U.S. Department of Commerce, Bureau of the Census, *The Social and Economic Status of Negroes in the United States*, 1970, p. 59. Data for 1973, U.S. Department of Labor, *Manpower Report of the President*, April, 1974, Table A-12, p. 269.

household employment also occurred during the period. The number of blacks so employed fell by almost 50 per cent (to 520 thousand), while the corresponding decline for whites was 16 per cent (to 833 thousand). In addition, the number of black nonfarm laborers declined by 7 per cent, while the total percentage of laborers increased somewhat.

Nonetheless, considerable disparity remains in black/white employment patterns. Blacks in 1973 still comprised a disproportionately small share of employed persons holding high paying, high status jobs. As shown in Table 2, blacks remain heavily concentrated in low paying, low status occupations. For instance, blacks still held about 1.6 million of the service jobs outside of private households in 1973, representing about one fifth of the total—about the same proportion as in 1960. The number of blacks holding operative jobs (semi-skilled) rose by 44 per cent (to about 2.0 million) compared with an expansion of only 16 per cent for all workers. Thus, the black share of the total increased from 12 per cent in 1960, to 13 per cent in 1973. These two categories alone accounted for a larger share of total black employment in 1973 than they did in 1960—when their share was about 38 per cent.

A closer look at where blacks are concentrated gives further insight into the nature and extent of their occupational upgrading during the last decade. An examination of industrial distributions of black employment, for example, reveals that black workers are heavily concentrated in the manufacturing sector of the economy. This is particularly true of black men. About 25 per cent of all black jobholders in 1973 were employed in manufacturing. The corresponding proportion for white workers was about the same. However, blacks represented about 21 per cent of the total construction workers and about 13 per cent of transport equipment operatives. Within these and other blue collar industries, black workers are generally found in the worse jobs—jobs requiring little skill, much physical strength and endurance, and few opportunities for advancement (see, Manpower Report of the President, 1974). Thus, while black workers, and particularly black males, have increased their share of blue collar jobs, they have done so largely in the least desirable and rewarding categories.

It would appear that, to a considerable extent, black males have been improving their occupational status only to the degree that upper level jobs have been created for white male workers within particular industries. Although the evidence bearing on this issue is limited and impressionistic, the conclusion does seem plausible on purely a priori

TABLE 4-2 EMPLOYED PERSONS BY MAJOR OCCUPATION GROUP AND COLOR (NUMBERS IN THOUSANDS)

Occupation	Total		Blacks		Per cent of total Number
	Number	Percentage Distribution	Number	Percentage Distribution	
Total Employed	84,409	100.0	8,061	100.0	9.5
White Collar Workers	40,386	47.8	2,302	28.6	5.7
Professional & Technical	11,777	14.0	684	8.5	5.8
Managers, Officials, & Prop.	8,644	10.2	280	3.5	3.2
Clerical Workers	14,548	17.2	1,171	14.5	8.0
Sales Workers	5,415	6.4	167	2.1	3.1
Blue Collar Workers	29,869	35.4	3,411	42.3	11.4
Craftsmen & Foremen	11,288	13.4	713	8.9	6.3
Operatives (except transport)	10,972	13.0	1,410	17.5	12.9
Transport Operatives	3,297	3.9	467	5.8	14.2
Nonfarm Laborers	4,312	5.1	821	10.1	19.0
Service Workers	11,128	13.2	2,130	26.4	19.1
Private Household	1,353	1.6	509	6.3	37.6
Other Service Workers	9,735	11.6	1,621	20.1	16.6
Farm Workers	3,027	3.6	219	2.7	7.2
Farmers & Farm Managers	1,664	2.0	51	0.6	3.1
Farm Laborers & Foremen	1,363	1.6	168	2.1	12.3

SOURCE: U.S. Department of Commerce, Bureau of the Census, *The Social and Economic Status of the Black Population in the United States*, 1973, p. 56.

grounds. To be sure, expansion of jobs at the upper levels in various blue collar industries has created vacancies at low and intermediate levels that could be filled by blacks and other minority workers. This development no doubt has been advantageous to employers who, because of the pressure resulting from government initiatives in minority employment opportunities, could appear to be responsive to these demands, and because replacing white workers with black and other minority workers in the lowest categories entailed no cost and no apparent threat to the job security of the former, many of whom now find themselves in a relatively better position vis-a-vis the latter.[2] Once hired, black employees are effectively denied advancement by unusually high criteria for promotion, or through internal arrangements that place blacks and whites in different promotional channels (Franklin and Tanzer, 1970).

There are typically two reasons given for black concentration in low and intermediate levels in blue collar and other occupational categories: lack of "human capital," and job discrimination (Harrison, 1974; Thurow, 1969; Tabb, 1970; Becker, 1971). Human capital refers to such factors as the level of educational attainment, job experience and skills, nutrition and health care, and other essential factors which enhance human potential. It is argued, for example, that black workers command less in the way of human capital than their white counterparts. And since a worker's productivity is assumed to be related to the amount of human capital he or she has possession of, the fewer resources among black workers is therefore alleged to explain their lower occupational status. Barbara Bergman (1968), for example, reports that "the value of the stock of human capital embodied in the average male adult Negro is on the order of $10,000 smaller than the human capital the average white male has possession of. For the Nation as a whole, this adds up to a deficiency of around $50 million of investment in the human capital of adult male Negro Americans, which would have been made had they been whites" (p. 263). While this notion provides a partial explanation, it will become increasingly untenable as blacks continue to enlarge the amount of their human capital, particularly in the field of education where, by 1970, young blacks (20–34) had reduced the education gap to less than half a year.

It is important to note that the deficit in human capital—the putative cause of black overrepresentation in low paying, low status occupations—is itself explained by systematic discrimination to which these workers are subject. In effect, social and economic discrimination determine the level of human capital at any given point in time and in turn influence the industrial and occupational location of black workers. Empirical estimates of the impact of discrimination on black employment patterns are generally speculative, but they do underscore the importance of the problem. Gary Becker's (1971) analysis of discrimination is perhaps the most sophisticated attempt to measure the impact of this factor. He argues that every employer has his price for hiring blacks which may be determined by what he terms a "discrimination coefficient," a crucial wage differential which would make the hiring of a white and an equally qualified black a matter of indifference to him. This wage differential takes into account the disutility cost involved in hiring blacks. In other words, because working with blacks entails a "psyche cost" to white workers (given the former's stigmatized status), black workers must either be "decompensated" (i.e., less pay and low position) if white employers are to hire them, or white workers must be "overcompensated" if they are to be induced to work with blacks (cf. Franklin and Tanzer, 1970).

The degree of discrimination may vary under certain conditions, as when the black-white ratio increases in any given area, or by the structure of a given industry, i.e., whether it is monopolistic (large firm) as against competitive (small firm) in operation. Becker demonstrates that monopolistic industries (defined as the four leading firms in an industry employing 50 per cent or more of the workers in that industry) have on the whole, a greater "taste for discrimination" than smaller, more competitive ones, given the former's greater market advantages, capital assets, etc. Applying this distinction to Southern industries, for example, Becker found that blacks were overrepresented in competitive industries (saw mills, logging, textiles, etc.) and underrepresented (if at all) in monopolistic industries (petroleum refining, railroads, tobacco processing, etc.). Using a different approach, Tanzer has shown how the extent of discrimination against blacks of either sex in Southern industries is highly correlated with the job structure of a given industry. "Specifically," he writes, "the greater the proportion of total jobs in an industry which are laborer jobs, the greater the proportion of Negroes found in the industry as a whole and in each occupational job category separately" (Franklin and Tanzer, 1970, p. 120).

Franklin and Tanzer (1970), however, offer an alternative framework for the analysis of discrimination against black workers. They suggest that the degree of discrimination is related to the technical conditions of production and operates within a social context in which "work relations between races are expected to correspond to a dominant-subordinate role pattern" (p. 122). Accordingly, labor-intensive modes of operation are more likely to generate discriminatory practices than capital-intensive ones. As they explain:

> Capital-intensive modes of production generally separate the product and/or services from the worker. Moreover, the technical conditions of production, such as big assembly plants and/or machines which are operated by one person and involves a repetitive process, tend to require a minimum of personal interaction on equal terms or interaction on terms in which the Negro has jobs vested with authority over whites. Therefore, the employer in capital-intensive operations has less reason to be concerned with the product-color connection which is made by the consumer or the breakdown of the dominant-subordinate human relations pattern which tends to operate as a barrier to the Negro's occupational mobility. (p. 122)

The structure and modes of production of various industries would both, then, seem to explain much of the observed variance between black and white workers in terms of occupational status and rates of job mobility. In these terms, the jobs available to black workers in blue collar occupations are not a random selection, even allowing for the alleged "dearth of human capital" possessed by these workers. On the contrary, as the data and analyses presented above makes clear, blacks tend to be concentrated very heavily in a few occupations and in low level positions. Indeed, on the basis of the most recent data available, it may not be too much to say that despite recent occupational gains, a "racial division of labor" still existed in the U.S. in 1974 (See, Manpower Report of the President, 1974).

It would be an error to conclude that only blacks employed in blue collar occupations are subject to employment discrimination. Assuming a greater investment of human capital in blacks employed in white collar occupations, one might expect a far more random distribution of blacks in this category than is actually the case. For instance, the occupational group of professional, technical, and kindred workers includes such diverse occupations as physicians, engineers, clergymen, school teachers, architects, social workers, and medical and dental technicians. Yet blacks remain heavily concentrated in teaching, social work, and the clergy. The traditional and continuing attraction of these fields is undoubtedly one explanation of this concentration, but the continuing difficulties encountered in gaining entry to graduate and professional schools is another (Poinsett, 1974). Furthermore, acquiring certification upon completion of professional training continues to be a serious problem in some fields. Income differentials between black and white workers of similar occupational status offer an additional basis upon which to infer the existence of job discrimination. For example, among professional, technical, and kindred workers in 1972, black males had a median income of $7,946 compared with $12,336 for white males—a ratio of .64. The median income for black managers and administrators was $9,141 compared with $12,825 for whites. For black male sales workers, the income differential was considerably worse: $3,201 compared with $8,304, or a ratio of only .39! Clearly, "occupational equality" has not meant "economic equality" for these workers.

The implications of labor market discrimination can more fully be seen in the patterns of intergenerational mobility between black and white workers. If, for example, the sons of black male workers could convert their inherited status into occupational status at the same rate that white sons do, in time blacks and whites would become increasingly alike in their job distributions. The percentage of sons of fathers with various occupational levels, whose own occupation is white collar, for blacks and whites is shown in Table 3. Inspection of

TABLE 4-3 PERCENTAGE OF BLACK AND WHITE MALES IN LABOR FORCE IN 1962 WHOSE OCCUPATION IS WHITE COLLAR, CLASSIFIED ACCORDING TO FATHER'S OCCUPATION LEVEL

Father's Occupation	Whites	Blacks
Higher white collar (professional, technical, managerial)	69.6	20.1
Lower white collar (clerical and sales)	59.4	23.6
Higher manual (craftsmen and foremen)	39.9	15.6
Lower manual (operatives, service workers, non-farm labor)	37.8	15.0
Farm (managers, laborers, foremen)	23.5	6.1
Not reported	36.3	8.9

SOURCE: James S. Coleman (1971), p. 14. Data are from research originally reported in Toward A Social Report (1969).

the table indicates that for blacks whose fathers were in the highest white collar occupations, only 20 per cent were themselves in white collar occupations. The same holds true for those in lower white collar jobs. In fact, at every level the divergence is more than twice as great for black sons than for white. It would seem that the occupational advantages which accrue to one generation of black workers are much less likely to be converted into "working capital" by the next.

At the 1960–73 rate of occupational upgrading, it would take several generations for blacks to achieve occupational equality with whites at most levels. Even if all discrimination were to end immediately, the accumulated economic and social liabilities resulting from past discrimination would continue to exert an independent influence on black occupational distributions. Using a simple mathematical model, the Markov-chain,[3] Liberson and Fuguitt (1967) have attempted to determine what impact an end to discrimination would have on black-white male occupational differences in terms of intergenerational occupational mobility. An end to discrimination is operationalized by assuming that both black and white mobility patterns are similar to those found to prevail for the total population. Beginning with the actual black-white occupational distributions for 1960, the authors traced the consequences of certain artificial assumptions on an intergenerational succession of fathers and sons thirty-five to forty-four years old. An alternative analysis was carried out (under the assumed relationship between education and occupational mobility) using education mobility data for blacks and whites, which was then converted into an additional set of occupational distributions. The results of both measures indicated that black and white distributions would converge rapidly in just one generation without race specific discrimination. For instance, the percentage of black male professionals would triple in a single generation in the absence of discrimination, while the percentage of managers, officials, and proprietors would more than quadruple. Nevertheless, it would be the year 2040 before complete equality is achieved in these occupational categories, and perhaps never in some other white and blue collar jobs.

To be sure, this study overstates the rate of occupational mobility for black male workers by assuming an immediate end to discrimination; however, it does serve to emphasize the stubbornness and size of the problem. While the past decade has witnessed striking improvements in the occupational status of black workers, it is not at all certain whether this trend will continue. In fact, there are some signs that the trend may reverse itself in the decades just ahead.

Youth Participation in the Labor Market

When the problem of unemployment is added to labor market discrimination, the prospect for continued and accelerating improvements in the occupational status of black workers does not look very promising. Conditions in this critically important dimension of economic life underscore the gaps in the prosperity which has occurred, and will undoubtedly influence the measure of overall economic well-being between the races for generations to come.

The positions of black workers on the job ladder of individual firms are adversely affected by intermittent labor force participation and by longer duration of unemployment that white workers. It is true, of course, that the worsening economic situation beginning in the early 1970's has resulted in a deterioration in the overall employment situation of all workers, but its effect on black youth has been a disaster. In 1973, the jobless rate was 8.9 per cent for black and other races, and 4.3 per cent for white workers. For black teenagers (16 to 19) the unemployment rate averaged about 30 per cent—more than 3 times the rate for black workers, 7 times the white adult unemployment rate, and more than twice the rate for white teenagers. But these figures mask the extent of the unemployment problem. An estimated 100,000 black youths are never found by the enumerators (Levitan and Taggart, 1971). An even greater disparity exists in central cities where estimates of youth unemployment range from 32 to 40 percent. The unemployment situation threatens to grow even worse as the very large number of black children now in big cities reach working ages, and as today's teenage blacks grow older (Manpower Report of the President, 1971).

Unemployment, however, is only one of the problems facing black youth, though serious in its implications once it is realized that many face the prospect of never experiencing gainful employment in their lifetime (Glazer and Moynihan, 1970; Feldstein, 1973).[4] By all measures of labor force activity black youth are worse off than other youth. On the whole, they tend to hold the worse jobs at the lowest wages, work fewer hours, and are more heavily concentrated in dead-end jobs (Harrison, 1972). The frequently cited liabilities of these youth and the serious obstacles to their labor force participation are

well known, though the chain of causation is perhaps less well understood. For instance, while inferior education, limited skills, a lack of
family resources, and discrimination are all cited as factors contributing to their severe employment problems, each may only be marginally important at any given point in time. Rather, these factors
are parts of a larger complex of factors which, when taken together,
constitute formidable barriers to labor market participation.

Of course, black youth do participate in the labor market economy, but it is the manner of their participation, not the question of
participation as such, which is at issue. Large numbers of urban black
youth (and adults) are trapped in a labor market where jobs are marginal, low paying, and unattractive. A goodly number of white youth
can also be found in such jobs but their opportunities to move to more
attractive higher status jobs are frequently greater (Friedlander,
1972). Where black youth have been able to breach the barriers to
more rewarding occupations and industries, they tend to move upward
at a much slower pace than their white counterparts. The fact that
black and white youth with similar education within the same industries have very different earnings, points to the existence of separate
tracking systems.

The unequal access of different groups in the labor force to
jobs with good wages and good advancement opportunities has led
to the development of a new labor market theory, referred to as the
"theory of the dual economy," or the "theory of primary and secondary labor markets" (Piore, 1969). The dual labor market theory
helps to explain why, in periods of "full employment," the rate of unemployment remains consistently high among black youth (and
adults), higher, in fact, in recent years than the national unemployment rate during the worst years of the depression in the 1930's (Killingsworth, 1969). According to this theory, the economy is stratified
into "primary" and "secondary" labor markets which are qualitatively
different in significant ways. In the primary labor market, working
conditions and workers' behavioral traits interact in such a way as to
produce high productivity, high wages, employment stability, equal
treatment in the administration of work rules, and systematic opportunities for job progression. By contrast the secondary labor market
is characterized by low productivity, low wages, poor working conditions, employment instability, and few if any opportunities for advancement. Black and other minority workers, according to this notion, with few skills and limited work experience are, to a large extent,

locked out of primary jobs and confined to the secondary labor market, a limitation which is both self-perpetuating and reinforcing.

The secondary labor market does not generally require skills of any great consequence, since technologies in this sector are rather simplistic. On the other hand, the casual and deadend nature of the job, breeds casual work habits, high turnover, and lack of motivation, which further handicap such workers and act to insure their confinement to the secondary market. Even those individuals who possess the behavioral traits required to function efficiently in primary jobs may be forced into secondary jobs because of superficial characteristics such as race, demeanor, accent, or low educational attainment, and may come over time to develop those behavioral traits associated with secondary workers. Moreover, it is not unlikely that employers encourage such traits in order to reduce labor costs, increase the margin of profit, and to insure an adequate labor supply. Because black youth are largely caught in secondary labor markets, stranded in entry-level jobs far below whites, and subject to on-the-job discrimination, the long-term effects on them are conspicuous.

The funneling of large numbers of black youth into secondary labor markets is the culmination of a tracking process begun in the schools. It is well recognized that schools play a major role in controlling the flow of manpower into the economy, and "tracking" is the principle technique for accomplishing this objective (See Bowles, 1972; Howe and Lauter, 1970). No less an authority on the American educational system than James Conant has recognized the essential function of tracking. In his *Slums and Suburbs* (1961), he argues that "in a heavily urbanized and industrialized free society, the educational experiences of youth should fit their subsequent employment" (p. 40). However, given the shortage of trained guidance personnel in large city schools, together with pupil and parental indifference, this ideal is especially difficult to accomplish; therefore, "the system of rigid tracks may be the only workable solution to a mammoth guidance problem" (p. 66). In spite of the best motives of those who favor this "solution" to the guidance and employment problem, tracking has served only to facilitate the channeling of urban youth of both races into the secondary labor market.

Tracking is part of the internal social structure of many urban school systems where interpersonal relations, authority, and attitudes mirror those of the factory and office (Carney, 1972). School socialization tends to place a high premium on discipline, punctuality, acceptance of authority outside the family, and individual accountability—behavioral traits which are essential for primary labor market participation. Moreover, differences in educational objectives and in expectations of school personnel resulting in differential socialization practices are found to exist in schools attended by pupils of different socioeconomic backgrounds (See, e.g., Kohl, 1968; Sexton, 1971; Gintis, 1971). In so-called "inner city" schools, attended mainly by working and lower class youth, there is typically less of an emphasis on discipline, punctuality, and personal accountability, and a greater tolerance for "irregular behavior" in recognition of the fact that these youth are unlikely candidates for primary jobs. The results can clearly be seen in the very large numbers of minority youth tracked into "general" and "vocational" programs as against "basic" or "college preparatory" ones (Howe and Lauter, 1970). The relatively high school drop out rate for inner city youth is unquestionably related to the recognition of the palpable realities of their situation: that they are being "cooled out" by the educational establishment, or that they are being conditioned to accept "the uncreative, routine kind of unskilled work which most of them will be required to perform after they 'graduate' " (Harrison, 1974, p. 283).

In these terms, the educational equality (measured in median years of schooling attained) which a growing number of young blacks have managed to achieve in recent years may not be matched by improved occupational status. Although an increasing number may be expected to gain access to primary jobs, increased educational investments may be no guarantee of employment security. As Harrison (1974) has observed: "with blacks crowded disproportionately into the secondary labor market, increasing educational investments ceteris paribus may only increase the effective supply of secondary labor, which might then drive black wages down even further" (p. 283). Hence, the return on investments in education at some levels may be far less, at least in the short run, for black youth than for white, especially for those located in the inner city. Indeed, it may very well be that a large number of young blacks will have to become considerably "overeducated" before they secure access to primary jobs.

In the absence of effective countermeasures, young black workers in central cities will find themselves increasingly isolated from the mainstream of economic activity. It is perhaps in partial recognition of the social and political implications of "structured" underemployment and unemployment that new federally sponsored programs have recently been initiated. The Public Employment Program (PEP), and the Comprehensive Employment and Training Act (CETA) were both initiated for the expressed purpose of dealing with these problems. The Public Employment Program, authorized by the Emergence Employment Act of 1971, is the first large-scale federally sponsored program of its kind and is mandated to create "transitional public service jobs for unemployed and underemployed individuals" (Manpower Report of the President, 1974, p. 151). PEP is specifically designed to serve those groups not covered by the Manpower Development and Training and Economic Opportunity Acts—welfare recipients, youth entering the labor force, older workers, Vietnam veterans, and workers with little or no command of English. It is interesting to note that almost 75 per cent of the total number of participants in this program in 1973 were high school graduates, a higher level of educational attainment than the civilian labor force at large (which was about 68 per cent in 1973), and a fact which underscores the growing employment problems of the better educated. The kinds of jobs supported by this program fall within the normal categories of clerical, service, and technical jobs, including recreation aides, clerk-typists, street and highway repairmen, housing and fire inspectors, park laborers, and maintenance helpers. The aim is to eventually move participants in the program into unsubsidized primary employment.

The Comprehensive Employment and Training Act passed in 1973, overlaps the PEP. The CETA provides funding for cities and towns where rates of unemployment are especially severe—6 per cent or higher and for 3 consecutive months. Like the Public Employment Program, CETA funds may be used for the creation of public service transitional jobs, and programs are to be "designed with a view toward —1) developing new careers, or 2) providing opportunities for career advancement, or 3) providing opportunities for continued training..." (Manpower Report, 1974, p. 157). As in PEP, programs funded under this Act must provide for the transition to unsubsidized employment.

Unfortunately, both PEP and the CETA sustain many of the weaknesses of the older Manpower Development and Training and Economic Opportunity Acts, and will no doubt fail (or "succeed" depending on one's point of view) for much the same reason (See, Levitan and Taggart, 1972). To begin with, none of these programs was designed to interfere with vested interests such as labor unions, state and local bureaucracies, or business establishments. Jobs created under these programs do not pose significant threats to regular employees since participants are only trained for jobs where there is a labor shortage. The CETA is quite explicit on this point: "jobs created can be at other than entry levels only if program agents have complied with applicable personnel procedures and collective bargaining agreements" (Manpower Report, 1974, p. 157). The possibility of meeting these requirements is rather remote since all such federal programs are considered "special" and therefore are not subject to operative employment procedures and union agreements. Furthermore, the creation of jobs at other than entry level runs counter to the well established seniority rule in most industries and occupations.

The experience of the last twelve years (since 1962 when the MDTA was started) has taught painful lessons that must be kept in mind when broad employment efforts are being contemplated. For one thing, brief crash training programs have generally failed to develop either the job skills or the job opportunities for the mass majority of their participants. In many instances, the very programs themselves have been appropriated by the business establishment and used to facilitate its own operation, that is, to recruit secondary workers for secondary jobs (Piore, 1970). The fact is that it is very difficult to create meaningful and productive jobs for youthful participants in the face of vested interest groups. Effective programs that attempt to link job training to primary job requirements run the risk of being rejected or isolated by the very establishments they seek to attract. At any rate, there is little evidence that the kind of training and temporary employment typically offered by such programs significantly improve chances of later employment (Wellman, 1970). Graduates generally are no less vulnerable to unemployment than those who have not undergone similar training, or those who lack work experience altogether.

Assuming that effective programs can and will be developed in the near future, given sufficient funding, programming, and personnel, the prospect of increasing the effective supply of jobs for black youth appears to be greatly diminished by two additional complicating factors: rapid growth of the young black and other minority populations in central cities, and the suburbanization of industry. The past decade has witnessed a virtual "population explosion" in the number of young blacks in central cities throughout America. For example, from 1960 to 1970, blacks aged 16 to 19 increased by 72 per cent (to 1.2 million), while the age category 20 to 24 increased by 66 per cent (to 1.3 million). By 1973, there were an estimated 2.7 million black youth between the ages of 16 and 25 in the nation's central cities. This trend is expected to continue for some time. Teenagers among blacks and other minority groups are expected to increase from about 2.1 million in 1970 to 2.6 million in 1980—a rise of 24 per cent. Among blacks aged 20 to 24, the number is expected to increase from 2 million in 1970 to about 3.1 million by 1980, or an increase of 36 per cent. This portentous population growth suggests that the job market situation of young workers will be much more favorable for white youth than for black during the present and coming decades. The number of white teenagers in the labor force is expected to increase by only 5 per cent between 1970 and 1980, while a 44 per cent rise is projected for black youth during this period (Manpower Report, 1974, p. 80).

The concentration of industrial growth and employment opportunities on the periphery of the city will undoubtedly exacerbate the job-finding problems of inner city residents. Industrial decentralization has accompanied the shift in population to the suburbs, and suburban economic growth has frequently exceeded that of central cities in recent years (Lewis, 1969). For instance, one study of eight metropolitan areas shows that between 1965 and 1967, central city employment grew at an annual rate of 3 per cent compared with 6 per cent in the suburbs (Fremon, 1970). The number of jobs in metropolitan areas has also been declining. Mooney (1969) has presented data showing that the percentage of jobs located in the central cities of the twenty-five largest metropolitan areas has declined from 68 per cent in 1948 to 59 per cent in 1963—and the decline continues. In addition, the employment mix of central cities jobs is being significantly altered by economic decentralization. Manufacturing, and the wholesale and retail trade, areas of large black employment concentration, have been particularly affected by employment declines. Between 1959 and 1967, almost 80 per cent of the employment growth in manufacturing took place in the suburbs. For wholesale and retail trade, the percentage was 78 and 68 respectively (Manpower Report, 1971).

The decline in blue collar jobs has been paralleled by an increase in white collar jobs (e.g., government, finance, real estate, etc.), open only to persons who have acquired the appropriate degree, diploma, certificate, or license. This trend will mean a further reduction in the number of jobs available to central city residents with limited skills, particularly young black males whose labor force participation rate has steadily declined in recent years (See Mooney, 1969).

Although these data may suggest pessimism concerning the prospects for increased labor force participation of black youth, the intent has been otherwise. It is clear that the employment problems of a large proportion of these youth (and adults) will not yield under existing efforts, and that a much more aggressive campaign will have to be undertaken in order to widen their employment opportunities both occupationally and geographically—and to eliminate the systematic retardation to which many are currently exposed. In a word, if the current cohorts of young black workers are not to be relegated to secondary jobs in the "post-industrial" society, the implementation of multidimensional programs on a scale necessary to alter significantly present realities would seem essential.

PROSPECTS FOR THE FUTURE

There is no clear-cut evidence that blacks are moving inexorably toward a position of occupational equality in the American economy. Indeed there is some reason to fear that their relative position at some levels will worsen in the years just ahead. But to suggest that the economic situation of a substantial number of blacks may grow worse rather than improve, flies in the face of that all-pervasive American strain of optimism and belief in accelerating favorable progress toward the "great society." Yet, while black occupational upgrading and employment progress have been prominent features of the "big picture" of the aggregate economy during the past decade, so also has economic regression. An overall appraisal of the black economic situation of the last decade can at best be described as mixed. That is, some things have improved markedly, while other have worsened. Both developments hold important implications for the future.

On the basis of current realities and a few reasonable assumptions about the overall rate of economic growth, it is possible to arrive at some estimates of the level and occupational distributions of employment of black workers several decades hence. The Bureau of Labor Statistics projects a sharp slowdown in overall economic growth beginning toward the end of the current decade and continuing throughout the 1980's (Aterman, 1973). This projection is based partly on changes in the growth of the population 16 years of age and over from which the work force is drawn. While the labor force grew at an annual rate of about 1.8 per cent during the 1960–1973 period, it will decline sharply to 1.1 per cent annually during the period 1980–90. At this decelerated rate, the labor force is estimated to reach 112.6 million by 1990. On this assumption, about 13 million black workers may be in the labor force in 1990 compared with 9.5 million in 1973. Hence, it is obvious that the projected reduction in the economic growth rate will have serious implications for the black labor force.

The expected slowdown in the rate of increase of the total labor force will be accompanied by several dramatic changes in composition as well. For instance, the number of young workers (16 to 24 years of age) is expected to decline on the average of 350,000 a year over the next decade, or from 23.8 million in 1980 to 20.3 million by 1990. However, the proportion of black youth in the labor force is expected to continue its upward climb. As noted earlier, the number of white teenagers in the labor force is projected to rise by only 5 per cent between 1970 and 1980. In contrast, a 44 per cent increase in the number of black youth in the labor force is expected during the same period. Thus, while the proportion of teenage workers entering the labor force is expected to peak around 1979, the proportion of black youth is expected to continue to grow. This means that a significant proportion of blacks seeking to enter the labor market in the next decade and beyond will be younger city residents from the less well off sectors of the black population—youth lacking in education, skills, and work experience. Consequently, the already critical employment situation among these youth will be intensified by these developments. Many will be pushed out of secondary jobs into the category of unemployables if the high rate of long term unemployment (e.g., 13 weeks or more) persists at the current level.

By 1980, the number of workers who will be qualified for and seeking advancement to high level occupations is expected to increase substantially, while the supply of workers available for low-level, low wage jobs may become much more limited. Among the factors contributing to this labor pattern of supply and demand are the rising level of educational attainment, the age distribution of the labor force, and increasing levels of employment of blacks and other minority groups. As previously noted, the educational attainment of blacks and whites has been converging over the last decade. The proportion of white adult workers (of both sexes) with at least 4 years of high school rose by almost 9 percentage points since the mid-1960's, climbing to 66.4 per cent in 1972. Over the same period, educational attainment for black and other races rose by 11.5 percentage points, reaching 45.2 per cent in 1972. As a result, the gap in educational attainment between blacks and whites in the labor force in 1972 was reduced to 21.2 percentage points. This rapid increase in educational attainment would suggest increasing homogeneity of occupational qualifications of black and white workers in the near future.

Ironically, at a time when black workers are increasing their level of educational attainment, the educational requirements demanded by employers have moved steadily upward (See Rosenthal, 1973), in effect widening the gap between the level of skills required and those offered by potential jobholders. If this upward trend continues (and there is every reason to believe that it will), black youth who fail to complete high school will be left still farther behind in the competition for entry level jobs than they are at present. Moreover, given the anticipated employment "squeeze" for college graduates by the end of the present decade, one may expect that the number of intermediate jobs which have traditionally gone to the less educated worker will become increasingly unavailable.

Projected trends in employment may also be expected to have a significant impact on the distribution of occupations within the black community. The favorable impact of these trends may not be felt throughout the entire occupational structure, however. The relative occupational standing of black and other minority workers in the labor force in 1970 was 66.3 per cent, or about two-thirds that of white workers. This represents an increase of more than one third between 1960 and 1970. Almost all of the increase was due to the rise in the proportion of black and other minority workers in white collar occupations, and a corresponding sharp reduction in the proportion of low wage occupational groups. The increase in the proportion of black workers employed in professional, technical, and clerical occupations may be expected to continue to account for much of the observed increase in the proportion of black white collar workers. For instance, blacks might hold about 10 per cent of the professional and technical jobs in 1980 compared with 6 per cent in 1973. This may rise to 13 per cent by 1990. Blacks may also raise their share of the managerial, officials, and proprietory jobs from 3.2 per cent in 1973 to roughly 3.9 per cent in 1985. Significant increases are also likely to be registered in sales and clerical occupations, though at a somewhat slower rate than was experienced over the 1960–73 period.

Despite these projected gains for black white collar workers, the occupational center of gravity for black workers may be expected to remain anchored to blue collar and service jobs for the foreseeable future. The proportion of all workers employed in blue collar jobs is expected to continue its downward movement—reaching about 32 per cent by 1985. The proportion of black workers in this category may also be expected to decline. Since the majority of blacks in this category are operatives (e.g., operators of heavy moving equipment, drivers of trucks, etc.), they will be hardest hit by the slowdown in the growth rate in manufacturing and by the continuing substitution of machinery for manual labor. The percentage of black workers so employed may decline from 13 per cent in 1973 to about 11 per cent by 1985. By 1985, black operatives may account for only 15 per cent of the black labor force compared with 18 per cent in 1973. By contrast, the proportion of service workers (excluding private household) may be expected to continue to rise during the next several decades. Expanding business activity, increasing leisure time, and population growth are among the major factors underlying increases in this category. In 1973, black workers accounted for 19 per cent of all service workers; by 1985 they may constitute 21 per cent. As is presently the case, these two categories will continue to make up a substantial share of total black employment.

Finally, the proportion of farmworkers of black and other races, which has already declined more rapidly than any other major occupational group (from 841 thousand in 1960 to 255 thousand in 1973), may decline even farther, reaching about 112 thousand by 1985.

These, of course, are projections not predictions of black employment and occupational distributions in the near future. As such, they do not anticipate unexpected developments in degree or kind. For instance, the long term effects of high rates of unemployment (as high as 30 per cent among urban black adult workers in 1974) on black workers resulting from the current recession, can not be determined with any degree of certainty, but will undoubtedly adversely affect the level of labor force participation and job mobility rates in incalculable ways. Nor is it possible to gauge the impact of technological changes which may cause employment to increase in some occupations and decrease in others. Variations in the growth rate among industries may also be counted on to influence the occupational distributions of the black labor force. For example, the proportion of blacks in the health fields may grow more rapidly over the next several decades than the proportion of blacks in the field of education, due to the moderate growth in the number of pupils (Rosenthal,

1973). Moreover, the extent to which the projected oversupply of college graduates—expected to be acute by 1980—will affect the future job situation of black white collar workers remains speculative, yet ominous in its consequences. And, most important of all, while the interaction between discriminatory practices and structural, nonracial factors, is difficult to know, these may be assumed to have a continuing significant influence on black/white occupational compositions and mobility.

These uncertainties notwithstanding, several significant conclusions can be drawn from the data presented above. It is clear, for example, that problems of employment and underemployment will continue to plague a large percentage, perhaps a majority, of black workers for decades to come—particularly youth and adults located in central cities. On the other hand, the well-educated and well-qualified can anticipate continued economic and occupational advancement, though at a somewhat slower pace than has occurred previously.

The jobless situation of a growing number of black males may be expected to parallel an absolute and relative increase in the number of families headed by females (which by 1971 had already climbed to 39.3 per cent in the central cities of metropolitan areas) during the next several decades. Since such families tend on balance to be worse off economically than other families (black or white), the impact of this trend will be considerable in terms of the overall economic well-being of the black community.

These developments will have the decided effect of widening the gap between those blacks with exploitable and tangible skills, and those who, for obvious reasons, have failed to acquire them—thus "deepening the schism" in the black community to which Brimmer (1969) has referred. This schism has already become apparent in the unequal distribution of income and in the overall rate of economic progress of the better educated. Although the social and political implications of this trend remain as yet unclear, a conservative view would suggest that they will be serious. For one thing, we can expect more wretchedness, unhappiness, and hopelessness, as large numbers of potential black workers encounter mounting difficulties in securing educational and economic opportunities. The results may be violence and terror with increasing frequency unless drastic curatives are applied with celerity.

The future grows out of a present that has been shaped by the past. The fate of black workers in "post-industrial" society will thus be determined in part by trends already discernible, and by developments yet to be spawned. In addition, that future will be shaped by concerted efforts made in the present to remove serious obstacles to employment opportunity. To be sure, the problems young black workers face are multidimensional and action in any single direction will prove inadequate. Improving urban education and job training, though essential, will not by themselves improve employment opportunities unless these are tied to employment requirements. Moreover, upgrading the quality of available jobs will be as important in meeting the employment needs of young and older workers as increases in the number of job openings. Subprofessional and "para-technical" careers are among the possible approaches in this area (See Pearl and Reissman, 1969). But expanding employment opportunities are dependent upon eliminating discrimination in the form of artificial barriers to employment, and this is as essential as improved education, training and job development.

Yet all such efforts may turn out to be no more than a series of Sisyphean exercises if there is validity in Rainwater's (1969) assertion that: "the central fact about the American underclass is that it is created by the operation of what in other ways is the most successful economic system known to man. It is not, in short, so much that the good system has not included the underclass, as that in the manner of its operation it produces and reproduces it" (p. 9). This view implies a shift of emphasis away from the alleged "deficiencies" of the black working class and toward a more critical examination of the defects in the socioeconomic system which consigns them to a relatively inferior position. It is perhaps this central fact, more than any other, that will ultimately determine the fate of black workers in the post-industrial society, and should therefore become our most pressing concern.

NOTES

1. Blacks constitute about 92 per cent of all persons in this group. Other races include Orientals and Native Americans. It is common when referring to the socioeconomic status of blacks to use the statistical data for blacks and other races where data are not available separately. Presumably, no serious distortion in the data is introduced by this practice. (Until now this problem was neatly handled by the term "nonwhite" in referring

to blacks and other races, a reference that speaks volumes on the character of race relations in America.) In the text, this practice is followed where data are unavailable for blacks specifically.

2. Of course, many employers derived substantial economic benefits from hiring minority workers in the form of federal subsidies and free publicity. Interestingly, as the pressure from Washington abated and public sentiments cooled toward such efforts, many employers found they could no longer lend their support to major advancements in this area. (See Tabb, 1970, Chap. 4).

3. The Markov-chain model assumes a set of observations (or experiments) that may be classified into a finite number of possible outcomes (or states). In addition, it assumes that "a given observation may move from one state to another over a time period t, and there is a sequence of such time periods. The probability that an observation will move from state i to state j between t and t+1 is given by p_{ij}. The basic assumption of the model is that the probability of moving from i to j depends only on the state at time t and that this probability is constant over the sequence of time intervals" (Liberson and Fuguitt, op. cit., p. 189).

4. For many inner-city youth presented with menial jobs at low wages and with no prospect of advancement, "hustling," i.e., illegal activities, has become a logical alternative. See, e.g., Barry Bluestone, "The Tripartite Economy: Labor Markets and the Working Poor," *Poverty and Human Resources,* July/August 1970, pp. 23–24.

REFERENCES

Alterman, Jack. 1973. "The United States Economy in 1985: An Overview of BLS Projections." *Monthly Labor Review* 96 (December): 3–7.

Becker, Gary. 1971. *The Economics of Discrimination.* Chicago: University of Chicago Press.

Bell, Daniel. 1973. *The Coming of Post Industrial Society.* New York: Basic Books.

Bergman, Barbara R. 1968. "Investment in the Human Resources of Negroes." *Federal Programs for the Development of Human Resources,* Washington, D.C.: Government Printing Office.

Bowles, Samuel. 1972. "Unequal Education and the Reproduction of the Social Division of Labor." In *Schooling in a Corporate Society,* edited by Martin Carnoy. New York: David McKay.

Brimmer, Andrew F. 1969. "The Black Revolution and the Economic Future of Negroes in the United States." *The American Scholar* 38 (Autumn): 629–43.

Coleman, James S. 1971. *Resources for Social Change.* New York: Wiley.

Conant, James B. 1961. *Slums and Suburbs.* New York: McGraw-Hill.

Feldstein, Martin S. 1973. "The Economics of the New Unemployment." *The Public Interest* 33 (Fall) : 3–42.

Franklin, Raymond, and Michael Tanzer. 1970. "Traditional Microeconomic Analysis of Racial Discrimination: A Critical View and Alternative Approach." In *Economics: Mainstream Readings and Radical Critiques,* edited by David Mermelstein. New York: Random House.

Fremon, Charlotte. 1970. "Central City and Suburban Employment Growth, 1965–67." Washington, D.C.: Urban Institute.

Friedlander, Stanley L. 1972. *Unemployment in the Urban Core: An Analysis of Thirty Cities with Policy Recommendations.* New York: Praeger.

Gintis, Herbert. 1971. "Education, Technology, and the Characteristics of Worker Productivity." *American Economic Review/Proceedings* (May) 266.

Glazer, Nathan, and Daniel P. Moynihan. 1970. *Beyond the Melting Pot.* Cambridge, Mass.: M.I.T.

Glenn, Norval D. 1963. "Some Changes in the Relative Status of American Nonwhites, 1940 to 1960." *Phylon* 24 (Summer) : 109–22.

Harrison, Bennett. 1974. "The Theory of The Dual Economy." In *The Worker in Post-Industrial Capitalism,* edited by Bertram Silverman and Murray Yanowitch. New York: Free Press.

————. 1972. *Education, Training, and the Urban Ghetto.* Baltimore: John Hopkins University Press.

Howe, Florence, and Paul Lauter. 1972. "How the School System is Rigged for Failure." In *The Capitalist System,* edited by Richard C. Edwards, Michael Reich, and Thomas E. Weisskopf. Englewood Cliffs, N.J.: Prentice-Hall.

Kemeny, John L., J. Laurie Snell, and Gerald L. Thompson. 1957. *Introduction to Finite Mathematics.* Englewood Cliffs, N.J.: Prentice-Hall.

Killingsworth, Charles. 1969. "Jobs and Income for Negroes." In *Race and Social Science,* edited by Irwin Katz and Patricia Gurin. New York: Basic Books.

Kohl, Herbert. 1967. *36 Children.* New York: New American Library.

Levitan, Sar A., and Robert Taggart. 1971. *The Job Crisis for Black Youth.* New York: Praeger.

————. 1972. "The Emergency Employment Act: An Interim Assessment." *Monthly Labor Review* 95 (June) : 3–11.

Lewis, Wilfred. 1969. *Urban Growth and Suburbanization of Employment— Some New Data.* Washington, D.C.: Brookings Institute.

Lieberson, Stanley, and Glenn V. Fuguitt. 1967. "Negro-White Occupational Differences in the Absence of Discrimination." *American Journal of Sociology* 73 (September) : 188–200.

Lyman, Stanford M. 1972. *The Black American in Sociological Thought.* New York: Capricorn Books.

Mooney, Joseph D. 1969. "Housing Segregation, Negro Employment, and

Metropolitan Decentralization: An Alternative Prospect." *Quarterly Journal of Economics* 83 (May) : 299–311.

Moynihan, Daniel P. 1972. "The Schism in Black America." *The Public Interest* 27 (Spring) : 3–24.

Pearl, Arthur and Frank Reisman. 1969. *New Careers for the Poor.* New York: Free Press.

Piore, Michael J. 1970. "Jobs and Training." In *The State and the Poor,* edited by Samuel Beer and Richard Barringer. Cambridge, Mass.: Winthrop.

Poinsett, Alex. 1974. "The 'Whys' Behind the Black Lawyer Shortage." *Ebony* 33 (December) : 95–104.

Rainwater, Lee. 1969. "Looking Back and Looking Up." *Trans-Action* 6 (February) : 9.

Rosenthal, Neal H. 1973. "The United States Economy in 1985: Projected Changes in Occupations." *Monthly Labor Review* 96 (December) : 18–26.

Sexton, Patricia C. 1971. "Education and Income: Senior High Schools." In *Problems in Political Economy: An Urban Perspective,* edited by David M. Gordon. Lexington, Mass.: D.C. Heath.

Spratlen, Thaddeus H. 1974. "The Record and Rhetoric of Black Economic Progress." *The Review of Black Political Economy* 4 (Spring) : 1–27.

Tabb, William K. 1970. *The Political Economy of the Black Ghetto.* New York: Norton.

Thurow, Lester. 1969. "Employment Gains and the Determinants of the Occupational Distribution of Negroes." In *Proceedings of a Conference on the Education and Training of Racial Minorities.* Madison, Wis.: University of Wisconsin Press.

U.S. Department of Labor. 1971. *Manpower Report of the President.* Washington, D.C.: Government Printing Office.

_____. 1974. *Manpower Report of the President.* Washington, D.C.: Government Printing Office.

Wattenberg, Ben J. and Richard M. Scammon. 1973. "Black Progress and Liberal Rhetoric." *Commentary* 55 (April) : 35–44.

Wellman, David. 1970. "Putting on the Youth Opportunity Center." In *Soul,* edited by Lee Rainwater. Chicago: Aldine.

THE NEW GHETTO MAN
A REVIEW OF RECENT EMPIRICAL
STUDIES*

Nathan Caplan

What clearly emerges from the recent research findings on Negroes is a picture of a new ghetto man: a black militant who is committed to the removal of traditional racial restraints by open confrontation and, if necessary, by violence; a ghetto man who is very different in his actions and sympathies from the Negro of the past and from the white ghetto dwellers of an earlier period in this country's history. He is a ghetto man whose characteristics are seldom recognized and understood by most white Americans. It is our purpose here to describe him based on existing empirical data—to determine what he is like as a person, how large a segment of the Negro community he represents, what he wants, and how he intends to get it.

Profile of the Black Militant

Political authorities tend to categorize militants who advocate social and economic change through open confrontations as "riffraff" —irresponsible deviants, criminals, unassimilated migrants, emotionally disturbed persons, or members of an underclass. The riffraff theory sees these militants as being peripheral to organized society, with no broad social or political concerns; it views the frustration that leads to rioting or other forms of militant confrontation as simply part of a long history of personal failure.

It is not difficult to understand why protestors are generally labelled in these terms. By attributing the causes of riots to individual

*From the *Journal of Social Issues* 26, no. 1 (C) (1970) : 59–73. Reprinted with permission of the author and the *Journal of Social Issues*.

deficiencies, the riffraff theory relieves white institutions of most of the blame. It suggests that individual militants should be changed through psychotherapy, social work, or, if all else fails, prolonged confinement. If protesting militants can be publicly branded as unable to compete successfully because of personal reasons, then their demands for system changes can be declared illegitimate with impunity. Authorities would have the right to use punitive and coercive forms of control in place of working to ameliorate structural deficiencies and injustices.

The data show, however, that the militants are no more socially or personally deviant than their nonmilitant counterparts. In fact, there is good reason to believe that they are outstanding on some important measures of socioeconomic achievement. Tomlinson (1968) concludes from his study that the militants are "the cream of urban Negro youth in particular and urban Negro citizens in general (p. 28)."

The Extent of Militancy

The available data run counter to the commonly held belief that militancy is characteristic of only a small fraction of the Negro community. Militancy in pursuit of civil rights objectives represents a considerable force in the ghetto. Its support approaches normative proportions.

As shown in Table 1, in a group of studies using related criterion variables about one third to one half of the ghetto residents surveyed express support for riots and militant civil rights positions. The proportion of persons reporting active participation in riots is less, but the data across studies are equally consistent if differences in methodology and data sources are taken into consideration. Based on random probability sampling of general population, survey data show the level of self-reported riot participation to be 15 percent for Watts (Sears and McConahay, 1970a), and 11 percent for Detroit (Caplan and Paige, 1968a). In Newark, where only males between the ages of fifteen and thirty-five were sampled, 45 percent of the respondents reported riot activity (Caplan and Paige, 1968a). The riot participation figure for males in the same age group from the general population sample surveyed in Detroit is practically identical with the Newark findings.

Interpolating from arrest records, Fogelson and Hill (1968)

TABLE 4-4   ATTITUDES EXPRESSED BY NEGROES RELATING TO RIOTS

Attitudes Expressed	Percent Study Sample	Locale and Source
A. RIOT SYMPATHY		
Do not view riots as "essentially bad"	50%	Nationwide, *Fortune,* 1967 (Beardwood, 1968)
In sympathy with rioters	54%	Fifteen American Cities (Campbell and Schuman, 1968)
Believe riots are helpful	30%	Houston, 1967 (McCord and Howard, 1968)
Believe riots are helpful	51%	Oakland, 1967 (McCord and Howard, 1968)
B. RIOT PARTICIPATION		
Active participation in Watts riot	15%	Watts (Sears and Mc-Conahay, 1970a)
Active participation in Detroit riot	11%	Detroit (Caplan and Paige, 1968a)
Active participation in Newark riot	45% (males, age 15-35)	Newark (Caplan and Paige, 1968a)
Active participation in riots	20%	Six major riot cities, 1967 (Fogelson and Hill, 1968)
Willingness to participate in riots	15%	Nationwide, *Newsweek* poll (Brink and Harris, 1966)
Advocated use of violence	15%	Fifteen American Cities (Campbell and Schuman, 1968)

estimated that 20 percent of ghetto residents participated in riots that occurred in their cities. Finally, two studies involving surveys in a number of different cities report that 15 percent of the ghetto population advocate or express willingness to participate in riots (Brink and Harris, 1966; Campbell and Schuman, 1968).

In most of these studies, riot sympathy and riot participation related to age and sex. The militant, particularly the rioter, is usually young and most likely male. In so far as it is possible to determine from the available literature, the differences between militants and nonmilitants to be discussed here hold up after age and sex are controlled.

Income—Absolute

According to one variety of the riffraff theory, the rioter is a member of a deprived underclass, part of the "hard core" unemployed —often out of work for long periods of time or chronically unemployable because he lacks skill or education. Having lost contact with the job market and all hope of finding work, he is economically at the very bottom of Negro society.

Data from the major research studies do not support this hypothesis. There is no significant difference in income between rioters and nonrioters. In fact, income and militancy are related only in the way Karl Marx predicted: In the main, the black *lumpenproletariat* is quiescent, not militant. The available data show that those in the lowest socioeconomic position are the least militant and the least likely to riot (Murphy and Watson, 1970; Caplan and Paige, 1968a; Darrow and Lowinger, 1967; Shulman, 1967).

The poorest of the poor are also low on those variables which show relationships with active protest. Caplan and Paige (1968a) found that the lowest income group tends to score low on black pride and more readily accepts the traditional deprecating Negro stereotypes. Campbell and Schuman (1968) reported a surprising degree of job satisfaction among those who are the most economically disadvantaged. Brink and Harris (1966) found that approval of "Black Power" was lowest among those in the poorest group. Only 13 percent of their low-income respondents approved of the term, compared with 31 percent in the lower middle-income and 26 percent in the middle and upper-income groups. Apparently, continued injustice and the severe withdrawal of resources increase a deprived group's dependency behavior and approval of those who control scarce resources. These findings argue strongly against an "underclass" or strictly economic interpretation of militancy and violent protest in the ghetto.

Income—Relative

Objective poverty in the sense of destitution is not the only issue associated with economic standing which has drawn research attention. The subjective meaning of one's wealth, or the absence of it, in relation to what others have, may also be important in producing the frustration that leads to unrest and rioting.

The widening gap between income levels of whites and blacks often has been cited as a possible cause for the present social unrest.

The assumption is that members of the black community are concerned not so much with what they have as with what they feel they deserve compared with the whites. Attention to the discrepancy arouses a sense of social injustice that generates the frustration leading to rioting.

In order to examine the relation of the racial economic gap to riot participation, Caplan and Paige (1968b) asked respondents whether they thought the income gap between Negroes and whites was increasing, remaining the same, or decreasing. They found that 45 percent of the rioters but 55 percent of the nonrioters said the gap was *increasing*. Although the difference between these groups is small, it is opposite in direction to what one would predict on the basis of a relative deprivation hypothesis. More important, when these respondents were questioned about the income gap between the wealthier and poorer Negroes, these percentages were reversed. Fifty-five percent of the rioters and 45 percent of the nonrioters said the gap between the very poor and the higher income level Negroes was increasing.

Thus the rioters are particularly sensitive to where they stand in relation to other Negroes, not to whites. If the "black capitalism" idea, as presently formulated, is carried out seriously as a remedial step to prevent further rioting, it is likely to increase this income gap among Negroes and thereby produce disturbing consequences.

Education

McCord and Howard (1968) found that educational attainment had no linear relationship to participation in civil rights activity although college-educated respondents in their study were the *least opposed* to the use of violence. Campbell and Schuman (1968) reported no relationship between education and expressed favorability toward riots. Conversely, Tomlinson (1970) found that militants in Watts had attained a higher level of formal education than their more conservative neighbors. Marx (1967) reported a linear relationship between education and militancy—the higher the respondent's education, the greater the likelihood that he would score high on militancy measures. Forty-two percent of the militants in his study had attended college.

There was a slight tendency for the Watts riot participants to be better educated than the nonparticipants but the difference is too small to be statistically reliable (Murphy and Watson, 1970). Finally, Caplan and Paige (1968a) reported that rioters in Detroit and

Newark were significantly higher on an educational achievement scale than the nonrioters.

Thus, while the average rioter was likely to be a high school dropout, data show that the average nonrioter was more likely to be an elementary school dropout. There is a significant relationship between schooling, militancy, and riot activity, but it is the militants and rioters who are better educated.

Employment

A major difficulty arises in interpreting the relationships between employment and militancy because researchers use varying definitions of unemployment and different criteria for ranking occupational skill levels. It is clear from the available evidence, however, that the militants are not the hardcore unemployed. Rather, the militants, particularly the rioters, have greater job dissatisfaction since they are continually on the margin of the job market, often employed but never for long.

Murphy and Watson (1970) found a tendency for unemployment to be higher among those who were active during the Watts riot although there was no relationship between riot sympathy and employment. Fogelson and Hill (1968) reported a 25 percent unemployment rate among riot arrestees and pointed out that this is about the same level of unemployment as in comparable samples in the open community.

In Detroit, Caplan and Paige (1968a) found that the unemployment rate for rioters and nonrioters was practically identical, about 31 percent. But in Newark where the respondents were all young males, unemployment was higher among rioters: 31 percent as compared to 19 percent. Further, in Newark the rioters held higher job aspirations than nonrioters and were also more likely to blame their employment failures on racial barriers rather than on personal deficiencies. The same study showed that the rioters were not chronically but only temporarily unemployed and were marginally related to the labor force, i.e., persons who tended to move in and out of the labor force several times throughout the year.

Social Integration and Values

Political theories often emphasize that the militant is isolated or cut off from the rest of the community. More parochial views speculate that the militant is a social deviant who is alienated from the more responsible elements and forces in the social environment. The date from these studies, however, do not support such views. At least two of the major studies show that the Negro who is militant in the pursuit of civil rights objectives is more likely to be the person best integrated into the black community.

Marx (1967) found a positive relationship between militancy and the number of organizational memberships held. In Detroit and Newark, Caplan and Paige (1968a) reported a similar relationship and, in addition, found that rioters socialized with their neighbors and others in the community more frequently than nonrioters. Finally, Marx (1967) and Caplan and Paige (1968a) demonstrated that the militants were more strongly identified with Negro cultural values and civil rights objectives than those in the black community who neither support nor participate in militant activities.

Neither Murphy and Watson (1970) nor Caplan and Paige (1968a) found any relationship between church attendance and riot participation. Marx (1967), however, found that militancy and church attendance related negatively.

Several of the studies included questions intended to show whether or not militancy and rioting are related to differences in support for an important American value: belief in work and the Protestant ethic. Rioters and nonrioters were virtually identical in their responses to most of these questions (Caplan and Paige, 1968a). About 75 percent of both groups in this study expressed the belief that hard work rather than luck or dependence upon help from others was important for achieving a successful life. Similarly, about 65 percent of the sample studied by Marx (1967) agreed that Negroes could get ahead through hard work.

Fogelson and Hill (1968) found that the crime rate for the riot arrestees was similar to that of the community as a whole. They did, however, report a difference with respect to the types of past offenses. Rioters tended to have committed less serious crimes.

Socialization

Several of the studies include information about some important elements of adjustment. The possibility that the frustrations of the militant may be caused by inadequate socialization because of family disorganization or migration has been investigated. Data on family background are available only in the study by Caplan and Paige (1968a) which found that there was essentially no difference between rioters and nonrioters in the presence of an adult male in the home during formative years.

Region of socialization has also been related to militancy in a number of different studies but the direction of the relationship is opposite to the riffraff hypothesis that rioters are most likely to be found among recent migrants to the urban area. On the contrary: The militant is no parvenu to the city. Rather, he is the long-term resident who knows urban life best.

Watts respondents born in California were more favorable to the riot (Murphy and Watson, 1970) and more likely to participate in it (Sears and McConahay, 1970a) than those who migrated to the area. Rioters in Detroit and Newark were more likely than nonrioters to have been born and raised in the North (Caplan and Paige, 1968a). In Detroit, six out of ten of the rioters, in contrast to three out of ten of the nonrioters, were born in that city. The distinction between region of socialization and riot participation is even more clearly drawn in the Newark data from the same study. There almost half of the nonrioters but only a quarter of the rioters had been born and raised in the South.

The readiness of the long-term northern-born ghetto resident to participate in riot activity is even more clearly defined in Fogelson and Hill (1968). In addition to finding that the arrestees were more likely to be northern born, they also discovered that the highest proportion of northern-born rioters and the lowest proportion of southern-born rioters were arrested on the first day of rioting. The arrestees on and after the third day represented the highest proportion of southern born and lowest proportion of northern born. Fogelson and Hill also noted a tendency for the southern born to be involved in less flagrant aspects of the riot. They were least likely to have been charged with "assault" and most likely to have been arrested for looting.

Finally, in their study of the meaning of "Black Power" carried out in Detroit, Aberbach and Walker (1968) found that northern-born Negroes more frequently define this concept in militant, political terms. Southern-born Negroes were less likely to view the slogan favorably and less likely to interpret it in a militant context.

Black Consciousness

Possibly the characteristic of the new ghetto man which has the most etiological significance for understanding the rise of militancy is his Black Consciousness. Both the Detroit and the Newark studies indicate that rioters have strong feelings of racial pride and even racial superiority (Caplan and Paige, 1968a, 1968b). They not only have rejected the traditional stereotype of the Negro but also have created a positive stereotype.

In both cities, rioters were more likely to view their race more positively than nonrioters on racial comparison items involving dependability, smartness, courage, "niceness," etc. For example, about one-half of rioters but less than one-quarter of nonrioters felt Negroes were "more dependable" than whites. Responses in these studies reflect a higher level of black pride among rioters; those who attempted to quell the disturbance and control the level of destruction deviate in the opposite direction. When the sample was divided into rioters, the uninvolved, and counter-rioters, the rioters were highest and counter-rioters were lowest on several measures of racial pride. Furthermore, half of the rioters and only a third of the nonrioters preferred to be called "black" rather than "colored," "Negro," or "Afro-American." Similarly, Caplan and Paige (1968a, 1968b) found a tendency for rioters to be stronger in the belief that all Negroes should study Negro history and African languages in the high schools.

Marx (1967) reported that militants prefer Negro newspapers and magazines, are better able to identify Negro writers and civil rights leaders, and have a more positive appreciation of Negro culture than nonmilitants. Darrow and Lowinger (1967) also encountered feelings of a new, positive Negro self-image among the rioters they studied. Consequently, these authors argue against the psychoanalytic interpretations of rioting which hold that participants release aggression associated with self-hatred.

This positive affirmation of racial identity is found not only among the militants but is widespread throughout the Negro community (Campbell and Schuman, 1968). Ninety-six percent of the sample in this study agreed that "Negroes should take more pride in Negro history." Also, four out of ten of the respondents thought that "Negro school children should study an *African* language" (italics mine).

Thucydides said long ago that social revolution occurs when old terms take on new meanings. The wisdom of this statement is apparent in the dramatic, recent change of the meaning for the term "black"—a word that has become a badge of intense pride which borders on racial superiority: "Black is Beautiful."

Attitudes Toward Whites

The fact that racial pride is so high in the black community and the suspicion that it may play a causal role in the rise of militancy raise questions about Negro attitudes towards whites. Do black pride and the desire for black self-development go hand-in-hand with white hatred? What is the overall attitude of the ghetto toward whites?

Although there are some slight inconsistencies in the findings, in general militancy does not appear associated with increased hostility toward whites; the black community as a whole is not markedly anti-white nor preoccupied by social cross-comparison with whites.

Marx (1967) found that militancy and anti-white attitudes were inversely related. The variables which were most closely related to militancy—intellectual sophistication, high morale, and a positive self-image—correlated negatively with anti-white sentiment. Marx concluded that "they don't hate (whites), but they don't like them either (p. 179) ." In an earlier study, Noel (1964) also found that those lowest in anti-white feelings were the most militant proponents of civil rights action. Although he presents no supporting data, Tomlinson (1970) also reported that the militants in the Watts study are not notably anti-white.

Murphy and Watson (1970) reported a slight tendency for the economically better-off riot participants to be more hostile towards whites. Caplan and Paige (1968a) similarly found the rioters to be slightly more anti-white, but equally hostile to more affluent Negroes. Also, it should be pointed out that several attempts to test if rioters are more likely to use whites as social comparative referents have found no support for this possibility.

When considered in the aggregate, the Negro community is probably far less anti-white than most whites are prepared to believe. Campbell and Schuman (1968) found little evidence of anti-white hostility in their study. Only 13 percent of their respondents wanted to live in an all black or mostly black neighborhood; only 6 percent believed that American Negroes should establish a separate black nation; and only 9 percent felt that Negroes should have as little as possible to do with whites. Furthermore, only 6 percent wanted Negro children to go to only Negro schools and 5 percent preferred to have only Negro friends. On the basis of responses to these and a number of similar items, Campbell and Schuman concluded: "Negroes hold strongly, perhaps more strongly than any other element in the American population, to a belief in nondiscrimination and racial harmony (p. 17) ."

In general, these findings are not different from the results of earlier studies. Noel and Pinkney (1964) found that 41 percent of Negroes sampled in four cities expressed no particular antipathy toward whites. Among the respondents in the nationwide survey by Brink and Harris (1966), 80 percent reported that they preferred to work with a racially mixed group; 68 percent preferred to live in an integrated neighborhood; 70 percent preferred to have their children attend school with white children; and only 5 percent supported Black Nationalism. Only about 4 percent of Marx's (1967) total sample supported pro-nationalistic statements.

In the Murphy and Watson (1970) and Caplan and Paige (1968b) studies, anti-white sentiment was most intense among riot participants when associated with perceived discrimination practices which restricted social and economic mobility for Negroes. Neither social envy of whites nor material greed motivates men to riot, but rather anger over the conditions that produce—and the practices that sustain—barriers denying Negroes the same freedoms and opportunities available to whites.

Political Attitudes

Almost all recent studies of Negro communities have included political items in their interview schedules and, without exception, the data show that militants are politically more sensitive and better informed than nonmilitants. They are not, however, politically alienated. What they want is what is already guaranteed by law, not a new political system.

Tomlinson (1970) reported that, compared with nonmilitants, militants in Watts were politically more active, more likely to refer to the riot in "revolutionary" terms, and less distrustful of elected officials. Marx (1967) found that almost twice as many militants as nonmilitants voted during the 1960 presidential election (31 percent vs. 17 percent). Sears (1970) and Sears and McConahay (1970b) reported that Watts arrestees and riot participants expressed greater political discontent and were more cynical of the responsiveness of local political powers to Negro grievances than nonrioter samples.

Caplan and Paige (1968a) found that rioters were more familiar with the identification of political personalities, more distrustful of politicians, and more likely to cite anger at politicians as a cause of the riot. In Newark, 44 percent of the rioters and 34 percent of the nonrioters reported "almost never" when asked if local government could be trusted "to do what is right." In Detroit, 42 percent of the rioters but only 20 percent of the nonrioters cited "anger with politicians" as a major cause of the riot.

The kinds of discontents that are felt most intensely by the militants reflect feelings that are widespread throughout the Negro community. Sears (1969) reported that 45 percent of the random sample of Watts residents said that "elected officials cannot generally be trusted (p. 21) "; this figure compares with 17 percent of a comparable white sample. Despite these discontents with political representation and the domination of the political system by whites, there is no evidence of broad rejection of the political system itself. Brink and Harris (1966) found that 74 percent of the Negroes in their sample expressed the desire to attain civil rights objectives through existing political channels. Also, Campbell and Schuman (1968) found no evidence indicating that Negroes want a new form of political functioning.

Fate Control

The final characteristic of the militant that must be given special emphasis can be called fate control or the power to maintain control over those environmental forces that affect one's destiny. Although none of the researchers conceptualize this variable as such, several findings imply its distinct character as well as its significance to the emergence of militancy in the ghetto.

For example, Marx (1967) identifies "intellectual sophistication" as one of the three variables most strongly related to militancy. He describes intellectual sophistication as greater knowledge of the world and a way of looking at the world. Two important related factors that make up this variable are a broad liberated world outlook and a great sensitivity to the way social factors shape human behavior. In essence, Marx stresses that the militant is more likely to be cognitively correct about the external forces that influence his behavior and how they impede his ability to effectuate personal goals.

Meyer (1968) concluded that Miami-area Negroes who scored high on militancy possess "... a strong feeling that they can and should shape their destinies" (p. 22). He based his interpretation on the association between the respondents' scores on militancy and their sense of personal and political efficacy. In a survey study of Los Angeles Negroes, Ransford (1968) found that "powerlessness," which he defines as "a low expectancy of costrol over events" (p. 583). was strongly related to the respondent's willingness to use violence. Those with the highest scores on powerlessness held the highest commitment to violence.

Crawford and Naditch (1968) reexamined Ransford's data along with data from two other survey studies. By combining power-lessness with Rotter's internal-external schema, they found that the more militant respondents were characterized by a high sense of personal efficacy and low control over external forces that affect the probability of achieving personal goals. Employing a similar analytical framework, Gurin *et al.* (1969) found a marked tendency for militancy among Negro students to be associated with the belief that they could not reach personal goals because of external or social systemic constraints. Finally, the blocked-opportunity theory which emphasizes environmental rather than personal factors as the cause of riots (Caplan and Paige, 1968b) is supported by the survey data from that study which found that rioters desire increased mastery over the distribution of resources rather than the mere acquition of resources.

Conclusions

There is a surprising degree of empirical regularity and basic coherence to the findings discussed here, even though they come from studies carried out in several parts of the country by different investigators employing various methodological approaches. This agreement allows us to draw some important conclusions with reasonable comfort and confidence in their validity, conclusions which should help achieve a better understanding of the militant and a safer evaluation of his behavior.

1. Militancy in the pursuit of civil rights objectives represents a considerable force within the ghetto. Its support approaches normative proportions and is by no means limited to a deviant and irresponsible minority.

2. The militant is a viable creature in search of practical responses to arbitrary institutional constraints and preemptions which deny him the same freedom and conventional opportunities as the white majority. He is the better educated but underemployed, politically disaffected but not the politically alienated. He is willing to break laws for rights already guaranteed by law, but under ordinary circumstances he is no more likely to engage in crime than his non-militant neighbor. He is intensely proud of being black, but nei-

ther desires revenge from whites nor is socially envious of them. He has little freedom or resources to effectuate his personal goals, but strongly desires freedom and ownership of his own life. Indeed, this new man of the ghetto is also the man of paradox.

3. The characteristics of the militants together with the large proportion of ghetto blacks who share their views certainly indicate that the fight for civil rights will not end with the recent riots. Even though the time and place of their occurrence may not be predictable nor their instrumental value always clear, the riots are neither random events nor marginal, temporary phenomena. The militants must be taken seriously and not simply treated as troublemakers.

4. With candor and a few frills, the Kerner Commission cited white racism as the major cause of ghetto riots. Undoubtedly, white racism is a root issue, but it has been present for over three hundred years and, therefore, is insufficient as a sole explanation of riots of such magnitude and intensity as occur at this point in time. The logic of scientific proof would require that we look for causal factors whose relationships are more contemporaneous.

The findings reviewed here suggest that Negroes who riot do so because their conception of their lives and their potential has changed without commensurate improvement in their chances for a better life. In the midst of squalor and despair, Negroes have abandoned the traditional stereotypes that made nonachievement and passive adaptation seem so natural. Rather, they have developed a sense of black consciousness and a desire for a way of life with which they can feel the same pride and sense of potency they now derive from being black. Without these changes in self-perception, the demands to be regarded and treated as an individual with the same liberties as white Americans would never have reached the intensity that they have today. If this interpretation of the research is correct, it could be argued that the riots and other forms of civil rights protest are caused by the self-discovery of the American Negro and his attempt to recreate himself socially in ways that are commensurate with this new image. This battle for greater personal rights can be expected to continue as long as the Negro's political, social, and economic efficacy is not aligned with his new and increasing sense of personal potency.

5. The limited data available at this time do not permit us to make fine grain projections about the maturation pattern of riot activity, the future forms of other protest activity, or their outcome. Possibly the most that one can say at this time about the meaning of these outbreaks is: First, they are more similar to the early slave-

ship uprisings than they are to the white-initiated interracial riots that occurred after World Wars I and II. Ghetto-locked blacks are claiming ownership of their behavior and are demanding the freedom and opportunity necessary to control their destiny. They are interested in bettering their position in American society; they are not interested in "white blood" or the glorification of violence. Second, it seems safe to conclude that the riots represent an elementary form of political activity. But, it must be emphasized that the political objectives are conservative. The militants are not rebelling against the system itself but against the inequities and contradictions of the system.

If this nation is serious about the application of democratic principles to human affairs, then it must increase the power of the black man to improve his position beyond anything now possible in American society. The stereotype of the Negro—which for seven generations has been used to destroy his initiative, motivation, and hope—is a reality apart from what these studies show him to be. He emerges in these studies as more American than those who built the ghetto and those who now maintain it. Unless this nation acts now to redress the balance in social and economic distance between the races, we will probably have lost forever the ideal of the democratic prospect and, like other nations in the past, will resort to what C. P. Snow calls "hideous crimes in the name of obedience." It is clear that the Negro will not give up the struggle for a better life. Unlike the Negro in the past, the present ghetto dwellers have neither the psychological defenses nor the social supports that permit passive adaptation to barriers that prevent implementation of their potential capabilities. In a sense, they are the hearing children of deaf parents.

NOTES

1. Adapted from a paper presented at the Second International Congress of Social Psychiatry, London, August, 1969.

REFERENCES

Aberbach, D., & Walker, L. The meanings of black power: A comparison of white and black interpretations of a political slogan. Paper presented at the meeting of the American Political Science Association, Washington, D.C., 1968.

Beardwood, R. The new Negro mood. *Fortune Magazine*, 1968, 77, 146–152.

Brink, W., & Harris, L. *Black and white*. New York: Simon and Schuster, 1966.

Campbell, A., & Schuman, H. Racial attitudes in fifteen American cities. Supplement Studies for The National Advisory Commission on Civil Disorders. Government Printing Office, 1968.

Caplan, N. S., & Paige, J. M. In O. Kerner, *et al. Report of The National Advisory Commission on Civil Disorders*. New York: Bantam Press, 1968, 127–137. (a)

Caplan, N. S. & Paige, J. M. A study of ghetto rioters. *Scientific American,* August 1968, 219 (2), 15–21. (b)

Crawford, T. J., & Naditch, M. Unattained and unattainable goals: Relative deprivation, powerlessness, and racial militancy. Paper presented at the meeting of the American Psychological Association, San Francisco, California, 1968.

Darrow, C., & Lowinger, P. The Detroit uprising: A psychosocial study. Paper presented at the meeting of the American Academy of Psychoanalysis, New York, 1967.

Fogelson, R. M., & Hill, R. B. Who riots? A study of participation in the 1967 riots. Supplement Studies for The National Advisory Commission on Civil Disorders, Government Printing Office, 1968.

Forward, J., & Williams, J. Internal-external control and black militancy. *Journal of Social Issues,* 1970, 26 (1).

Gurin, P., Gurin, G., Lao, R., & Beattie, M. Internal-external control in the motivational dynamics of Negro youth. *Journal of Social Issues,* 1969, 25 (3), 29–53.

Marx, G. T. *Protest and prejudice: A study of belief in the black community.* New York: Harper and Row, 1967.

McCord, W., & Howard, J. Negro opinions in three riot cities. *American Behavioral Scientist,* March/April, 1968, 11 (4), 24–27.

Meyer, P. Negro militancy and Martin Luther King: The aftermath of martyrdom. Washington, D.C.: *Knight Newspapers,* 1968.

Murphy, R. J. & Watson, J. M. The structure of discontent. In N. E. Cohen (Ed.), *The Los Angeles riots: A socio-psychological study.* New York: Praeger, 1970.

Noel, D. L. Group identification among Negroes: An empirical analysis. *Journal of Social Issues,* 1964, 20 (2), 71–84.

Noel, D. L., & Pinkney, A. Correlates of prejudice: Some racial differences and similarities. *American Journal of Sociology,* 1964, 69 (6), 609–622.

Ransford, H. E. Isolation, powerlessness, and violence: A study of attitudes and participation in the Watts riot. *American Journal of Sociology,* 1968, 73, 581–591.

Sears, D. O. Political attitudes of Los Angeles Negroes. In N. E. Cohen (Ed.), *The Los Angeles riots: A socio-psychological study.* New York: Praeger, 1970.

Sears, D. O., & McConahay, J. B. Riot participation. In N. E. Cohen (Ed.), *The Los Angeles riots: A socio-psychological study.* New York: Praeger, 1970. (a)

Sears, D. O., & McConahay, J. B. The politics of discontent. In N. E. Cohen (Ed.), *The Los Angeles riots: A socio-psychological study.* New York: Praeger, 1970. (b)

Shulman, J. Ghetto residence, political alienation and riot orientation. Unpublished manuscript, Cornell University, 1967.

Tomlinson, T. M. The development of a riot ideology among urban Negroes. *American Behavioral Scientist,* March/April, 1968, 11 (4), 27–31.

Tomlinson, T. M. Militance, violence, and poverty: Ideology and foundation for action. In N.E. Cohen (Ed.), *The Los Angeles riots: A socio-psychological study.* New York: Praeger, 1970.

JOBS AND THE NEGRO FAMILY:
A REAPPRAISAL*

Edwin Harwood and Claire C. Hodge

Louise Meriwether's recent novel, *Daddy Was a Number Runner*, deals with an adolescent Negro girl in Harlem at the depth of the Depression. Although the young heroine manages to fend off a variety of local predators—mostly whites who make sexual advances—she proves powerless to prevent the disintegration of her family, a process that becomes the dramatic anchor in the book's plot. When her father stumbles hard against New York's job-scarce labor market, her mother starts work as a domestic for a suburban housewife, at first for a few half-days a week, but, towards the end of the novel, on almost a full-time basis. She knows it wounds Dad's pride, but the children must eat. What little Dad does manage to earn, by running numbers slips for the racketeers, he squanders on bets. The conclusion is foregone. Bitter at his wife's taking relief and going to work as a domestic, he fades from the home and becomes "a street-corner man."

None will deny that tragedies of this kind occurred. None will deny that economic recessions have posed serious problems for Negro city dwellers all along. Yet Meriwether's tale of woe relies heavily on a prevalent—and largely erroneous—stereotype of the Negro's economic condition. This is to the effect that, relative to their menfolk, Negro women have enjoyed an advantage in the urban labor market, and that in this their situation has differed sharply from that of working-class whites. Recent fantasies about "internal colonialism" have sharpened this stereotype to the point where it is sometimes said that the black man has been kept down in order to keep him in line, and that black women have been allowed a freer economic adjustment as a part of this same strategy. These and other such notions have helped fuel the animosities of black militants during the past decade. What better justification could there be for the rage of angry young men if, as Richard Rubenstein claims in his thinly-veiled apology for black violence, *Rebels in Eden*, "young [Negro] men have been degraded by this lack of control over their lives—by their inability to get or keep jobs and the need to send their women out to clean Goldberg's floor."

This stereotype is so familiar, and so widely-accepted, that it is hard to believe it could be false. Yet false is what available evidence shows it to be. Today, even in the poorest urban neighborhoods, Negro men enjoy a clear economic superiority over Negro women, as the findings of the United States Bureau of Labor Statistics' 1968–9 Urban Employment Survey demonstrated. Moreover, and more surprising, all the evidence we have for past periods offers no significant support for the assumption that Negro women ever were advantaged in the search for jobs.

Since 1890, when separate tabulations for whites and Negroes first became available, every decennial census has revealed Negro men to have enjoyed a markedly greater diversification of jobs than Negro women. In the urban or nonagricultural labor force, this difference is particularly striking. While Negro men could be found in substantial numbers in jobs in every major industry, Negro women were concentrated in just a handful of the several hundred occupational classifications. As late as 1930, of 1.3 million Negro women in nonagricultural jobs, over one million (or roughly 85 percent) were in domestic and personal service occupations. Over half were "laundresses not in laundries" and servants in private households. Of the Negro men outside agriculture, by contrast, less than 25 percent (425,000 of over 2 million) were to be found in the domestic and personal service classification. When, after studying Harlem's working population at the turn of the century, George Edmund Haynes concluded that Negroes would, when given the opportunity, expand their job horizons, he could only have been referring to Negro men. For his statistics showed that over half of the men had moved into jobs in firms and businesses, whereas 90 percent of all Negro female workers in his canvass were still confined to domestic and personal service jobs.

Taking economic dominance in its most literal sense, we might ask who held the supervisory and managerial jobs available to Negro workers then. Men did. With the exception of restaurants and boarding and lodging houses, Negro females in supervisory positions are rarely to be found at all in 1930. Second, and most contrary to popular belief, Negro men outnumbered women by heavy margins in white-collar clerical occupations (as did white men in relation to white women a generation ago). In 1930, Negro men in clerical occupations numbered almost 30,000 compared with 11,000 Negro women. In the single category, "Clerks" (except "clerks" in stores) the census located over 20,000 Negro males but only 5,000 Negro females in that year. In sum, *the historical pattern of occupational and earnings differences between the sexes reveals a striking similarity between whites and blacks, and not the reversal of roles or, as one writer phrased it, the "unnatural superiority" of women* that so many scholars have allowed themselves to believe without a careful review of the facts.

When it is argued that higher proportions of Negro women than men hold white-collar jobs today, it is forgotten that the same holds true of female whites in relation to men—simply because our economy employs more cashiers, "girl fridays," and telephone opera-tors than it does lawyers, physicians, and corporation executives. Women moved into these more numerous white-collar occupations as men took better-paying jobs in other sectors of the economy, including blue-collar jobs. It is *not* true, as is often assumed, that female white-collar workers, black or white, earn more than male blue-collar work-ers. In 1969, annual earnings for Negro men in white-collar, blue-collar, and service (excluding private household) occupations were higher on average than earnings for Negro women in clerical and sales jobs. In the top bracket of the earnings scale, Negro female pro-fessional workers rank third, following Negro male professionals and managerial workers. However, these women, who are predominantly elementary and secondary school teachers, nurses, or medical and health technicians, are only 10 percent of all employed Negro women; they earn on average a mere $17 more per year than Negro male crafts-men and foremen. Twice as many Negro women are still to be found in the lowest paying of all job classifications, private household work.

Thus, the facts simply do not support the notion that the Ne-gro man had a rougher go in the urban labor market than the Negro woman. On the contrary, his economic problems shrivel by comparison with hers. If she had to work, she found a limited range of jobs to choose from, most of them in private households, which paid the low-est wages. In New York City 70 years ago, more than half (53 percent) of the Negro women in service work earned less than five dollars a week, whereas only 28 percent of Negro male service workers had earnings that low. Elevator operator, butler, fireman, houseman, even "usefulman," paid better than "general housework, chambermaid, and laundress."

The argument for the Negro female's advantaged labor market position fails precisely where one might expect it to be strongest—in times of economic depression. Consider the facts turned up by the Division of Social Research of the Works Progress Administration (WPA). A thorough study of urban workers on relief in 79 major cities in the early 1930's was published in the two-volume study, *Urban Workers on Relief*. We learn:

1. The single occupational group that had the heaviest representation among relief applicants was "servants." Women, and particularly Negro women, were disproportionately represented in the unskilled service jobs included in that category. Among Negro women, a large majority were general houseworkers and laundresses.

2. Negro women on relief were twice as apt to be employed at the time of the study as Negro men on relief—but they enjoyed no special economic advantage because of that fact. The WPA researchers point out that the women earned less than men (17 cents an hour against the male's 25 cents an hour). And because she worked fewer than half the median hours her working male counterpart obtained in a week (17 hours for her; 35 for him), her median *weekly* earnings ($2.80) were less than half of what he earned ($6.30).

To argue that Negro women had the edge in the Depression labor market simply because at any given time she was more apt to get some job in unskilled service work is to rest the argument for her superiority on a shallow and incomplete statistic. In any case white men faced the same situation in relation to white females. Negro men may very well have been unemployed for longer stretches, but *when they did get jobs they worked more hours per week and earned substantially more money, such that in the aggregate they may very well have been doing much better by far than Negro women.* What proponents of the "dominant-female" view have never established is crucial: Did the female domestic work more days during the course of a given *year* in and out of depressions? The fact that in a given week she could often locate some job does not prove that she had more work over a longer span. Did she receive anywhere near the annual earnings received by a male laborer? According to Charles S. Johnson, research di-

rector for the National Urban League, women domestics in Water-
bury, Connecticut were averaging three dollars a day in 1923 in work
"that could rarely be secured for more than four days a week." Wages
for Negro men averaged $4.38 per day; men in skilled manual jobs
earned as much as five dollars and six dollars per day.

3. What the WPA researchers chose to emphasize in their study is even
   more significant in view of the strenuous attempt scholars have made
   to stress the differences in the adjustments of blacks and whites to
   a recession. The WPA study emphasized that *both* Negro and white
   males were unemployed for longer stretches than their female counterparts because *both* white and Negro men had a more diverse
   occupational distribution. This meant that, though they enjoyed
   the higher earnings that jobs in industrial and commercial firms
   paid in good times, they would suffer longer stretches of unemployment during a recession. It is reasonable to think that the
   casual service employment which women willingly took was not
   an acceptable alternative to either the white or black male worker,
   in any case. Reports issued by the United States Employment Service during the Depression years showed that a large proportion
   of the job placements in household work were for very short periods, often only for a given day, which supports the WPA's finding that most women obtained casual laboring jobs characterized
   by high turnover. Household workers in Wisconsin, for example,
   were so poorly paid that the state set a minimum weekly wage of
   $6 for a 50 hour week if board alone was furnished. We have no
   comparable data on the conditions of employment and pay in service jobs available to men, but we can be reasonably sure that the
   male janitor or porter, for example, would have been guaranteed
   a job of longer duration at higher pay.

The irony here is that the facts gathered by the WPA research
team require something on the order of an about-face in our thinking.
If Negro men had made even *further* advances in occupations and
earnings, and hence in expectations as well, beyond what they had already achieved, then they would have experienced *longer* stretches of
unemployment. They would have been more reluctant to take casual
low-paying jobs. *Their problem of finding an acceptable job would
have approached in severity that of white males who held the record
for unbroken spells of unemployment!*

Clearly, it was because more reform-minded scholars wanted
to do the Negro good, not ill, that they were led consistently to emphasize the *differences* between white and black Americans in their perfor-

mances in the labor market. Only thus could special remedial action urged on the Negro's behalf have a plausible basis. Moreover, the troublesome issue of Negro marital instability had to be explained. If this could be linked to an economic plight not shared by white Americans, then it followed that most scholars would first seek out and then emphasize some critical difference observed in the adjustment of blacks and whites to the labor market.

It is important to keep two facts in mind: First, that an economic explanation was not logically compulsory for understanding family instability. E. Franklin Frazier's early monograph, *The Negro Family in Chicago,* hardly mentions employment handicaps—let alone handicaps peculiar to the Negro—in accounting for the disintegration of families in the slum. If Frazier later changed his mind, it was most probably because others were changing theirs, and his professors at the University of Chicago no longer insisted that the adjustment of Negro migrants—whom Frazier called peasants—fit the same model they had used earlier to explain the adjustment of European peasants who had come to Chicago from Poland and southern Italy. (Then, family disintegration was attributed to the clash between a secular urban and a traditional agrarian ethos.)

Secondly, even granting that the antecedent of an aberrant social pattern might be an aberrant economic pattern, was there one and only one important and critical difference between whites and blacks in their relation to the occupational order? Was it not possible that some other difference had been overlooked that might explain the instability of Negro marriages just as well?

If it is hard to imagine that the working Negro woman could resent her husband, or he her, on the basis of the jobs, wages, and the amount of work she could command in relation to him, then we must turn to another clue in trying to answer the riddle of the urban North's peculiar institution—the matriarchal Negro family. For clearly it was the woman who faced near insurmountable obstacles in getting jobs beyond the level of unskilled domestic work, and this heavy concentration of Negro women in domestic service suggests an intriguing alternative explanation. She had not just a second job, but a job in a second *household,* with a second family. How this competition between obligations to two households could tear at the fabric of her own family's solidarity we can just imagine—not alone in the burden of doing double duty with long hours spent away from her own home, but also in the continual awareness of the differences in living standards, the competition of dual loyalties and possibly of dual affections.

If the status of the employing household mattered to the domestic, how might this have affected her perception of the conditions in her own? Negro women at service in Carlisle, Pennsylvania, a contributor to *Gunton's Magazine* (January, 1896) observed, "will only serve in a Negro family when hard pressed for money, and then for a few days only." If, as the writer suggests, the domestic was accustomed to taking home foodstuffs from her employer's table, such considerations of status would make sense. Might it also, along with all the other invidious comparisons to be made, condition her to think less highly of the breadwinner in her own family? Or, taking the problem from the other end: Did her husband find her efforts at home less than satisfactory because she had to do so much for the other household? It is hard, perhaps impossible, to arrive at clear-cut answers to these questions. We can only hypothesize that if Negro women had had access to a broader range of jobs beyond household work fewer complications would have entered into the picture.

It is instructive that white female houseworkers, including the many European immigrant women who took domestic jobs, seem to have solved the dual-household problem by staying single for as long as they worked, and then quitting domestic service upon marriage. Doubtless the strong sentiments of Catholicism about the requirements of normal family life insured this outcome in the case of the Irish, for example, who had a tradition of delaying marriage until economic conditions permitted. The available evidence on this point is sketchy, but a 1925 study of working women in four cities revealed that domestics in Passaic, New Jersey, who were overwhelmingly native or foreign-born whites, were much more apt to be single at the time of the canvass than were domestics in Jacksonville, Florida, who were overwhelmingly black. Whereas almost half (45 percent) of Jacksonville domestics were either married or married but separated, only a quarter (24 percent) of Passaic's domestics were thus classified. Mary V. Robinson's report to the Women's Bureau in the United States Department of Labor a year earlier established two facts from a survey of applicants for domestic work in Baltimore: Negro women were clearly reluctant to take jobs that required living in. Only 36 percent of the black women stated a willingness to do so, whereas 80 percent of white females were prepared to live in. Mary Robinson related this fact to another—namely, the significantly higher proportion of

Negro women compared with white females who remained in domestic service after marriage—and she came to a judgment about the difficulties of carrying the work of two households that should not surprise us:

> [Matrimony] usually means added responsibilities which tend to demand more time than many women in domestic service are able to find for such important private matters, especially if they are compelled to live in the home of employers or to have the usual hours of labor expected in domestic service. When women live in the homes of their employers, they rarely have opportunity to go to their own homes more than once or twice a week, and can have little private life with their families. . . .

At the turn of the century, a researcher assigned to canvass Sandy Springs, Maryland, reported to the United States Department of Labor that he found a tragic division between the Negro woman's "real family" and her "economic family" (the employing household) that her heavy concentration in domestic work had caused. Noting the heavy turnover of domestic workers and how better wages in the bigger cities north lured girls away, he concluded that "the future of the Negro race would seem to be more in danger from a certain general looseness of the younger generations of women than from lawlessness of the younger generations of men."

Certainly more research is needed to settle this historical issue. Again returning to the 1930 Census we find industrial cities in which a very low proportion of Negro women are holding jobs—Flint, Gary and Youngstown, for example. Perhaps domestic work was harder to find in small industrial cities than in the large northern cities having a wealthier citizenry. Were marriages correspondingly more stable in cities where, regardless of the women's interest in or need of work, jobs for domestics simply did not exist in the number needed? We do not know.

Accepting this alternative view of the Negro family problem does not require that we refuse to consider the Negro male's hardships, or their effect on his role in the family. Certainly if his rents had been lower and his wages higher, fewer of his women would have found it necessary to seek out domestic jobs. And it is quite proper to think that family stress would be closely associated with cyclical business fluctuations that affected the man's employment, as Daniel P. Moynihan showed in his 1965 report, *The Negro Family: The Case for National Action*. But we still need to know why Negroes, of all groups, were disproportionately affected in their family life by bad times that in their season hit *every* working-class group, and hit much harder in times past than now. This requires looking for that combination of unique historical experiences peculiar to many Negro Americans. The "peculiar institution" of the south, slavery, was very probably the most important factor in the emergence of the peculiar institution of the urban north, the female-headed family. But if an economic cause is to be sought in addition, we suggest that it may have been the Negro woman's handicaps in the labor market, not the man's.

THE BLACK FAMILY
AND SOCIAL CLASS*

Charles V. Willie

Blacks often are stereotyped as a homogeneous population exhibiting a common way of life. Nine black families of varying income levels were studied to determine similarities and differences in life style. Middle-class blacks were found to be affluent conformists, working-class blacks respectable marginals who achieve upward mobility by their wits, and lower-class blacks exhibited a lack of commitment arising out of fears of trusting in an untrustworthy society. Black and white families were seen to share a common value system but adapt to the society differently because of racial discrimination and social class distinctions.

It has been difficult to understand the black family in America because most writers fail to deal with it one its own terms. Usually the black family is compared to or contrasted with the white family.

Scholars who follow this approach do so, they say, because racism is a pervasive experience in the United States which none can escape. But the author's upbringing, in a black community in Dallas, Texas, taught him that all blacks did was not necessarily a reaction to the actions of whites.

Indeed, reference groups for many blacks consisted of other blacks—black family members, black neighbors, black friends, black church members, and black club members. Social sanctions, norms, and behavior standards were generated by these groups.

The Sunday School Superintendent of the church attended by

*From the *American Journal of Orthopsychiatry* 44 (January, 1974) : 50–60. Reprinted with permission of the editors and Charles Willie, Professor, The Graduate School of Education, Harvard University, Cambridge, Massachusetts.

the family of orientation of the author organized Christmas parties at the church for the children and Labor Day picnics in the country for the teenagers and young adults. He gave neckties to boys who graduated from high school and went on to college and saved cereal box tops for the young. He delivered chicken dinners, which were prepared by the women of the church, to the homes of neighbors. He was a janitor in a building where automobiles were sold and serviced. He was an ordained clergyman with limited training of less than a high school education. His limited education and unskilled occupation were probably a manifestation of racism. But in Oak Cliff, a black community in Dallas, he was never looked upon as a victim. To the children in the author's community he was the Reverend J. I. Farrar —a decent, kind, and courteous gentleman, a man interested in children, and a man to whom one could always turn for help. It was the Reverend Farrar's love for the church, community, and children that was partly responsible for teaching them how to love others, despite the presence of racism. The interaction between the Reverend Farrar and his community is a common story about local black leaders throughout this nation; it is not necessarily a reaction to whites.

My interest in understanding the way of life of blacks independent of any reference to the way of life of whites is due to a desire 1) to extricate the social and behavioral sciences from a white ethnocentric perspective, and 2) to increase their contribution to the understanding of social change. Innovations in life-styles, including family life-styles, often develop among minority populations in the society before they are adopted by the majority. Such innovations may not be recognized when the way of life of the majority is looked upon as the "ideal type" and the behavior of others is considered deviant.

Method

During the past few years we have compiled approximately 200 case studies of black families, many southern migrants or descendant of southern migrants who now live in the northeastern region of the United States. The case studies were obtained as an assignment for students enrolled in a course on "The Black Family." The responsibility for locating a black family was that of each student. Many students interviewed families in their home towns scattered throughout the region. They interviewed families who were friends, referred to them by friends, referred by an agency, or selected at random by knocking on the door of a stranger. Students were provided with an interview schedule that requested specific information about economic, social and demographic characteristics, family customs, aspirations of parents for children, and patterns of authority within the family. Interviewers were black and white undergraduate students.

Out of the 200 or more case studies, nine were selected for detailed analysis in this paper as a composite representation of three income groups. Household income was the primary basis for more or less arbitrarily selecting three families each for middle-income, marginal-income, and lower-income groups. Utilized in this study were the student reports that contained the most complete and detailed descriptions. We cannot claim to have randomly selected the families for analysis. But we can say that the bias of the investigator was not the basic factor that determined whether or not a family was included among the nine for intensive study. The income groups studied ranged from $3000 to $6000 (low-income), $6000 to $10,000 (marginal-income), and $10,000 to $20,000 (middle-income). Essentially, this study is an example of inductive analysis. Two variables—race and economic status—were used. Since blacks often are referred to as if they were a homogeneous group, nine families of the same race but of different income groups were studied to determine if, in fact, their way of life, customs, and practices were similar. Probability sampling, of course, would be necessary if the goal had been to make generalizations about the frequency of certain behavior forms within the total black population. This was not our goal. Thus, less rigor in the process of selecting the families for intensive analysis was possible.

Social class refers to style of life as well as economic resources. No operational definition of social class was developed for this study. The middle-class, working-class, and lower-class categories referred to later in this paper were derived from the analysis. The composite picture for the three families in each of the income groups was different from the style of life of black families in other income groups. Only the composite picture of the style of life for a social class is given. Detailed information on each of the nine families is presented elsewhere in a book-length manuscript.[3] The three social classes included in this study represent about 75% of all blacks. Not included are the upper middle class and the upper class, probably few in number, and at the other end of the stratification hierarchy, the under class—20% to 25% of all blacks.

Middle Class: The Affluent Conformists

Middle-class status for most black families is a function of dual employment of husband and wife. Black men and women have relied heavily on the public sector for employment at livable wages.

The public school has been an employment haven for black working wives. It has provided steady and continuous work and often has been the one occupational role in the family which has enabled it to lay claim to a professional style of life. Because of educational requirements, black female teachers of middle-class families are likely to be more highly educated than their male spouses. The length of employment of professional working wives is likely to be as long as that of their husbands, with only brief interruptions for childbearing. The numbers of children in black middle-class families tend to be small, ranging from one to three, but more often two or less. Thus, the black woman, in a public sector job with prescribed yearly increments and retirement benefits and with only a few interruptions in her labor force status, tends to draw a decent income by the time she reaches middle age.

Continuity in employment also is a characteristic of black men in middle-class families. Public sector jobs, especially in the postal service, have been a source of support and security over the years. Some black men have, however, received financially rewarding professional positions in industry.

The economic foundation for middle-class black families is a product of the cooperation of the husband and wife. Their way of life is a genuine illustration of a team effort. Few, if any, family functions, including cooking, cleaning, and buying, are considered to be the exclusive prerogative of the husband or wife. Probably the best example of the liberated wife in American society is the wife in the black middle-class family. She and her husband have acted as partners out of necessity and thus have carved out an equalitarian pattern of interaction in which neither husband nor wife has ultimate authority. He or she alone could not achieve a comfortable style of life, because of racial discrimination and the resulting income limitations of the kinds of jobs available to most blacks. Together they are able to make it, and this they have done. In the 1970s middle-class black families earned $10,000 to $20,000 a year—the joint income of husband and wife.

Such income is lavishly spent on a home and on the education of children. Unless restricted by racial discrimination, middle-class black families tend to trade in older homes for new structures as their income and savings increase. Thus, families in the income range mentioned above are likely to be found in houses valued from $25,000 to $35,000. The real expense in housing, however, is in the up-to-date furnishings and modern appliances. For most middle-class black families, their home is their castle and it is outfitted as such.

Because work is so consuming for the husband and wife, little time is left for socializing. Most families have nearby relatives—usually the reason for migrating to a particular city. They visit relatives occasionally, may hold membership in a social organization, participate regularly in church activities, and spend the remainder of their free time in household upkeep and maintenance chores.

In most middle-class black families, one member almost always has attended college. Often both have attended college. The husband and wife struggled and made great sacrifices to complete their formal education. Not infrequently, college and graduate school are completed on a part-time basis after adulthood and while the husband or wife, who also may be a parent, is employed full-time. Parents who have experienced these struggles and hardships know that their middle-class status, which usually is not achieved until middle age, is directly correlated with their increased education. New jobs, especially public school teaching, and salary increments can be traced directly to the added schooling. Education has been a major contributor to upward mobility for blacks.

Because education and, consequently, economic affluence are so closely tied together for middle-class black households, parents tend to go all out for their offspring. Particularly do they wish their children to go to college immediately after graduating from high school so that they will not have to struggle as long as did their parents whom middle-class status eluded during young-adult years. An ambition of most parents is to give to their children opportunities they did not have.

As a starter, almost all children in middle-class households are given music lessons. Daughters, in particular, are expected to learn to play a musical instrument, usually the piano. Recreational skills are developed, too. Most children in middle-class black families are expected to work around the house for an allowance. Families try to inculcate in their children positive attitudes toward work and thrift.

Active involvement in community affairs that take on the characteristics of a movement is not the cup of tea for most black middle-class, middle-aged adults. Their adolescent children may be deeply involved in various liberation movements but seldom are the parents.

Middle-class black families in America, probably more so than any other population group in this society, manifest the Puritan orientation toward work and success that is characteristic of our basic values. For them, work is a consuming experience. Little time is left for recreation and other kinds of community participation, except regular involvement in church affairs. The way of life of black middle-class Americans is a scenario patterned after Weber,[2] except that most blacks have little capital other than the house they own, which, of course, is their primary symbol of success.

Working Class: The Innovative Marginals

Family life in the black working class is a struggle for survival that requires the cooperative efforts of all—husband, wife, and children. Income for black working-class families ranged from $6000 to $10,000 during the 1970s. This is hardly enough for luxury living when the family size is considered. Black working-class families tend to be larger families, consisting of five or more children.

There is some indication that the size of the family is a source of pride for the parents, especially the father and maybe the mother too. The bearing and rearing of children are considered to be an important responsibility, so much so that black working-class parents make great personal sacrifices for their families. They tend to look upon children as their unique contribution to society, a contribution they are unable to make through their work roles, which at best are semi-skilled. The family size of the black working-class also may be a function of age at marriage, usually before twenty-one for the wife and mother and often during the late teens. Husbands tend to assume parenthood responsibilities early too; often they are only one or two years older than their spouses.

The cohesion of the black working-class family results not so much from understanding and tenderness shown by one for the other as from the joint and heroic effort to stave off adversity. Without the income of either parent or the contributions of children from part-time employment, the family would topple back into poverty.

The parents in black working-class families are literate but of limited education. Most have completed elementary school but may be high school drop-outs. Seldom do any have more than a high school education. This is the educational level they wish their children to achieve, although some families hope that one or two of the smarter children in their brood will go on to college. The jobs they wish for their children also are those that require only a high school or junior college education, like work as a secretary, nurse, mechanic, or bank messenger.

Racial discrimination, on the one hand, and insufficient education, on the other, have teamed up to delimit the employment opportunities for black working-class families. Their mobility from rural to urban areas and from the South to the North usually has been in search for a better life. Families tend to be attracted to a particular community because of the presence of other relatives who sometimes provided temporary housing.

In general, the moves have opened up new opportunities and modest advancement such as from gas station attendant to truck driver, or from farm laborer to dairy tanker. The northern migration has resulted in some disappointments, too. On balance, new employment opportunities have resulted from the move from South to North, particularly for wives who have found work in institutional settings such as hospitals more profitable than private household work. Nursing aide and cooking jobs have been outlets for women and have enabled them to supplement the family income.

One sacrifice that the members of black working-class families have made so as to pull out of and stay beyond the clutches of poverty is to give up on doing things together as a family. Long working hours and sometimes two jobs leave little time for the father to interact with family members. In some households, the husband works during the daytime and the wife works during the evening hours. In other families, children work up to twenty hours a week after school and on weekends. These kinds of work schedules mean that the family as a unit is not able to share any meals together, except possibly on Sunday.

Despite the hardships, there is a constancy among the members of black working-class families that tends to pull them through. Some husbands and wives have been married more than two decades; they tend to have been residents of their neighborhoods for ten or more years and to have worked for the same employer over a long period of time. Though their earnings are modest, this continuity in area of residence and in other experiences has stabilized these families and enabled their members to accumulate the makings of a tolerable existence without the losses that come from frequent stops and starts.

Another stabilizing experience is the home that some black working-class families own. Rather than renting, many are paying mortgages. Their homes may range in value from $10,000 to $15,000, may be located in isolated rural or unsightly urban areas, and may be in a poor state of exterior repair but neat and clean on the inside. Home ownership for black working-class families is not so much a symbol of success as an indicator of respectability.

Black working-class parents boast of the fact that their children are good and have not been in trouble with the police. They also have a strong sense of morality, which emphasizes "clean living." The home they own is part of their claim to respectability. The owned home is one blessing that can be counted. It is a haven from the harsh and sometimes unfriendly world.

There is little time for community activities for black working-class families. Most spare time is devoted to associating with household members or with nearby relatives. Religion is important; but participation in church activities is limited to regular or occasional attendance at Sunday worship services. The mother in such families tries to maintain tenuous contacts with at least one community institution, such as the school. She even may be a member of the Parents-Teachers Association but is not deeply involved in organizational maintenance work as a volunteer.

Black working-class parents do well by their children if no special problems are presented. Their comprehension of psychological maladaption, however, is limited. These problems are dealt with by a series of intended remedial actions that seem to be of little assistance in solving the child's real problem and usually result in frustration both for the parent and for the offspring. Black working-class families have learned to endure; and so they bear with the afflictions of their members—those they do not understand as well as those with obvious sources of causation.

Cooperation for survival is so basic in black working-class families that relationships between the husband and wife take on an equalitarian character. Each knows that his or her destiny is dependent upon the actions of the other. Within the family, however, husbands and wives tend to have assigned roles, although in time of crisis, these roles can change. The husband tends to make decisions about financial expenditures, including the spending of money for furniture. He also has basic responsibility for household upkeep. The father is the chief advisor for the boys. The mother tends to be responsible for the cooking and cleaning, although she may delegate these chores to the children. She is the chief advisor for the girls. She also maintains a liaison relationship with the school and may be the adult link between the family and the church if the father is not inclined to participate.

We tend to think in terms of upward mobility in American society. Indeed, this is what many working-class families are—households moving out of poverty into respectability; households that emphasize mobility, goal, and purpose; households committed to making a contribution to society by raising and maintaining a family of good citizens. This, of course, involves a struggle. But the struggle may be a function of the ending of good times rather than the overcoming of adversity. A black working-class family may be of a lower-income household on its way up or a middle-income household on its way down. A middle-income family beset with illness, for example, could slip into the working-class status due to reduction in income and the requirement for change in style of living. How often this occurs, we do not know. It does occur often enough to keep the working class from becoming a homogeneous lot. For this and other reasons, one should not expect to find a common philosophical orientation within the working-class.

Lower Class: The Struggling Poor

The most important fact about black lower-class families is their low-income status; it forces them to make a number of clever, ingenious, and sometimes foolish arrangements to exist. These range from extended households consisting of several generations under one roof to taking in boarders or foster children for pay. Boyfriend-girlfriend relationships between adults often assume some parental functions when children are involved, while the participants maintain their autonomy unfettered by marital bonds. Because every penny counts, poor households often do whatever they must do to bring money in. Conventional practices of morality may be set aside for expedient arrangements that offer the hope of a livable existence. The struggle among poor families is a struggle for existence. All else is secondary. Family income tends to vary from $3000 to $6000, and more often than not the household does not receive public welfare.

The struggle is severe and there is little margin for error. Black low-income families learn to live with contingency. They hope for little and expect less. Parents love their children but seldom understand them. Men and women become sexually involved but are afraid to entrust their futures to each other. There is much disappointment. The parents in broken families often have broken spirits—too broken to risk a new disappointment. For this reason, black lower-class parents often appear to be uncommitted to anyone or to anything when in actuality they are afraid to trust.

Movement is constant, as if one were afraid to stay put and settle down. Jobs, houses, and cities are changed; so are spouses and boyfriends and girlfriends. Unemployment is a constant specter. The womenfolk in the household usually find employment as maids or private household workers. The males are unskilled factory workers or maintenance men between periods of no work at all.

Marriage may occur at an early age, as early as sixteen years for some girls. The first child is sometimes born before the first marriage. Others tend to come in rapid succession. Some families have as many as eight or more children, while others are smaller. When the burdens of child care, illness, and unemployment strike at the same time, they often are overwhelming. Drinking, gambling, and other escape behavior may increase. A fragile love and capacity for endurance are shattered, and the man in the house moves out, no longer able to take it. One more failure is experienced.

The parents in black lower-class families are grade school or high school dropouts. Neither spouse has more education than the other. Thus, parents in lower-class families sometimes hold themselves up to their children as failures, as negative images of what not to do. There is only limited ability to give guidance concerning what ought to be done. Thus, children are advised not to marry early, not to drop out of school, and not to do this and not to do that. There is admonition but little concrete effort at prevention.

Scapegoating is a common way of explaining deviant behavior in children. Juvenile delinquency may be attributed to the disreputable parent. The mother on location seldom knows what to do. Although little love may exist between parents, there is fierce loyalty between mothers and offspring, and between grandmothers, and children. The children come first. Mothers will extend every effort to take care of their sons and daughters, even into adulthood. Grandparents are excellent babysitters. They are expected to teach their grandchildren good manners and other fundamentals.

A strong custom of brothers and sisters helping each other exists in the lower class. The problem is that siblings are struggling too. About the most one can do for the other is share already overcrowded living quarters when a new member comes to town or when a two-parent family breaks down. The move from one city to another often is for the purpose of being near kinsmen. There is strong loyalty between siblings and a standing obligation to help.

Little participation in any community association is seen. Religion is important for some black lower-class families. But for others, it is no more than a delusion. Those who attend church regularly tend to engulf their lives with religion and especially with affirmations about its saving grace and reward system after death. Some shy away from the church as one more disappointing promise that has copped out on the poor without really helping. Black lower-class people are seldom lukewarm about religion. They are either all for it or all against it, although the latter are reluctant to deny their children religious experience, just in case there is more to it than was realized.

It is hard for a poor black family to overcome poverty; so much is lined up against it. If illness or unemployment do not drain away resources, there is a high probability that old age will.

Conclusion

We turn now to a theoretical discussion of the differences that have been observed. In his classical article, "Social Structure and Anomie," Robert Merton[1] identified five kinds of adaptations by individuals to social organizations: conformity, innovation, ritualism, retreatism, rebellion. We shall discuss three of the adaptations to explain the way of life of the three different social classes. The conformist acknowledges the legitimacy of societal values and goals and also accepts the means that are sanctioned and prescribed for achieving them. The innovationist believes in the socially sanctioned goals but must improvise new and different means. The retreatist gives up on the socially sanctioned values and goals as well as the means and, therefore, is declared to be in a state of anomie or normlessness. This theoretical formulation provides a helpful way conceptually for approaching an understanding of the differences between middle-class, working-class, and lower-class black families.

Middle-class black families subscribe to the basic values and goals in American society and utilize appropriately prescribed means for their achievement. Its members are success-oriented, upwardly mobile, materialistic, and equalitarian. They consume themselves in work and leave little time for leisure. Education, hard work, and thrift are accepted as the means for the achievement of success. Property, especially residential property, is a major symbol of success. This is the American way and the prevailing way of life to which the middle-class black family in America conforms. Thus, its members may be called conformists.

Black working-class families also have internalized the basic values and goals of this nation. They too are success-oriented and upwardly mobile. However, their symbol of success differs from that of the black middle-class. The welfare of the total family is the principal measure of effective functioning. A black working-class family is successful if it is respectable. A family is respectable when its members are well-fed, well-clothed, and well-housed, and do not get into trouble with the police.

The location and value of a house is not so important. Home ownership is important but home value is something else. In the latter respect, the black working class differs from the black middle class, in which an expensive home is the symbol of success.

Almost everything that the black working-class parents do to achieve success and respectability is extraordinary, compared with the black middle class. Their education is limited; their occupations are unskilled; their income is modest; and their families are relatively larger. Yet they dream the impossible dreams about doing for their children what they could not do for themselves. By hook or crook, they—the parents—manage to do it when others said it couldn't be done. The members of the working class are the creative innovationists of our times. They strive to achieve the societal values and goals, are deficient in the possession of socially sanctioned means, but somehow overcome.

The black lower class is fatalistic. No note of hope does it sing. Failure and disappointment recur repeatedly, as if they were a refrain. Unable to deal with the difficulties presented, black lower-class families withdraw. The parents appear to be uninvolved with anyone or anything. They have retreated from social organizations but not necessarily from all social relations for we know of their loyalty to their children.

The retreatist behavior of black lower-class families is sometimes described as being in opposition to the basic values and goals of social organization—a rejection of that which is socially sanctioned. This may not be the case, however, but only the way it appears. Presumably, lower-class households, like the working class, wish for family cohesion. The tie between mother and offspring is a residual family relationship indicative of this desire. Presumably, also, lower-class families, like the middle class, wish for material comforts and new experiences. Spending sprees and impulse traveling are indicative of these desires.

Because of inadequate resources, lower-class families dare not hope for the fulfillment of their wishes in a systematic and regularized way. To protect themselves from more disappointment, denial of the wish for improvement is one approach and poking fun at the struggle for social mobility is another.

A fuller explanation of the retreatist behavior of the lower class requires examination of the interaction between objective and subjective dimensions of social structure. Despite the rhetoric about self-reliance and self-sufficiency, the family members of the working class and the middle class did not make it on their own unassisted by the social system. They acknowledged their interdependence, and asked for and received help when they needed it. Upward social mobility involves giving and receiving from others. The poor are given precious little in our society and so their capacity to receive is under-developed. In the giving of help, we learn to love. In the receiving of assistance, we learn to trust. Because the poor have been given so little in society, the poor have not learned how to receive—which is to say, the poor have not learned how to trust.

We learn to trust before we learn to love. Love involves commitment to persons, social groups, and social organizations. The members of lower-class families can commit themselves to persons, especially the mothers to their offspring and the siblings to each other; but they cannot commit themselves to a society they have never learned to trust. Thus, the retreatist behavior of the lower-class may be a manifestation of the absence of trust rather than a rejection of social organization in favor or social disorganization.

This paper clearly demonstrates that it is inappropriate to say, "a black family is a black family is a black family." Styles of life do vary among blacks by social class. Recognition of this should serve as a corrective against stereotyping black ways of life.

The neat way in which the different black family life-styles by social class fit into the theoretical model developed by Robert Merton for explaining variation in adaptations to the social organization also suggests that all black families, including the middle-class, the working-class, and the lower-class, participate in a common system of values shared by all families, including blacks and whites in the United States.

Finally, there was evidence of limited opportunities available to blacks due largely to racial discrimination. This was a common experience of most black families of all social classes. A frequent manifestation of racial discrimination was the delimitation of economic opportunity. Inadequate financial resources frequently resulted in the joint participation of husband and wife in the labor force—a circumstance more or less pervasive among black families, especially those who were upwardly mobile.

On the basis of this analysis, one may conclude 1) that black and white families in America share a common value system, 2) that they adapt to the society and its values in different ways, largely because of racial discrimination, and 3) that the unique adaptation by blacks is further differentiated by variations in style of life by social class.

Our initial assumption that the way of life of blacks in America can be understood independent of their involvement with whites appears to be unwarranted. Moreover, the life-styles of different social classes cannot be understood apart from the rest of society.

Referring to the interdependence of blacks and whites in America, this paper ends with the statement of a modified version of the wisdom of Eliza Doolittle, created by George Bernard Shaw. She said that she discovered the difference between a flower girl and a lady is not so much how she acts but how she is treated. Our revised version emphasizes *both* personal action *and* social reaction. We assert that the difference between the families of racial groups in the United States, and the difference between the families of various social classes within the racial groups are a result of how each family acts *as well as* how each family is treated.

References

1. Merton, R. 1949. Social Structure and Social Theory. Free Press, New York. (p. 133)
2. Weber, M. 1948. The Protestant Ethic and the Spirit of Capitalism. George Allen and Unwin, London.
3. Willie, C. 1976. A New Look at Black Families. General Hall, Bayside, N.Y.

VARIATIONS IN THE FATHER ROLE IN COMPLETE FAMILIES OF THE NEGRO LOWER CLASS*

David A. Schulz

In spite of the fact that there are numerous studies of the Negro in America, very few have been concerned primarily with the family.[1] Those that have taken the family as a central concern[2] have not been based upon intensive studies such as, for example, Oscar Lewis' studies of poor families in Mexico.[3] Indeed, it is common to think of lower-class Negro families in terms of a simple "fatherless-complete" typology.[4] Consequently Hylan Lewis had to say recently, "in focusing on family homes ... the present father tends to be forgotten. Forgotten also is the fact that we know very little about him."[5]

Negro family structure has been studied more intensively in the Caribbean. Here the work has been motivated to a large extent by a concern to determine if patterns of nonresidential mating do or do not indicate a breakdown or "disorganization" of the family—a concern originating in the markedly high rates of illegitimacy.[6]

Several types of mating patterns are described. Hyman Rodman, for example, found that the natives of Coconut Village distinguished between three types of "marital" relations: "friending," "living," and "married."[7] Friending was a nonresidential pattern similar to one called "visiting" by Roberts and Braithwaite.[8]

The concern of the present study, however, is to describe and analyze some of the variations in the husband-father role in the category that is ordinarily thought of as "married."[9]

*From *Social Science Quarterly* 49 (December, 1968) : 651–59. Reprinted with permission from the author and the *Social Science Quarterly*.

The Sample

The field work focused upon 10 lower-class Negro families living in a large public housing project in a midwestern city. Five of the families were complete, five were fatherless.[10] The age of the parents ranged from 33 to 55. All except two families had teenage children living in the households. The size of the families varied from six to 18 persons and the households from five to 18 persons. The latter included some kin at times but no other boarders. Although about 88 persons lived in these households during most of the study, only three of the households remained relatively stable in size. Data were collected on all household members and most family members.

Methodology

The majority of the data on these households were collected by means of participant observation[11] and open-ended interviewing. While the researcher did not live with the families, he did spend about 250 ten-hour days on site interacting with the family members in various ways—sometimes obviously studying them and asking direct questions, at other times just enjoying their company at home, in a bar, or on the street. Extensive biographies were taken of all parents and many teenaged members of the households, and the assessment of the role played by the father in each household was based upon information obtained from most, if not all, family members plus observations of family interaction. All periods of the waking day were covered in most families, and in one the researcher was invited to spend the night.

Whenever possible a tape recorder was used to record conversations and interviews. Notes were made on all encounters. To supplement the information obtained from family members and to provide additional perspectives on the families, data were obtained from the files of the Housing Authority, the schools, and the police.

A Typology of Marginality

As an exploratory study attempting to document the variety to be found in lower-class Negro family life, the first objective was to describe each family. This objective alone could easily result in ten case studies. Indeed, each family has enough distinctive characteristics to be considered by some researchers as a separate culture.[12] To dichotomize the 10 families simply into "complete" and "fatherless," however, is to grossly oversimplify. A useful compromise can be achieved if one looks at the husband-father role in terms of several significant variables: (1) the "strength" of the conjugal bond, (2) the support given by the father to his family and (3) the relationship of the father to the children. At this stage of the research, none of these variables was rigorously defined or measured, but an immense amount of qualitative data[13] has enabled the researcher to make and support judgments about the relative placement of these families along the dimension of adult male marginality. The 10 families suggest six types. This article describes the three types of "complete" families.[14]

THE INDISCREET FREE-MAN

The most marginal type of father observed is the indiscreet free-man.[15] What is apparent in his relationship to his family is a split in allegiance between his legitimate family and one or more "illegitimate" families. This outside interest is continually paraded before his wife and family either in a constant, chiding reference to the "other woman" or by the deliberate engineering of an encounter with her. His interests outside the family are reflected in his spending on behalf of the other woman and, if he has had children by her, a regular amount of money may be set aside each month in their behalf —regardless of whether or not the court has intervened—or, more commonly, he will buy shoes, clothing, and gifts for them from time to time. Such a father's interests have repercussions upon his legitimate children, creating an intensified kind of sibling rivalry with his "outside" children who, in some instances, are known personally by his legitimate children. Life within such families is thus one of constant conflict and bickering. That the family stays intact at all is probably related to (1) the advancing age of the wife which, combined with her many children, makes her less and less attractive to other men and more and more destined to head a household should her husband leave, (2) her continuing hope that he will reform his ways, and (3) his positive, if sporadic contributions in support and affection to his family.

Two families fit this type: the Pattersons and the Boikens. Illustration from the Patterson case will suffice. They had been married 22 years; he was 45, she was 42. They had 18 children including eight "outsiders."[16] All but two were his by other women. Their present household included eight children in age from 9 to 19. Mr. Patterson's earnings as a machine operator for a local automobile manufacturer accounted for $5,593 of the family's $6,072 annual income; his wife's earnings accounted for the balance. He was in complete charge of the money and allowances, expecting his wife to live within her allowance, adequate or not.

About four years ago he left his family to live with another woman by whom he sired two children. Prior to that, in 1965, his wife had had him put in the workhouse for six months for nonsupport while he was living with another woman. His spending, even when he was at home, extended to his several "outside" children, a fact that was fully and painfully known by his wife and legitimate children. When he was at home he generally was shunned by his family and usually ate alone.

He once commented on his marriage:

> I would say that if I had to do it all over again, I don't think I would select this route that I have gone. It hasn't been too pleasant at all times. I mean there's a ruling to everything. You can't run what's in the house and what's on the outside of the house both at the same time ... so I don't know whether I came in the house too much or whether I stayed on the outside too long. It's a problem somewhere. ... I don't think it would get serious enough where it would cause another separation. ... [You] make the best out of what you have. ... I can walk, shun them, a lot easier than the other person could shun me.

His wife's account of their marriage reflected his indiscretion more vividly:

> Well before we came to the city my husband and I were separated three times on the sake of fighting. He used to fight me all the time. He was in the city about nine months before I came. When I came up he was living with another woman at my uncle's house. ... I have never walked out in front of him, but this lady he used to live with, he have had her right out in front of my door. ... I asked him not to do it again because he seemed like he was boasting about it. And the next time he did it ... I got a gun and started down the steps and he ran down there by the car. But by the time I got down under the building he had done pulled off.

His relationships with his children were also strained, particularly those with his older boys, who generally took the side of their mother against him. Their oldest boy once lived with the family, but he moved out about midway in this study in order to avoid a fight with his father, who at the last encounter had "hit him up side of the head with a shoe." After that Patterson's wife claimed that when he walked in the door, "the actual sight of him made me nervous... because I had a fear of his ways."

The older girls, on the other hand, tried to cover up the family feuding as much as possible, stressing the fact that their father "will still give" to them. His 18-year-old daughter, B., noted "every family has its ups and downs ... some parents be arguing and fighting all the time ... but they don't hardly quarrel. ... One of them will walk away from it. I guess because they have us and don't want to be setting a bad example in front of us." The implied denial could not, even for B., cover up Patterson's obvious and flagrant infidelity, which lay at the base of the family conflict. Mr. Patterson's indiscretion as a free-man made his home all but intolerable for him, and a source of embarrassment and hurt for his wife and children as well.

THE DISCREET FREE-MAN

In contrast to the indiscreet free-man, the discreet free-man's "cutting out" is clearly a secondary concern, which he does not use to antagonize his wife and children. As a result his indiscretions are understood and both partners are likely to admit "we get along well enough." His relationship to his children is not particularly impaired as a result of his interests outside the home and they often look upon him as an ideal father. Typically, just as he is able to cover up or minimize his activities with other women, so also he is able to carry on deviant activities such as gambling or pimping without these appreciably interfering with his home life. The relationship can be considered as a separate type, therefore, because it does not result simply from the fact that the "old man" has not been caught yet. His indiscretions are known to his wife and family, but he manages in such a way as not to antagonize them, and thus maintains a relatively comfortable relationship with his legitimate family, which persists over time.

Two families fit this type: The Washingtons and the Bardwells. The Washingtons can provide the illustration. The researcher knew them for over three and one-half years and only toward the end of the study discovered why he knew comparatively little about them. Mr. Washington, 51, and seven of his boys had long police records connected mainly with gambling and narcotics. The father had once been "sent up" for possession of lottery equipment. Nevertheless, the home was neat, well kept, and his children well mannered. An impression of warmth and intimacy was characteristic of their interactions.

He and his wife, who was 47, had been married 26 years and for 19 of these years Mr. Washington had been the major wage earner. During the time of the study he supplemented his wife's earnings as a domestic through efforts at odd jobs and through gambling. Neither source of income was reported in the family's annual income of $4,370. The Washingtons had 12 children including two "outsiders" born before they married.

Mr. Washington said that he had managed to stay married 26 years because "we don't raise a lot of cain. If a little something happens we don't jump down each other's throat." He expressed his conception of marital fidelity in a way that implied he "cuts out" but does not play the field and does not brag about his antics in front of his wife:

> I am this type of fellow. I talk to anyone before my wife or behind my wife. But just to go out and say I've got a bunch of women and that type of thing, that's all baloney.... I see some women that look good to me, sure, and if you push it you can get caught in the right corner and you might step out. You're human and you're a good one if you don't. If you just go out and strive directly for that then you're going to find somebody that wants to do these things. The average woman that does it ain't doing it because she likes to but because she wants to do something just like you ... something different ... it's not a big deal.

His wife presented a complementary picture of tolerating his discreet outside activities:

> I think I've been a nice lady. I ain't bragging on myself, but it takes a steady head I guess. I never was a wild person and like to get in the streets. I stayed home and took care of my children ... I didn't leave my children to nobody.

One impressive indicator of the control parents were able to exercise over themselves and their children was their willingness not to exchange gifts at Christmas time. Mr. Washington said, "It's pretty rough when you know everybody else is receiving them and giving them and you're not ... but if you understand life ... you just have to grit your teeth and say, 'Well we doing the best we can, and thank the Lord.' "

Finally, instead of denouncing his delinquent children, as many parents did, Mr. Washington said of his oldest boy, who had the longest record, "He's just another one of my kids regardless of the troubles he's been in. Maybe he made a mistake and maybe he didn't. Maybe he just got the wrong break. That happens too. Sometimes to the best of people."

The family, despite what went on outside, was a central concern for all its members, and Mr. Washington's discretion in handling what went on outside was a major factor in its continuing relative stability.

THE MONOGAMOUS FATHER

The last type of father is called the monogamous type because he is proud of the fact that he is able to say, "Where you see me, you will see my wife." This type, although rare in fact, is reflected in the data in numerous references to its desirability. In such a family the father does not "cut out" and if he has had any "outside" children they are the result of youthful indiscretions and not of his violation of monogamous marriage. His home and family are his major concerns and receive his constant attention. Typically, such fathers have good relationships with their children and high status in the family regardless of their ability to earn a living.

Only one family fitted this type in the data: the Fraziers. They had been married 20 years, were the least urbanized of the families studied (lived in the city only seven years) and were the only family in which the father was younger than the mother. He was 37, she 40. He, nevertheless, was an advocate of the patriarchal type of family and his wishes in this regard were respected.[17] Because of illiteracy and a fear of the streets the family spent most of its time inside the small row apartment it had rented in the heart of the city—the last of five residences in which they lived during the last two years of the study. Mr. Frazier received disability checks and his wife received ADC, giving the family an annual income of $4,896 for a family of 11.

For both of the Fraziers "cutting out" was unheard of. They believed that for the parents to do so would result in their complete inability to control their children. Mr. Frazier said:

> I have been to lots of houses and I've seen some pretty rough deals with kids. I'll tell you what that come from. That comes from mother and daddy. If you do any and everything over your child you can't expect no better can you? ... I don't let my children see me do no wrong thing. ... I'm not playing [cutting out]. I ain't got nane that can tell you that today. They ain't never seen daddy come in here drunk, cussing, clowning, or nothing. They'll tell you that right now. Daddy is going to come in here as he leaves.

Being thus strong believers in teaching children by example rather than precept, both Fraziers labored to keep themselves respectable "in front of the children" for they knew that the accusation "Mamma, you and Daddy do it" had no acceptable reply—"It ain't nothing for us to say." Thus despite his educational handicaps and his poor earning power, Mr. Frazier was very well thought of in his family and his children were well behaved. The Frazier family was a warm, intimate shelter from the harsh realities of the street and if they had the legitimate earning capacity to become upwardly mobile, such a family would have followed the style of living more characteristic of the working-class nuclear family. Ironically, however, given their economic status, their conception of appropriate family living was a handicap in teaching the children how to cope with the world in which they found themselves. Thus they obtained a degree of intimacy at the expense of acquiring effective survival techniques.

MARGINALITY AND THE MODE OF LEGITIMATING AUTHORITY

An interesting aspect of the internal dynamics of these families was the fact that each type of father made his claim to hold authority in the household on somewhat different grounds.

1. The monogamous father tended to legitimate his authority on the basis of two more or less equal aspects of his relationship to the external world: his ability as an adequate provider (or the fact that his inability to provide was "understood"), and his ability to say, "There ain't nane that can speak slack of me"—that is, he was an adequate model for respectable behavior. He was not an adaptive strategist because he had been able to "make it" by legitimate means and because his principles prohibited him from being one.

2. The "discreetly free" fathers, on the other hand, tended to legitimate their authority within the household on the basis of being warm, loving "pals" to their children and expressive companions to more instrumentally oriented wives. They tended also to be able to muster respect for their ability to cope with the environment by means of manipulative strategies such as gambling, "working game" on friends, and discreet affairs with other women, which provided them with victories their sons would have liked to emulate. They were, or at one time had been, adequate providers and their current disability was understood by their families. They expressed concern for "skeletons" in the family closet, indicating they would have liked to draw upon past respectable behavior to provide an example for their children, but could not.

3. The "indiscreet" fathers had least control over their children because they had little to justify their authority. If they were able to provide for their family, this ability was marred by their split in allegiance. If they were unable, their disability was not accepted and they had to prefabricate an instrumental role in order to protect themselves in this vulnerable area—thus Mr. Boiken, though unemployed, thought of himself as earning $150 a week, the amount earned by the construction crew with which he once worked. They generally had little justification for authority on the basis of their expressive ability, and none as a model for traditional respectable behavior.

Conclusion

In an exploratory study based primarily upon such a small number of families the conclusions drawn can only be suggestive. However, the father in lower-class Negro families does not appear to be simply subordinate to his wife, as the term "matriarchal" would indicate and the term "matrifocal" might imply. His status, these data suggest, depends not only upon his capacity to earn a living and his further willingness to share that living with his family, but also upon the degree of his adherence to the norms of monogamous marriage, his ability to cope with the harsh realities of the ghetto, and his capacity to be a pal to his children. The family that seems best able to survive as a family unit in a situation where there is little hope of upward mobility or of sufficient income from legitimate sources is the family that is best able to cope with its environment as it presents itself. In such a family the father is typically the discreet free-man.

The cohesiveness of such families in spite of their extreme openness to the life of the street was a source of constant amazement to the researcher, and the extent of the father's influence, particularly as a model for effective coping behavior, was greater than expected.

Notes

1. Studies such as Allison Davis and John Dollard, *Children of Bondage* (Washington, D.C.: American Council of Education, 1940); Abram Kardiner and Lionel Ovesey, *The Mark of Oppression* (New York: Norton, 1951); and Hertha Reise, *Heal the Hurt Child* (Chicago: University of Chicago Press, 1962) concentrate on the children. Those such as Kenneth Clark, *Dark Ghetto* (New York: Harper and Row, 1965); Hylan Lewis, *Blackways of Kent* (Chapel Hill: University of North Caro-

lina Press, 1955) ; and St. Clair Drake and Horace Cayton, *Black Metro-polis* (New York: Harcourt, Brace and World, 1945) consider the family as a small portion of a much broader concern for community studies, although Lewis does develop a family typology based on genealogical data.

2. For example E. Franklin Frazier's *The Negro Family in the United States* (Chicago: University of Chicago Press, 1939) is based largely upon census data and other gross indices of family life combined with the author's own intuitive interpretation of their meaning. It is not based on an examination of how particular families function. The one intensive participant observation study of the Negro lower class by Elliot Liebow (*Tally's Corner* [Boston: Little, Brown, 1967]) only touches upon the family as its main concern is with "corner men."

3. *The Children of Sanchez* (New York: Random House, 1961) and *Five Families* (New York: Science Editions, Inc., 1962).

4. This tendency is heightened by the accessibility of Census data. A good idea of the extent to which this dichotomy is considered central to the study of the lower-class Negro family is provided in Thomas Pettigrew, *Profile of the Negro American* (Princeton, N.J.: D. Van Nostrand, Inc., 1964) on page 15 and following. The issue of the relevance of this simple typology was brought forward in the controversy over the Department of Labor's *The Negro Family: The Case for National Action*, now attributed to Daniel Patrick Moynihan.

5. Lee Rainwater and William Yancy, *The Moynihan Report and the Politics of Controversy* (Boston: MIT Press, 1967), p. 322.

6. For a summary of this work see Raymond T. Smith, "Cultural and Social Structure in the Caribbean: Some Recent Work on Family and Kinship Studies" in *Comparative Studies in Society and History* (The Hague, The Netherlands: Mouton & Co., Oct., 1963).

7. "Marital Relationships in a Trinidad Village," *Journal of Marriage and Family Living*, 23 (May, 1961), pp. 166–170.

8. "A Cross-Mating Table for a West Indian Population," *Population Studies*, 14:3 (1961).

9. John F. Cuber and Peggy B. Harroff develop a fivefold typology of marriage for the upper middle class that parallels in several respects this attempt, particularly in their discussion of the "conflict habituated" type of marriage which seems similar to this study's "indiscreet free-man." See "The More Total View: Relationships Among Men and Women of the Upper Middle Class," in Hyman Rodman, ed., *Marriage, Family and Society: A Reader* (New York: Random House, 1961).

10. In the project 54 percent of the families were headed by females. See Jerome Stromberg, *A Preliminary Report on Housing and Community Experience: Occasional Paper no. 1* (St. Louis: The Social Science In-

stitute of Washington University, 1966). Lefcowitz estimates that only about 23 percent of the entire lower-class Negro family population was headed by females in 1960. See "Poverty and Negro-White Family Structure," paper presented to the White House Conference, "To Fulfill These Rights," 1965.

11. In point of fact neither detached observation nor totally immersed participation was ever achieved: the working balance always tended toward one or the other pole.

12. Jules Henry, "An Anthropological Approach to Cultural Idiosyncratic and Universal Factors in Behavior," *American Anthropologist.*

13. The researcher's personal notes on observations and interviews exceed 2,500 type-written pages and the data on the larger study exceed 20,000 pages.

14. The researcher is greatly indebted to Lee Rainwater's "notes" entitled "Three Patterns of Separateness and Connectedness in Lower-Class Families: A Typology" although the typology presented in this study is a modification of his. The sixfold typology derived from these families is as follows: monogamous, discreet free-man, indiscreet free-man, quasi-father, supportive biological father, and supportive companion. A seventh and most marginal type, the pimp, was described by the family members but not observed. The last four types are discussed in David A. Schulz and Lee Rainwater, "The Role of the Boyfriend in Lower-Class Negro Life," paper presented to the Midwest Sociological Society, Des Moines, Iowa, 1967.

15. This type resembles the type of father described as Jesus Sanchez by Lewis in *Children of Sanchez.*

16. As the term is used in the project it means "outside a particular relationship" which ordinarily terminated in marriage—not simply "outside of wedlock."

17. In his article "The Impact of Urban Civilization upon Negro Family Life." *American Sociological Review,* 2 (1939), E. Franklin Frazier described a type of family organization originating in rural southern communities of Negro, white, and Indian ancestry that was relatively isolated from the main currents of Negro life and that maintained a strictly patriarchal tradition. The Fraziers seem to have been influenced by this tradition.

SELECTED
BIBLIOGRAPHY

Adams, Russel, ed. *Great Negroes, Past and Present,* 3d ed. Chicago: Afro-American Publishers, 1969.

Agar, Michael H. *Ripping and Running: A Formal Ethnography of Urban Heroin Addicts.* New York: Academic Press, 1973.

Aptheker, Herbert. "Frederick Douglass Calls for Black Suffrage in 1866," *The Black Scholar* 5 (December 1973-January 1974) : 10–16.

Austin, L. J. *The Black Man in the United States and the Promise of America.* Chicago: Scott, Foresman & Company, 1970.

Axelson, L. J. "Working Wife: Differences in Perception Among Negro and White Males," *Journal of Marriage and the Family* 32 (August 1970) : 457–64.

Baldwin, James. *Notes of a Native Son.* Boston: Beacon Press, 1955.

————. *Nobody Knows My Name.* New York: Dial, 1961.

————. *The Fire Next Time.* New York: Dell Publishing Co., 1964.

Baraka, Imamu Amiri. *Blues People: Negro Music in White America.* New York: Morrow, 1963.

Bennett, Lerone. *Before the Mayflower.* Chicago: Johnson Publishing Co., 1962.

————. *What Manner of Man; A Biography of Martin Luther King, Jr.* Chicago: Johnson Publishing Co., 1964.

————. *Confrontation: Black and White.* Chicago: Johnson Publishing Co., 1965.

————. "Nat's Last White Man," in John H. Clarke, ed. *William Styron's Nat Turner.* Boston: Beacon Press, 1968, pp. 3–16.

Bergman, Peter M. *The Chronological History of the Negro in America.* New York: Harper & Row, 1969.

Billingsley, Andrew. *Black Families in White America.* Englewood Cliffs, N.J.: Prentice-Hall, 1968.

Bims, Hamilton. "Why Black Men Die Younger," *Ebony* 30 (December 1974) : 45–52.

"Black Composers," *Newsweek,* April 15, 1974, p. 82.

Blackwell, James E., *The Black Community: Diversity and Unity.* New York: Dodd, Mead & Co., 1975.

Bond, Jean C., and Patricia Perry. "Has the Black Man Been Castrated?" *Liberator Magazine* 9 (May 1969) : 4–8.

Bontemps, Arna, and Jack Control. *Frederick Douglass: Slave-Fighter, Freeman.* New York: Alfred A. Knopf, 1959.

Booker, S. S. *Black Man's America*. Englewood Cliffs, N.J.: Prentice-Hall, 1964.

Brietman, George. *The Last Year of Malcolm X: The Evolution of a Revolutionary*. New York: Merit Pub., 1967.

Brotz, Howard. *The Black Jews of Harlem. Negro Nationalism and the Dilemmas of Negro Leadership*. New York: Free Press of Glencoe, 1964.

Brown, Claude. *Manchild in the Promised Land*. New York: Macmillan, 1965.

Brown, H. R. *Die Nigger Die*. New York: Dial Press, 1970.

Bullins, Ed; Ben Caldwell; Ronald Milner; and LeRoi Jones, eds. *Black Quartet: Four New Black Plays*. New York: The New American Library, 1970.

Cade, Toni, ed. *The Black Woman*. New York: New American Library, 1970.

Calverley, Edwin E. "Negro Muslims in Hartford," *Muslim World* 55 (1965) : 340–55.

Carmichael, Stokely, and Charles Hamilton. *Black Power: The Politics of Liberation in America*. New York: Vintage, 1967.

Carter, Robert L. "The Black Lawyer," *Humanist* 29 (September-October 1969) : 12–16.

Caute, David. *Frantz Fanon*. New York: Viking Press, 1970.

Chambers, Bradford, ed. *Chronicles of Black Protest*. New York: The New American Library, 1969.

Chrisman, Robert. "The Black Soldier," *The Black Scholar* 5 (October 1973).

Clark, Kenneth B. "The Cry of the Ghetto," *Dark Ghetto*. New York: Harper & Row, 1965.

Clarke, John H. ed. *Malcolm X: The Man and His Times*. New York: Macmillan, 1969.

———. "Marcus Garvey: The Harlem Years," *The Black Scholar* 5 (December 1973-January 1974) : 17–23.

Clayton, Edward T. *Martin Luther King: The Peaceful Warrior*. Englewood Cliffs, N.J.: Prentice-Hall, 1964.

Cleaver, Eldridge. *Soul On Ice*. New York: Dell Publishing Co., 1968.

Cobb, Charles E. "Behavior Modification in the Prison System," *The Black Scholar* 5 (May 1974) : 41–44.

Cromwell, John W. *The Negro in American History: Men and Women Eminent in the Evolution of the American of African Descent*. New York: Johnson Reprint Corporation, 1969.

Cronon, Edmund D. *Black Moses: The Story of Marcus Garvey and the Universal Negro Improvement Association*. Madison: University of Wisconsin Press: 1955.

Cruse, Harold W. *The Crisis of the Negro Intellectual*. New York: William Morrow, 1967.

Curtis, James L. *Blacks, Medical Schools, and Society*. Ann Arbor: The University of Michigan Press, 1971.

Daniel, W. Harrison. "Southern Presbyterians and the Negro in the Early National Period," *The Journal of Negro History* 58 (July 1973): 291–312.

Deane, Paul C. "The Persistence of Uncle Tom: An Examination of the Image of the Negro in Children's Fiction Series," *Journal of Negro Education* 37 (spring 1968): 140–45.

Drake, St. Clair, and Horace R. Cayton. *Black Metropolis.* New York: Harper & Row, 1962.

Du Bois, W. E. B. *The Souls of Black Folk: Essays and Sketches.* Chicago: McClurg, 1903.

————. *The College-Bred Negro American.* Atlanta, Georgia: Atlanta University Press, 1910.

————. *The Negro American Artisan.* Atlanta, Georgia: Atlanta University Press, 1913.

————. *The Gift of Black Folk. Negroes in the Making of America.* Boston, Stratford Co., 1924.

————. *Black Reconstruction in America, 1860-1880.* New York: Harcourt Brace, 1935.

————. *The Autobiography of W. E. B. Du Bois.* New York: International Publishers, 1968.

Ebert, Alan. "Roundtree," *Essence* (March 1974): 64, 70, 81.

Edwards, Harry. *The Revolt of the Black Athlete.* New York: Free Press, 1969.

————. "The Black Athlete: 20th Century Gladiators for White America," *Psychology Today* 7 (November 1973): 43–47, 50–52.

Ellison, Ralph. *Invisible Man.* New York: Random House, 1952.

————. *Shadow and Act.* New York: Random House, 1964.

Erickson, Erik. "Memorandum on Identity and Negro Youth," *Journal of Social Issues* 20:29–42.

Essien-Udom, E. U. *Black Nationalism: The Search for an Identity in America.* Chicago: University of Chicago Press, 1962.

Fair, Ronald. *We Can't Breathe.* New York: Harper & Row, 1974.

Fax, E. C. *Garvey: Story of a Pioneer Black Nationalist.* New York: Dodd, Mead & Co., 1972.

Forman, James. *Sammy Young, Jr.: The First Black College Student to Die in the Black Liberation Movement.* New York: Grove Press, 1968.

Foster, Frances S. "Changing Concepts of the Black Woman," *Journal of Black Studies* 3 (June 1973): 433–54.

Franklin, John Hope. *From Slavery to Freedom,* rev. ed. New York: Alfred Knopf, 1960.

————. *The Emancipation Proclamation.* Garden City, N.Y. Doubleday & Co., 1963.

Frazier, Edward F. *The Negro Church in America.* New York: Schocken Books, 1963.

Fuller, Hoyt W. "The Question of Aesthetics," *Black World* 24 (December 1974) : 49–50.

Gayle, Addison. *The Black Situation*. New York: Dell Publishing Co., 1970.

————. *Bondage, Freedom, and Beyond: The Prose of Black Americans*. Garden City, N.Y.: Doubleday & Co., 1971.

————. "The Son of My Father," in Abraham Chapman, ed. *New Black Voices*. New York: New American Library, 1972, pp. 524–38.

Glock, Charles Y. "The Role of Deprivation in the Origin and Evolution of Religious Groups," in Robert Lee and Martin E. Marty, eds., *Religion and Social Conflict*. New York: Oxford University Press, 1964.

Golden, Bernette, "Black Women's Liberation," *Essence* 4 (February 1974) : 36–37, 75–76, 86.

Goldston, Robert. *The Negro Revolution*. New York: The Macmillan Co., 1968.

Gregory, Dick. *The Shadow That Scares Me*. New York: Doubleday, 1968.

Grier, William H., and Price M. Cobbs. *Black Rage*. New York: Basic Books, 1968.

Griffin, John Howard. *Black Like Me*. New York: Houghton Mifflin, 1961.

Hannerz, Ulf. "Growing Up Male," in *Soulside*. New York: Columbia University Press, 1969, pp. 118–38.

————. "Roots of Black Manhood," *Transaction* 6 (October 1969) : 12–21.

————. "What Ghetto Males Are Like: Another Look," in N. E. Whitten and J. F. Sewed, eds., *Afro-American Anthropology*. New York: The Free Press, 1970, pp. 313–27.

Hare, Nathan. *The Black Anglo-Saxons*. New York: Marzani & Munsell, 1965.

————. "The Frustrated Masculinity of the Negro Male," in Robert Staples, ed., *The Black Family*. Belmont, Cal.: Wadsworth Publishing Co., 1971, pp. 131–34.

————. "A Study of the Black Fighter," *The Black Scholar* 3 (November 1971) : 2–8.

Harper, Frederick D. "The Influence of Malcolm X on Black Militancy," *Journal of Black Studies* 1 (June 1971) : 387–402.

Hauser, Stuart T. *Black and White Identity Formation*. New York: Wiley, 1971.

Hayden, Robert, ed. *Kaleidoscope: Poems by American Negro Poets*. New York: Harcourt, Brace and World, 1967.

Hayden, Robert C. *Seven Black American Scientists*. Redding, Mass.: Addison-Wesley Co., 1970.

Hedgeman, Anna A. *The Trumpet Sounds: A Memoir of Negro Leadership*. New York: Holt, Rinehart, & Winston, 1964.

Heiss, Jerold. *The Case of the Black Family: A Sociological Inquiry*. New York: Columbia University Press, 1975.

Henderson, George. "Role Models for Lower Class Negro Boys," *Personnel and Guidance Journal* 46: 6–10.

Hernton, Calvin. *Coming Together: White Hate, Black Power and Sexual Hangups.* New York: Random House, 1971.

Hernton, Calvin C. "The Negro Male," in *Sex and Racism in America.* Garden City, N.Y.: Doubleday & Co., 1964, pp. 55–79.

Hirsh, Selma. "The Negro: Why Whites Fear Him," *Science Digest,* October 1963, pp. 12–17.

Hopkins, Thomas J. "The Role of the Agency in Supporting Black Manhood," *Social Work* 18 (January, 1973) : 53–58.

Huggins, Nathan I. *Harlem Renaissance.* New York: Oxford University Press, 1971.

Hughes, Langston. *Famous American Negroes.* New York: Dodd Mead, 1954.

―――――, and Milton Meltzer. *A Pictorial History of the Negro in America,* 3d ed., New York: Crown Publishers, 1968.

Jeffers, Lance. "Afro-American Literature, the Conscience of Man," *The Black Scholar* 2 (January 1971) : 47–53.

Johnson, James Weldon. *Autobiography of an Ex-Coloured Man.* New York: Hill and Wang, 1960.

Jones, Christopher W. *Listen Pilgrim.* Milwaukee: Bruce Publishing Company, 1968.

Jones, Howard O. *Shall We Overcome? A Challenge to Negro and White Christians.* Westwood, N.J.: F. H. Revell Co., 1966.

Killens, John Oliver. "Explanation of the Black Psyche," in Arnold Adoff, ed., *Black on Black.* New York: The Macmillan Co., 1968, pp. 137–45.

―――――. *Black Man's Burden.* New York: Simon & Schuster, 1970.

King, Coretta Scott. *My Life With Martin Luther King, Jr.* New York: Holt, Rinehart & Winston, 1969.

King, Martin Luther, Jr. *Stride Toward Freedom.* New York: Harper and Row, 1958.

―――――. *Why We Can't Wait.* New York: Harper and Row, 1964.

Knight, Etheridge, ed. *Black Voices from Prison.* New York: Pathfinder Press, 1970.

Kochman, Thomas, ed. *Rappin' and Stylin' Out: Communication in Urban Black America.* Chicago: University of Illinois Press, 1972.

Ladenburg, Thomas J., and William S. McFeeley. *The Black Man in the Land of Inequality.* New York: Hayden Book Co., 1969.

Ladner, Joyce A. *Tomorrow's Tomorrow: The Black Woman.* New York: Doubleday & Co., 1971.

Leggett, John C. "Working Class Consciousness, Race, and Political Choice," *American Journal of Sociology* 69 (September 1963) : 171–76.

Lester, Jules. *To Be a Slave.* New York: Dial Press, 1968.

Lewis, Lillian. "The Sensual Male," *Mystique* 1 (September 1974) : 32–33, 60–62, 77.

Liebow, Elliot. *Tally's Corner.* Boston: Little, Brown & Co., 1967.

Lincoln, C. Eric. *The Black Muslims in America*. Boston: Beacon Press, 1961.

————. *My Face Is Black*. Boston: Beacon Press, 1964.

————. *Is Anybody Listening to Black America?* New York: Seabury Press, 1968.

Littlejohn, David. *Black on White: A Critical Survey of Writing by American Negroes*. New York: The Viking Press, 1969.

Littleton, Arthur C., and Mary W. Burger, eds. *Black Viewpoints*. New York: New American Library, 1971.

Lyman, Stanford M. *The Black American in Sociological Thought*. New York: Capricorn Books, 1972.

Malcolm X (with the assistance of Alex Haley). *The Autobiography of Malcolm X*. New York: Grove Press, 1965.

Meier, August, and Elliott Rudwick. *CORE: A Study in the Civil Rights Movement 1942-1968*. New York: Oxford University Press, 1973.

Meredith, James. *Three Years in Mississippi*. Bloomington, Ind.: Indiana University Press, 1966.

Muse, Benjamin. *The American Negro Revolution: From Nonviolence to Black Power, 1963-1967*. Bloomington, Ind.: Indiana University Press, 1968.

The National Advisory Commission on Civil Disorders, *Report of the National Advisory Commission on Civil Disorders*. New York: Bantam Books, 1968.

Nelson, S., et al. *The Black Man and the Promise of America*. Chicago: Scott, Foresman & Co., 1970.

Nichols, C. H. *Black Men in Chains*. Westport, Conn.: Lawrence Hill, 1970.

O'Daniel, T. B., ed. *Langston Hughes, Black Genius: A Critical Evaluation*. New York: William Morrow, 1971.

Palmer, Edward. "Black Police in America," *The Black Scholar* 5 (October 1973) : 19–27.

Parker, Seymour, and Robert J. Kleiner. "Social and Psychological Dimensions of the Family Role Performance of the Negro Male," *Journal of Marriage and the Family* 31 (August 1969) : 500–506.

Parks, Gordon. *A Choice of Weapons*. New York: Harper and Row, 1966.

Patterson, Raymond R. *26 ways of Looking at a Black Man*. New York: Award Books, 1969.

Paul, Tony. "Black Power and White Women," *Pageant* 23 (October 1967) : 6–12.

Pfautz, Harold W. "The New 'New Negro': Emerging American," in Doris Y. Wilkinson, ed., *Black Revolt: Strategies of Protest*. Berkeley, Calif.: McCutchan Publishing Co., 1968, pp. 35–45.

Poole, Elijah (Elijah Muhammed). *Message to the Black Man in America*. Chicago: Muhammad Mosque of Islam No. 2, 1965.

Poussaint, Alvin. "Sex and the Black Male," *Ebony* 27 (August 1972) : 114–118.

————. "The Black Administrator in the White University," *The Black Scholar* 6 (September 1974) : 8–14.

————. *Why Blacks Kill Blacks*. New York: Emerson Hall Publishers, Inc., 1972.

————, and J. L. Jackson. "Rap on Self Hatred," *Ebony* 28 (December 1972) : 118–20.

Proctor, Samuel. *The Young Negro in America: 1960-1980*. New York: Association Press, 1966.

Quarles, Benjamin A. *Frederick Douglass*. Washington, D.C.: Associated Publishers, 1948.

————. *The Negro in the American Revolution*. Chapel Hill, N.C.: University of North Carolina Press, 1961.

Rainwater, Lee, ed. *Soul*. Chicago: Aldine, 1970.

Ramsey, Paul. *Christian Ethics and the Sit-in*. New York: Association Press, 1961.

Redding, J. Saunders. *On Being Negro in America*. New York: Bobbs-Merrill, 1962.

Robinson, L. *The Black Millionaires*. Louisville, Ky.: Pyramid Press, 1972.

Rudwick, Elliot M. *The Unequal Badge: Negro Policemen in the South*. Atlanta: Southern Regional Council, 1962.

Samuels, Gertrude. "Five Angry Men Speak Their Minds," *New York Times Magazine,* May 17, 1964.

Saunders, Mary J. "Anti-Cult Deprogramming Full of Emotion," *St. Paul Sunday Pioneer Press, Family Life Section,* December 15, 1974, 1, 6.

Scanzoni, John H. *The Black Family in Modern Society*. Boston: Allyn and Bacon, 1971.

Schockley, Ann A., and Sue P. Chandler. *Living Black American Authors*. New York: R. R. Bowker Company, 1973.

Schulz, David A. "Variations in the Father Role in Complete Families of the Negro Lower Class," *Social Science Quarterly* 49 (December 1968): 651–59.

Sizemore, Barbara. "Sexism and the Black Male," *The Black Scholar* 11 March/April 1973) : 2–11.

Sleeper, Charles, F. *Black Power and Christian Responsibility: Some Biblical Foundations for Social Ethics*. Nashville: Abingdon Press, 1969.

Smith, Robert P. "William Cooper Nell: Crusading Black Abolitionist," *The Journal of Negro History* 55 (July 1970) : 182–99.

Spike, Robert W. *The Freedom Revolution and the Churches*. New York: Associated Press, 1965.

Staples, Robert, ed. "Educating the Black Male at Various Class Levels for Marital Roles," *The Family Coordinator* 30 (April 1970) : 164–67.

Sterling, Dorothy, and Benjamin Quarles. *Lift Every Voice.* New York: Doubleday, 1965.

Taylor, Ronald L. "Psychosocial Development Among Black Children and Youth: A Reexamination," *American Journal of Orthopsychiatry* 46 (January 1976) : 4–19.

————. "Psychosocial Development Among Black Youth: A Conceptual Framework," *Journal of Black Studies* (1976) .

Ten Houten, Warren D. "The Black Family: Myth and Reality," *Psychiatry* 33: 145–73.

"That Black Man-White Woman Thing," *Ebony* 25 (August 1970) : 130–33.

"The Black Male," *Ebony* 27 (August 1972) (Special issue) .

Thomas, Piri. *Down These Mean Streets.* New York: The New American Library, 1971.

Tousky, Curt, and William J. Wilson. "Work Attachment Among Black Men," *Phylon* 32 (spring 1971) : 23–30.

Truck, Samuel, Jr. "A Model for Working with Black Fathers," *American Journal of Orthopsychiatry* 41 (April 1971) : 465–72.

Turner, Darwin T., and Jean M. Bright, eds. *Images of the Negro in America: Selected Source Materials for College Research Papers.* Boston: D. C. Heath, 1965.

Vontress, Clemmont E. "The Black Male Personality," *The Black Scholar* 10 (1971) : 10–16.

Washington, Joseph R. *Black Religion: The Negro and Christianity in the U.S.* Boston: Beacon Press, 1964.

Weaver, Harold D. "Paul Robeson: Beleaguered Leader," *The Black Scholar* 5 (December 1973-January 1974) : 25–32.

Welsing, Frances Cress. "On 'Black Genetic Inferiority,'" *Ebony* 29 (July 1974) : 104–5.

————. "The 'Conspiracy to Make Blacks Inferior,'" *Ebony* 29 (September 1974) : 84–94.

Wiggins, William H. "Jack Johnson As Bad Nigger: The Folklore of His Life," *The Black Scholar* 2 (January 1971) : 35–46.

Wilkinson, Doris Y. "Racial Socialization Through Children's Toys: A Socio-historical Examination," *Journal of Black Studies* 5 (September 1974) : 96–109.

————, (ed.) . *Black Revolt: Strategies of Protest.* Berkeley, Calif.: McCutchan Publishing Co., 1969.

————, (ed.) . *Black Male/White Female.* Cambridge, Mass.: Schenkman Publishing Co., 1975.

————, and Patricia Kane. "Survival Strategies: Black Women in *Ollie Miss* and *Cotton Comes to Harlem,*" *Critique: Studies in Modern Fiction* 16 (1974) : 101–9.

Williams, Daniel T. *The Black Muslims in the United States: A Selected*

Bibliography. Tuskegee, Ala.: Hollis Burke Fissell Library, Tuskegee Institute, 1964. (Supp., 1966.)

Williams, John A. *The Man Who Cried I Am.* New York: The New American Library, 1972.

Willie, Charles V., and Joan D. Levy. "Black Is Lonely," *Psychology Today* 5 (May 1972): 50–52, 76–80.

Woodson, Carter G. "The New Type of Professional Man Required," in *The Mis-Education of the Negro.* Washington, D.C. Associated Publishers, 1933, pp. 173–80.

―――――. *The Negro Professional Man and the Community.* Washington, D.C.: Association for the Study of Negro Life and History, 1934.

―――――. *Negro Makers of History,* revised by Charles H. Wesley. Washington, D.C.: Associated Publishers, 1958.

Word, Francis, and Val Gray. "The Black Artist—His Role in the Struggle," *The Black Scholar* 2 (January 1971): 23–32.

Wright, Nathan, ed. *What Black Educators Are Saying.* San Francisco: Leswing Press, 1970.

Wright, Richard. *Native Son.* New York: Harper, 1940.

―――――. *White Man—Listen!* Garden City, N.Y.: Doubleday, 1957.

Young, A. S. N. *Great Negro Baseball Stars.* New York: Barnes & Noble, 1953.

Young, Louis C. "Are Black Men Taking Care of Business?" *Essence* 4 (April 1974): 40–44, 73, 75, 94.

Young, Whitney M., Jr. *Beyond Racism: Building an Open Society.* New York: McGraw-Hill, 1969.

Zinn, Howard. *SNCC: The New Abolitionists.* Boston: Beacon Press, 1964.

AUTHOR INDEX

SUBJECT INDEX

The Editors:

DORIS YVONNE WILKINSON is an associate professor in the Department of Sociology and Anthropology, Macalester College, St. Paul. She is a recognized authority on the black experience in America; author of *Black Male/White Female* and *Social Structure and Assassination: The Sociology of Political Murder,* published in 1974; author of *Workbook for Introductory Sociology*; editor of *Black Revolt: Strategies of Protest.* Dr. Wilkinson is a member of a number of organizations that include the Caucus of Black Sociologists and Sociologists for Women in Society.

RONALD LEWIS TAYLOR has been an assistant professor of sociology at the University of Connecticut at Storrs since 1972. Previously he was a lecturer in sociology at Boston University, dean of men at Bethune-Cookman College, and a research assistant for the U.S. Department of Labor. Dr. Taylor is a member of the Society for the Study of Social Problems, American Sociological Association, Eastern Sociological Society, and American Association of University Professors.